Volume 2

Created by
Svetlana Chmakova

HAMBURG // LONDON // LOS ANGELES // TOKYO

Dramacon Vol. 2
Created by Svetlana Chmakova

Digital Toning Assistant - J. Dee Dupuy
Lettering - Erika "Skooter" Terriquez
Graphic Designer - Chris Tjalsma
Cover Design - Chris Tjalsma

Editor - Lillian Diaz-Przybyl
Digital Imaging Manager - Chris Buford
Pre-Production Supervisor - Erika Terriquez
Art Director - Anne Marie Horne
Production Manager - Elisabeth Brizzi
Managing Editor - Vy Nguyen
VP of Production - Ron Klamert
Editor-in-Chief - Rob Tokar
Publisher - Mike Kiley
President and C.O.O. - John Parker
C.E.O. and Chief Creative Officer - Stuart Levy

A **TOKYOPOP** Manga

TOKYOPOP Inc.
5900 Wilshire Blvd. Suite 2000
Los Angeles, CA 90036

E-mail: info@TOKYOPOP.com
Come visit us online at www.TOKYOPOP.com

ISBN: 1-59816-130-X

First TOKYOPOP printing: October 2006
10 9 8 7 6 5 4 3 2 1
Printed in the USA

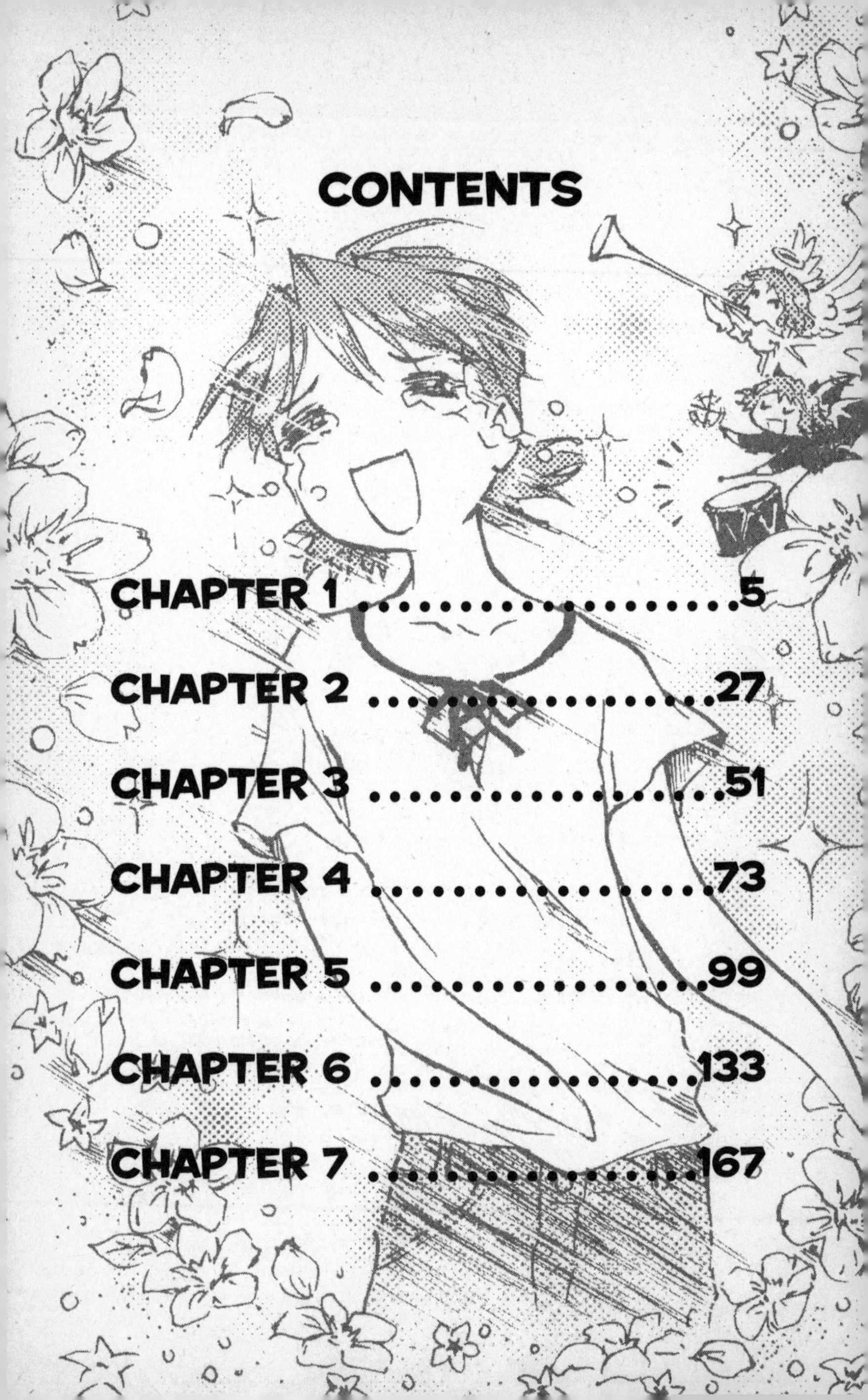

CONTENTS

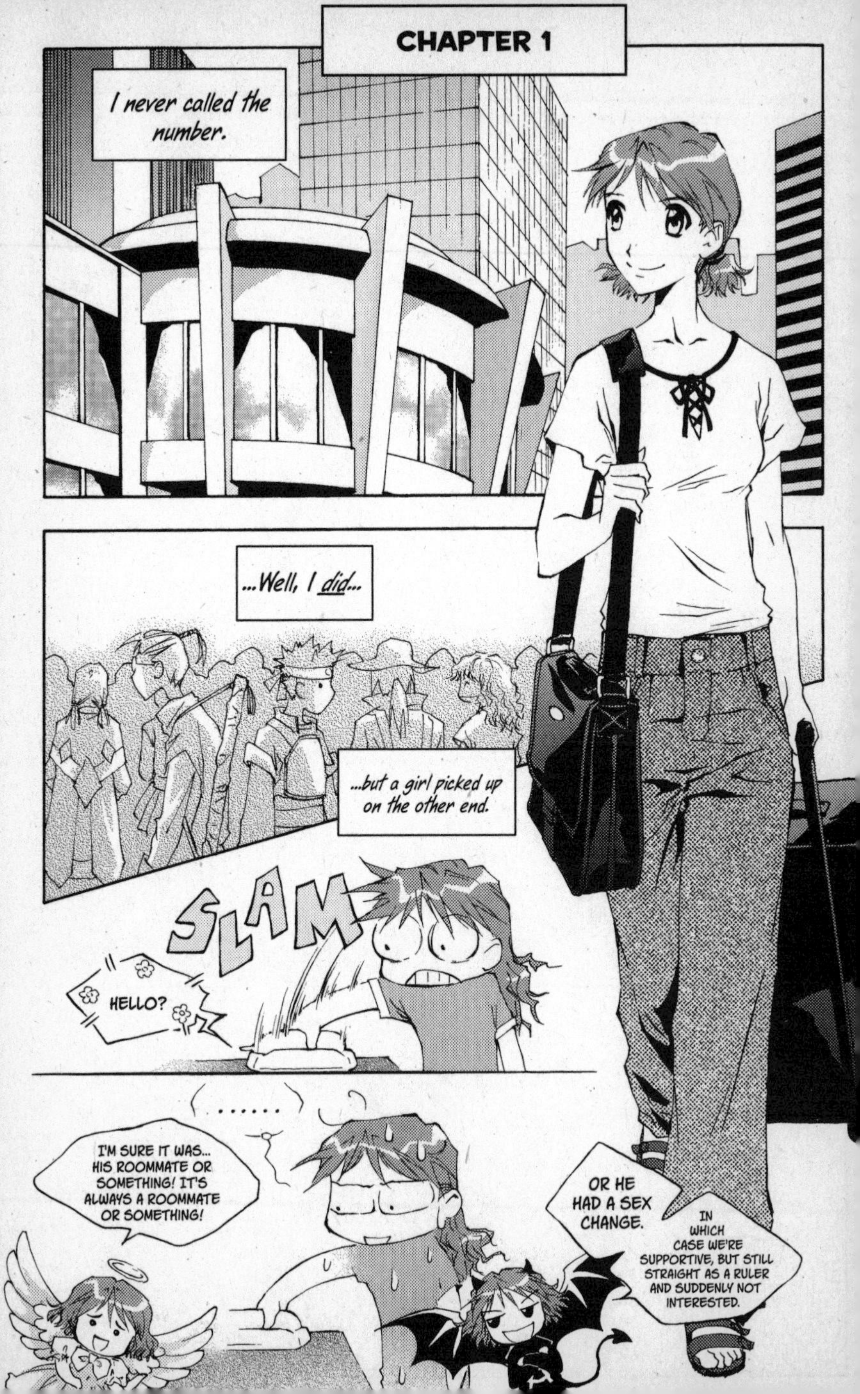
CHAPTER 1
I never called the number.
...Well, I did...
...but a girl picked up on the other end.
SLAM
HELLO?
(......)
I'M SURE IT WAS... HIS ROOMMATE OR SOMETHING! IT'S ALWAYS A ROOMMATE OR SOMETHING!
OR HE HAD A SEX CHANGE.
IN WHICH CASE WE'RE SUPPORTIVE, BUT STILL STRAIGHT AS A RULER AND SUDDENLY NOT INTERESTED.

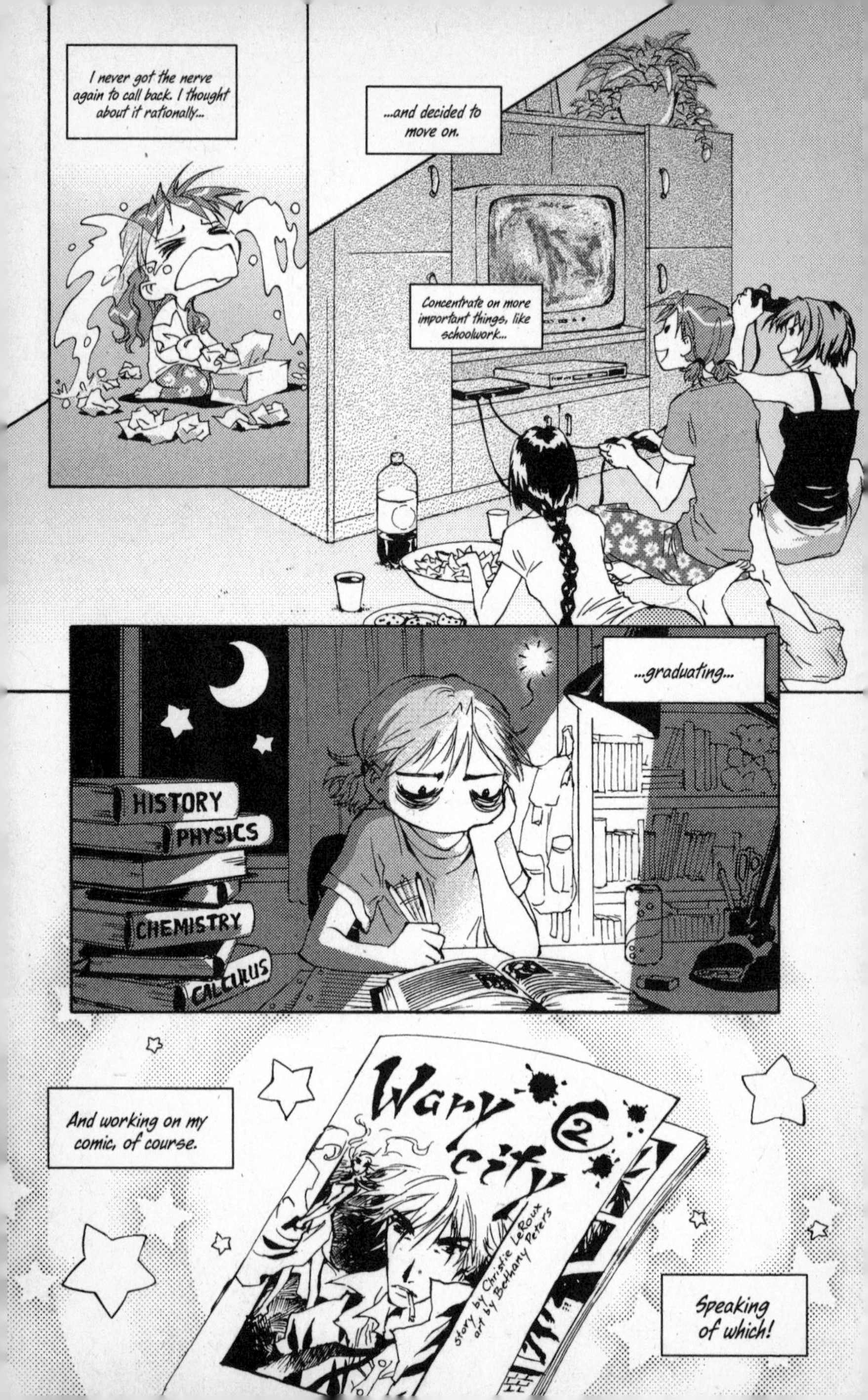
I never got the nerve again to call back. I thought about it rationally...
...and decided to move on.
Concentrate on more important things, like schoolwork...
HISTORY
PHYSICS
CHEMISTRY
CALCULUS
...graduating...
And working on my comic, of course.
Wary City 2
story by Christie LeRoux
art by Bethany Peters
Speaking of which!

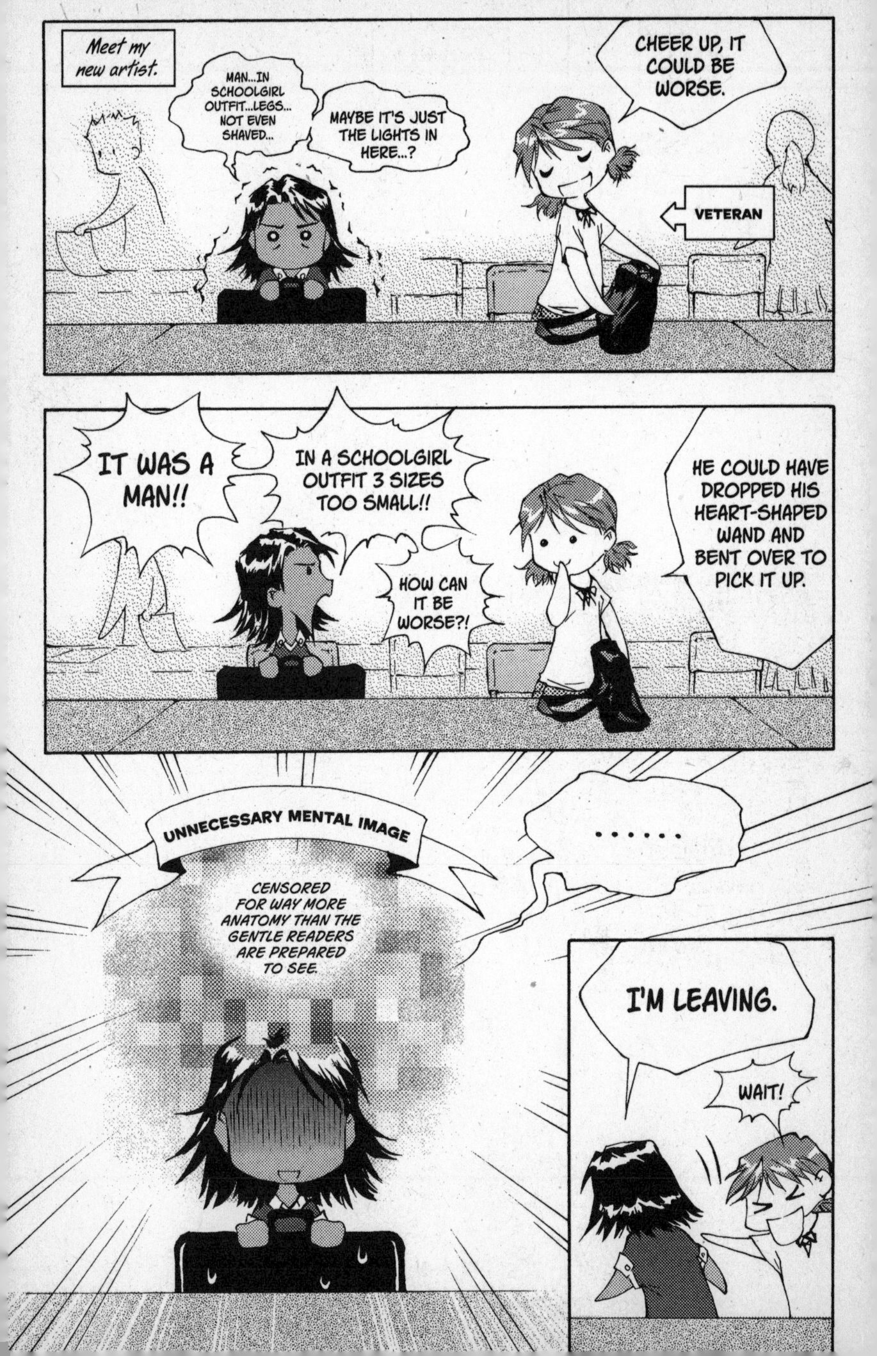
Meet my new artist.
MAN...IN SCHOOLGIRL OUTFIT...LEGS... NOT EVEN SHAVED...
MAYBE IT'S JUST THE LIGHTS IN HERE...?
CHEER UP, IT COULD BE WORSE.
VETERAN
IT WAS A MAN!!
IN A SCHOOLGIRL OUTFIT 3 SIZES TOO SMALL!!
HOW CAN IT BE WORSE?!
HE COULD HAVE DROPPED HIS HEART-SHAPED WAND AND BENT OVER TO PICK IT UP.
UNNECESSARY MENTAL IMAGE
CENSORED FOR WAY MORE ANATOMY THAN THE GENTLE READERS ARE PREPARED TO SEE.
......
I'M LEAVING.
WAIT!

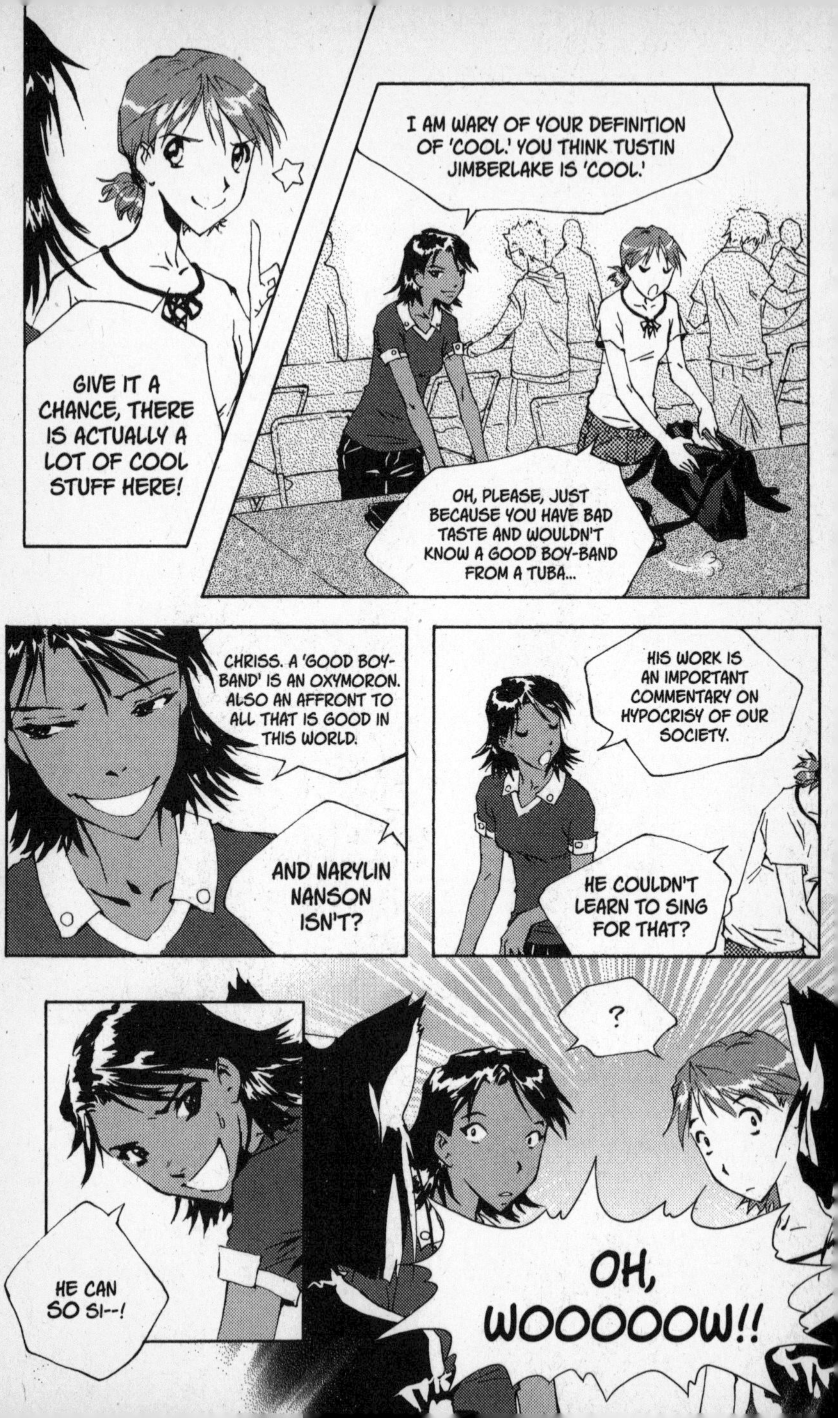
GIVE IT A CHANCE, THERE IS ACTUALLY A LOT OF COOL STUFF HERE!
I AM WARY OF YOUR DEFINITION OF 'COOL.' YOU THINK TUSTIN JIMBERLAKE IS 'COOL.'
OH, PLEASE, JUST BECAUSE YOU HAVE BAD TASTE AND WOULDN'T KNOW A GOOD BOY-BAND FROM A TUBA...
CHRISS. A 'GOOD BOY-BAND' IS AN OXYMORON. ALSO AN AFFRONT TO ALL THAT IS GOOD IN THIS WORLD.
AND NARYLIN NANSON ISN'T?
HIS WORK IS AN IMPORTANT COMMENTARY ON HYPOCRISY OF OUR SOCIETY.
HE COULDN'T LEARN TO SING FOR THAT?
HE CAN SO SI--!
?
OH, WOOOOOW!!

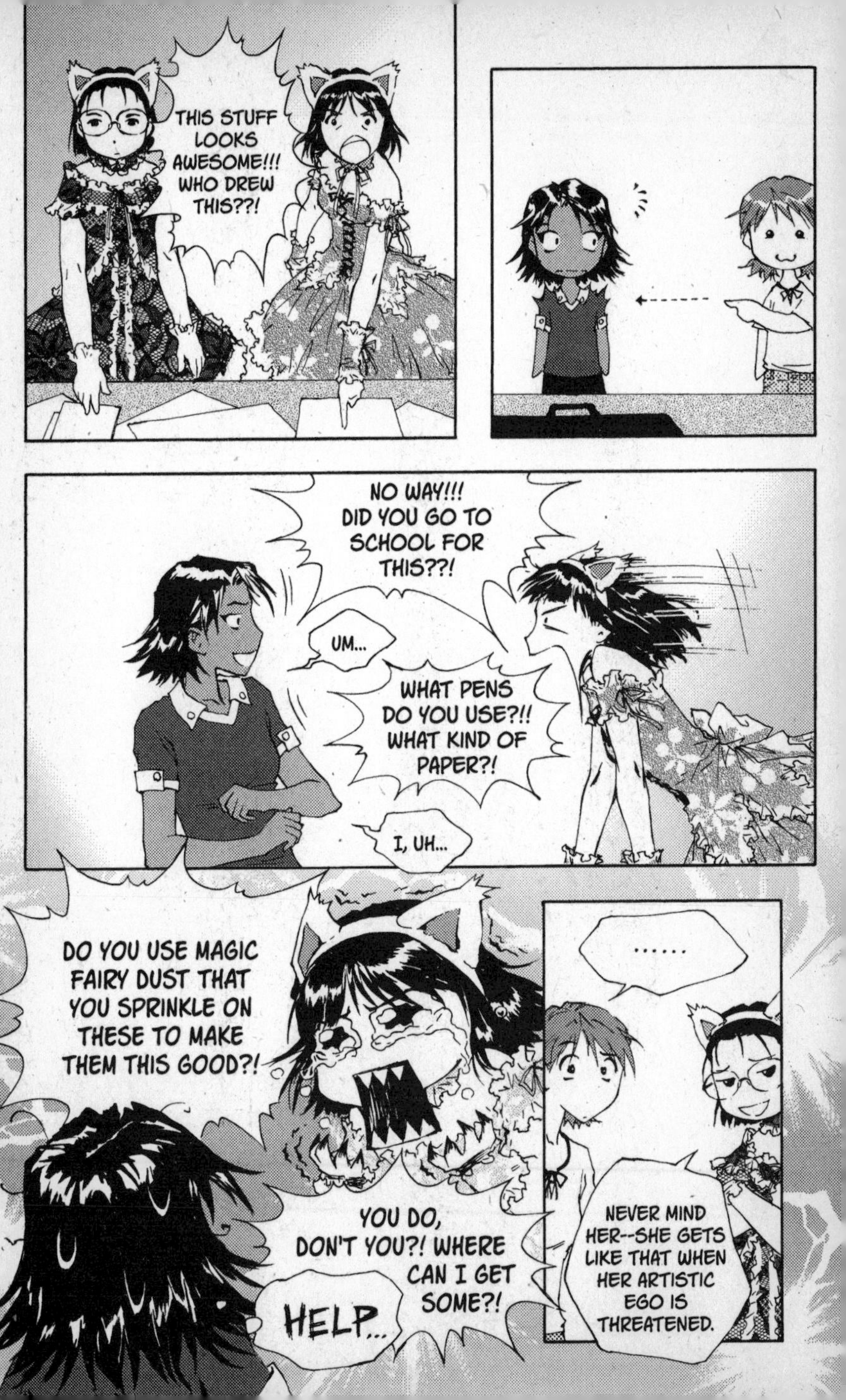
THIS STUFF LOOKS AWESOME!!! WHO DREW THIS??!
NO WAY!!! DID YOU GO TO SCHOOL FOR THIS??!
UM...
WHAT PENS DO YOU USE?!! WHAT KIND OF PAPER?!
I, UH...
DO YOU USE MAGIC FAIRY DUST THAT YOU SPRINKLE ON THESE TO MAKE THEM THIS GOOD?!
YOU DO, DON'T YOU?! WHERE CAN I GET SOME?!
HELP...
......
NEVER MIND HER--SHE GETS LIKE THAT WHEN HER ARTISTIC EGO IS THREATENED.

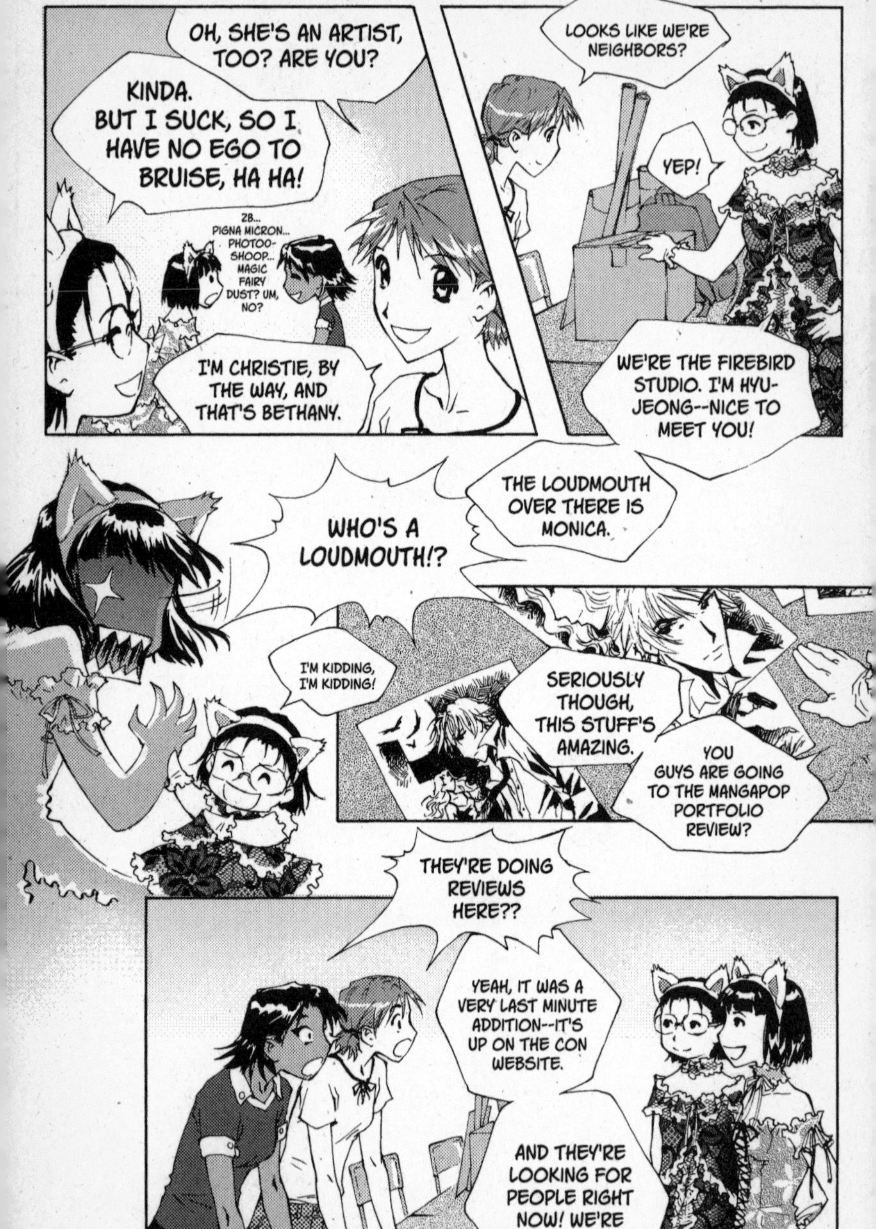
OH, SHE'S AN ARTIST, TOO? ARE YOU?
KINDA. BUT I SUCK, SO I HAVE NO EGO TO BRUISE, HA HA!
2B... PIGNA MICRON... PHOTOO-SHOOP... MAGIC FAIRY DUST? UM, NO?
I'M CHRISTIE, BY THE WAY, AND THAT'S BETHANY.
LOOKS LIKE WE'RE NEIGHBORS?
YEP!
WE'RE THE FIREBIRD STUDIO. I'M HYU-JEONG--NICE TO MEET YOU!
THE LOUDMOUTH OVER THERE IS MONICA.
WHO'S A LOUDMOUTH!?
I'M KIDDING, I'M KIDDING!
SERIOUSLY THOUGH, THIS STUFF'S AMAZING.
YOU GUYS ARE GOING TO THE MANGAPOP PORTFOLIO REVIEW?
THEY'RE DOING REVIEWS HERE??
YEAH, IT WAS A VERY LAST MINUTE ADDITION--IT'S UP ON THE CON WEBSITE.
AND THEY'RE LOOKING FOR PEOPLE RIGHT NOW! WE'RE TOTALLY GOING.

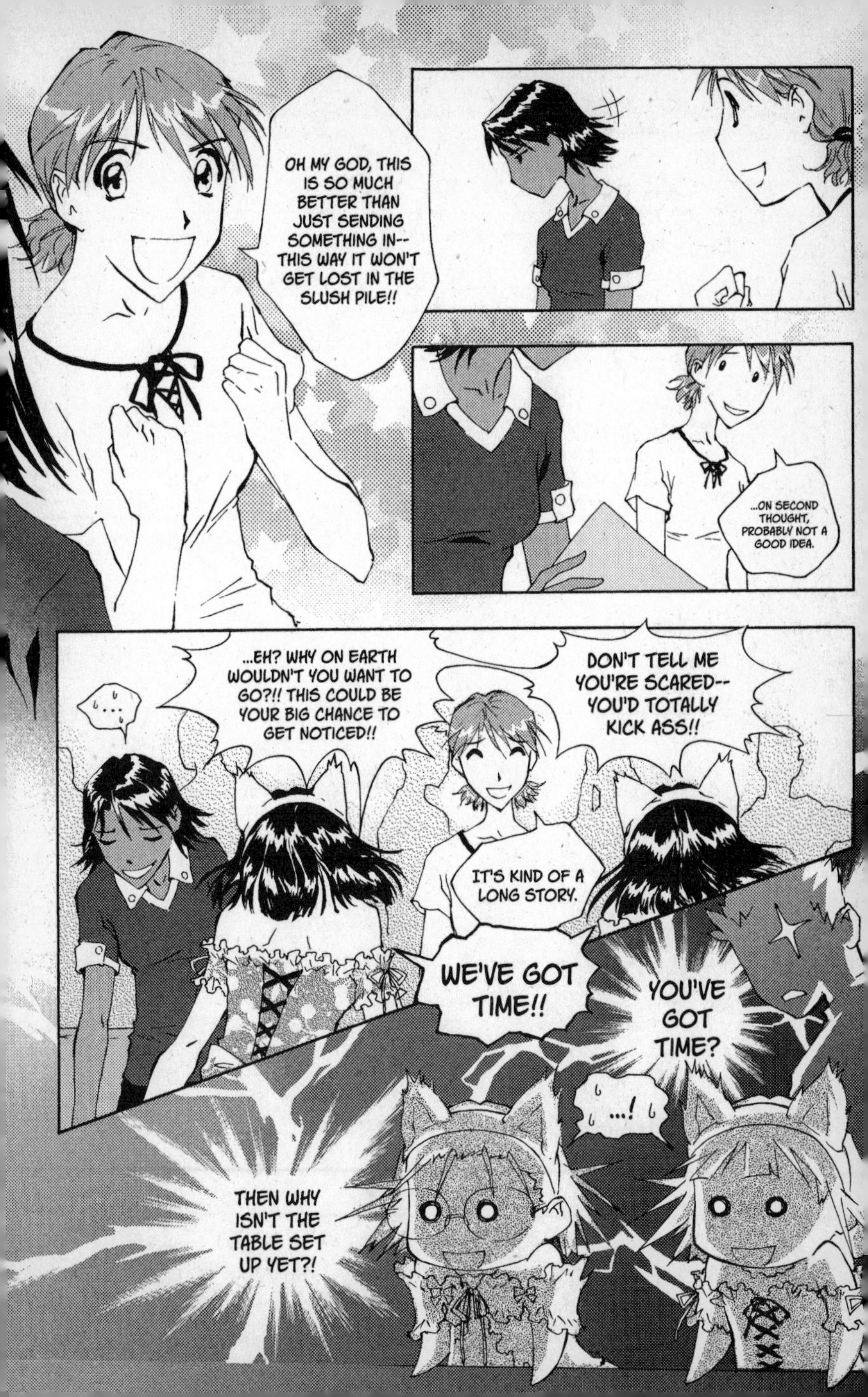
OH MY GOD, THIS IS SO MUCH BETTER THAN JUST SENDING SOMETHING IN-- THIS WAY IT WON'T GET LOST IN THE SLUSH PILE!!
...ON SECOND THOUGHT, PROBABLY NOT A GOOD IDEA.
...
...EH? WHY ON EARTH WOULDN'T YOU WANT TO GO?!! THIS COULD BE YOUR BIG CHANCE TO GET NOTICED!!
DON'T TELL ME YOU'RE SCARED-- YOU'D TOTALLY KICK ASS!!
IT'S KIND OF A LONG STORY.
WE'VE GOT TIME!!
YOU'VE GOT TIME?
...!
THEN WHY ISN'T THE TABLE SET UP YET?!

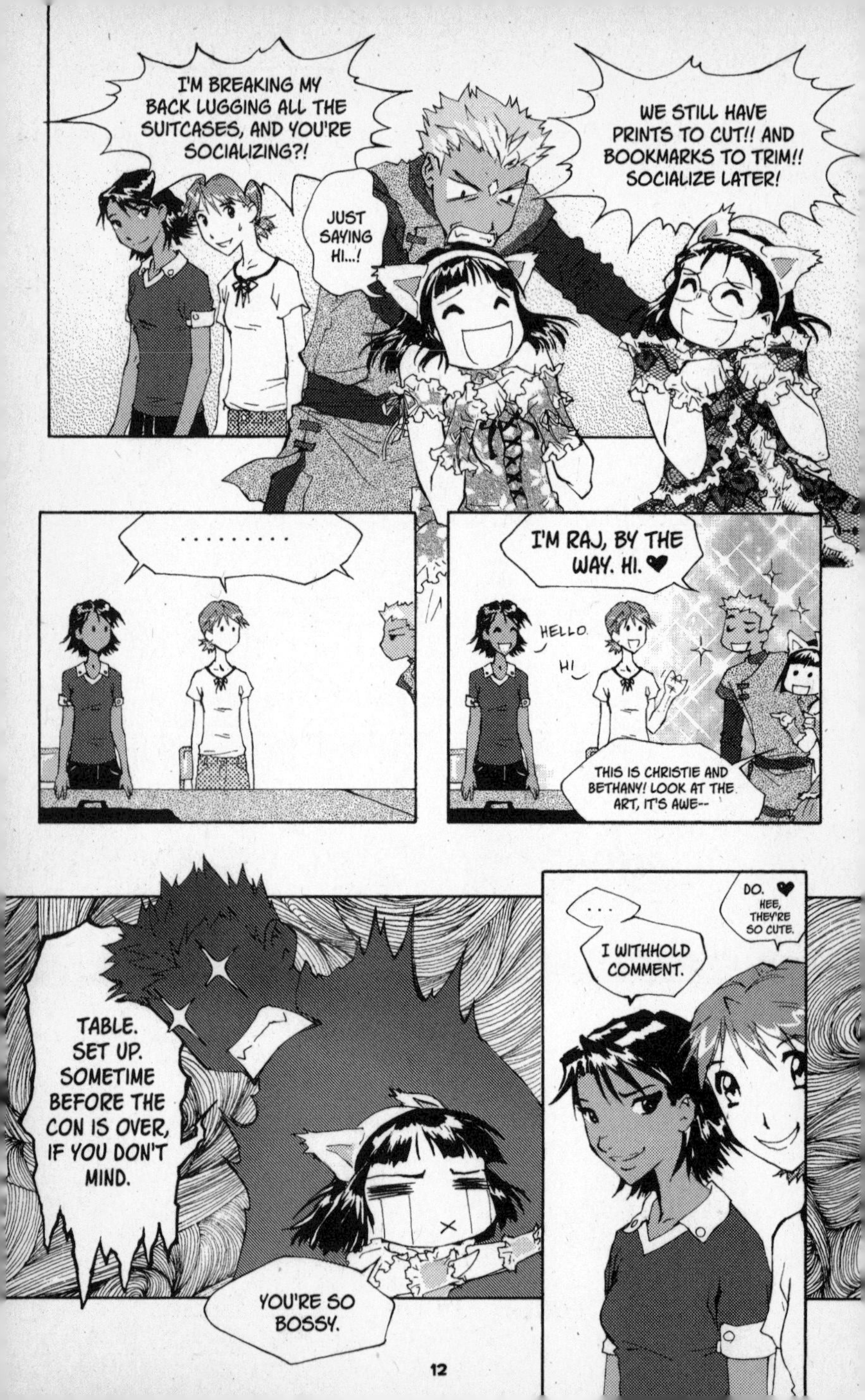
I'M BREAKING MY BACK LUGGING ALL THE SUITCASES, AND YOU'RE SOCIALIZING?!
JUST SAYING HI...!
WE STILL HAVE PRINTS TO CUT!! AND BOOKMARKS TO TRIM!! SOCIALIZE LATER!
. . . .
I'M RAJ, BY THE WAY. HI. ❤
HELLO.
HI!
THIS IS CHRISTIE AND BETHANY! LOOK AT THE ART, IT'S AWE--
TABLE. SET UP. SOMETIME BEFORE THE CON IS OVER, IF YOU DON'T MIND.
YOU'RE SO BOSSY.
. . .
I WITHHOLD COMMENT.
DO. ❤
HEE, THEY'RE SO CUTE.

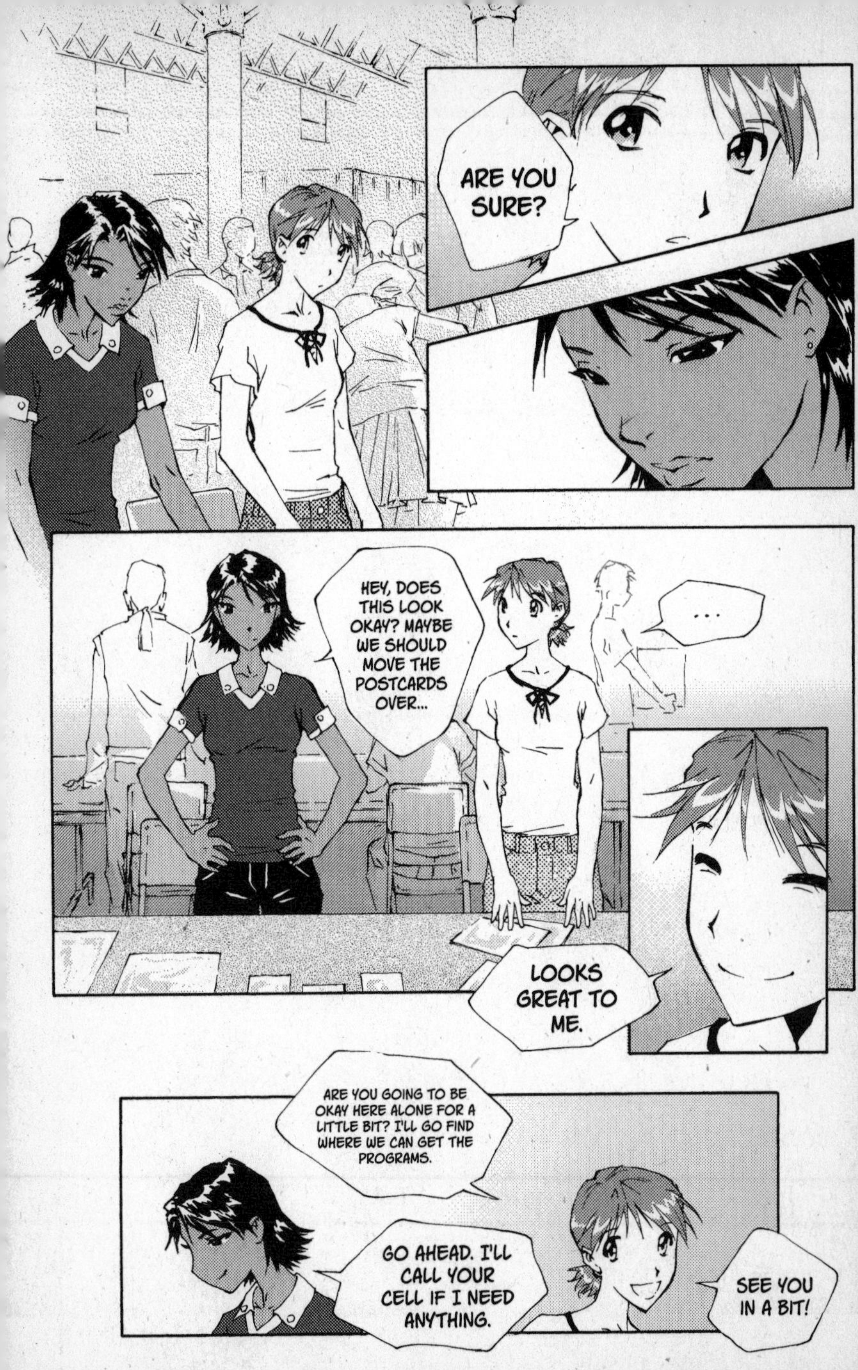
ARE YOU SURE?
HEY, DOES THIS LOOK OKAY? MAYBE WE SHOULD MOVE THE POSTCARDS OVER...
...
LOOKS GREAT TO ME.
ARE YOU GOING TO BE OKAY HERE ALONE FOR A LITTLE BIT? I'LL GO FIND WHERE WE CAN GET THE PROGRAMS.
GO AHEAD. I'LL CALL YOUR CELL IF I NEED ANYTHING.
SEE YOU IN A BIT!

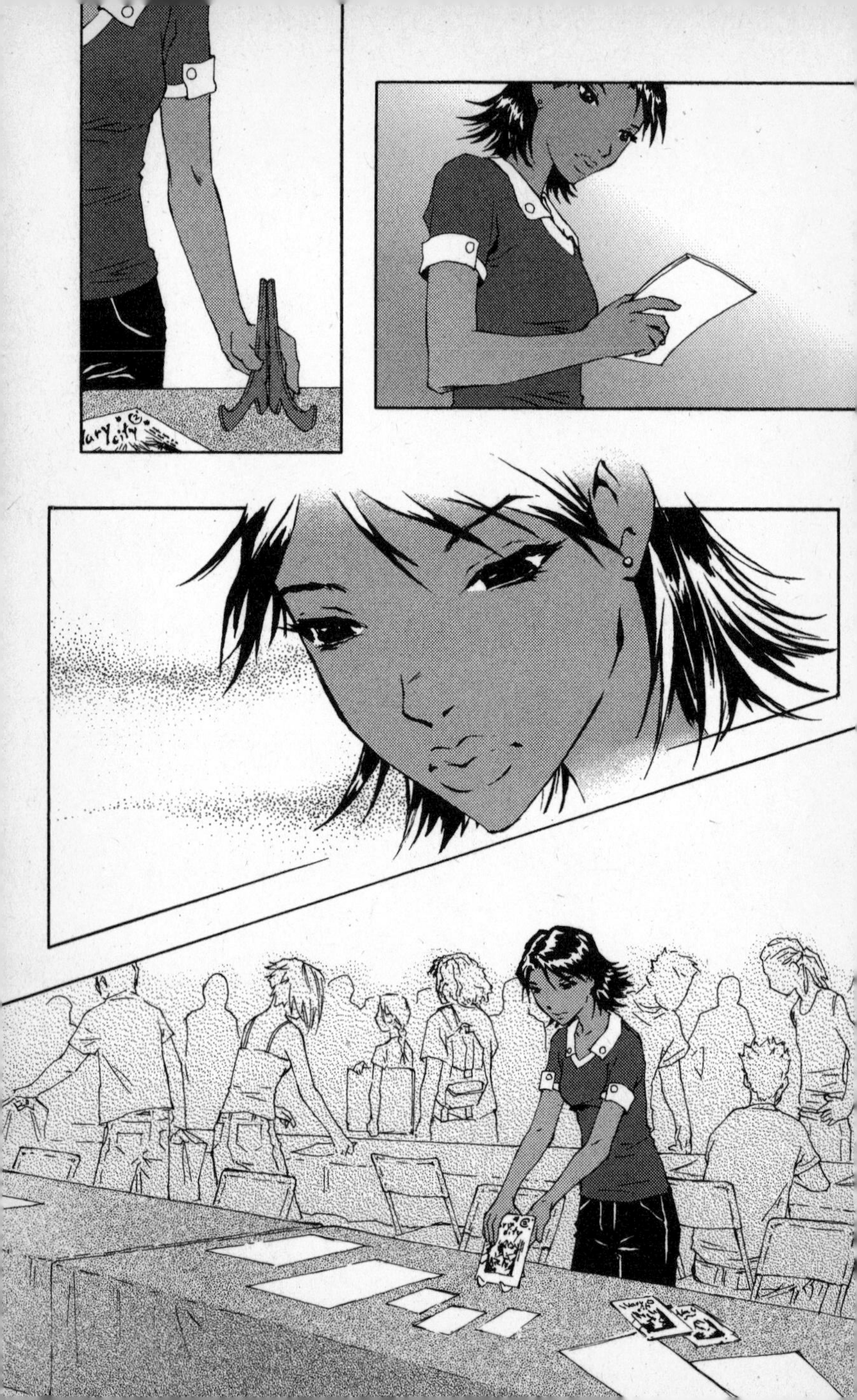

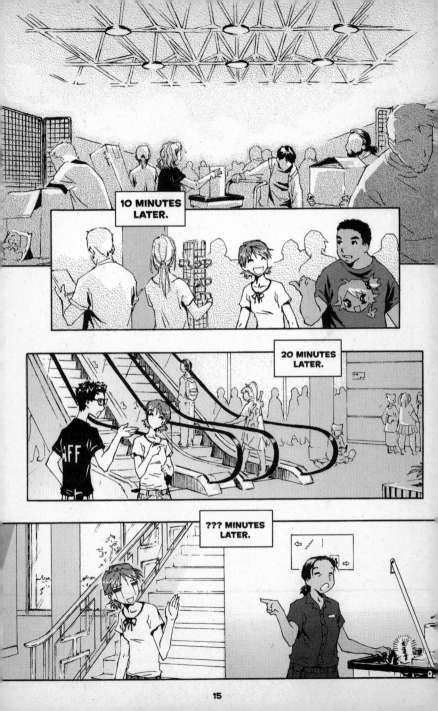

10 MINUTES LATER.

20 MINUTES LATER.

??? MINUTES LATER.

15

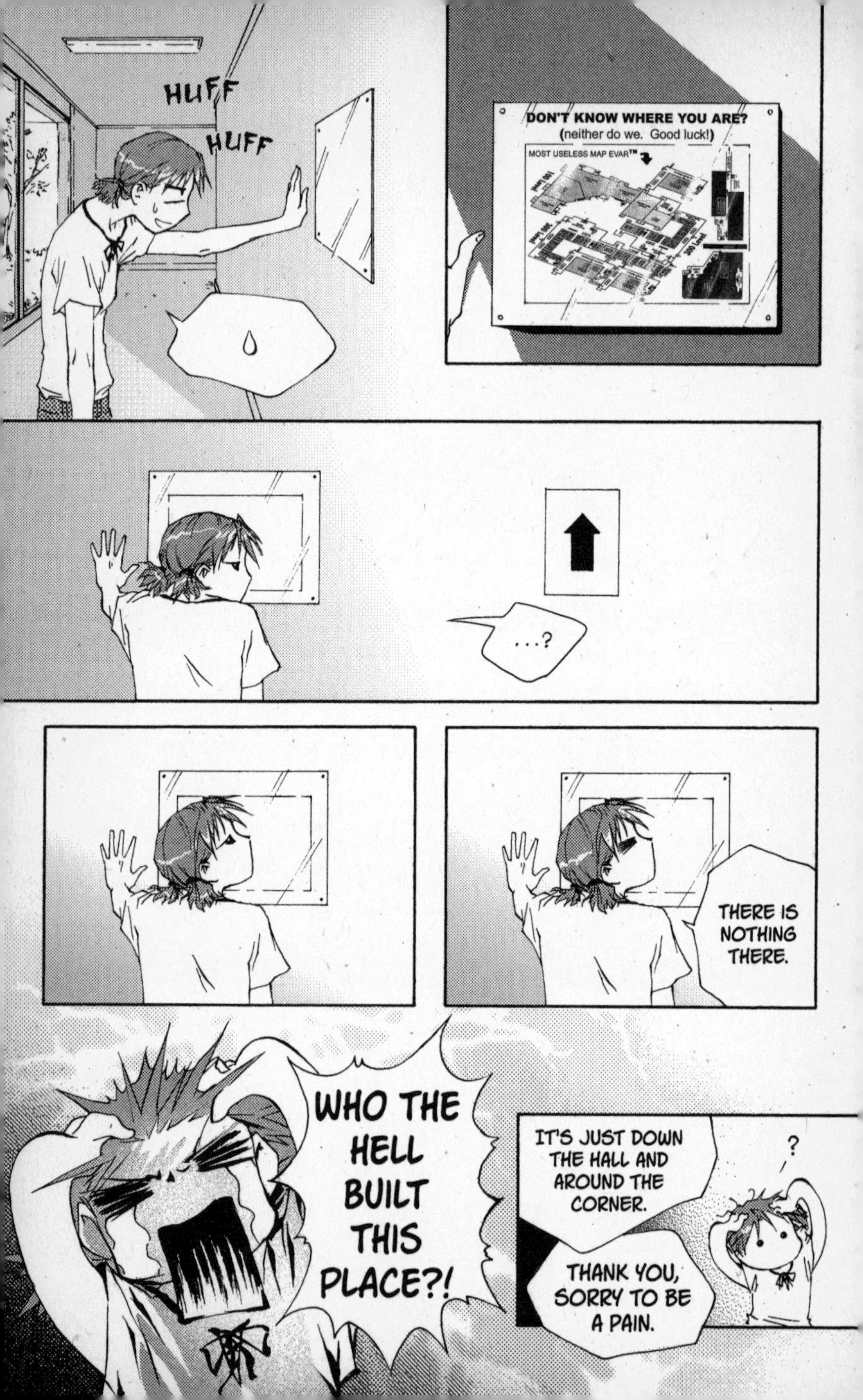
HUFF
HUFF
DON'T KNOW WHERE YOU ARE?
(neither do we. Good luck!)
MOST USELESS MAP EVAR™
...?
THERE IS NOTHING THERE.
WHO THE HELL BUILT THIS PLACE?!
IT'S JUST DOWN THE HALL AND AROUND THE CORNER.
THANK YOU, SORRY TO BE A PAIN.
?

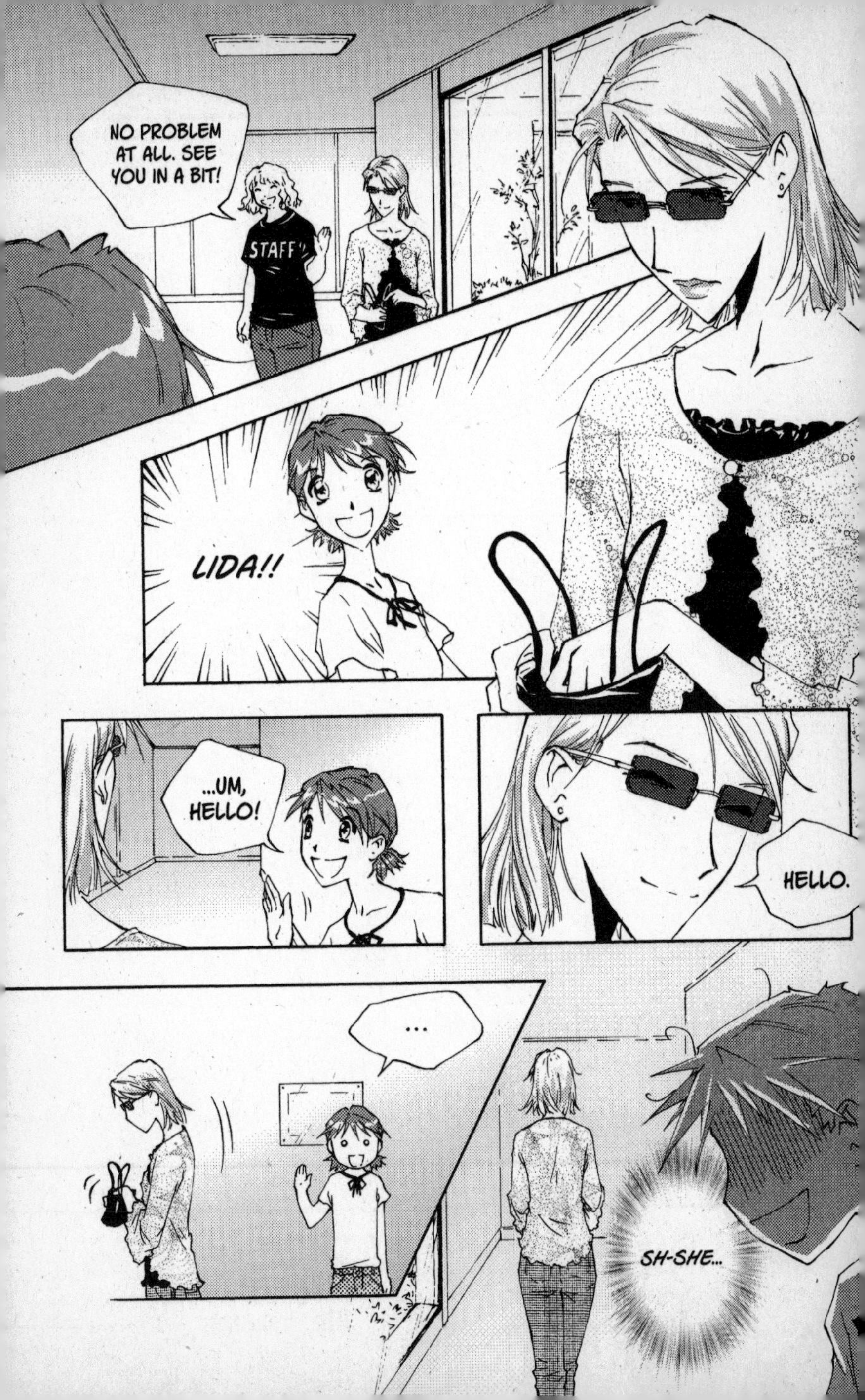
NO PROBLEM AT ALL. SEE YOU IN A BIT!
STAFF
LIDA!!
...UM, HELLO!
HELLO.
...
SH-SHE...

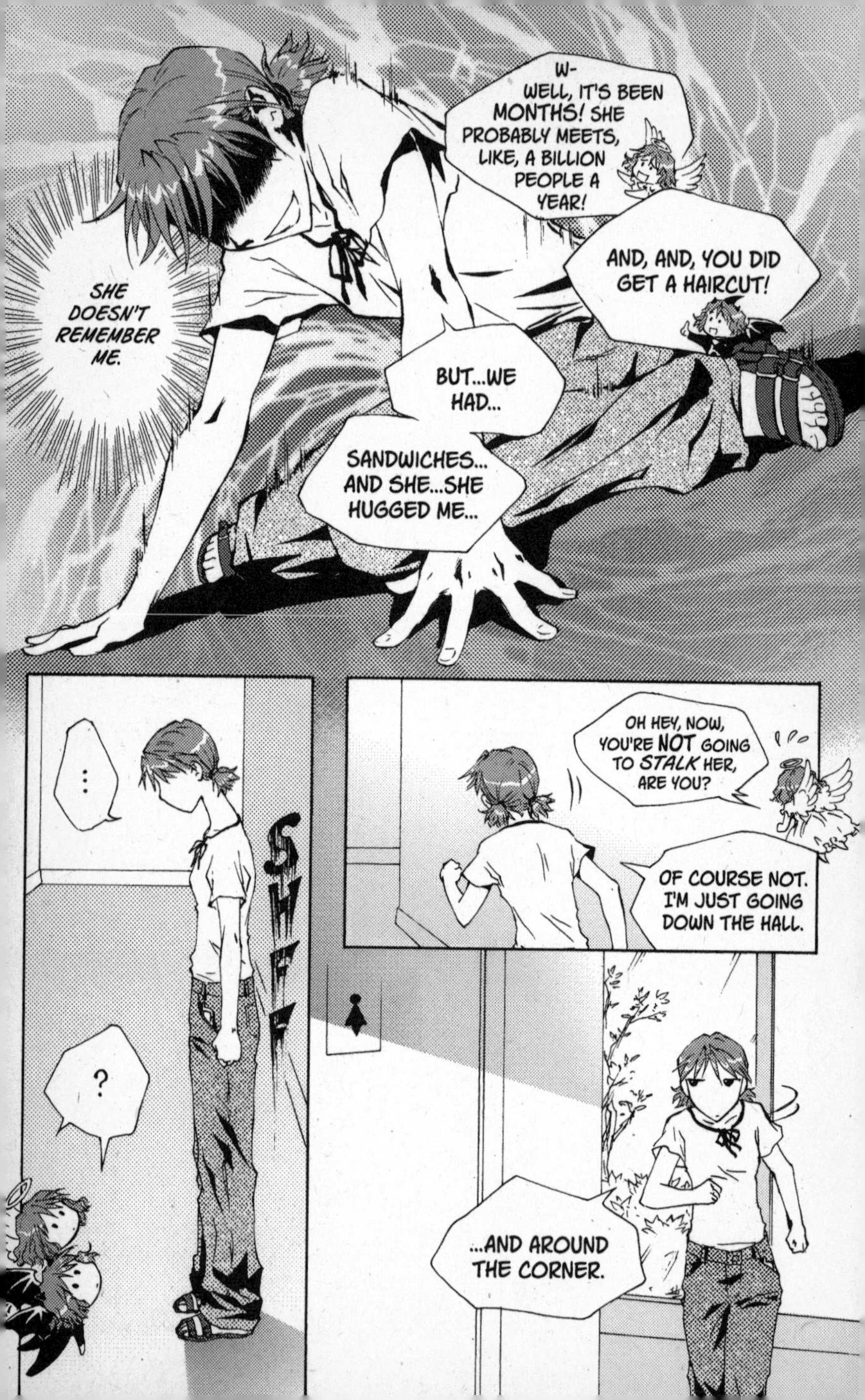
SHE DOESN'T REMEMBER ME.
W- WELL, IT'S BEEN MONTHS! SHE PROBABLY MEETS, LIKE, A BILLION PEOPLE A YEAR!
AND, AND, YOU DID GET A HAIRCUT!
BUT...WE HAD...
SANDWICHES... AND SHE...SHE HUGGED ME...
...
?
OH HEY, NOW, YOU'RE NOT GOING TO STALK HER, ARE YOU?
OF COURSE NOT. I'M JUST GOING DOWN THE HALL.
...AND AROUND THE CORNER.

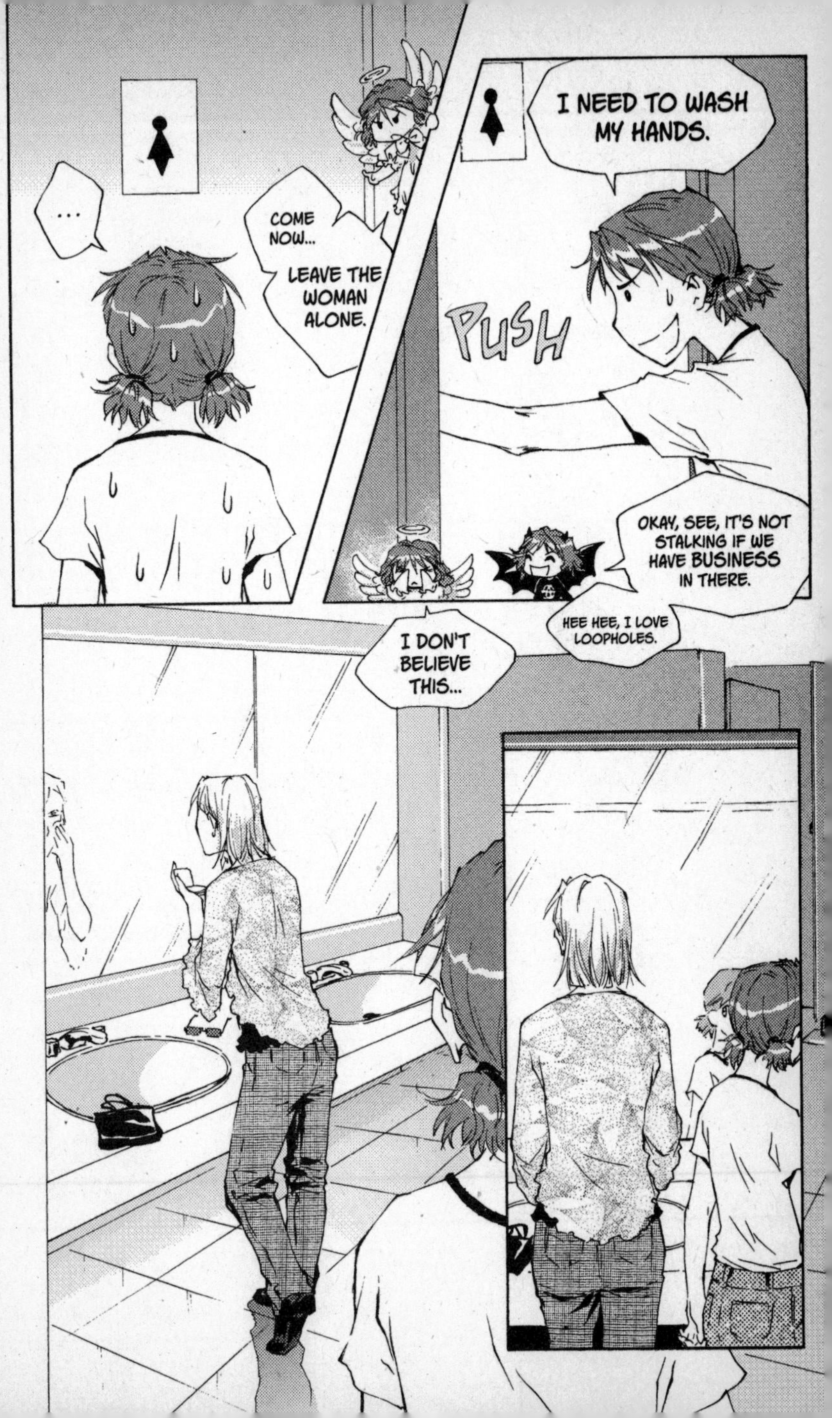
...
COME NOW...
LEAVE THE WOMAN ALONE.
I NEED TO WASH MY HANDS.
PUSH
OKAY, SEE, IT'S NOT STALKING IF WE HAVE BUSINESS IN THERE.
HEE HEE, I LOVE LOOPHOLES.
I DON'T BELIEVE THIS...

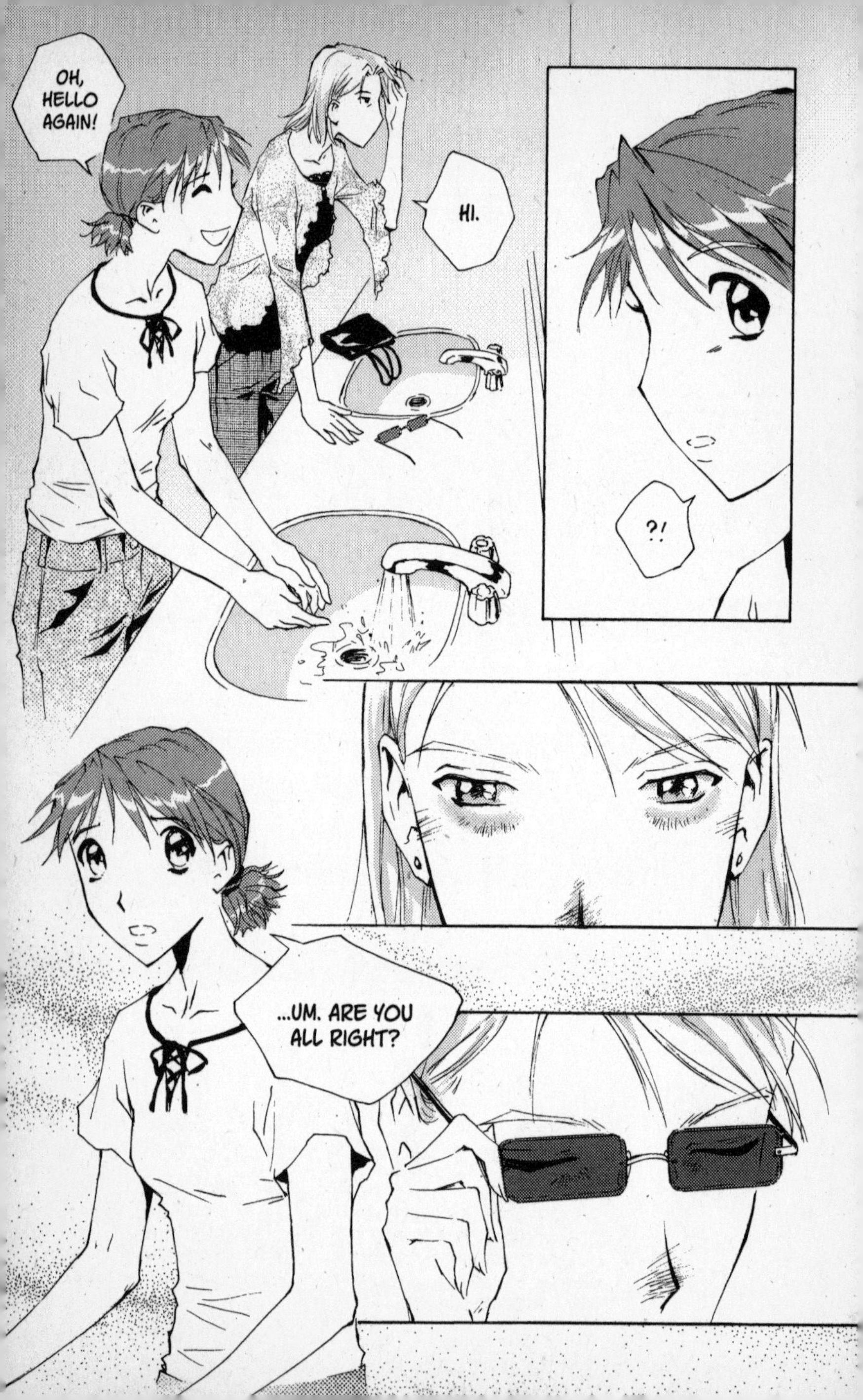
OH, HELLO AGAIN!
HI.
?!
...UM. ARE YOU ALL RIGHT?

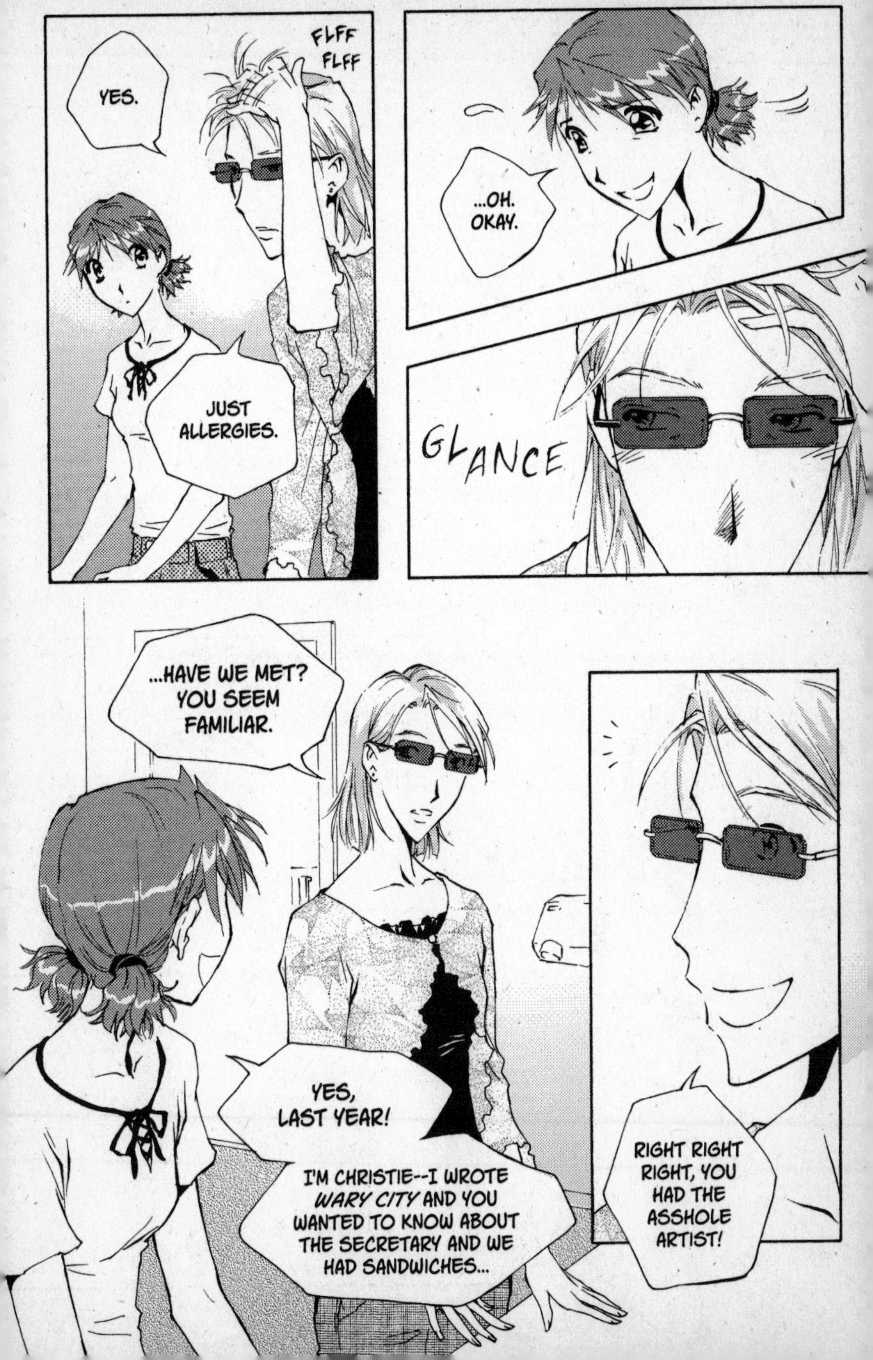
YES.
FLFF FLFF
JUST ALLERGIES.
...OH. OKAY.
GLANCE
...HAVE WE MET? YOU SEEM FAMILIAR.
YES, LAST YEAR!
I'M CHRISTIE--I WROTE *WARY CITY* AND YOU WANTED TO KNOW ABOUT THE SECRETARY AND WE HAD SANDWICHES...
RIGHT RIGHT RIGHT, YOU HAD THE ASSHOLE ARTIST!

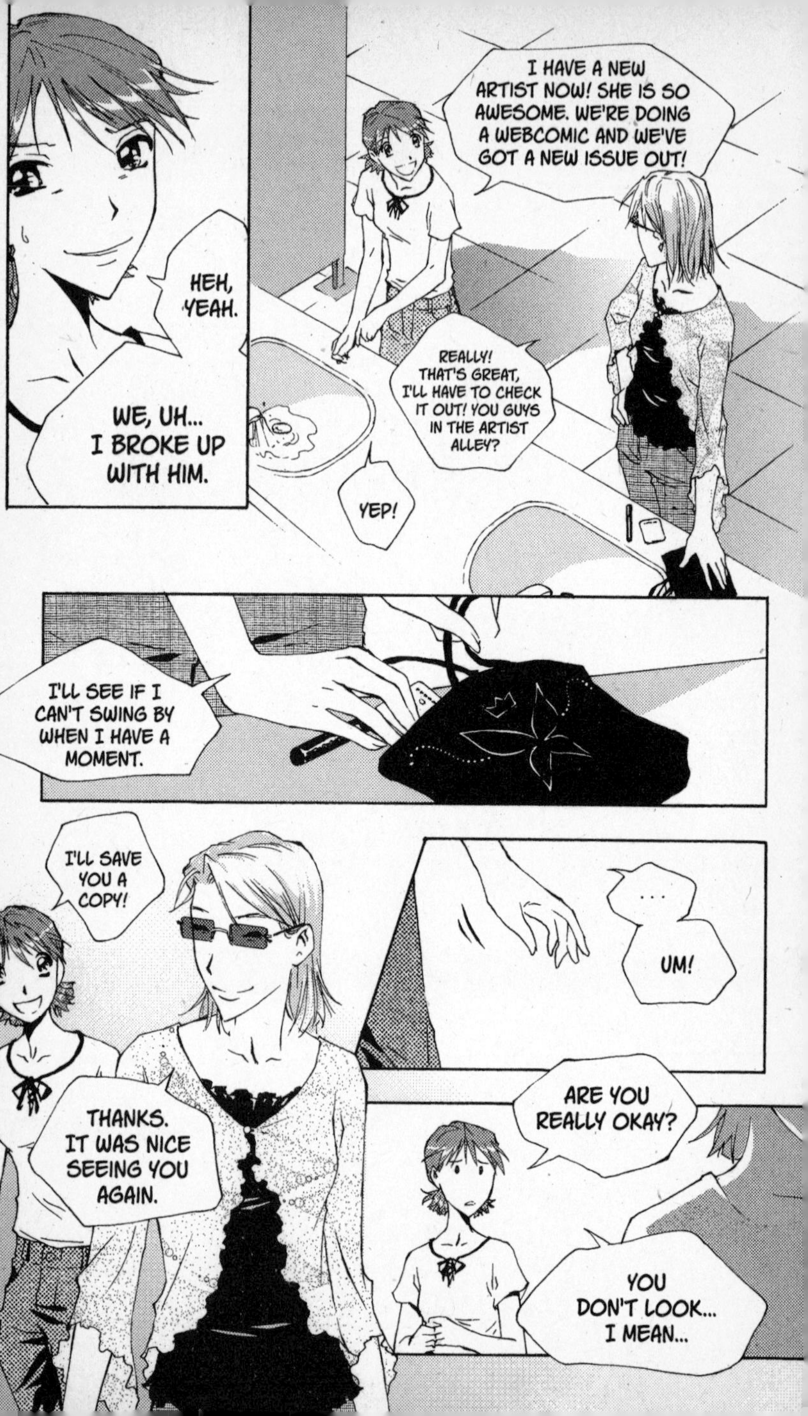
HEH, YEAH.
WE, UH... I BROKE UP WITH HIM.
I HAVE A NEW ARTIST NOW! SHE IS SO AWESOME. WE'RE DOING A WEBCOMIC AND WE'VE GOT A NEW ISSUE OUT!
REALLY! THAT'S GREAT, I'LL HAVE TO CHECK IT OUT! YOU GUYS IN THE ARTIST ALLEY?
YEP!
I'LL SEE IF I CAN'T SWING BY WHEN I HAVE A MOMENT.
I'LL SAVE YOU A COPY!
THANKS. IT WAS NICE SEEING YOU AGAIN.
...
UM!
ARE YOU REALLY OKAY?
YOU DON'T LOOK... I MEAN...

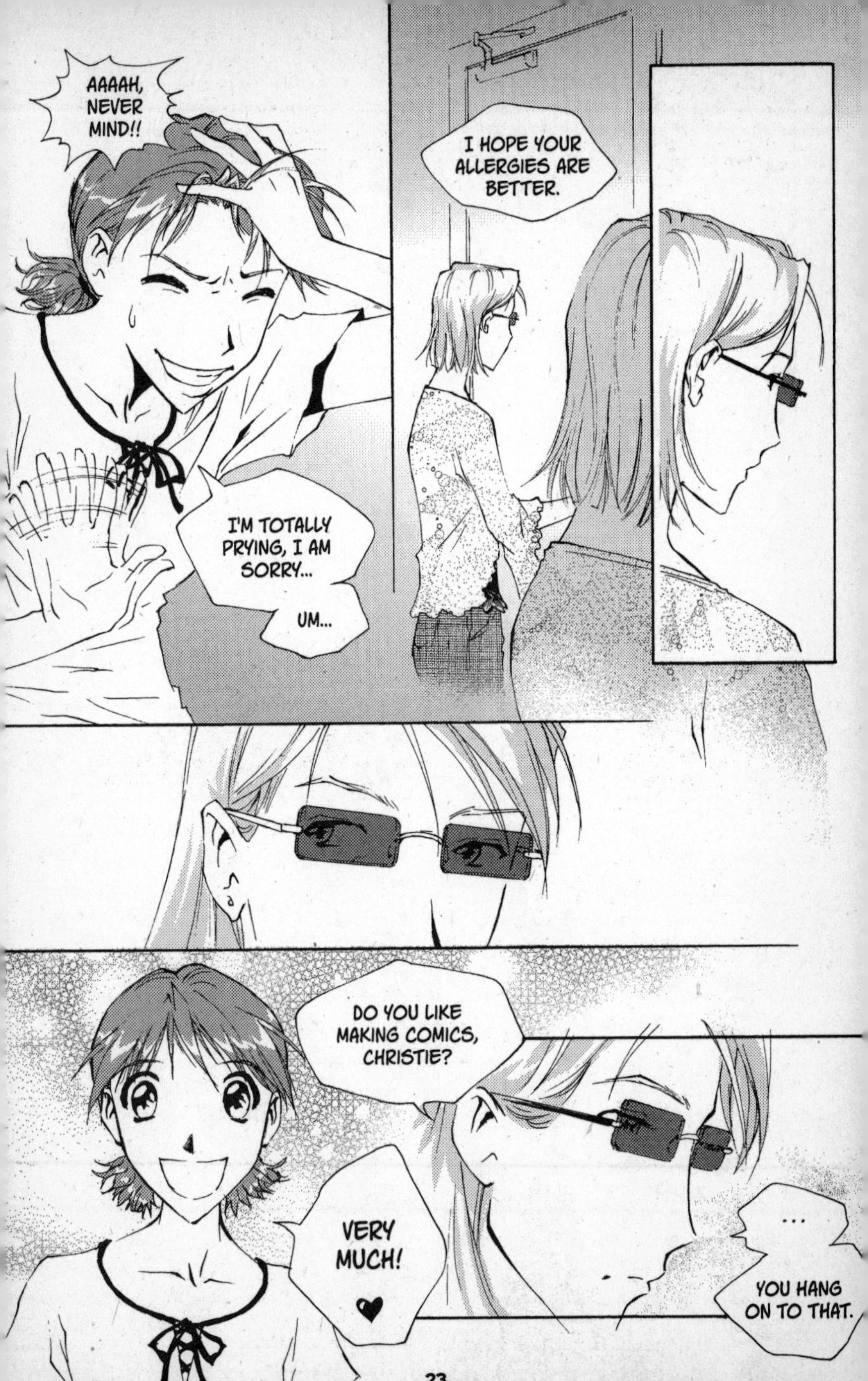
AAAAH, NEVER MIND!!
I'M TOTALLY PRYING, I AM SORRY...
UM...
I HOPE YOUR ALLERGIES ARE BETTER.
DO YOU LIKE MAKING COMICS, CHRISTIE?
VERY MUCH! ♥
...
YOU HANG ON TO THAT.

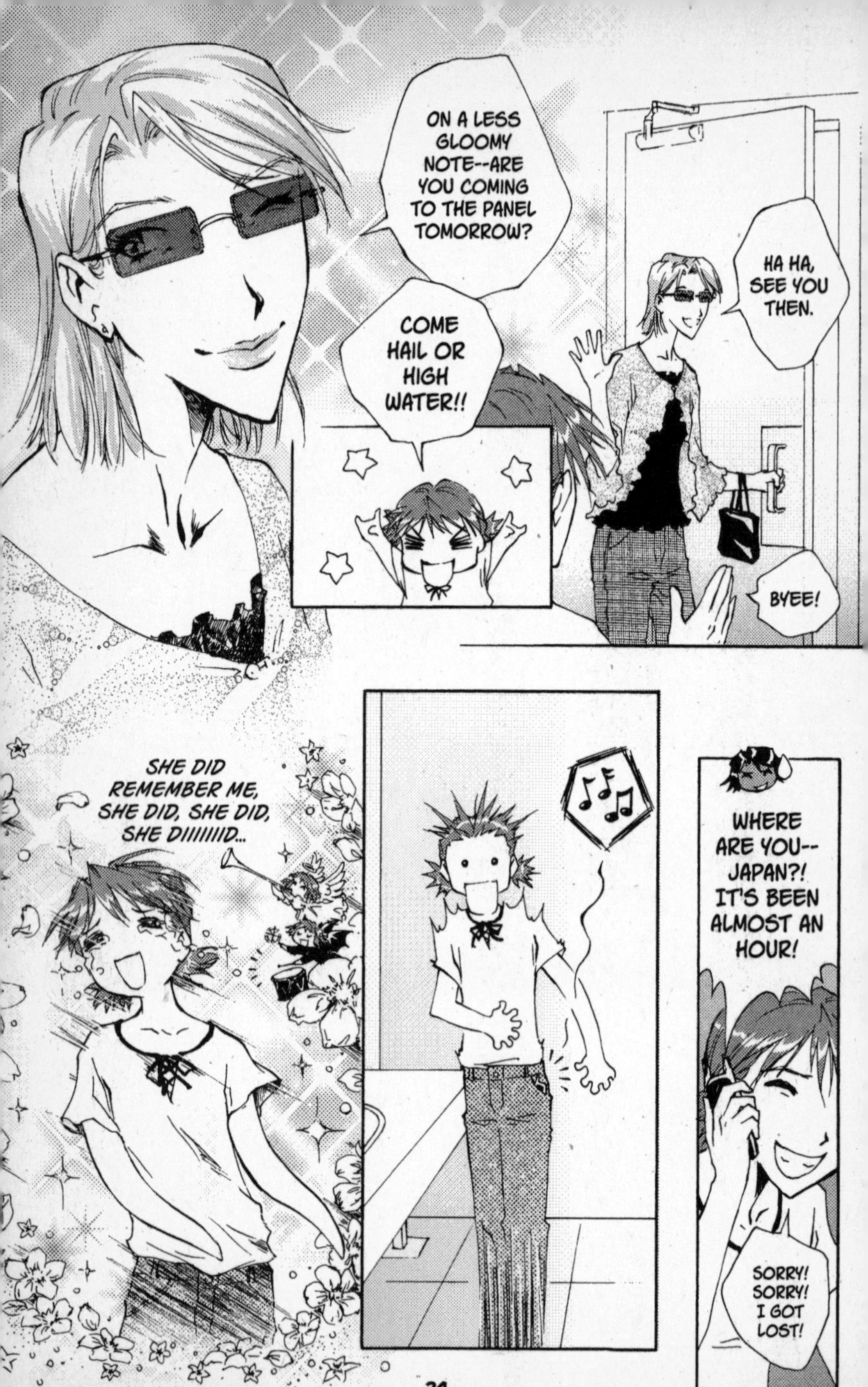
ON A LESS GLOOMY NOTE--ARE YOU COMING TO THE PANEL TOMORROW?
COME HAIL OR HIGH WATER!!
HA HA, SEE YOU THEN.
BYEE!
SHE DID REMEMBER ME, SHE DID, SHE DID, SHE DIIIIIIID...
WHERE ARE YOU--JAPAN?! IT'S BEEN ALMOST AN HOUR!
SORRY! SORRY! I GOT LOST!

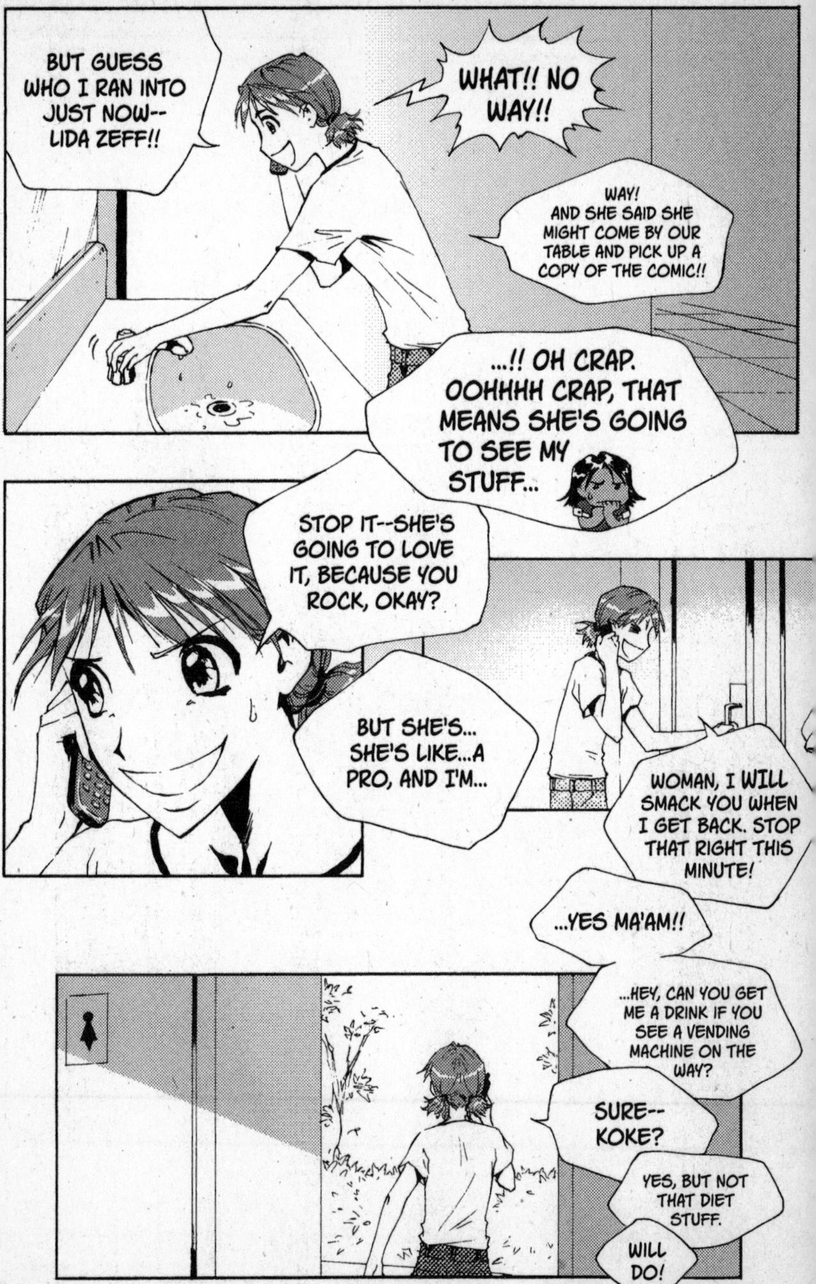
BUT GUESS WHO I RAN INTO JUST NOW-- LIDA ZEFF!!
WHAT!! NO WAY!!
WAY! AND SHE SAID SHE MIGHT COME BY OUR TABLE AND PICK UP A COPY OF THE COMIC!!
...!! OH CRAP. OOHHHH CRAP, THAT MEANS SHE'S GOING TO SEE MY STUFF...
STOP IT--SHE'S GOING TO LOVE IT, BECAUSE YOU ROCK, OKAY?
BUT SHE'S... SHE'S LIKE...A PRO, AND I'M...
WOMAN, I WILL SMACK YOU WHEN I GET BACK. STOP THAT RIGHT THIS MINUTE!
...YES MA'AM!!
...HEY, CAN YOU GET ME A DRINK IF YOU SEE A VENDING MACHINE ON THE WAY?
SURE-- KOKE?
YES, BUT NOT THAT DIET STUFF.
WILL DO!

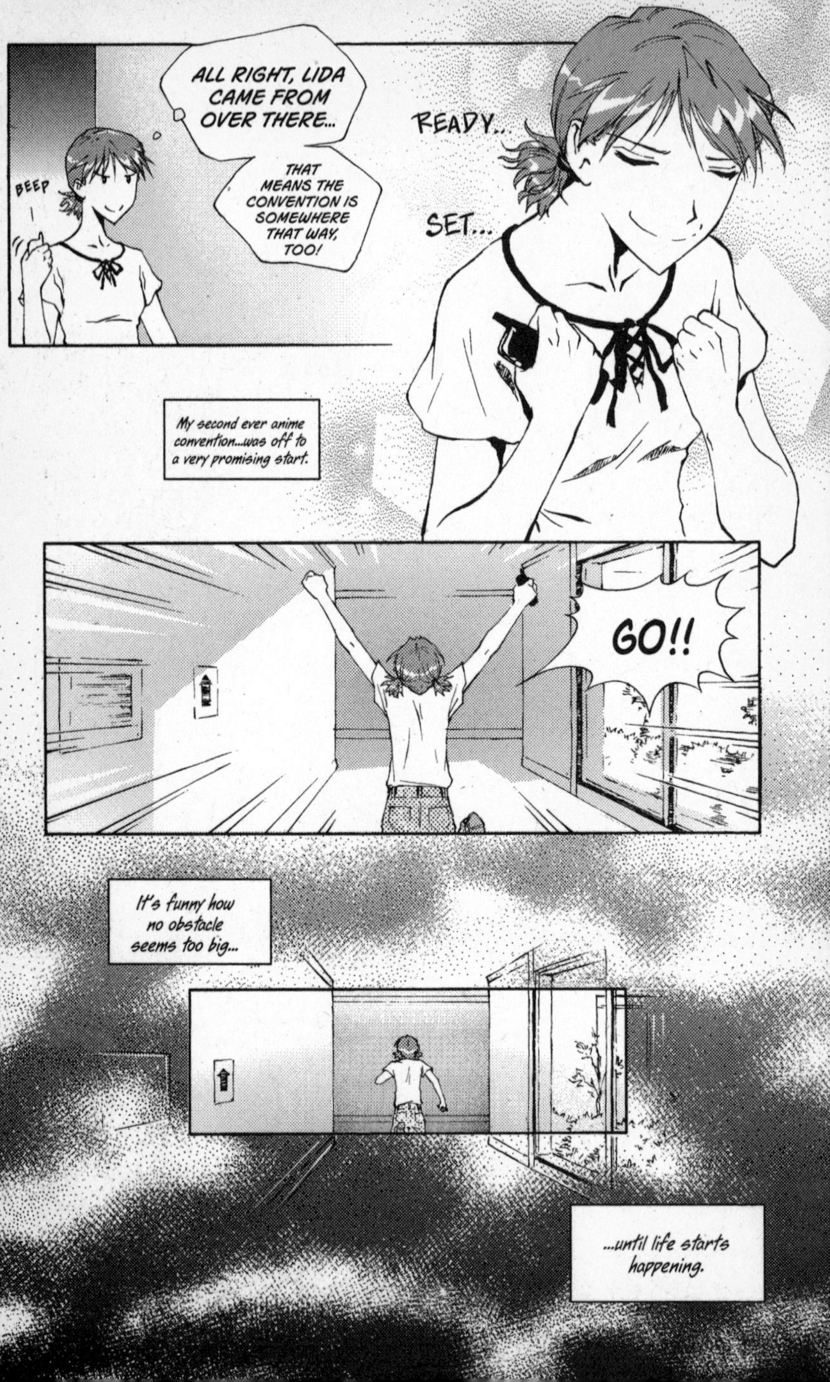
BEEP
ALL RIGHT, LIDA CAME FROM OVER THERE...
THAT MEANS THE CONVENTION IS SOMEWHERE THAT WAY, TOO!
READY...
SET...
My second ever anime convention...was off to a very promising start.
GO!!
It's funny how no obstacle seems too big...
...until life starts happening.

CHAPTER 2

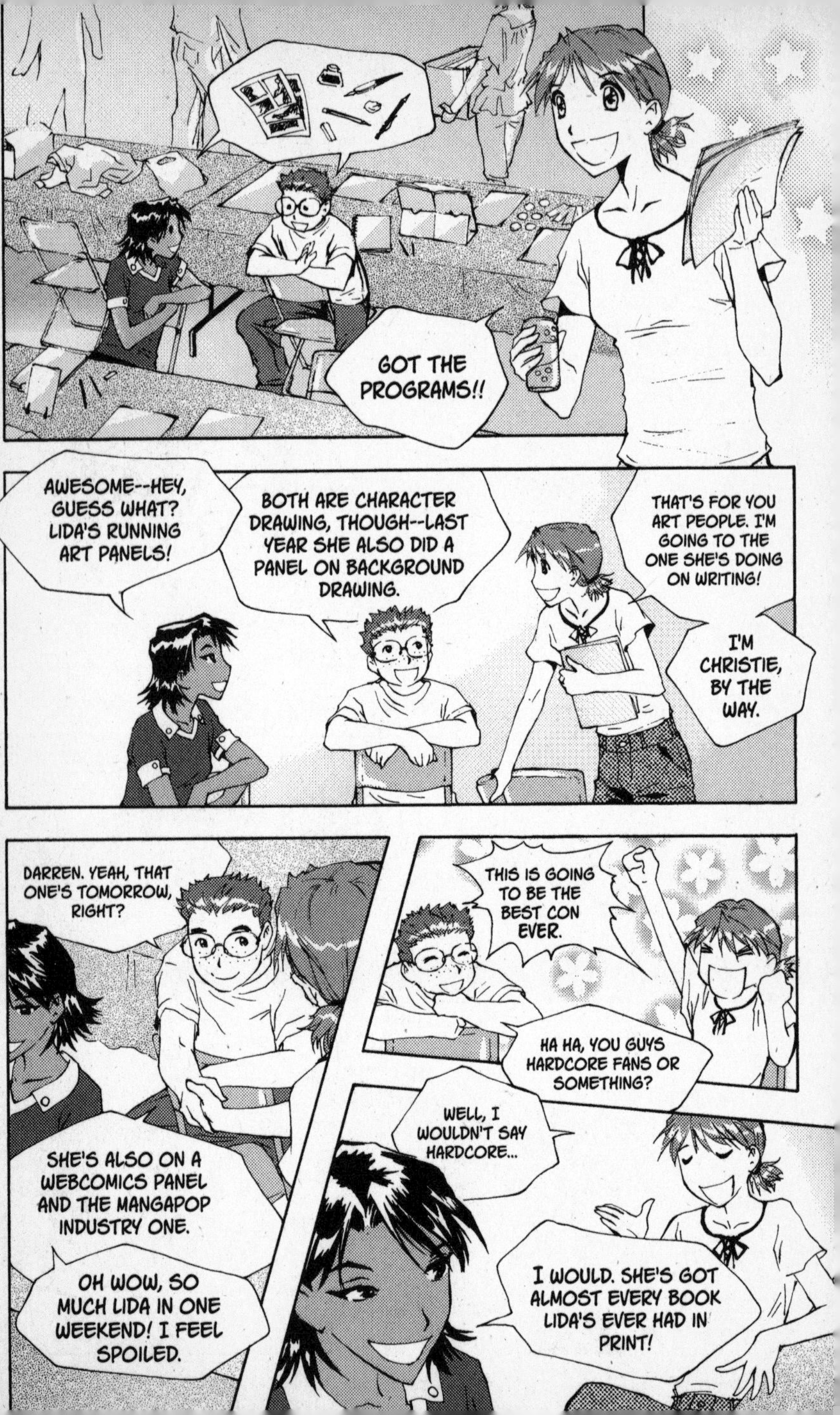
GOT THE PROGRAMS!!
AWESOME--HEY, GUESS WHAT? LIDA'S RUNNING ART PANELS!
BOTH ARE CHARACTER DRAWING, THOUGH--LAST YEAR SHE ALSO DID A PANEL ON BACKGROUND DRAWING.
THAT'S FOR YOU ART PEOPLE. I'M GOING TO THE ONE SHE'S DOING ON WRITING!
I'M CHRISTIE, BY THE WAY.
DARREN. YEAH, THAT ONE'S TOMORROW, RIGHT?
SHE'S ALSO ON A WEBCOMICS PANEL AND THE MANGAPOP INDUSTRY ONE.
OH WOW, SO MUCH LIDA IN ONE WEEKEND! I FEEL SPOILED.
THIS IS GOING TO BE THE BEST CON EVER.
HA HA, YOU GUYS HARDCORE FANS OR SOMETHING?
WELL, I WOULDN'T SAY HARDCORE...
I WOULD. SHE'S GOT ALMOST EVERY BOOK LIDA'S EVER HAD IN PRINT!

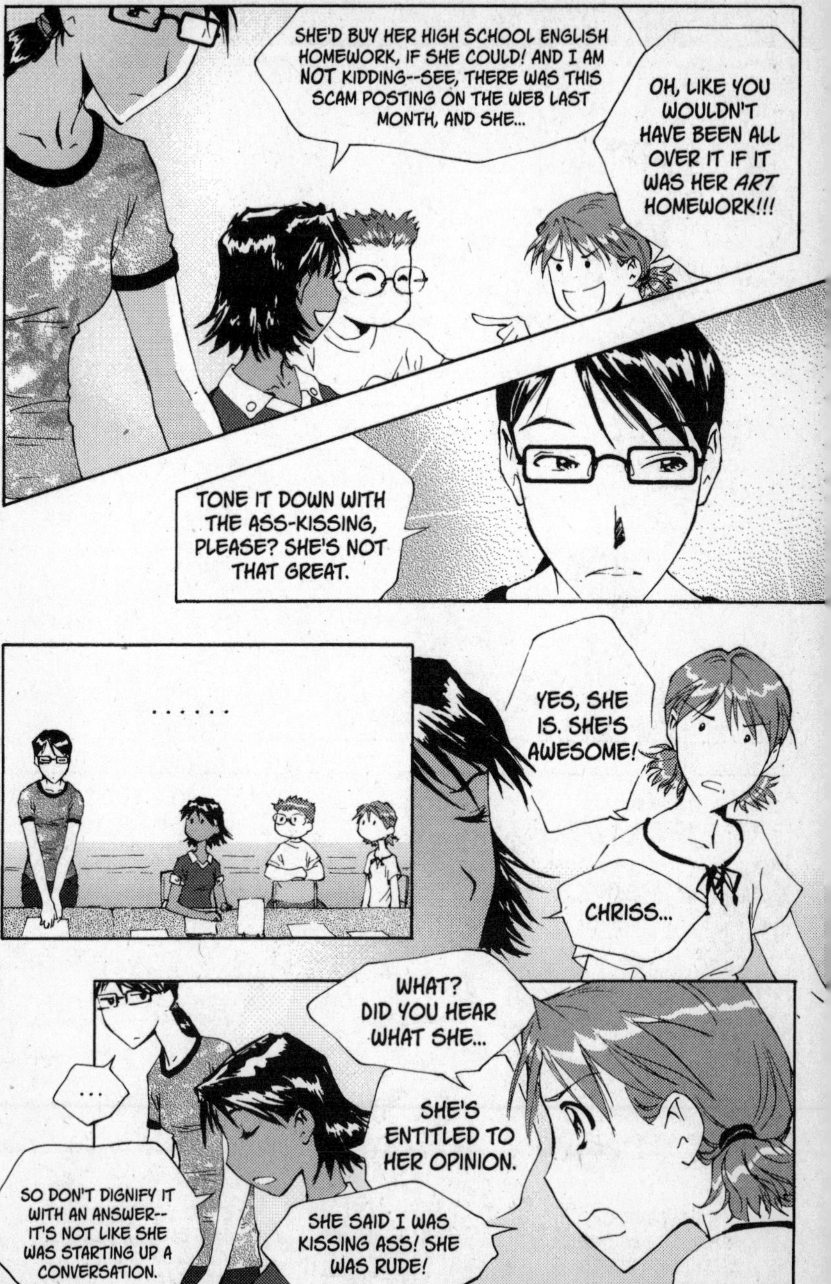

SHE'D BUY HER HIGH SCHOOL ENGLISH HOMEWORK, IF SHE COULD! AND I AM NOT KIDDING--SEE, THERE WAS THIS SCAM POSTING ON THE WEB LAST MONTH, AND SHE...
OH, LIKE YOU WOULDN'T HAVE BEEN ALL OVER IT IF IT WAS HER *ART* HOMEWORK!!!
TONE IT DOWN WITH THE ASS-KISSING, PLEASE? SHE'S NOT THAT GREAT.
......
YES, SHE IS. SHE'S AWESOME!
CHRISS...
...
WHAT? DID YOU HEAR WHAT SHE...
SHE'S ENTITLED TO HER OPINION.
SO DON'T DIGNIFY IT WITH AN ANSWER-- IT'S NOT LIKE SHE WAS STARTING UP A CONVERSATION.
SHE SAID I WAS KISSING ASS! SHE WAS RUDE!

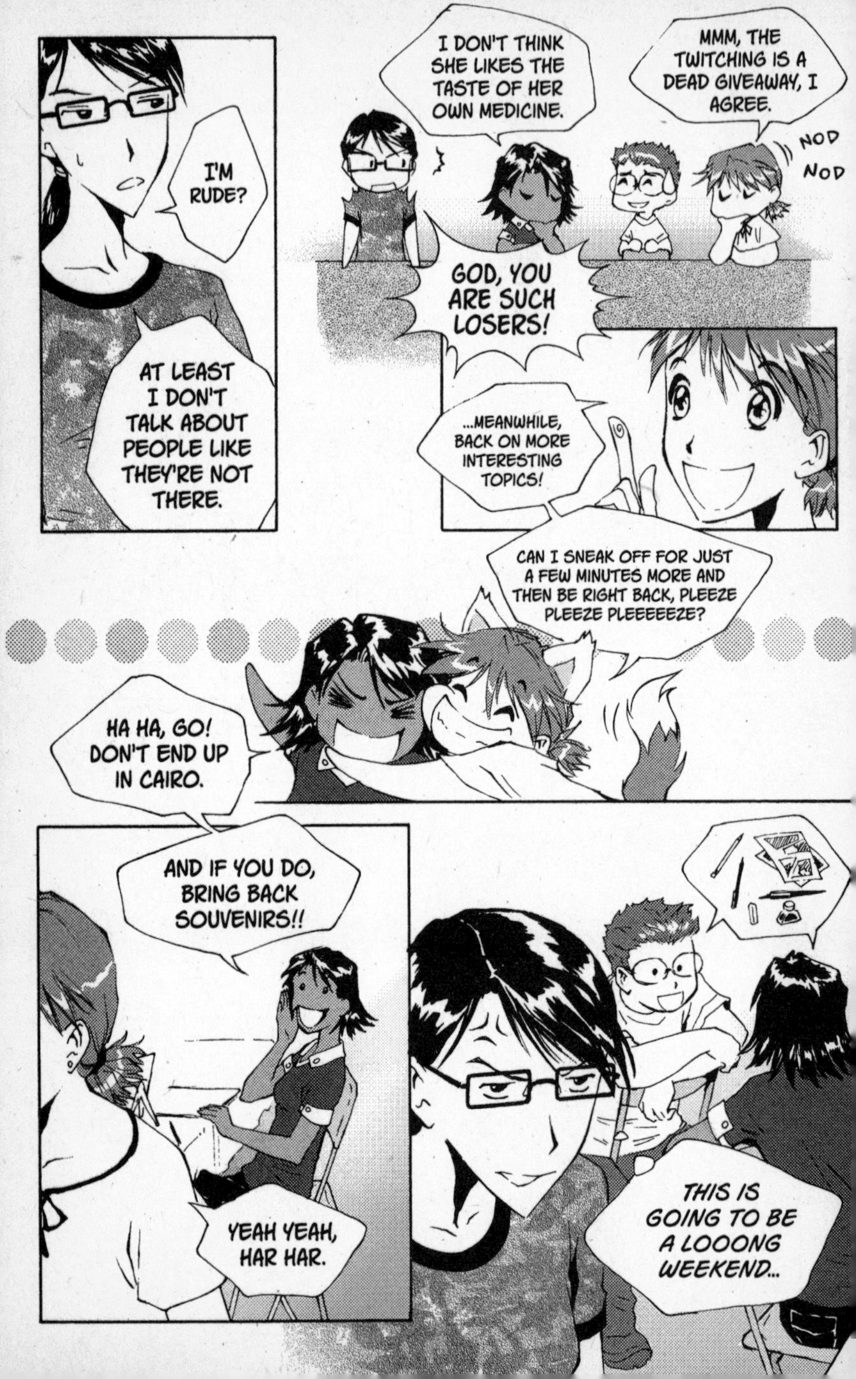
I'M RUDE?
AT LEAST I DON'T TALK ABOUT PEOPLE LIKE THEY'RE NOT THERE.
I DON'T THINK SHE LIKES THE TASTE OF HER OWN MEDICINE.
MMM, THE TWITCHING IS A DEAD GIVEAWAY, I AGREE.
NOD NOD
GOD, YOU ARE SUCH LOSERS!
...MEANWHILE, BACK ON MORE INTERESTING TOPICS!
CAN I SNEAK OFF FOR JUST A FEW MINUTES MORE AND THEN BE RIGHT BACK, PLEEZE PLEEZE PLEEEEEZE?
HA HA, GO! DON'T END UP IN CAIRO.
AND IF YOU DO, BRING BACK SOUVENIRS!!
YEAH YEAH, HAR HAR.
THIS IS GOING TO BE A LOOONG WEEKEND...

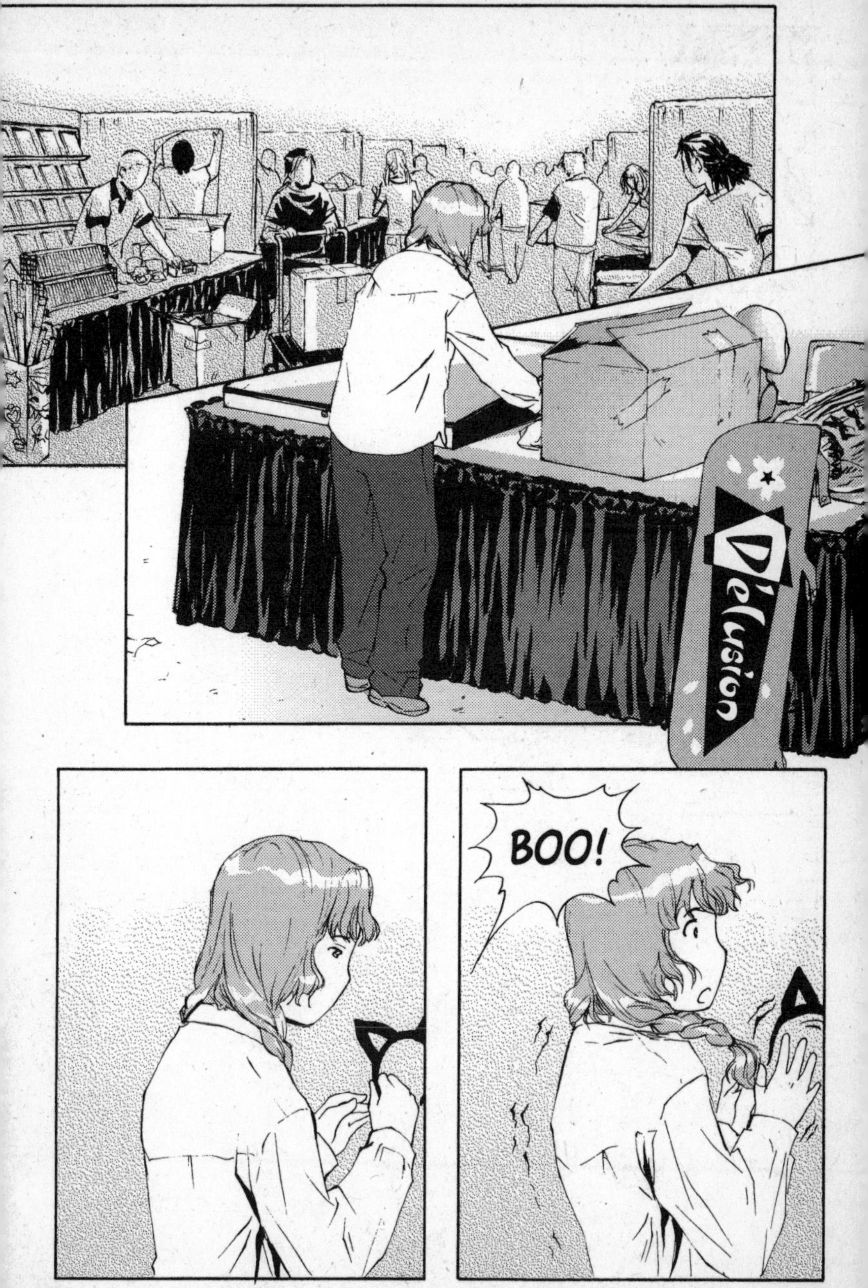
Delusion
BOO!

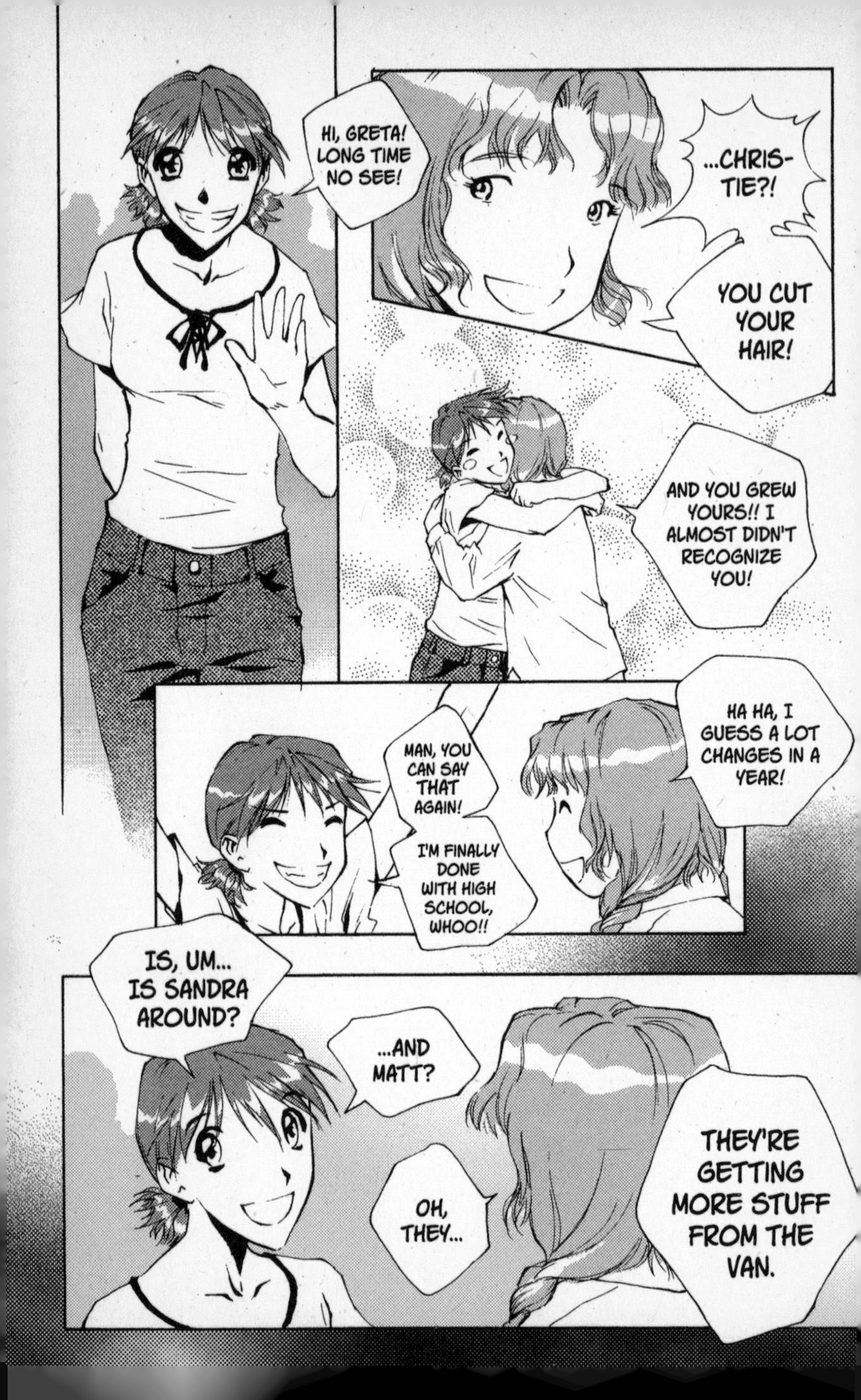
HI, GRETA! LONG TIME NO SEE!
...CHRIS-TIE?!
YOU CUT YOUR HAIR!
AND YOU GREW YOURS!! I ALMOST DIDN'T RECOGNIZE YOU!
MAN, YOU CAN SAY THAT AGAIN!
I'M FINALLY DONE WITH HIGH SCHOOL, WHOO!!
HA HA, I GUESS A LOT CHANGES IN A YEAR!
IS, UM... IS SANDRA AROUND?
...AND MATT?
OH, THEY...
THEY'RE GETTING MORE STUFF FROM THE VAN.

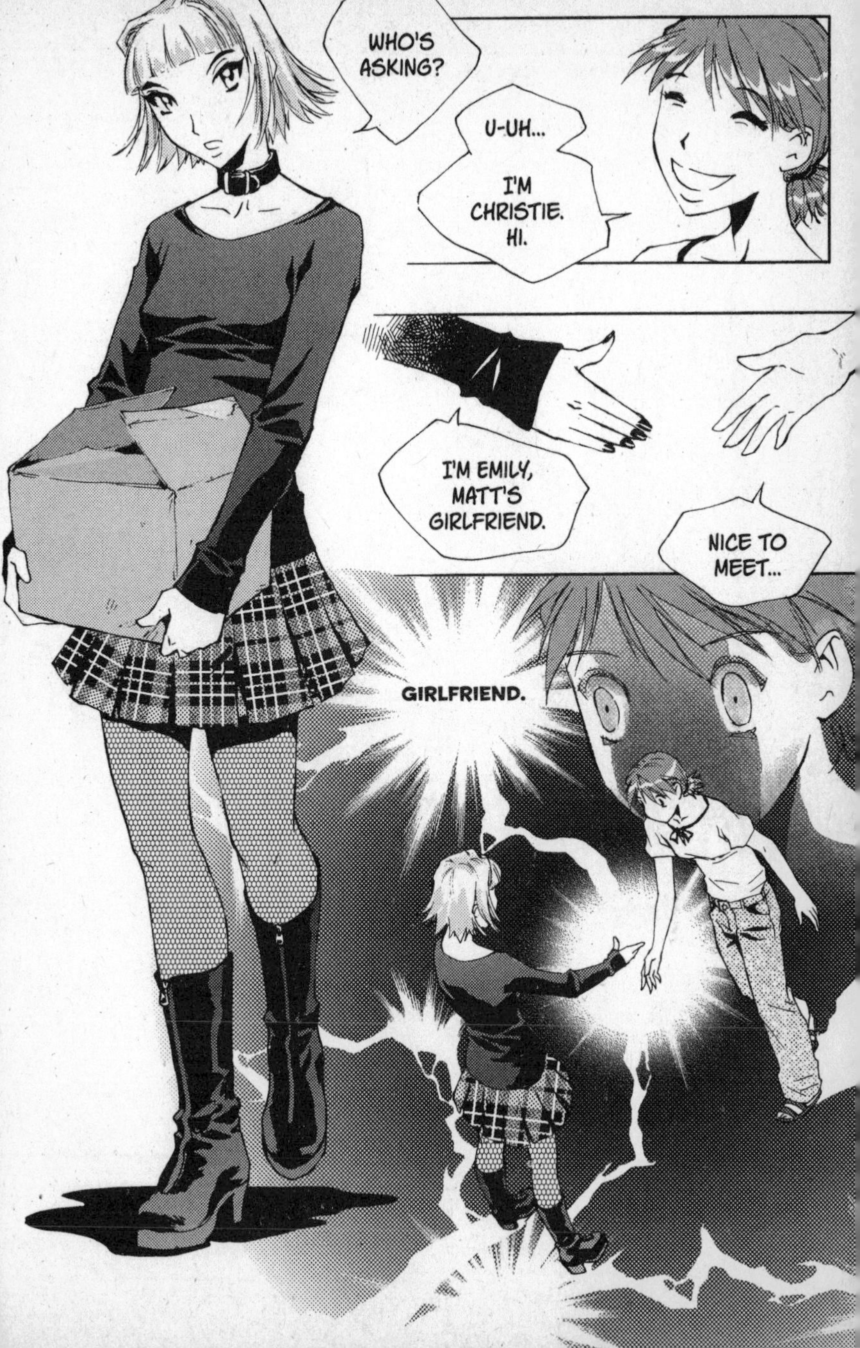
WHO'S ASKING?
U-UH...
I'M CHRISTIE. HI.
I'M EMILY, MATT'S GIRLFRIEND.
NICE TO MEET...
GIRLFRIEND.

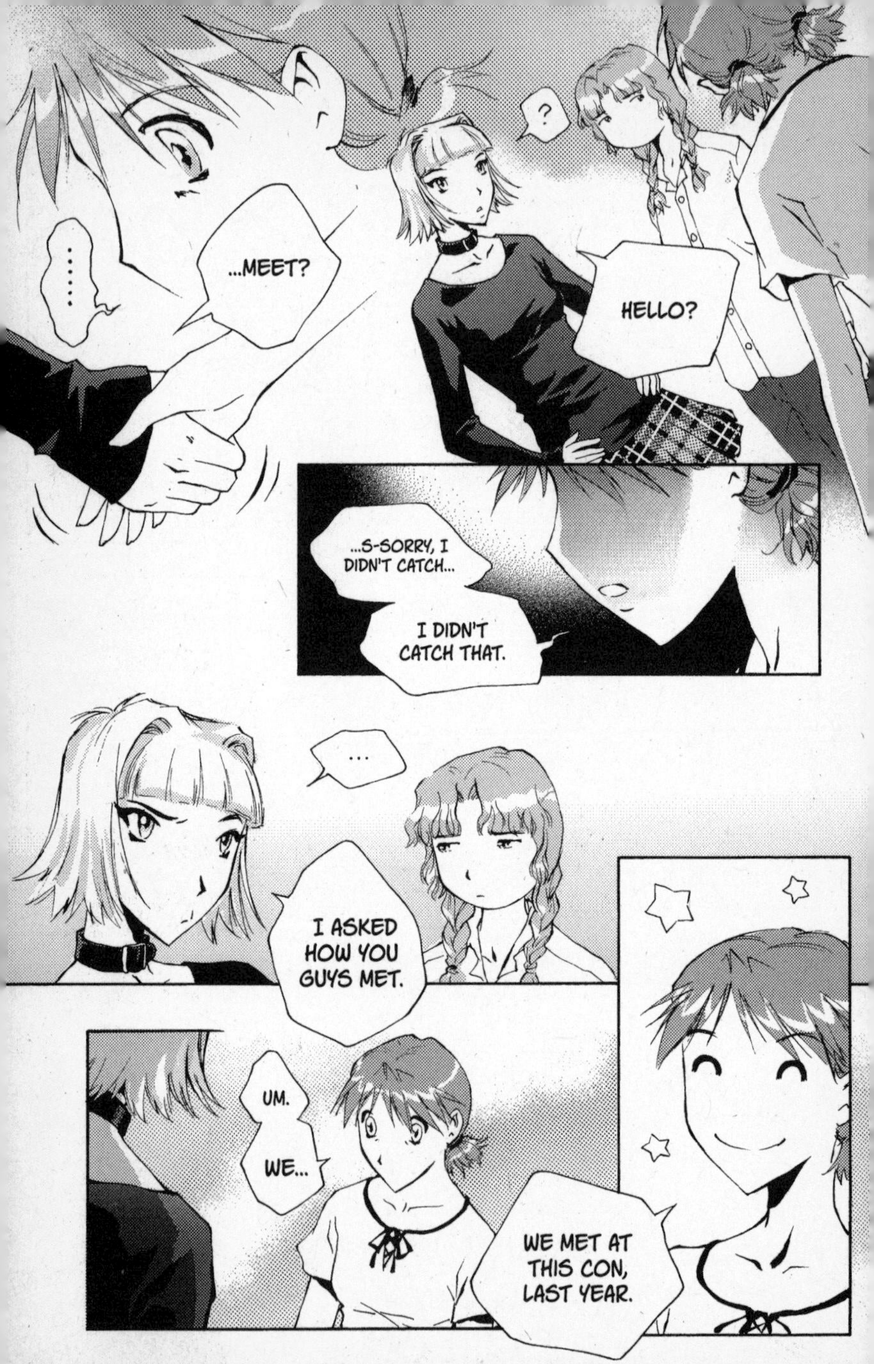
......
...MEET?
?
HELLO?
...S-SORRY, I DIDN'T CATCH...
I DIDN'T CATCH THAT.
...
I ASKED HOW YOU GUYS MET.
UM.
WE...
WE MET AT THIS CON, LAST YEAR.

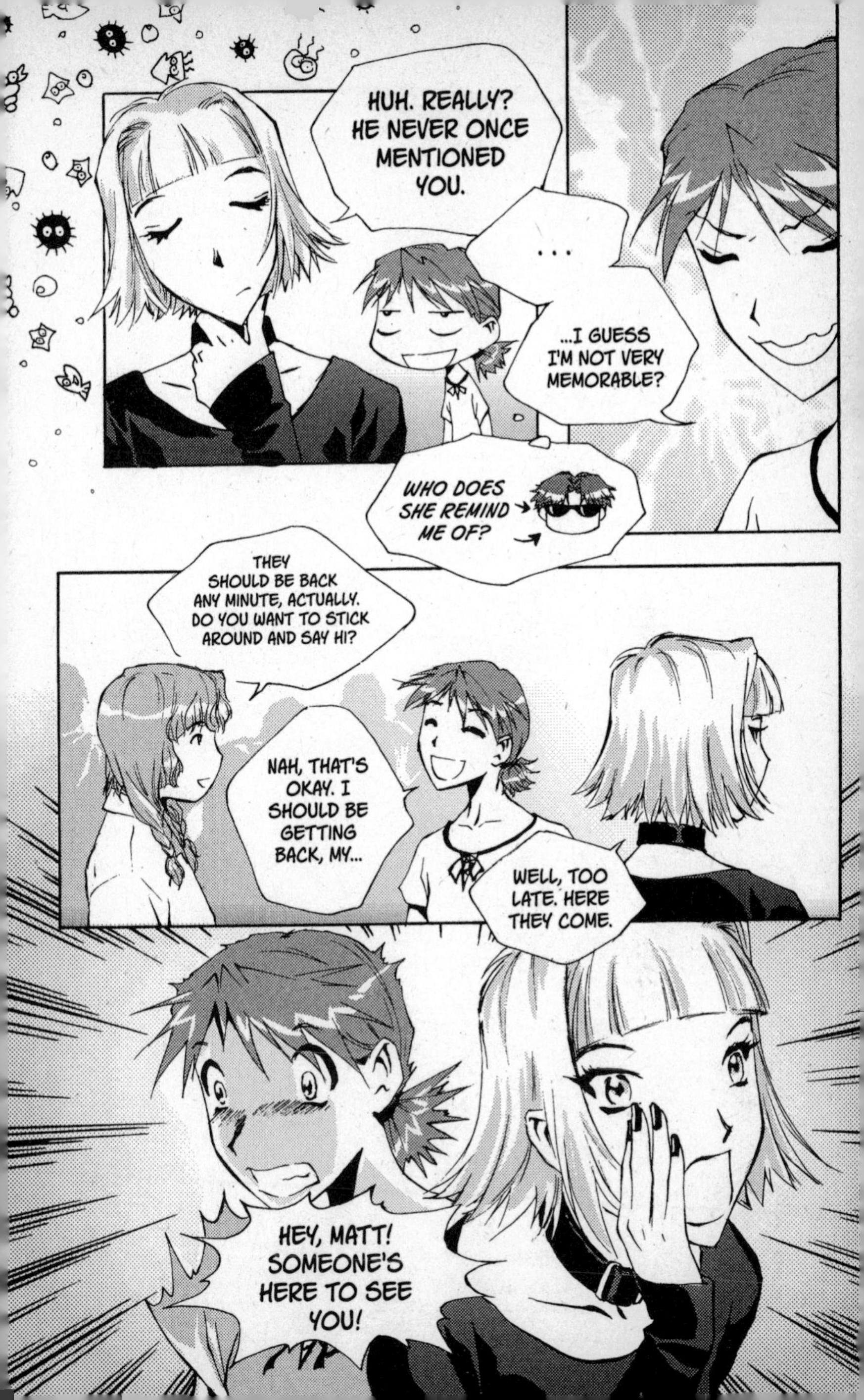
HUH. REALLY? HE NEVER ONCE MENTIONED YOU.
...
...I GUESS I'M NOT VERY MEMORABLE?
WHO DOES SHE REMIND ME OF?
THEY SHOULD BE BACK ANY MINUTE, ACTUALLY. DO YOU WANT TO STICK AROUND AND SAY HI?
NAH, THAT'S OKAY. I SHOULD BE GETTING BACK, MY...
WELL, TOO LATE. HERE THEY COME.
HEY, MATT! SOMEONE'S HERE TO SEE YOU!

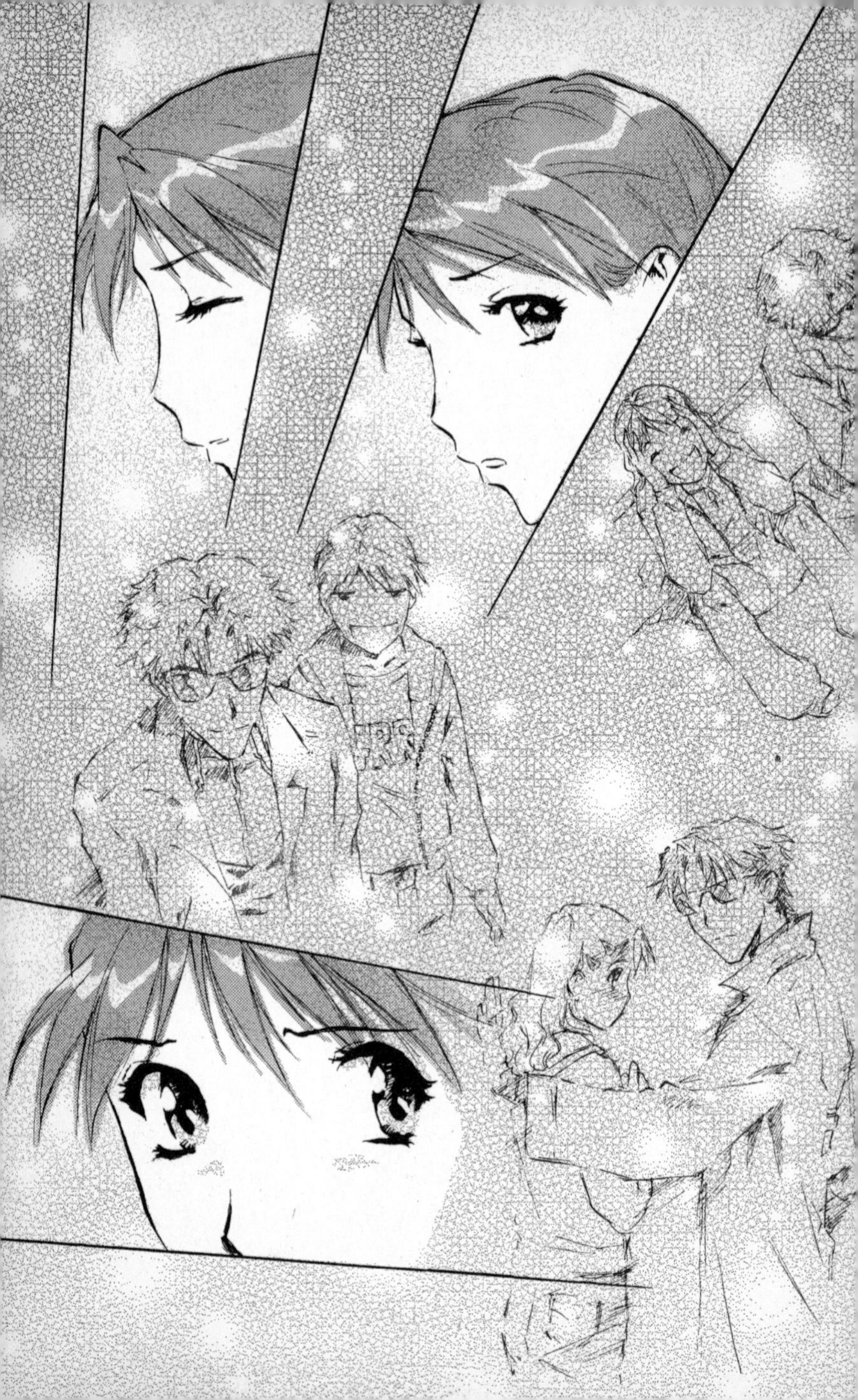

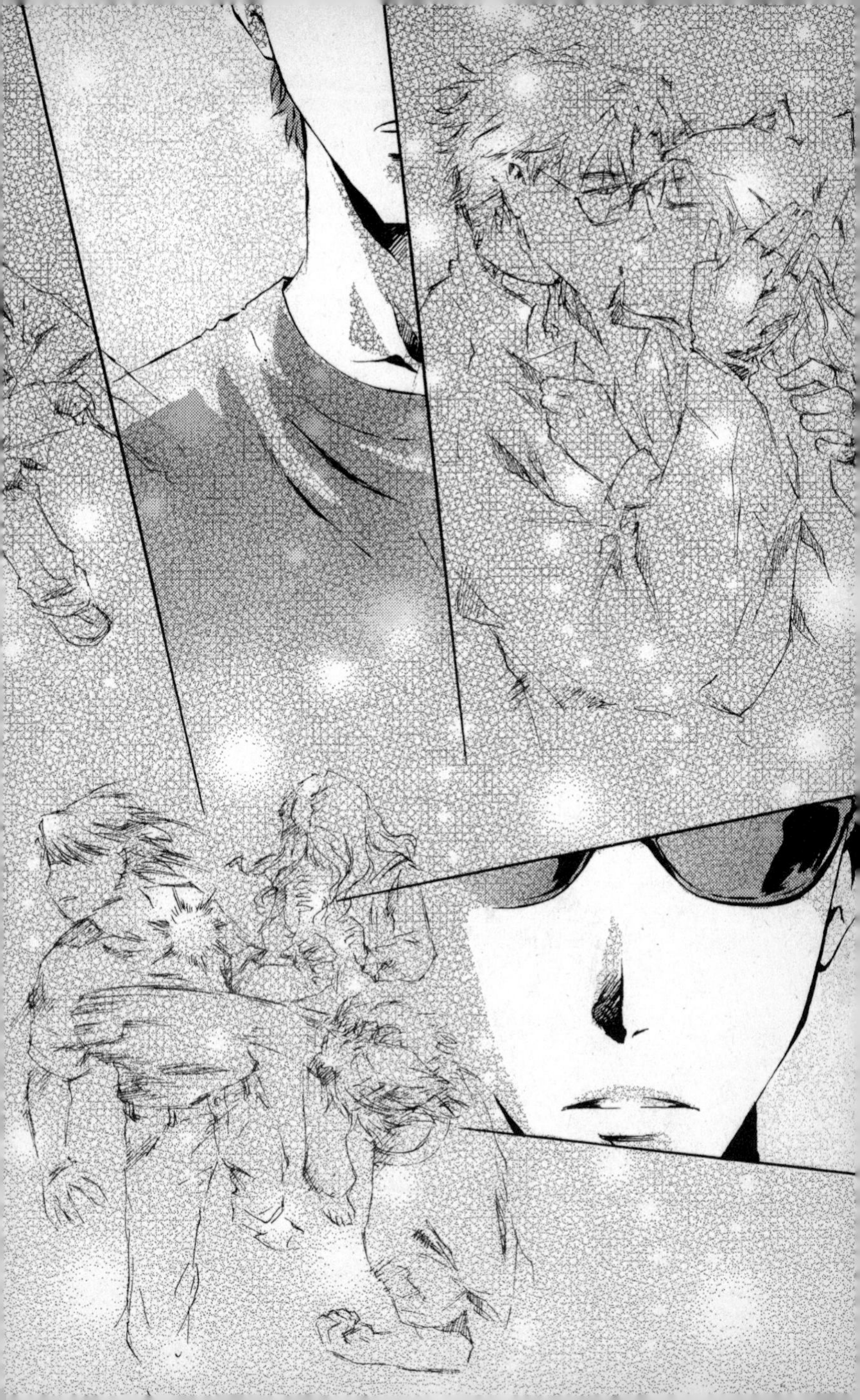

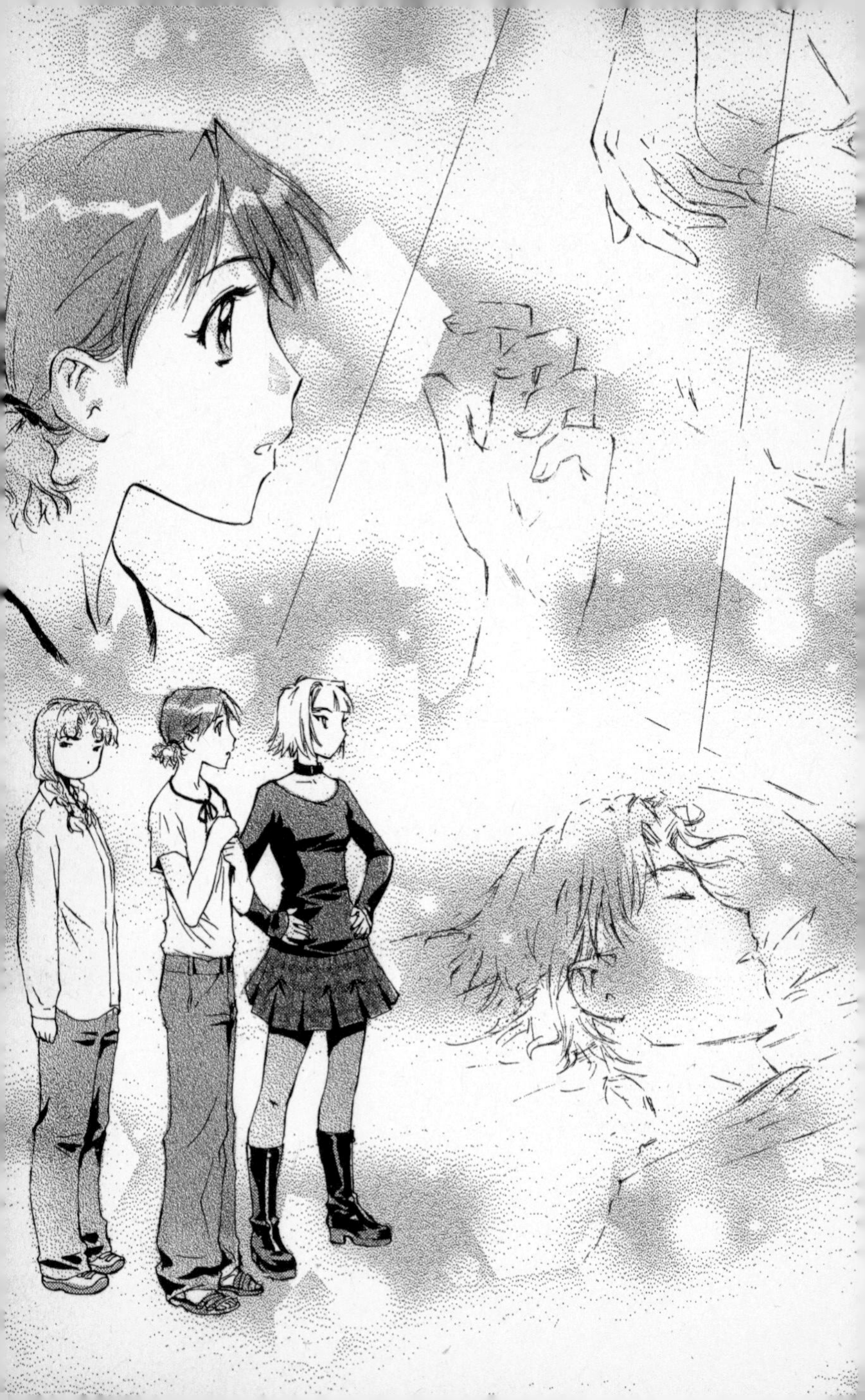

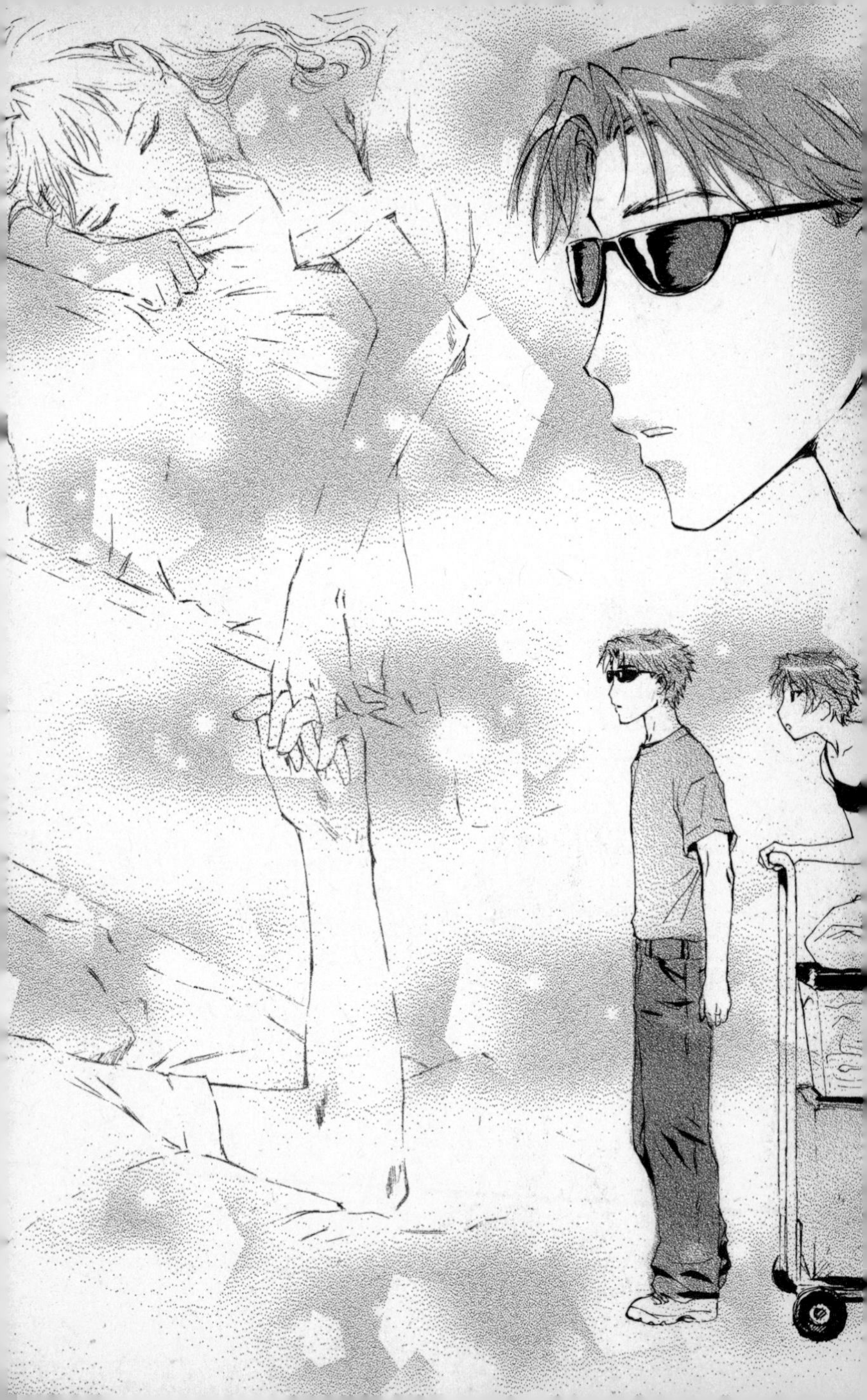

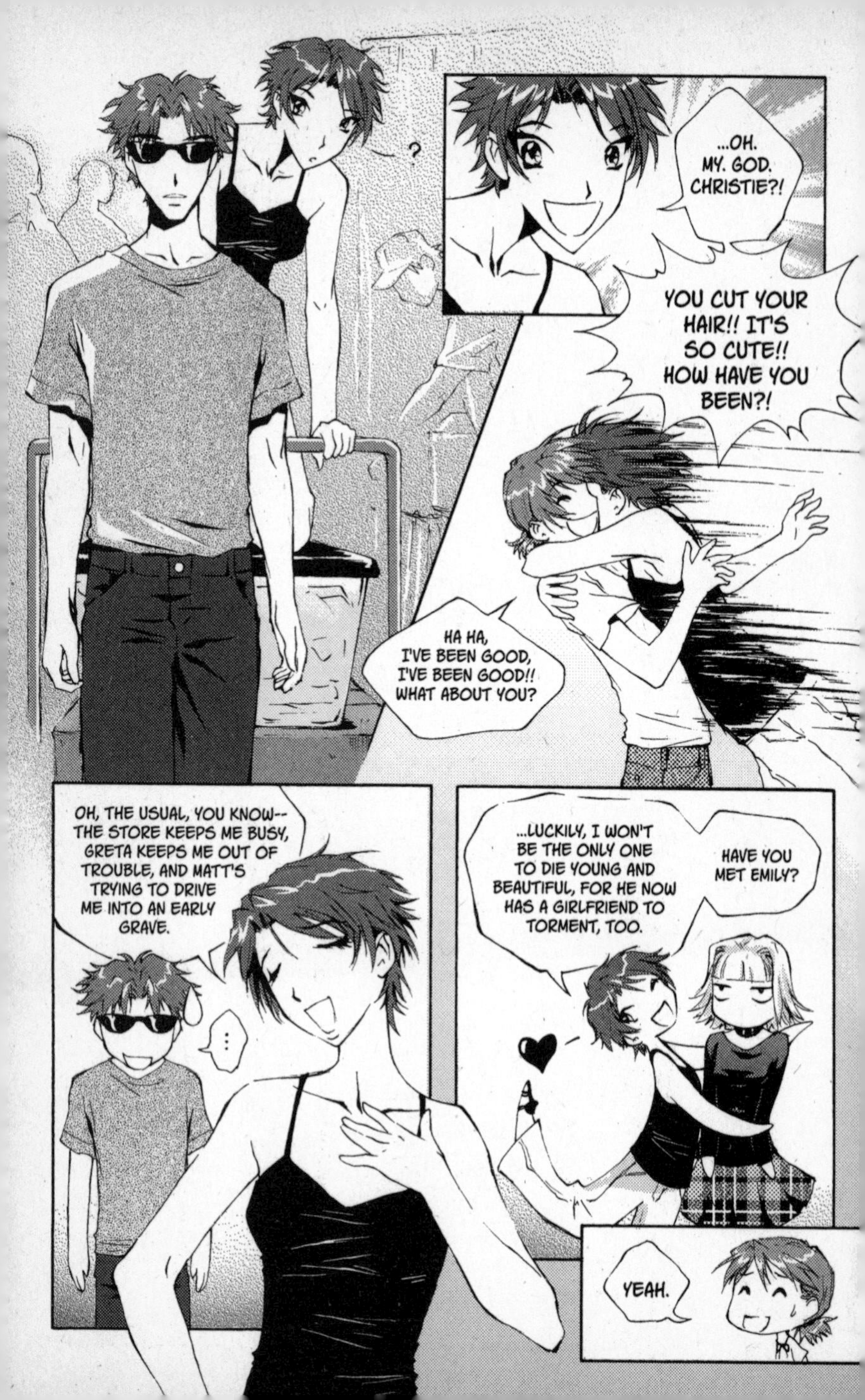
?
...OH. MY. GOD. CHRISTIE?!
YOU CUT YOUR HAIR!! IT'S SO CUTE!! HOW HAVE YOU BEEN?!
HA HA, I'VE BEEN GOOD, I'VE BEEN GOOD!! WHAT ABOUT YOU?
OH, THE USUAL, YOU KNOW-- THE STORE KEEPS ME BUSY, GRETA KEEPS ME OUT OF TROUBLE, AND MATT'S TRYING TO DRIVE ME INTO AN EARLY GRAVE.
...
...LUCKILY, I WON'T BE THE ONLY ONE TO DIE YOUNG AND BEAUTIFUL, FOR HE NOW HAS A GIRLFRIEND TO TORMENT, TOO.
HAVE YOU MET EMILY?
YEAH.

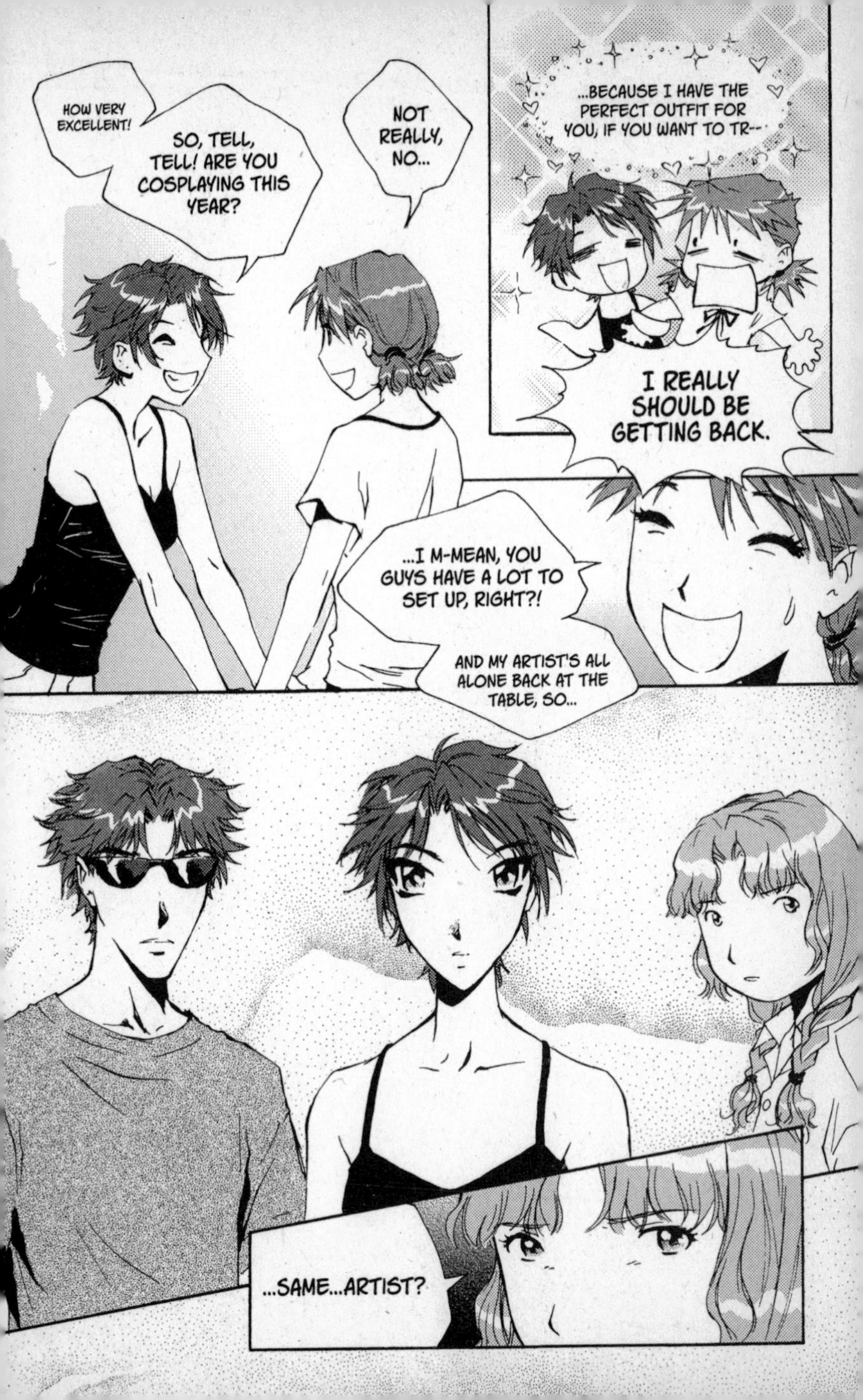
HOW VERY EXCELLENT!
SO, TELL, TELL! ARE YOU COSPLAYING THIS YEAR?
NOT REALLY, NO...
...BECAUSE I HAVE THE PERFECT OUTFIT FOR YOU, IF YOU WANT TO TR--
I REALLY SHOULD BE GETTING BACK.
...I M-MEAN, YOU GUYS HAVE A LOT TO SET UP, RIGHT?!
AND MY ARTIST'S ALL ALONE BACK AT THE TABLE, SO...
...SAME...ARTIST?

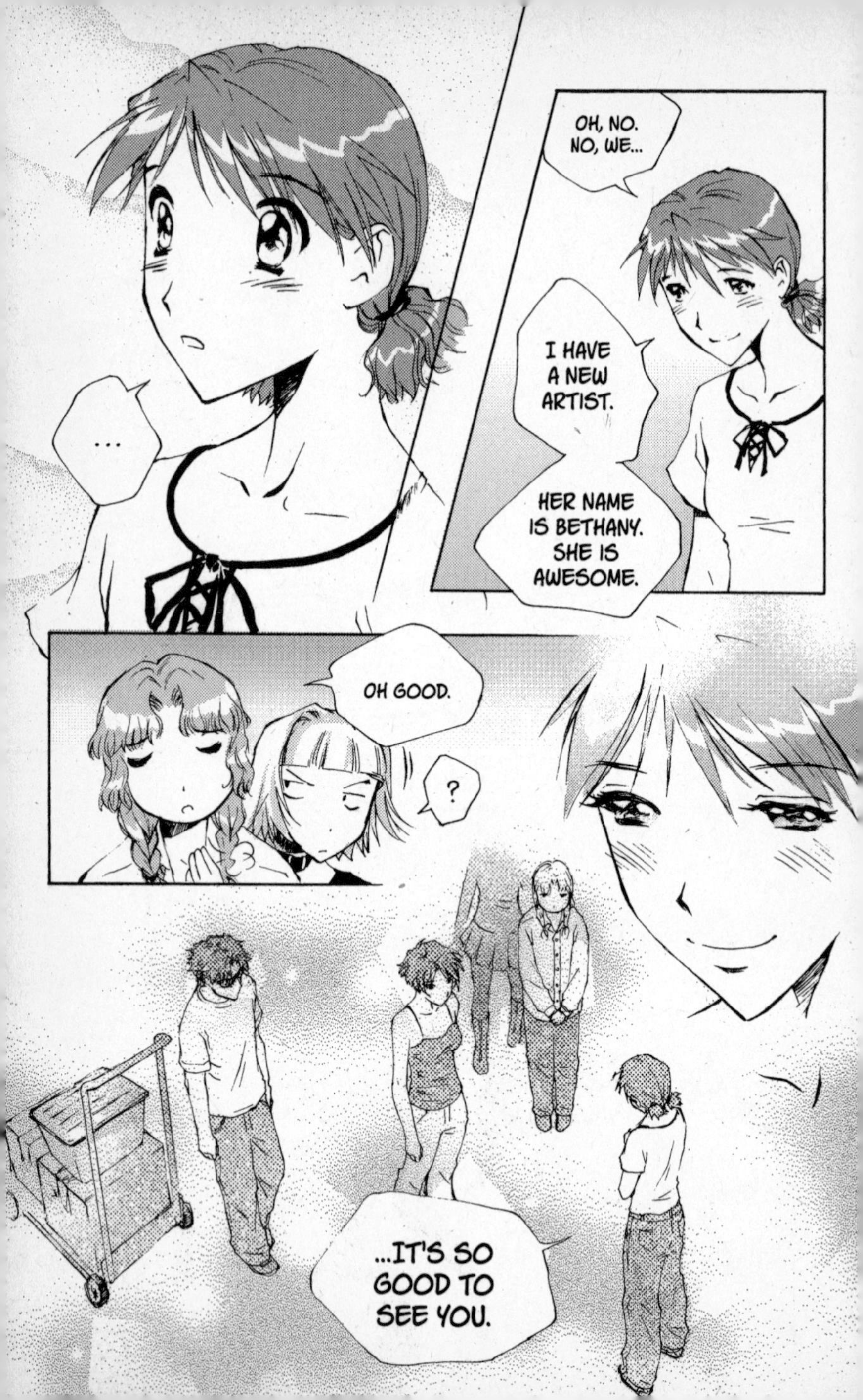
...
OH, NO. NO, WE...
I HAVE A NEW ARTIST.
HER NAME IS BETHANY. SHE IS AWESOME.
OH GOOD.
?
...IT'S SO GOOD TO SEE YOU.

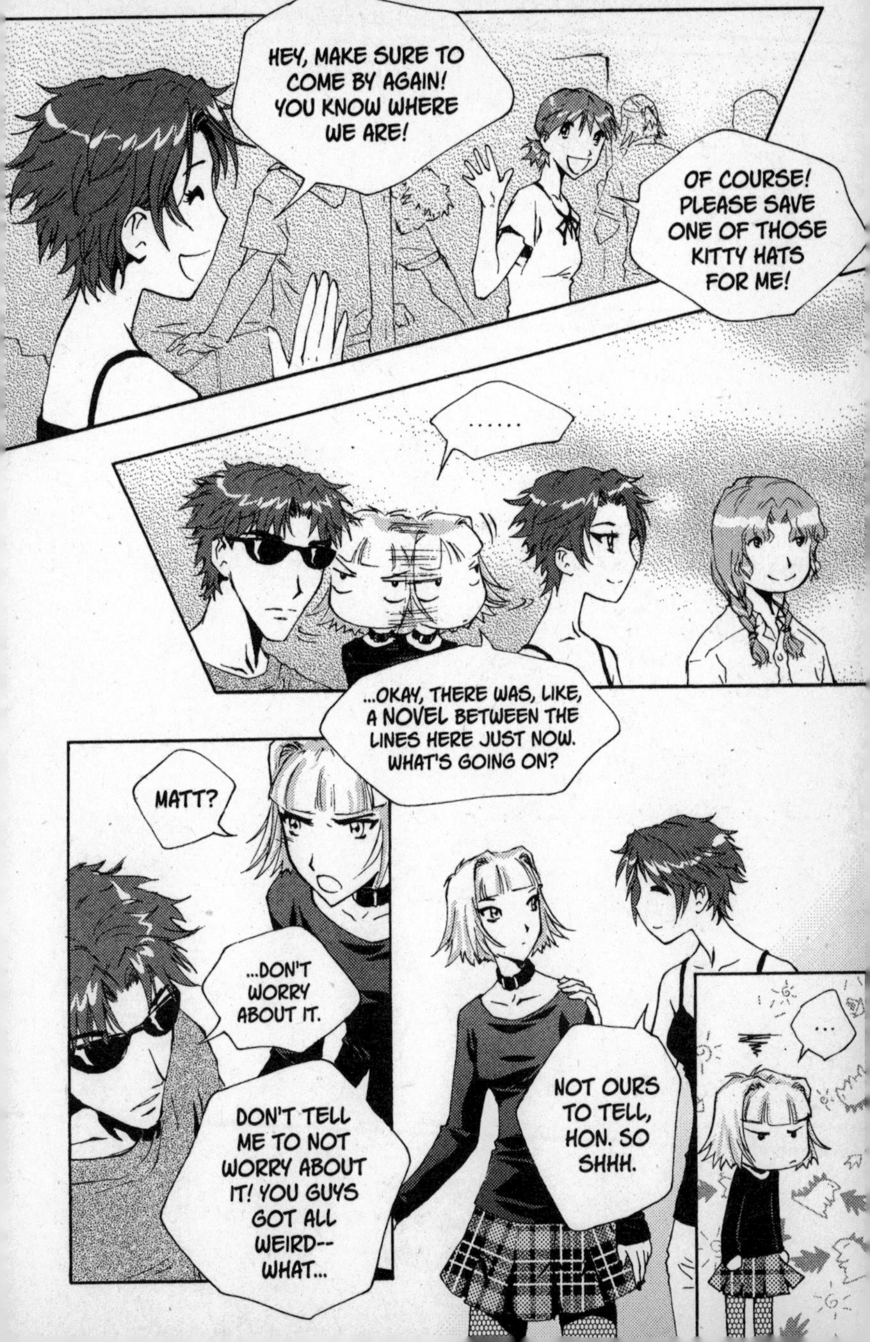
HEY, MAKE SURE TO COME BY AGAIN! YOU KNOW WHERE WE ARE!
OF COURSE! PLEASE SAVE ONE OF THOSE KITTY HATS FOR ME!
......
...OKAY, THERE WAS, LIKE, A NOVEL BETWEEN THE LINES HERE JUST NOW. WHAT'S GOING ON?
MATT?
...DON'T WORRY ABOUT IT.
DON'T TELL ME TO NOT WORRY ABOUT IT! YOU GUYS GOT ALL WEIRD-- WHAT...
NOT OURS TO TELL, HON. SO SHHH.
...

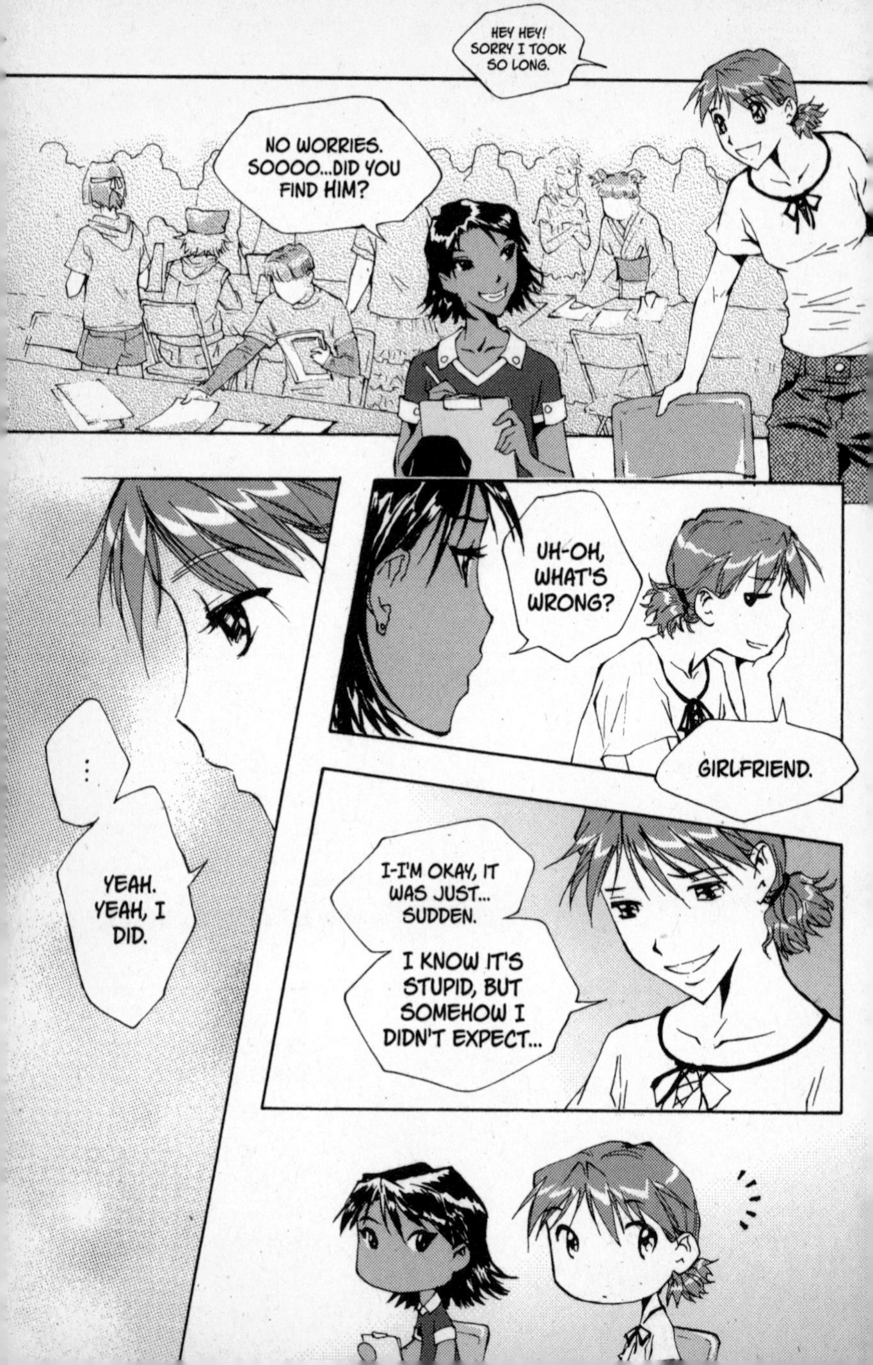
HEY HEY! SORRY I TOOK SO LONG.
NO WORRIES. SOOOO...DID YOU FIND HIM?
...
YEAH. YEAH, I DID.
UH-OH, WHAT'S WRONG?
GIRLFRIEND.
I-I'M OKAY, IT WAS JUST... SUDDEN.
I KNOW IT'S STUPID, BUT SOMEHOW I DIDN'T EXPECT...

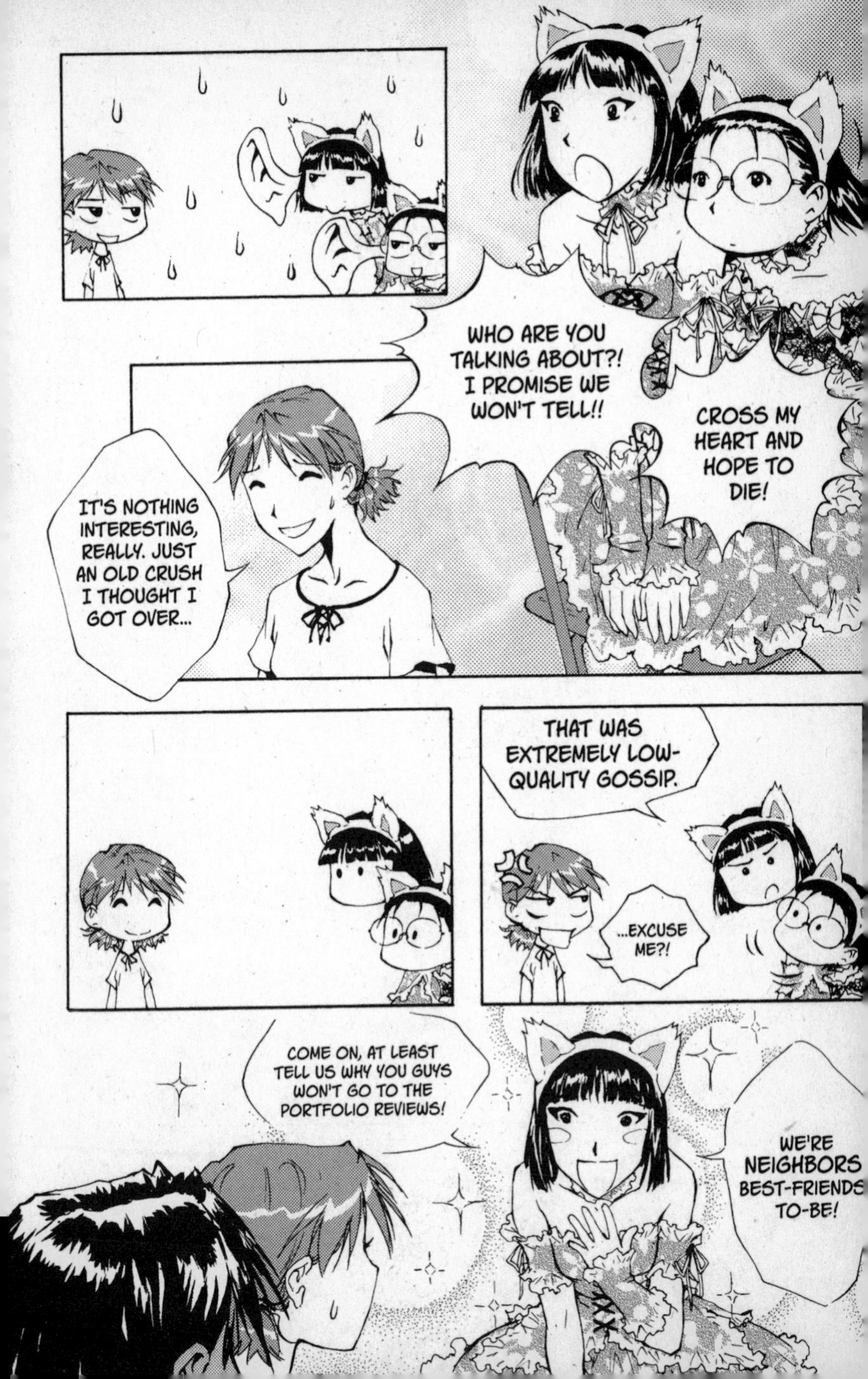
WHO ARE YOU TALKING ABOUT?! I PROMISE WE WON'T TELL!!
CROSS MY HEART AND HOPE TO DIE!
IT'S NOTHING INTERESTING, REALLY. JUST AN OLD CRUSH I THOUGHT I GOT OVER...
THAT WAS EXTREMELY LOW-QUALITY GOSSIP.
...EXCUSE ME?!
COME ON, AT LEAST TELL US WHY YOU GUYS WON'T GO TO THE PORTFOLIO REVIEWS!
WE'RE NEIGHBORS BEST-FRIENDS TO-BE!

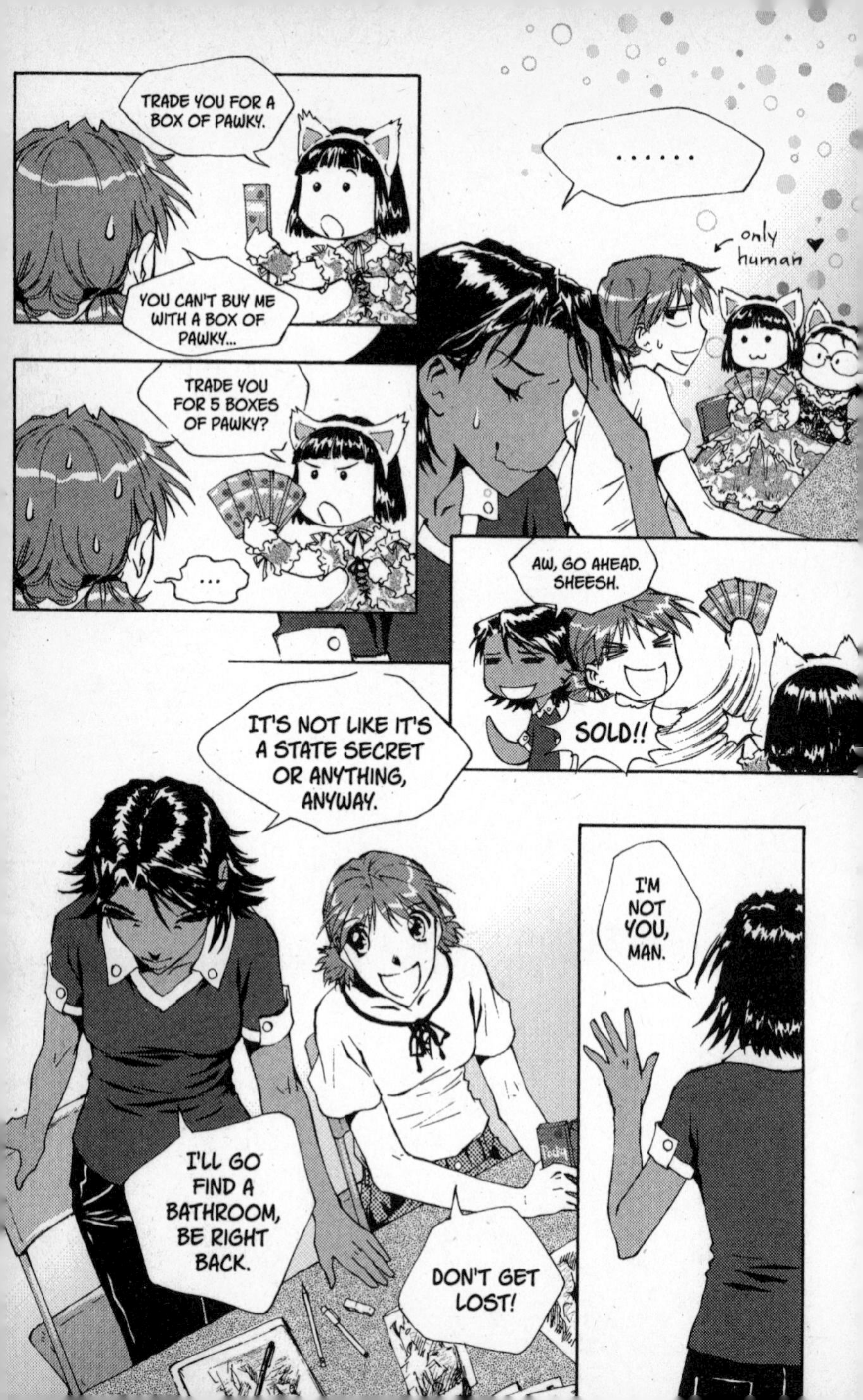

TRADE YOU FOR A BOX OF PAWKY.
YOU CAN'T BUY ME WITH A BOX OF PAWKY...
TRADE YOU FOR 5 BOXES OF PAWKY?
...
....
only human
AW, GO AHEAD. SHEESH.
SOLD!!
IT'S NOT LIKE IT'S A STATE SECRET OR ANYTHING, ANYWAY.
I'LL GO FIND A BATHROOM, BE RIGHT BACK.
DON'T GET LOST!
I'M NOT YOU, MAN.

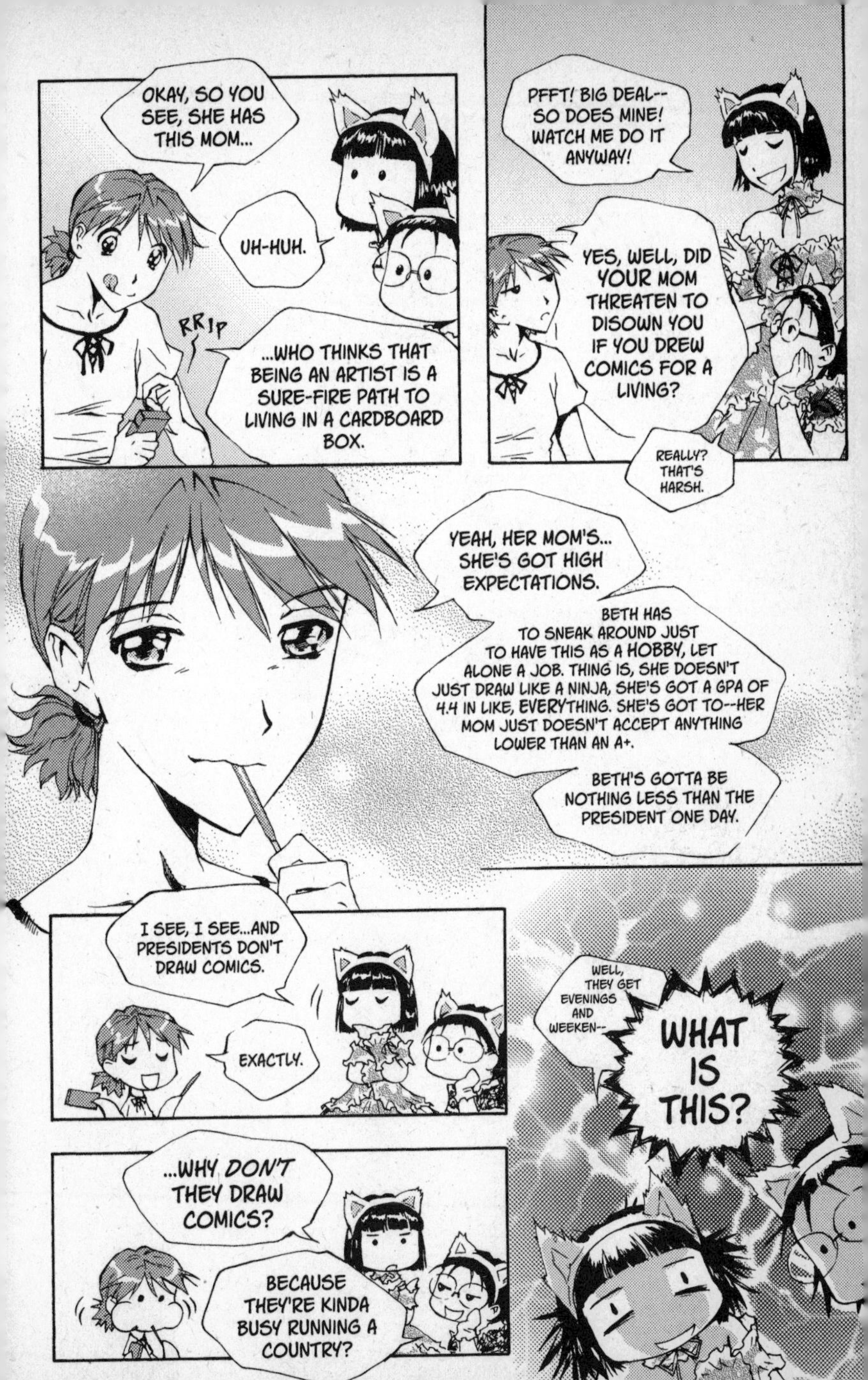
OKAY, SO YOU SEE, SHE HAS THIS MOM...
UH-HUH.
RRIP
...WHO THINKS THAT BEING AN ARTIST IS A SURE-FIRE PATH TO LIVING IN A CARDBOARD BOX.
PFFT! BIG DEAL--SO DOES MINE! WATCH ME DO IT ANYWAY!
YES, WELL, DID YOUR MOM THREATEN TO DISOWN YOU IF YOU DREW COMICS FOR A LIVING?
REALLY? THAT'S HARSH.
YEAH, HER MOM'S... SHE'S GOT HIGH EXPECTATIONS.
BETH HAS TO SNEAK AROUND JUST TO HAVE THIS AS A HOBBY, LET ALONE A JOB. THING IS, SHE DOESN'T JUST DRAW LIKE A NINJA, SHE'S GOT A GPA OF 4.4 IN LIKE, EVERYTHING. SHE'S GOT TO--HER MOM JUST DOESN'T ACCEPT ANYTHING LOWER THAN AN A+.
BETH'S GOTTA BE NOTHING LESS THAN THE PRESIDENT ONE DAY.
I SEE, I SEE...AND PRESIDENTS DON'T DRAW COMICS.
EXACTLY.
...WHY DON'T THEY DRAW COMICS?
BECAUSE THEY'RE KINDA BUSY RUNNING A COUNTRY?
WELL, THEY GET EVENINGS AND WEEKEN--
WHAT IS THIS?

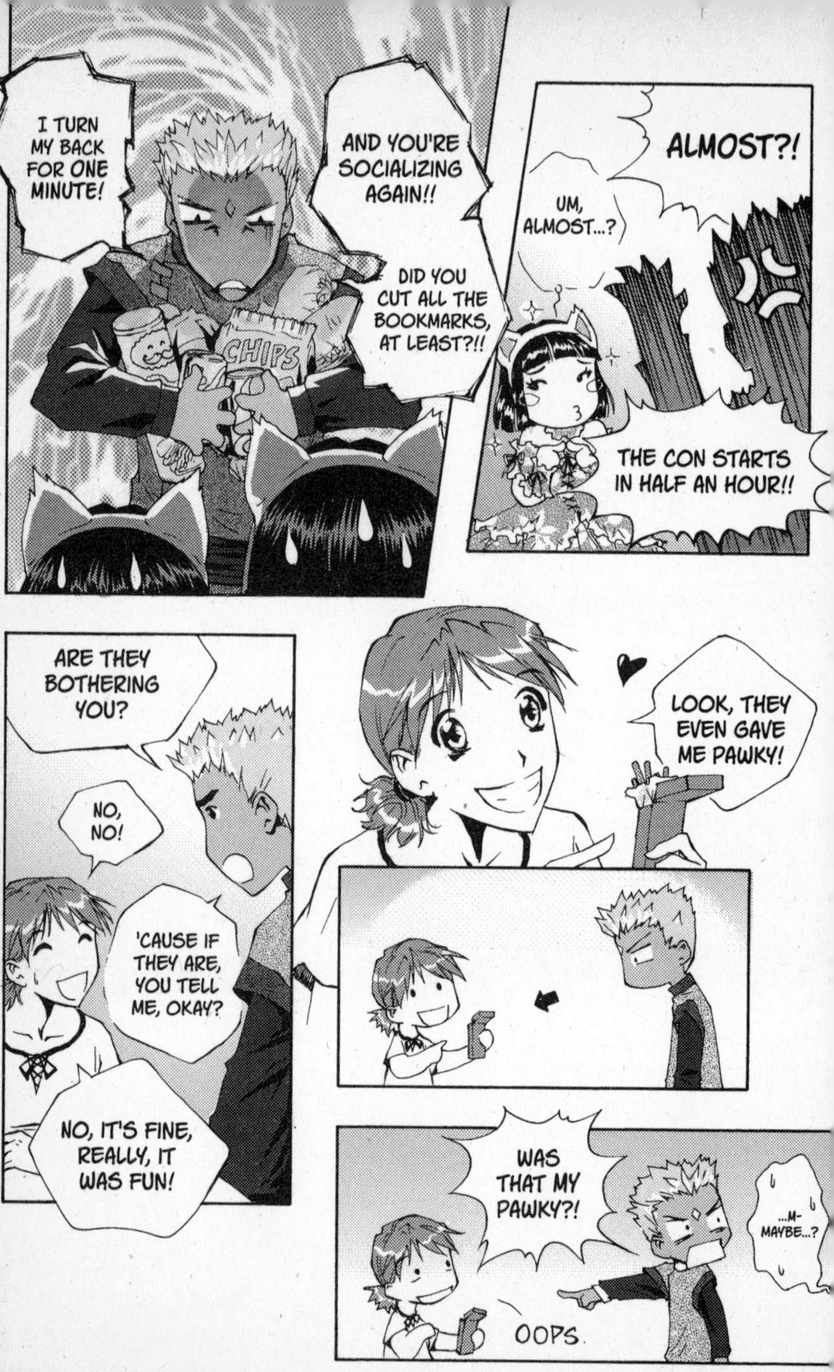
I TURN MY BACK FOR ONE MINUTE!
AND YOU'RE SOCIALIZING AGAIN!!
DID YOU CUT ALL THE BOOKMARKS, AT LEAST?!!
UM, ALMOST...?
ALMOST?!
THE CON STARTS IN HALF AN HOUR!!
ARE THEY BOTHERING YOU?
NO, NO!
'CAUSE IF THEY ARE, YOU TELL ME, OKAY?
NO, IT'S FINE, REALLY, IT WAS FUN!
LOOK, THEY EVEN GAVE ME PAWKY!
WAS THAT MY PAWKY?!
...M-MAYBE...?
OOPS.

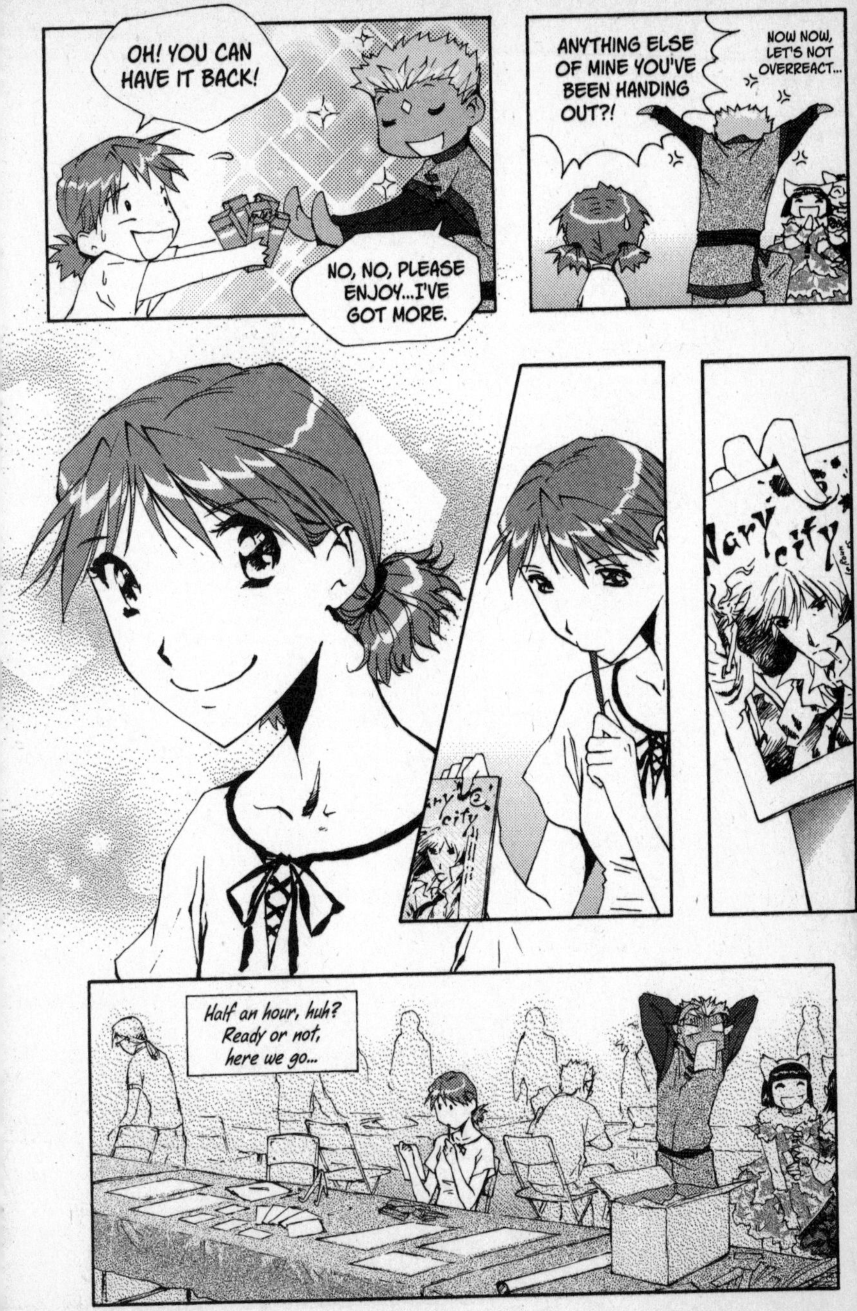
OH! YOU CAN HAVE IT BACK!
NO, NO, PLEASE ENJOY...I'VE GOT MORE.
ANYTHING ELSE OF MINE YOU'VE BEEN HANDING OUT?!
NOW NOW, LET'S NOT OVERREACT...
Half an hour, huh? Ready or not, here we go...

CHAPTER 3

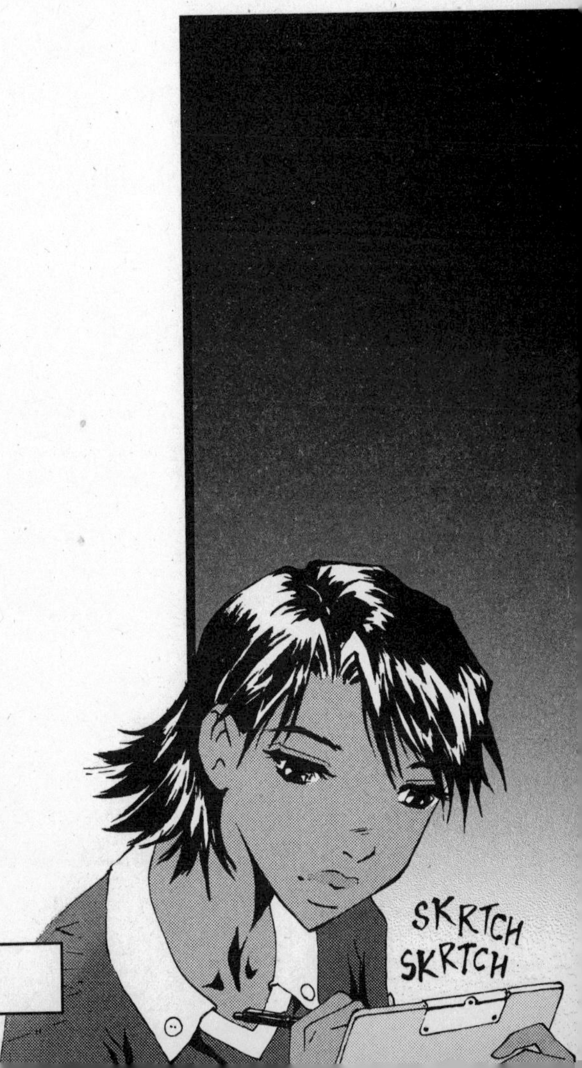
SKRTCH
SKRTCH

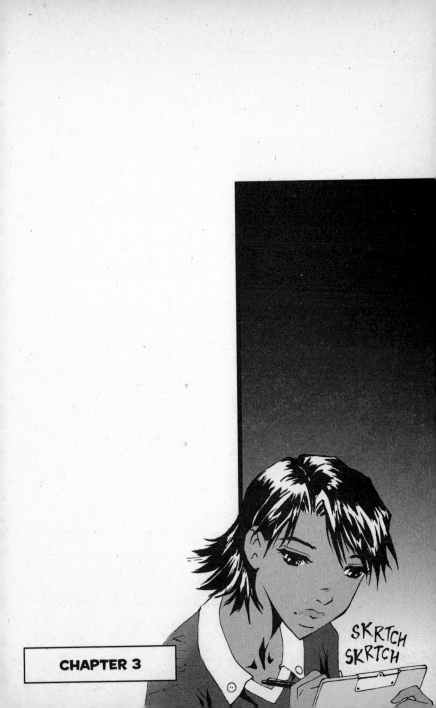

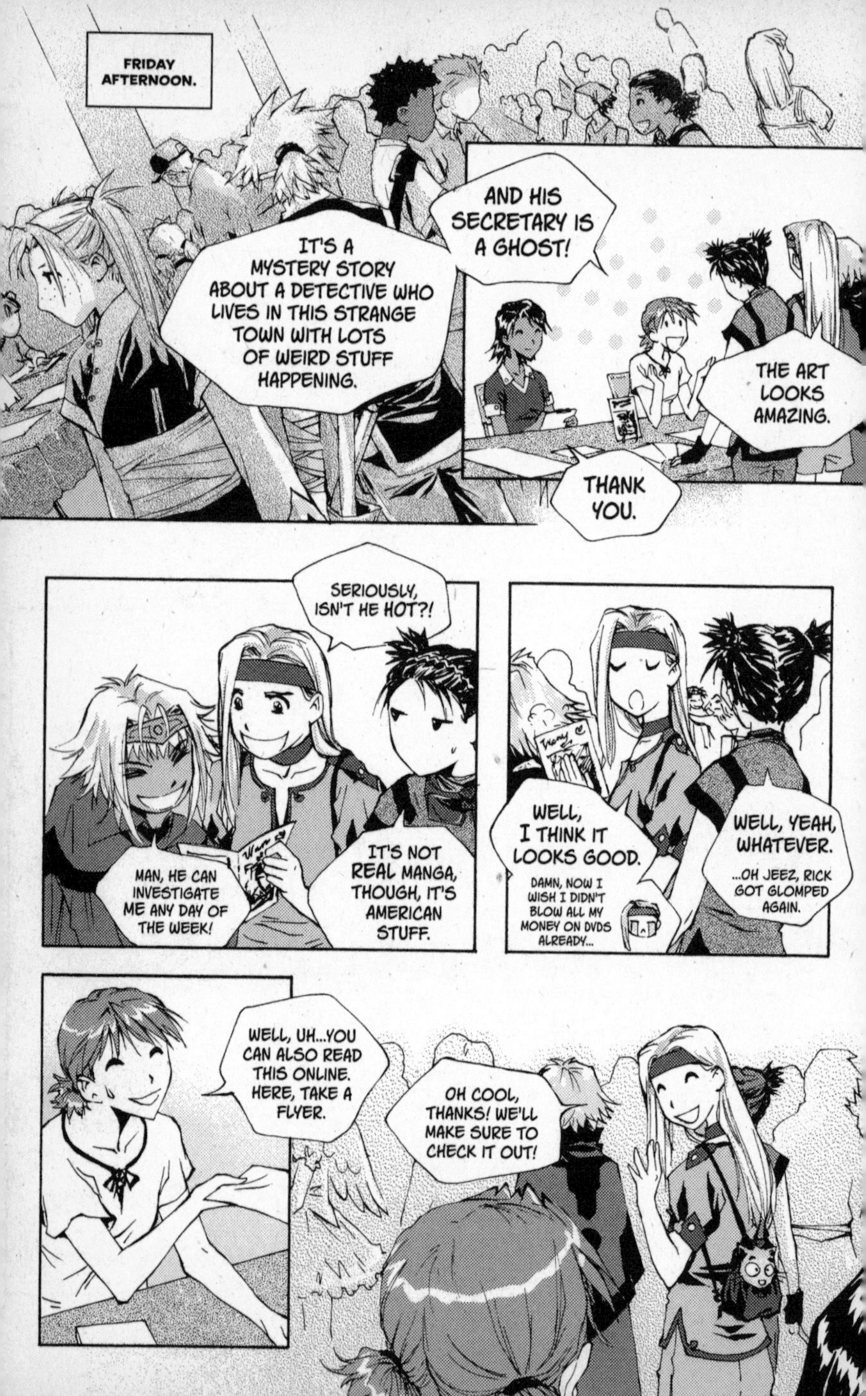
FRIDAY AFTERNOON.
IT'S A MYSTERY STORY ABOUT A DETECTIVE WHO LIVES IN THIS STRANGE TOWN WITH LOTS OF WEIRD STUFF HAPPENING.
AND HIS SECRETARY IS A GHOST!
THE ART LOOKS AMAZING.
THANK YOU.
SERIOUSLY, ISN'T HE HOT?!
MAN, HE CAN INVESTIGATE ME ANY DAY OF THE WEEK!
IT'S NOT REAL MANGA, THOUGH, IT'S AMERICAN STUFF.
WELL, I THINK IT LOOKS GOOD.
DAMN, NOW I WISH I DIDN'T BLOW ALL MY MONEY ON DVDS ALREADY...
WELL, YEAH, WHATEVER.
...OH JEEZ, RICK GOT GLOMPED AGAIN.
WELL, UH...YOU CAN ALSO READ THIS ONLINE. HERE, TAKE A FLYER.
OH COOL, THANKS! WE'LL MAKE SURE TO CHECK IT OUT!

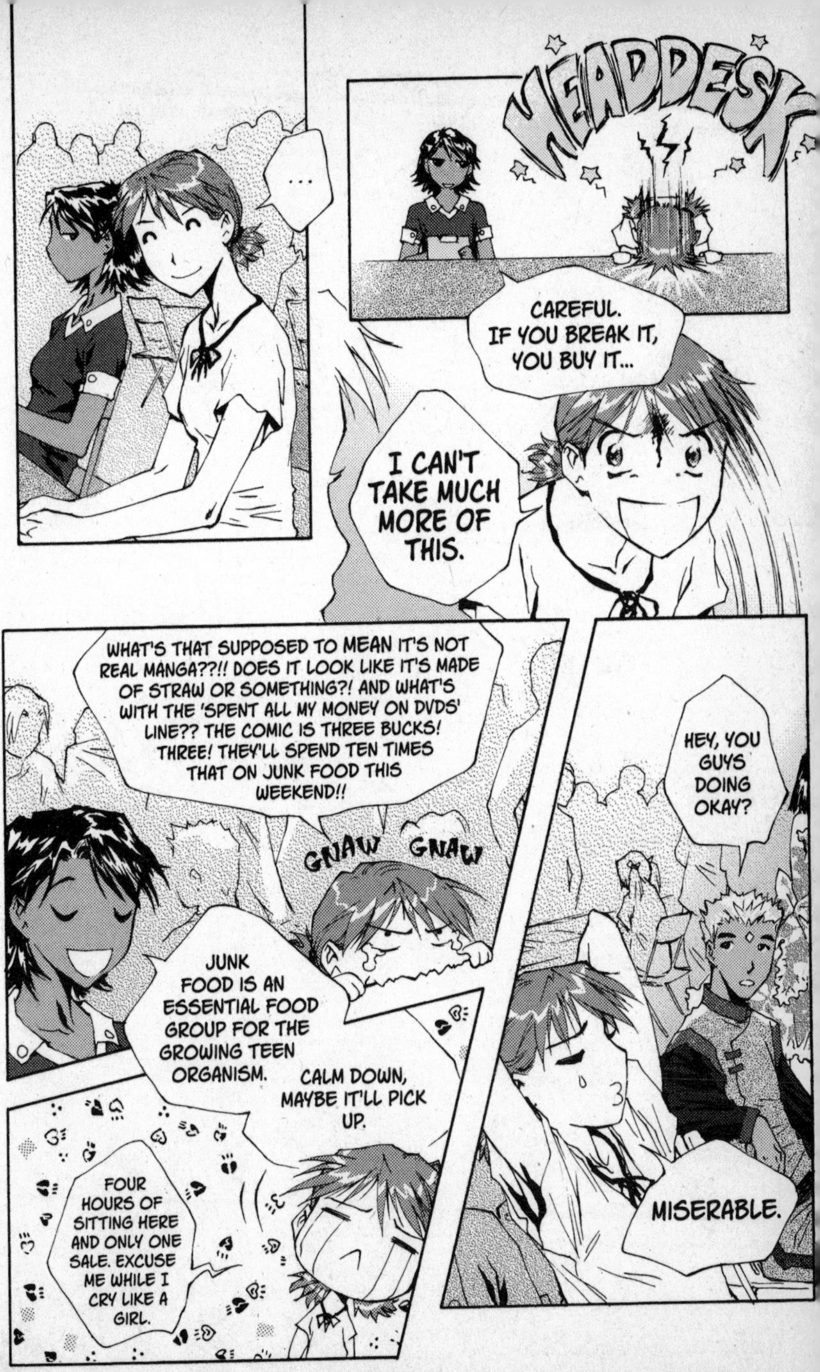
...
HEADDESK
CAREFUL. IF YOU BREAK IT, YOU BUY IT...
I CAN'T TAKE MUCH MORE OF THIS.
WHAT'S THAT SUPPOSED TO MEAN IT'S NOT REAL MANGA??!! DOES IT LOOK LIKE IT'S MADE OF STRAW OR SOMETHING?! AND WHAT'S WITH THE 'SPENT ALL MY MONEY ON DVDS' LINE?? THE COMIC IS THREE BUCKS! THREE! THEY'LL SPEND TEN TIMES THAT ON JUNK FOOD THIS WEEKEND!!
GNAW GNAW
JUNK FOOD IS AN ESSENTIAL FOOD GROUP FOR THE GROWING TEEN ORGANISM.
CALM DOWN, MAYBE IT'LL PICK UP.
FOUR HOURS OF SITTING HERE AND ONLY ONE SALE. EXCUSE ME WHILE I CRY LIKE A GIRL.
HEY, YOU GUYS DOING OKAY?
MISERABLE.

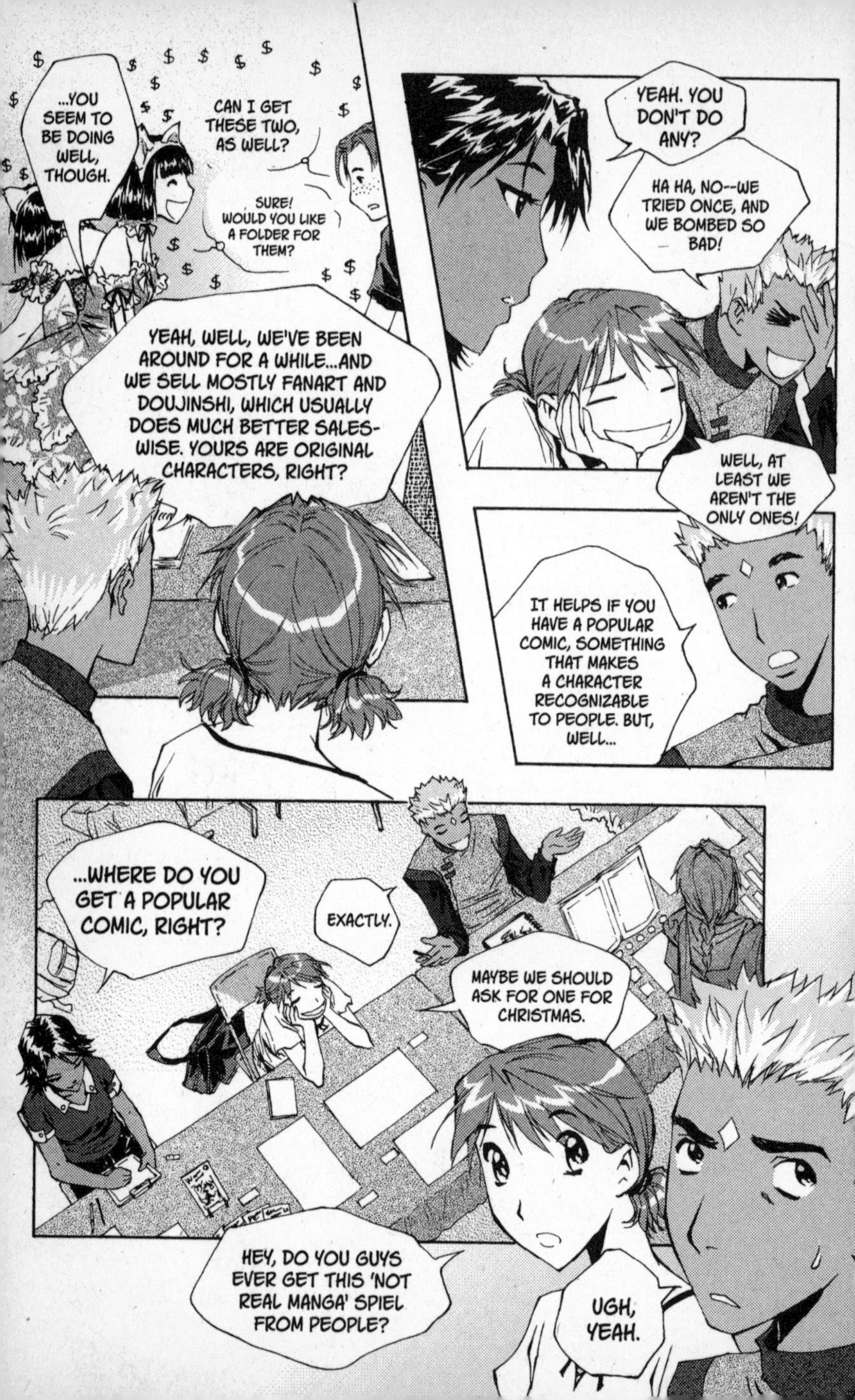
...YOU SEEM TO BE DOING WELL, THOUGH.
CAN I GET THESE TWO, AS WELL?
SURE! WOULD YOU LIKE A FOLDER FOR THEM?
YEAH, WELL, WE'VE BEEN AROUND FOR A WHILE...AND WE SELL MOSTLY FANART AND DOUJINSHI, WHICH USUALLY DOES MUCH BETTER SALES-WISE. YOURS ARE ORIGINAL CHARACTERS, RIGHT?
YEAH. YOU DON'T DO ANY?
HA HA, NO--WE TRIED ONCE, AND WE BOMBED SO BAD!
WELL, AT LEAST WE AREN'T THE ONLY ONES!
IT HELPS IF YOU HAVE A POPULAR COMIC, SOMETHING THAT MAKES A CHARACTER RECOGNIZABLE TO PEOPLE. BUT, WELL...
...WHERE DO YOU GET A POPULAR COMIC, RIGHT?
EXACTLY.
MAYBE WE SHOULD ASK FOR ONE FOR CHRISTMAS.
HEY, DO YOU GUYS EVER GET THIS 'NOT REAL MANGA' SPIEL FROM PEOPLE?
UGH, YEAH.

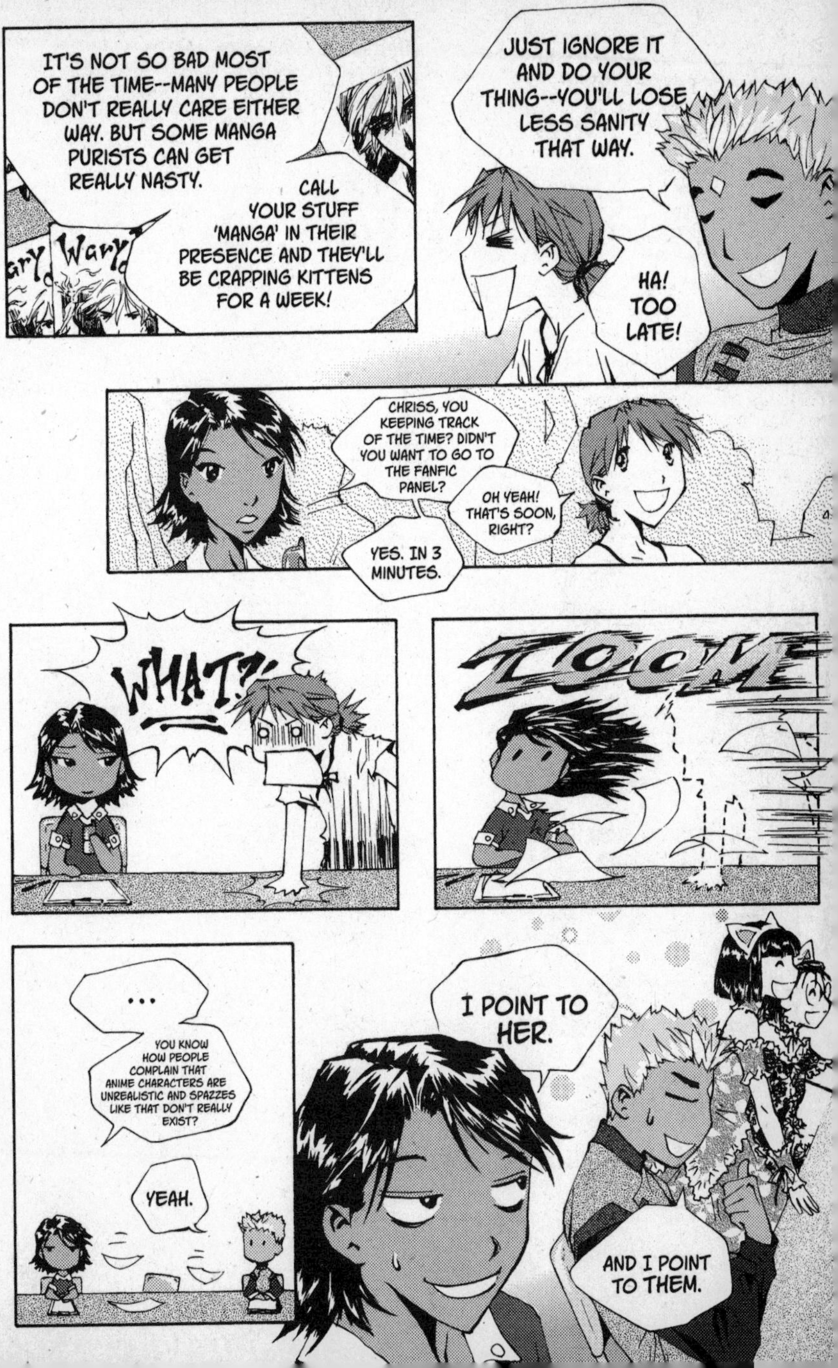
IT'S NOT SO BAD MOST OF THE TIME--MANY PEOPLE DON'T REALLY CARE EITHER WAY. BUT SOME MANGA PURISTS CAN GET REALLY NASTY.
Wary
Wary
CALL YOUR STUFF 'MANGA' IN THEIR PRESENCE AND THEY'LL BE CRAPPING KITTENS FOR A WEEK!
JUST IGNORE IT AND DO YOUR THING--YOU'LL LOSE LESS SANITY THAT WAY.
HA! TOO LATE!
CHRISS, YOU KEEPING TRACK OF THE TIME? DIDN'T YOU WANT TO GO TO THE FANFIC PANEL?
OH YEAH! THAT'S SOON, RIGHT?
YES. IN 3 MINUTES.
WHAT?!
ZOOM
...
YOU KNOW HOW PEOPLE COMPLAIN THAT ANIME CHARACTERS ARE UNREALISTIC AND SPAZZES LIKE THAT DON'T REALLY EXIST?
YEAH.
I POINT TO HER.
AND I POINT TO THEM.

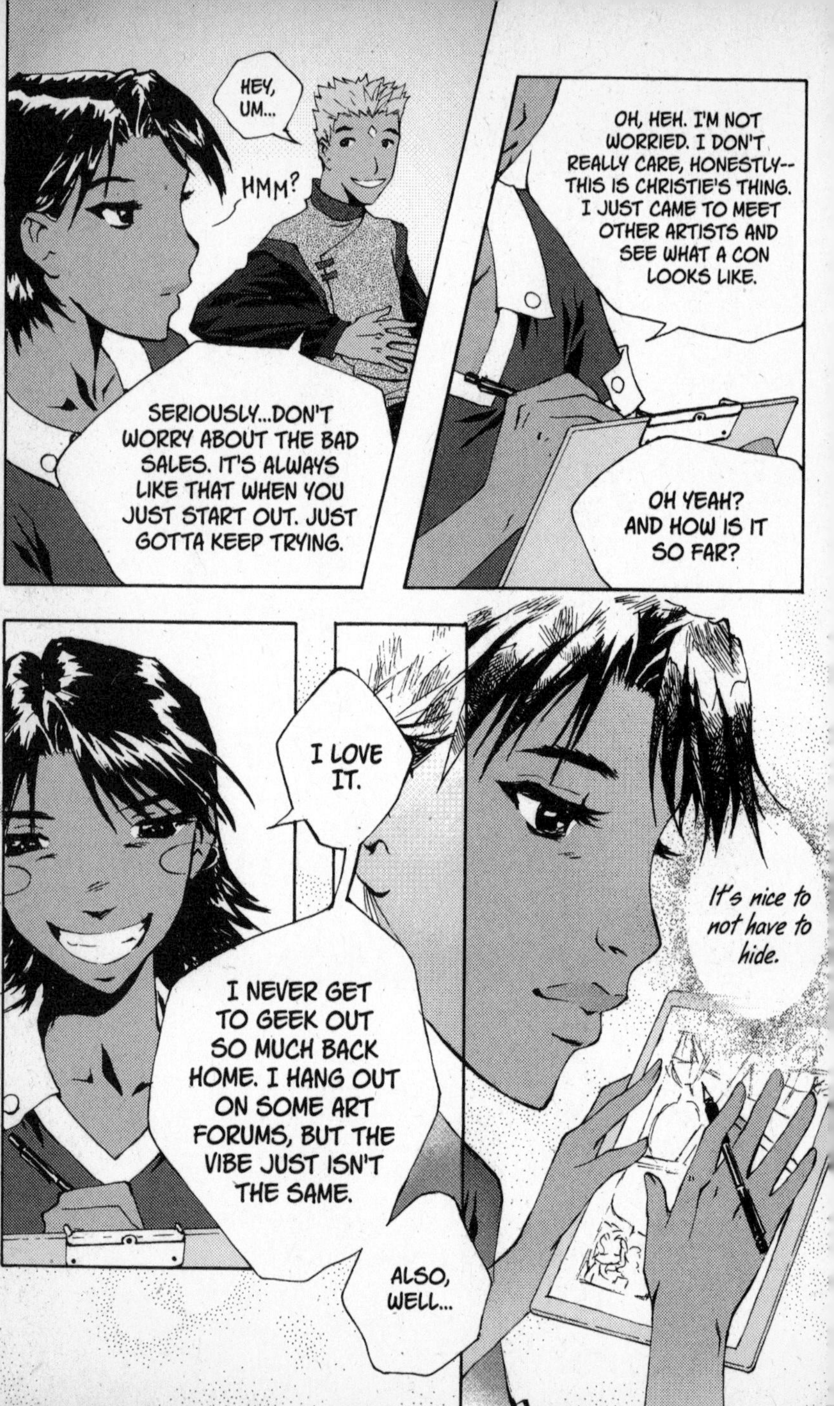
HEY, UM...
HMM?
SERIOUSLY...DON'T WORRY ABOUT THE BAD SALES. IT'S ALWAYS LIKE THAT WHEN YOU JUST START OUT. JUST GOTTA KEEP TRYING.
OH, HEH. I'M NOT WORRIED. I DON'T REALLY CARE, HONESTLY--THIS IS CHRISTIE'S THING. I JUST CAME TO MEET OTHER ARTISTS AND SEE WHAT A CON LOOKS LIKE.
OH YEAH? AND HOW IS IT SO FAR?
I LOVE IT.
I NEVER GET TO GEEK OUT SO MUCH BACK HOME. I HANG OUT ON SOME ART FORUMS, BUT THE VIBE JUST ISN'T THE SAME.
ALSO, WELL...
It's nice to not have to hide.

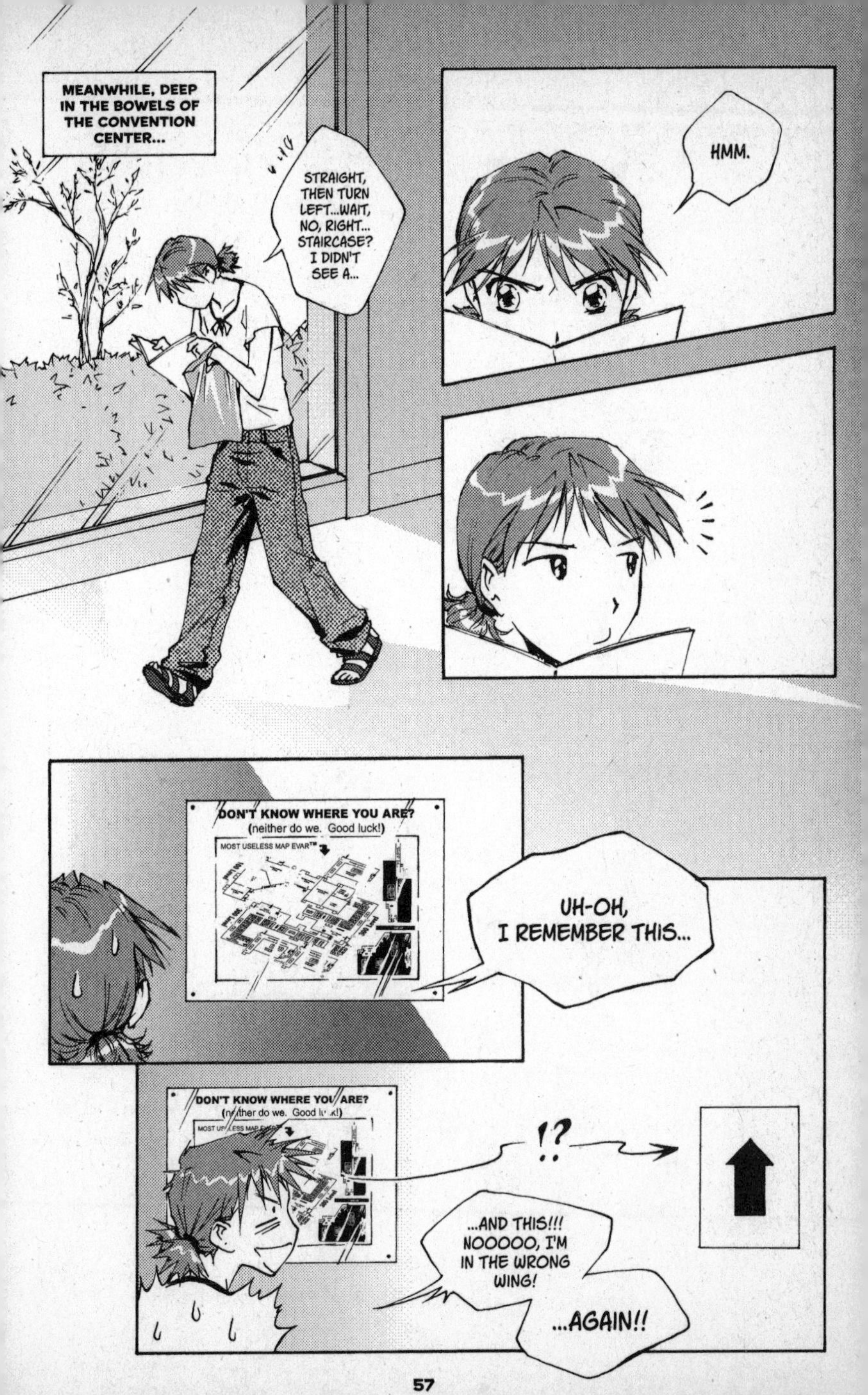
MEANWHILE, DEEP IN THE BOWELS OF THE CONVENTION CENTER...
STRAIGHT, THEN TURN LEFT...WAIT, NO, RIGHT... STAIRCASE? I DIDN'T SEE A...
HMM.
DON'T KNOW WHERE YOU ARE?
(neither do we. Good luck!)
MOST USELESS MAP EVAR™
UH-OH, I REMEMBER THIS...
!?
...AND THIS!!! NOOOOO, I'M IN THE WRONG WING!
...AGAIN!!

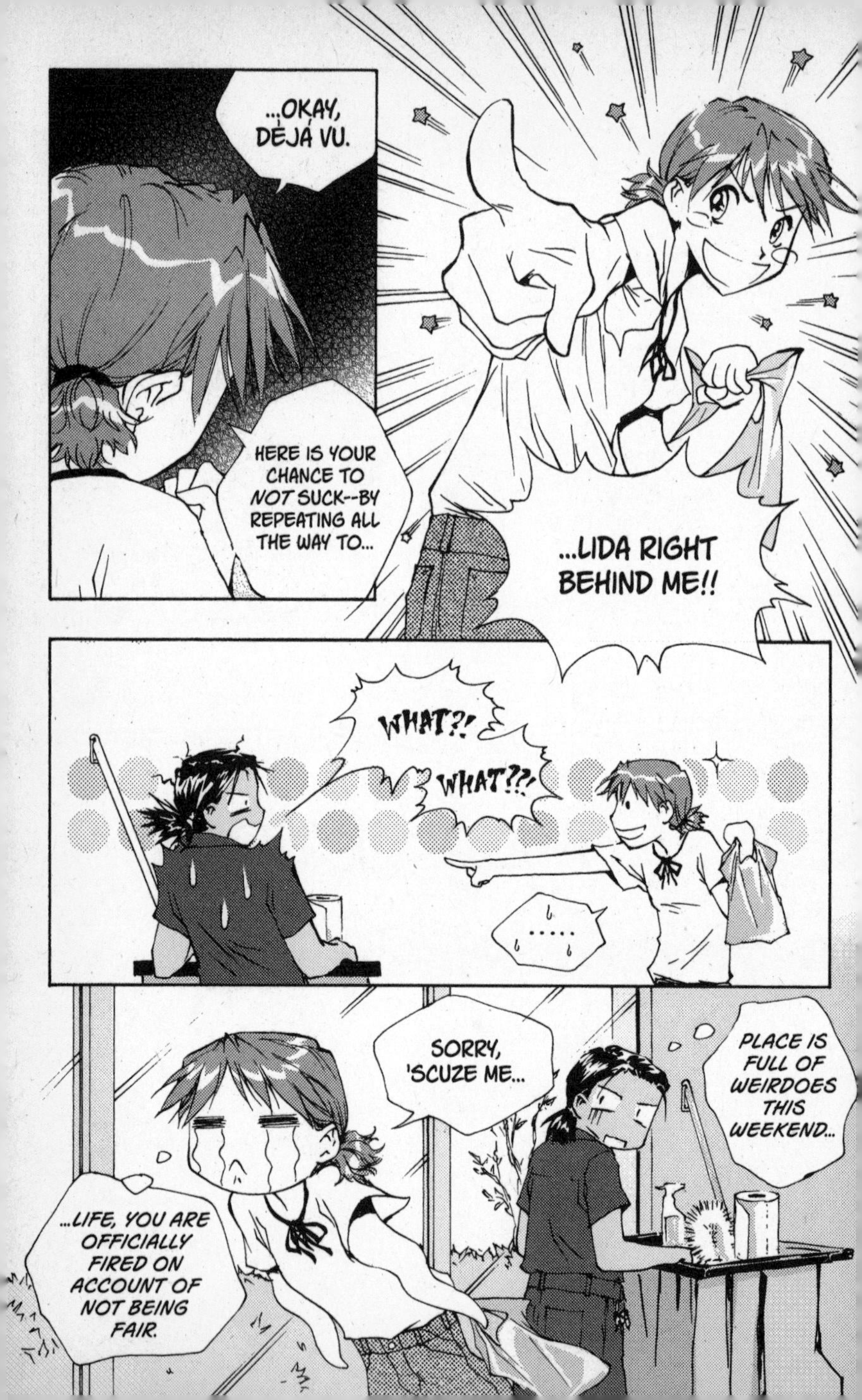
...OKAY, DÉJÀ VU.
HERE IS YOUR CHANCE TO *NOT* SUCK--BY REPEATING ALL THE WAY TO...
...LIDA RIGHT BEHIND ME!!
WHAT?!
WHAT??!
.....
SORRY, 'SCUZE ME...
PLACE IS FULL OF WEIRDOES THIS WEEKEND...
...LIFE, YOU ARE OFFICIALLY FIRED ON ACCOUNT OF NOT BEING FAIR.

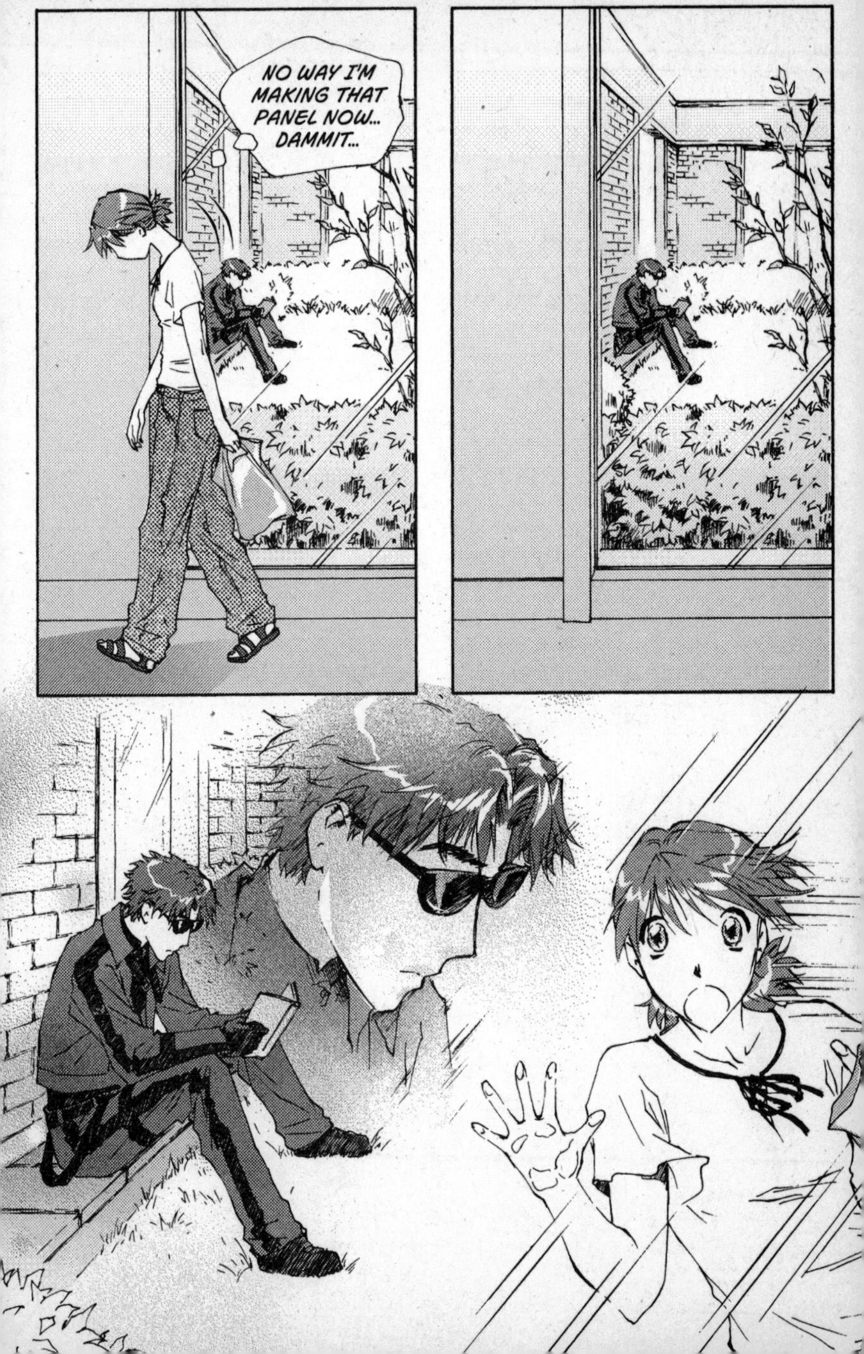
NO WAY I'M MAKING THAT PANEL NOW... DAMMIT...

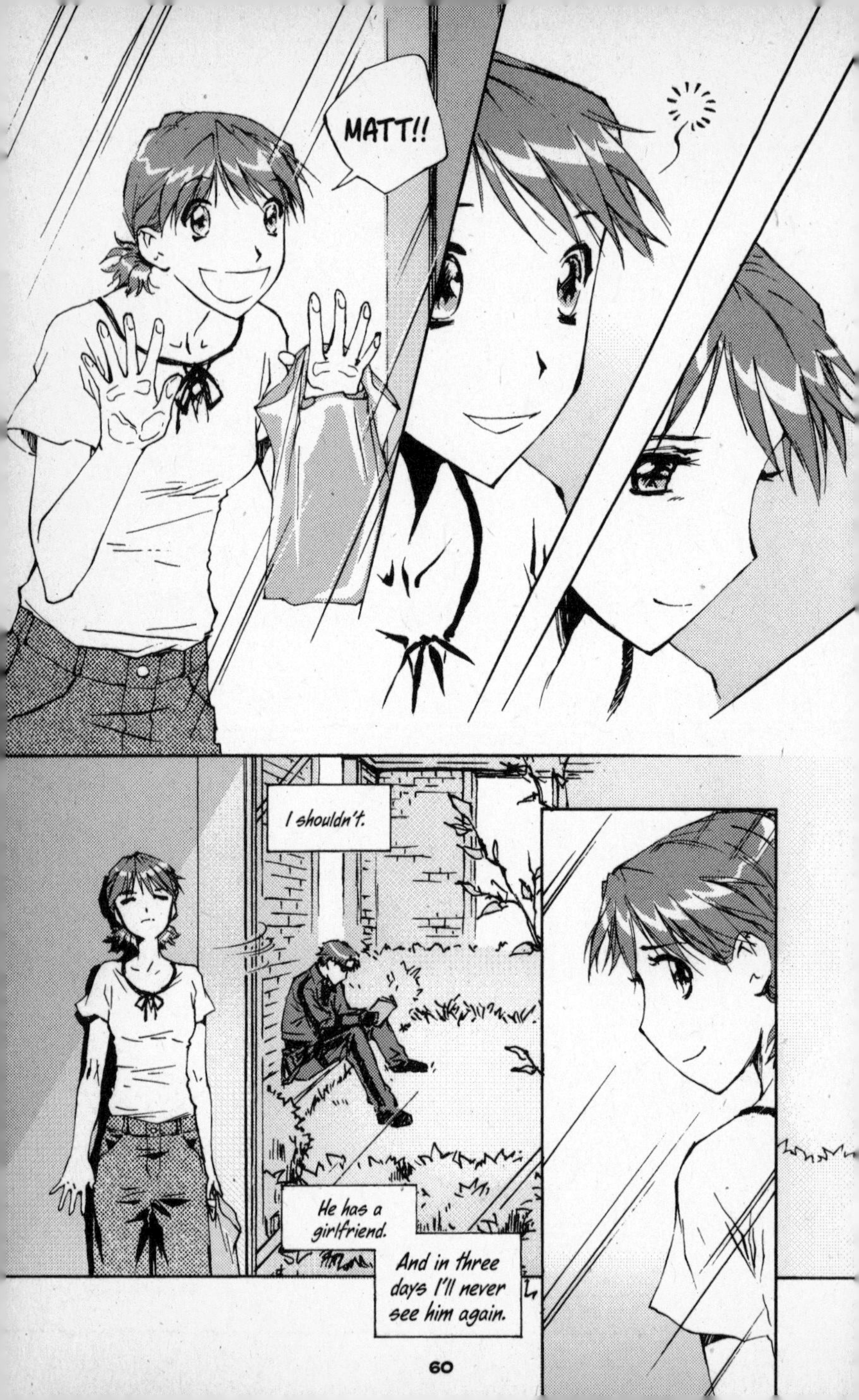
MATT!!
I shouldn't.
He has a girlfriend.
And in three days I'll never see him again.

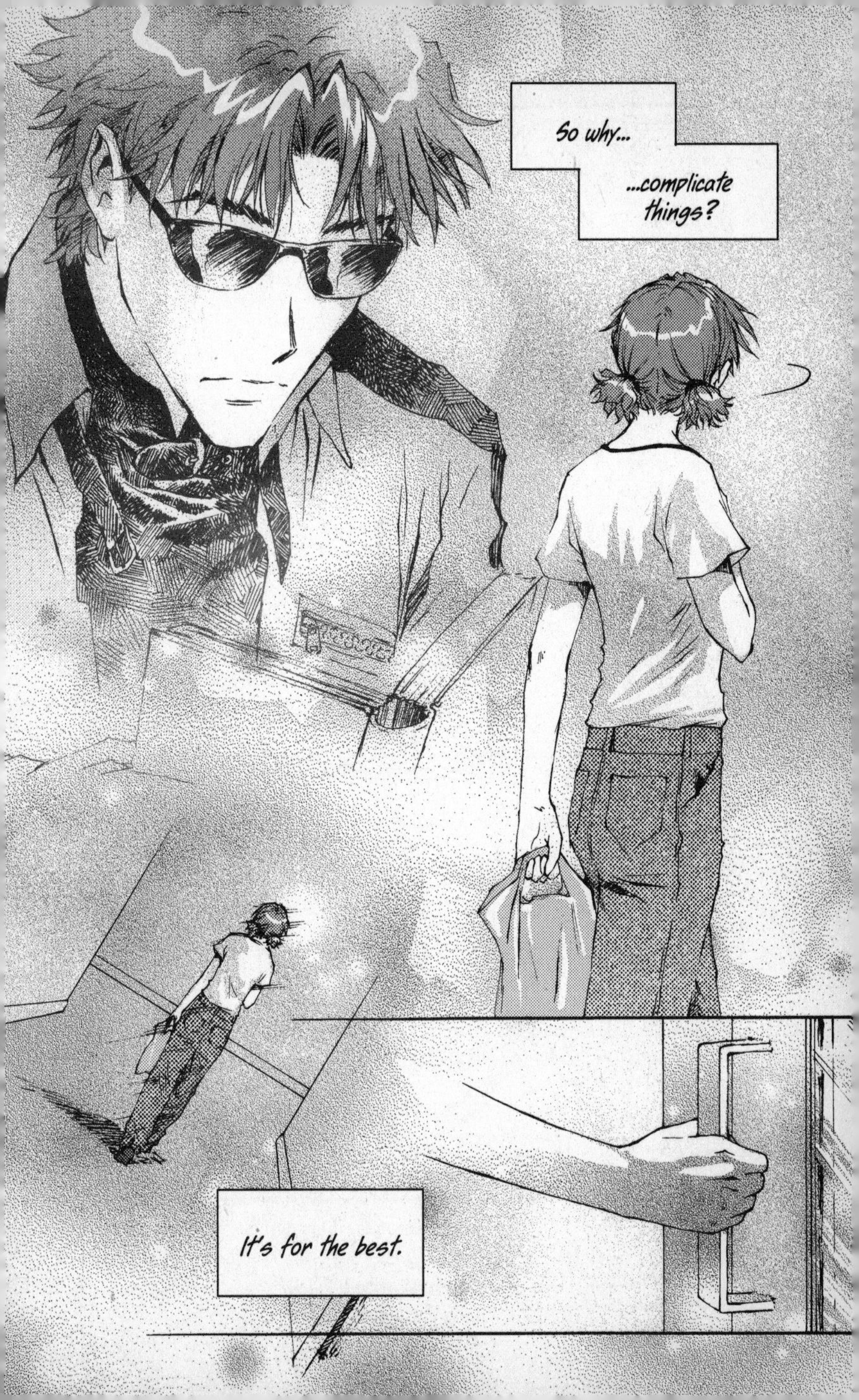
So why...
...complicate things?
It's for the best.

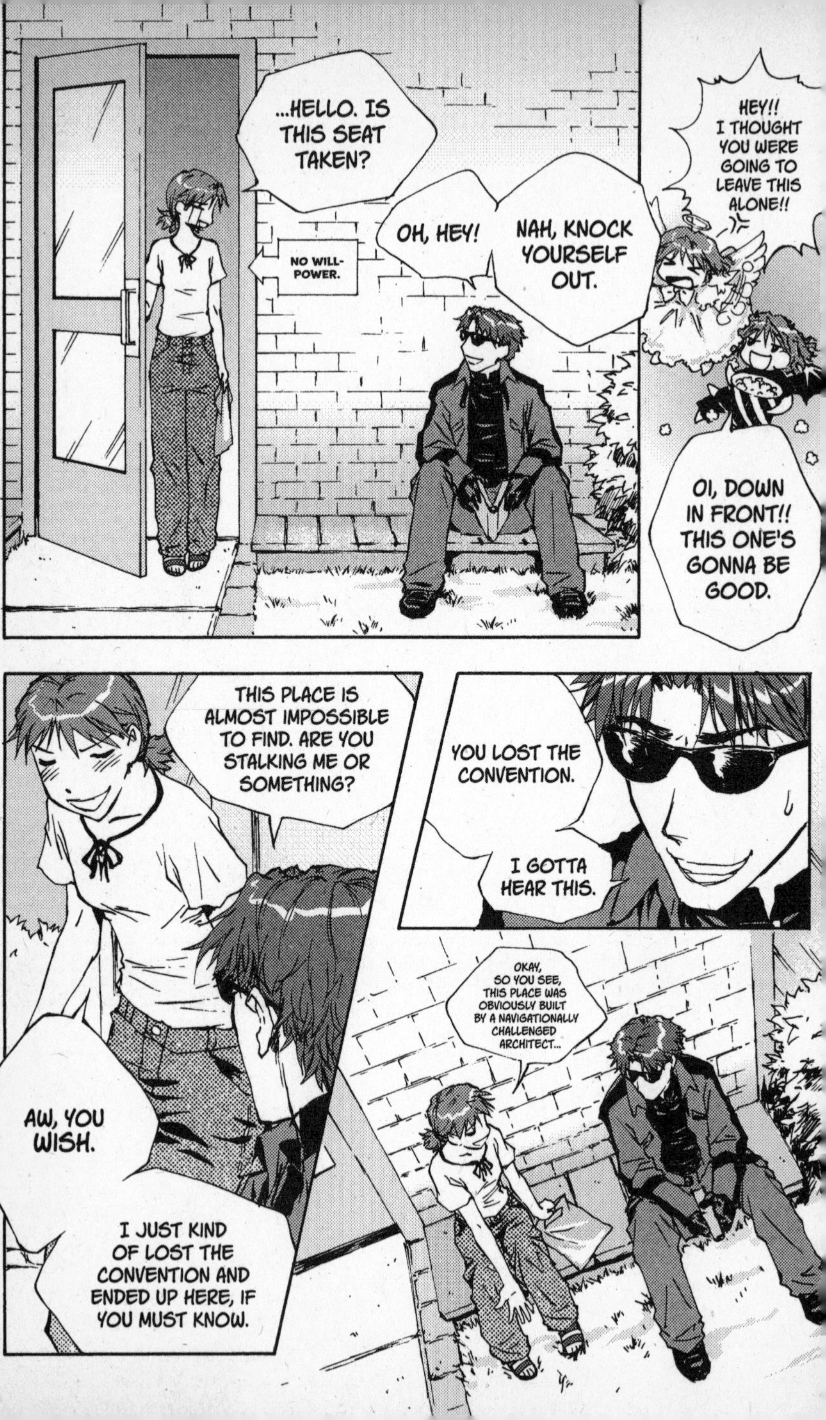
...HELLO. IS THIS SEAT TAKEN?
NO WILL-POWER.
OH, HEY!
NAH, KNOCK YOURSELF OUT.
HEY!! I THOUGHT YOU WERE GOING TO LEAVE THIS ALONE!!
OI, DOWN IN FRONT!! THIS ONE'S GONNA BE GOOD.
THIS PLACE IS ALMOST IMPOSSIBLE TO FIND. ARE YOU STALKING ME OR SOMETHING?
AW, YOU WISH.
I JUST KIND OF LOST THE CONVENTION AND ENDED UP HERE, IF YOU MUST KNOW.
YOU LOST THE CONVENTION.
I GOTTA HEAR THIS.
OKAY, SO YOU SEE, THIS PLACE WAS OBVIOUSLY BUILT BY A NAVIGATIONALLY CHALLENGED ARCHITECT...

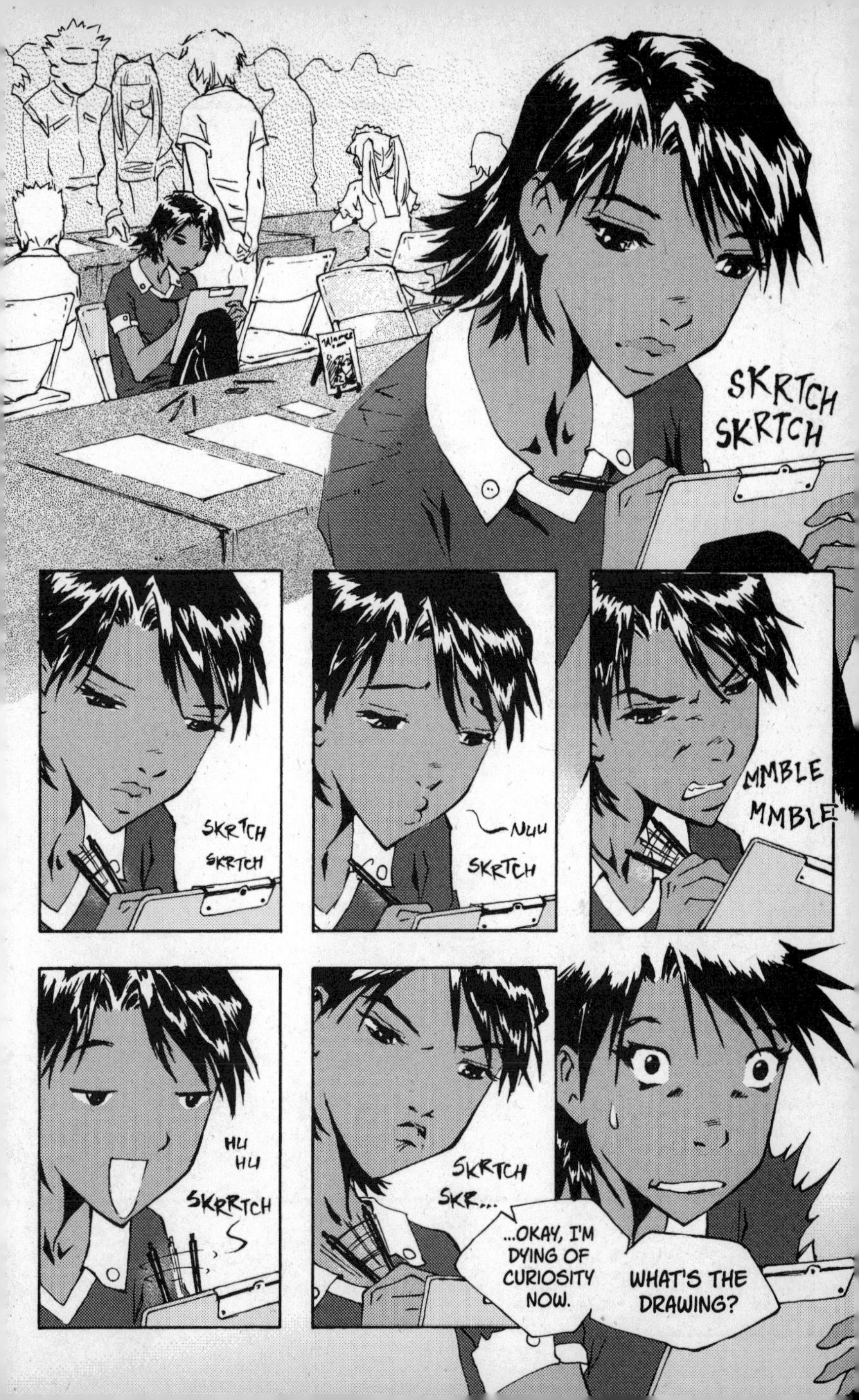
SKRTCH SKRTCH
SKRTCH SKRTCH
NUU
SKRTCH
MMBLE MMBLE
HU HU
SKRRTCH
SKRTCH SKR...
...OKAY, I'M DYING OF CURIOSITY NOW.
WHAT'S THE DRAWING?

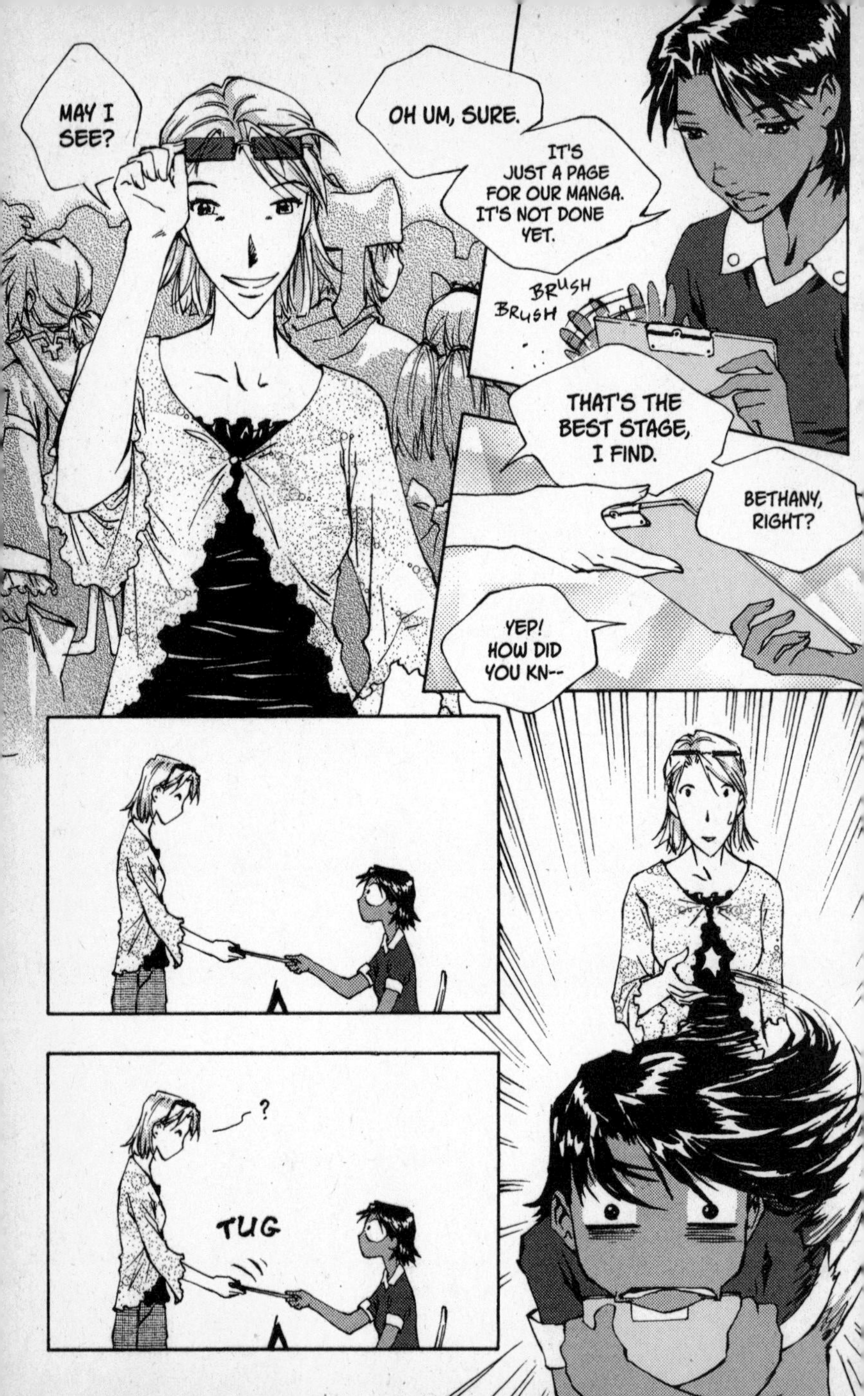
MAY I SEE?
OH UM, SURE.
IT'S JUST A PAGE FOR OUR MANGA. IT'S NOT DONE YET.
BRUSH BRUSH
THAT'S THE BEST STAGE, I FIND.
BETHANY, RIGHT?
YEP! HOW DID YOU KN--
?
TUG

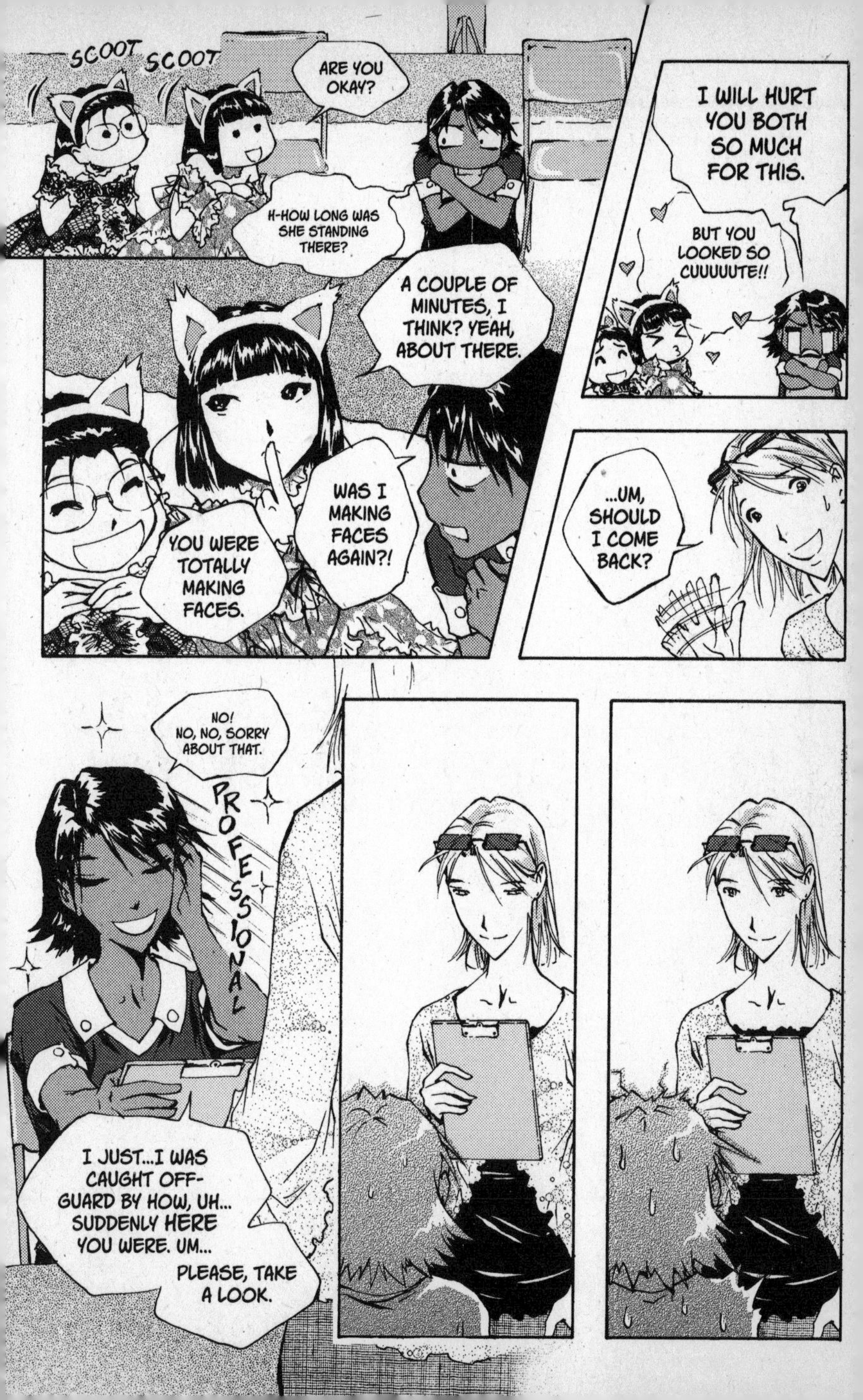
SCOOT SCOOT
ARE YOU OKAY?
H-HOW LONG WAS SHE STANDING THERE?
I WILL HURT YOU BOTH SO MUCH FOR THIS.
BUT YOU LOOKED SO CUUUUUTE!!
A COUPLE OF MINUTES, I THINK? YEAH, ABOUT THERE.
WAS I MAKING FACES AGAIN?!
YOU WERE TOTALLY MAKING FACES.
...UM, SHOULD I COME BACK?
NO! NO, NO, SORRY ABOUT THAT.
PROFESSIONAL
I JUST...I WAS CAUGHT OFF-GUARD BY HOW, UH... SUDDENLY HERE YOU WERE. UM...
PLEASE, TAKE A LOOK.

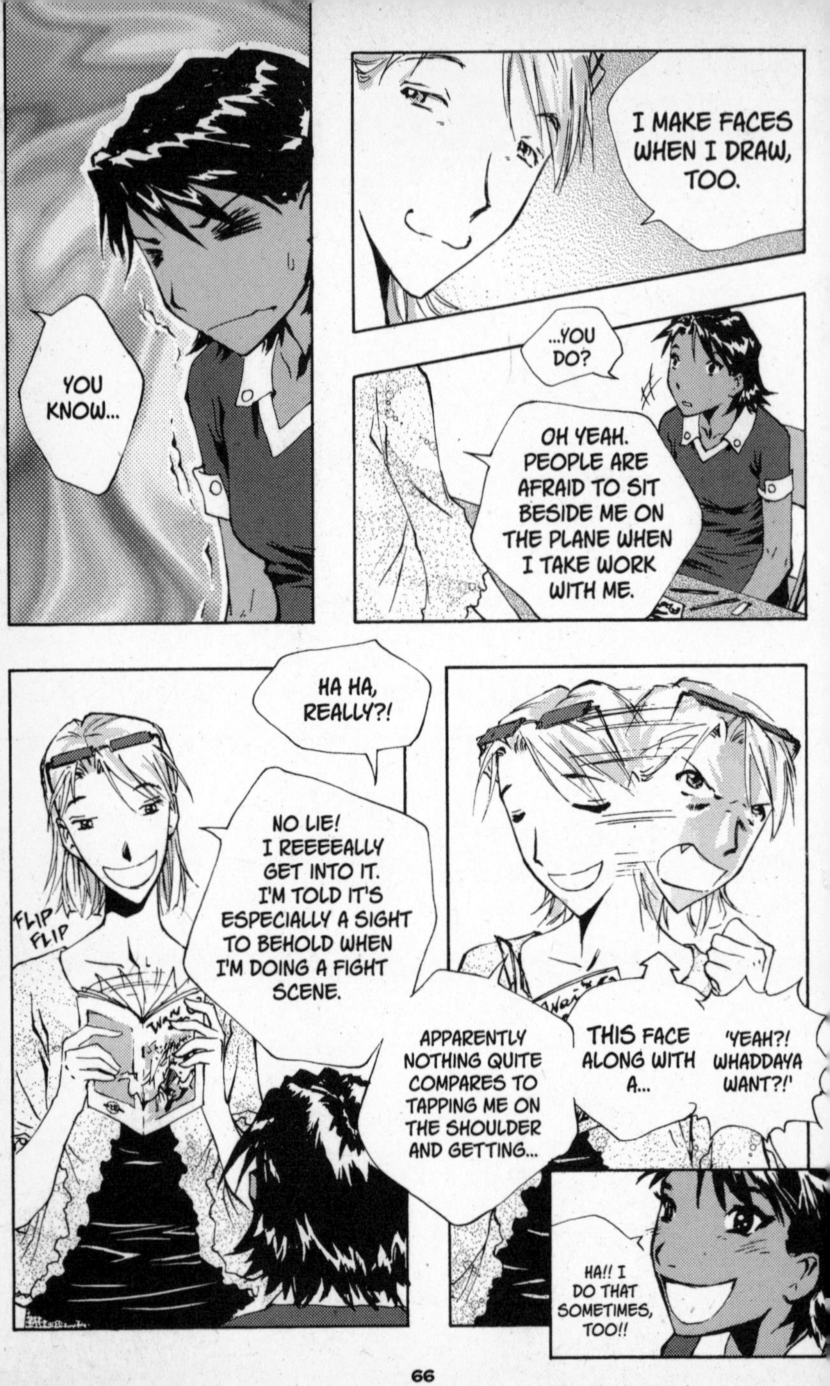
YOU KNOW...
I MAKE FACES WHEN I DRAW, TOO.
...YOU DO?
OH YEAH. PEOPLE ARE AFRAID TO SIT BESIDE ME ON THE PLANE WHEN I TAKE WORK WITH ME.
HA HA, REALLY?!
FLIP FLIP
NO LIE! I REEEEALLY GET INTO IT. I'M TOLD IT'S ESPECIALLY A SIGHT TO BEHOLD WHEN I'M DOING A FIGHT SCENE.
APPARENTLY NOTHING QUITE COMPARES TO TAPPING ME ON THE SHOULDER AND GETTING...
THIS FACE ALONG WITH A...
'YEAH?! WHADDAYA WANT?!'
HA!! I DO THAT SOMETIMES, TOO!!

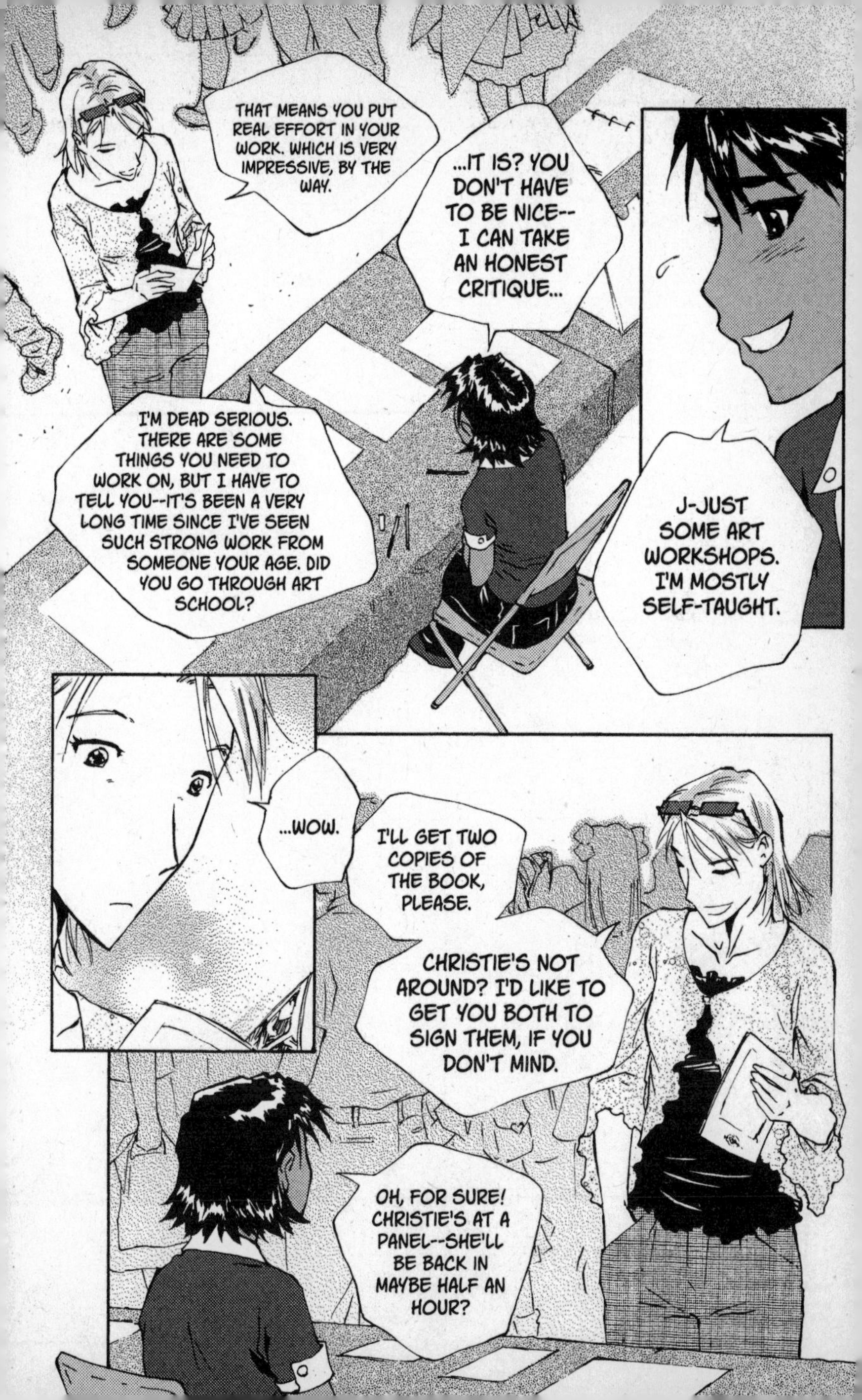
THAT MEANS YOU PUT REAL EFFORT IN YOUR WORK. WHICH IS VERY IMPRESSIVE, BY THE WAY.
...IT IS? YOU DON'T HAVE TO BE NICE-- I CAN TAKE AN HONEST CRITIQUE...
I'M DEAD SERIOUS. THERE ARE SOME THINGS YOU NEED TO WORK ON, BUT I HAVE TO TELL YOU--IT'S BEEN A VERY LONG TIME SINCE I'VE SEEN SUCH STRONG WORK FROM SOMEONE YOUR AGE. DID YOU GO THROUGH ART SCHOOL?
J-JUST SOME ART WORKSHOPS. I'M MOSTLY SELF-TAUGHT.
...WOW.
I'LL GET TWO COPIES OF THE BOOK, PLEASE.
CHRISTIE'S NOT AROUND? I'D LIKE TO GET YOU BOTH TO SIGN THEM, IF YOU DON'T MIND.
OH, FOR SURE! CHRISTIE'S AT A PANEL--SHE'LL BE BACK IN MAYBE HALF AN HOUR?

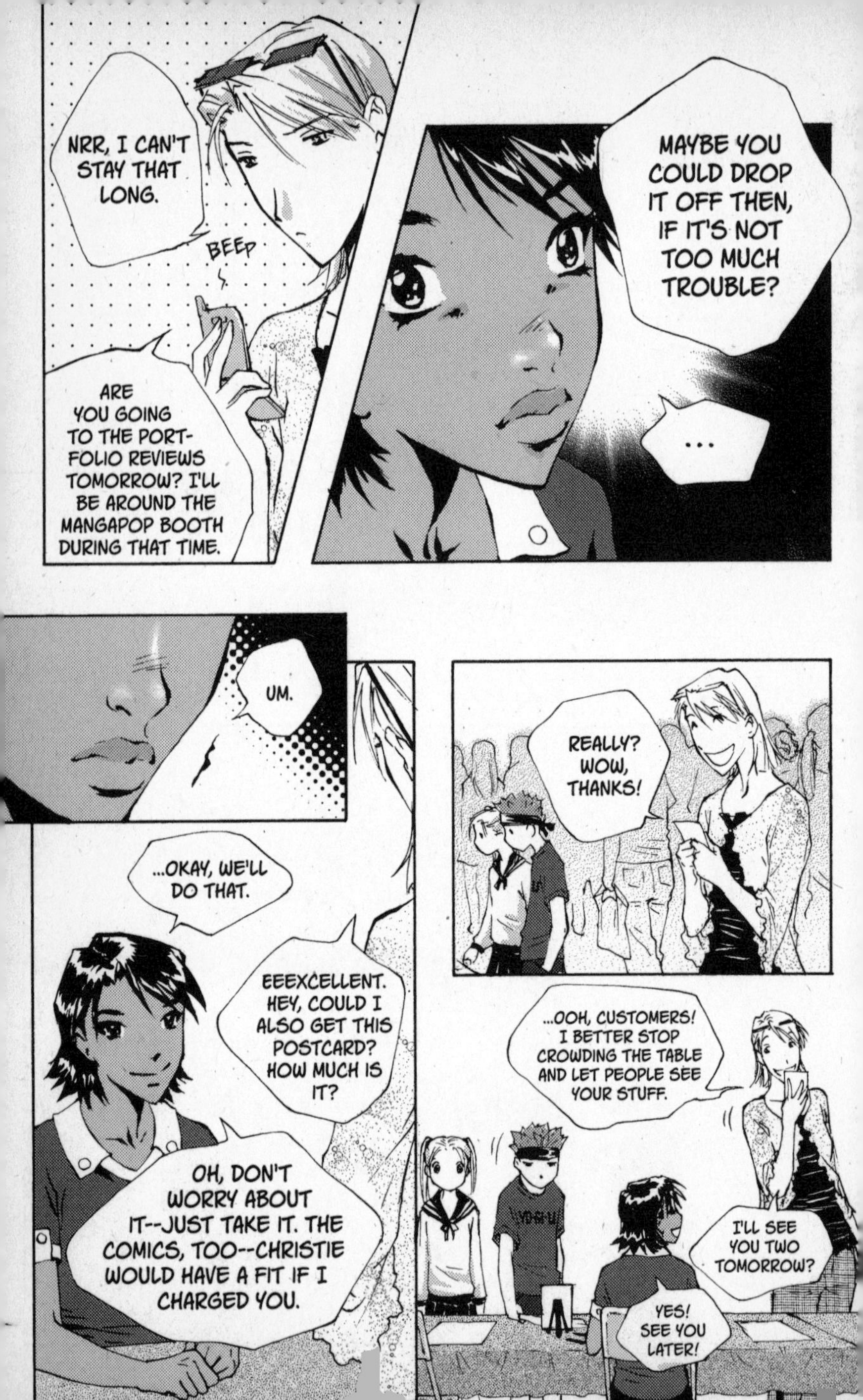
NRR, I CAN'T STAY THAT LONG.
BEEP
ARE YOU GOING TO THE PORT-FOLIO REVIEWS TOMORROW? I'LL BE AROUND THE MANGAPOP BOOTH DURING THAT TIME.
MAYBE YOU COULD DROP IT OFF THEN, IF IT'S NOT TOO MUCH TROUBLE?
...
UM.
...OKAY, WE'LL DO THAT.
EEEXCELLENT. HEY, COULD I ALSO GET THIS POSTCARD? HOW MUCH IS IT?
OH, DON'T WORRY ABOUT IT--JUST TAKE IT. THE COMICS, TOO--CHRISTIE WOULD HAVE A FIT IF I CHARGED YOU.
REALLY? WOW, THANKS!
...OOH, CUSTOMERS! I BETTER STOP CROWDING THE TABLE AND LET PEOPLE SEE YOUR STUFF.
I'LL SEE YOU TWO TOMORROW?
YES! SEE YOU LATER!

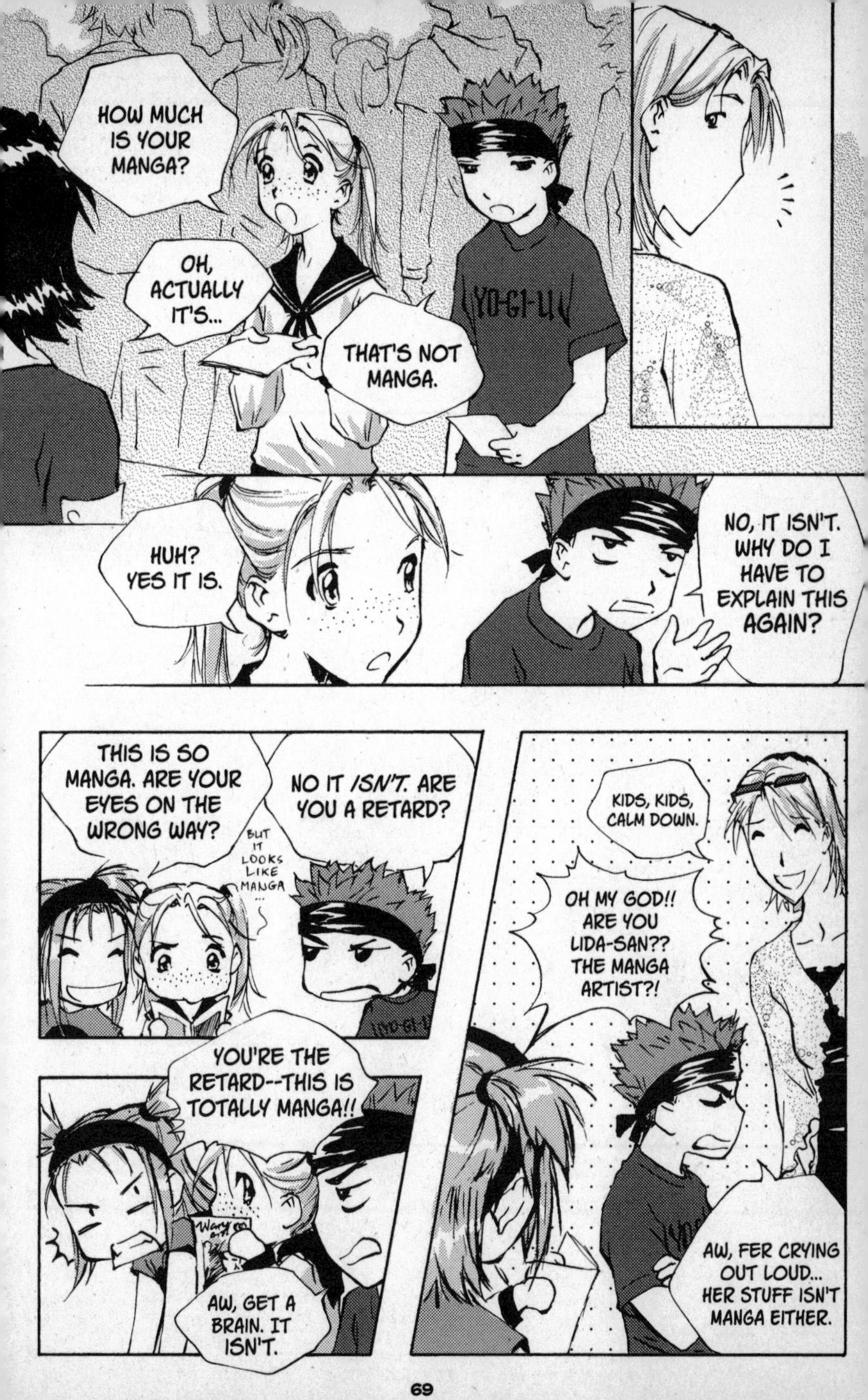
HOW MUCH IS YOUR MANGA?
OH, ACTUALLY IT'S...
THAT'S NOT MANGA.
HUH? YES IT IS.
NO, IT ISN'T. WHY DO I HAVE TO EXPLAIN THIS AGAIN?
THIS IS SO MANGA. ARE YOUR EYES ON THE WRONG WAY?
NO IT *ISN'T*. ARE YOU A RETARD?
BUT IT LOOKS LIKE MANGA...
YOU'RE THE RETARD--THIS IS TOTALLY MANGA!!
AW, GET A BRAIN. IT ISN'T.
KIDS, KIDS, CALM DOWN.
OH MY GOD!! ARE YOU LIDA-SAN?? THE MANGA ARTIST?!
AW, FER CRYING OUT LOUD... HER STUFF ISN'T MANGA EITHER.

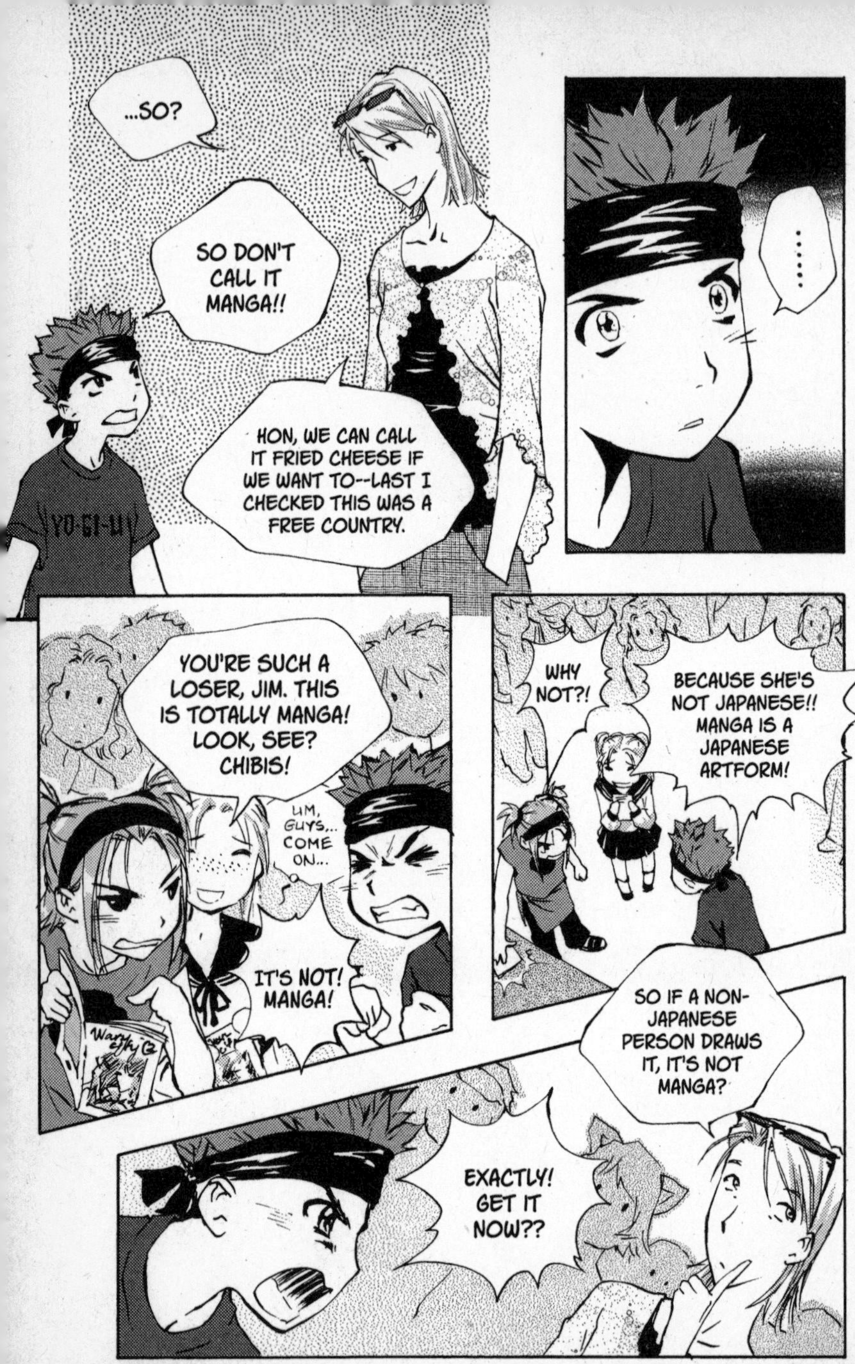
...SO?
SO DON'T CALL IT MANGA!!
HON, WE CAN CALL IT FRIED CHEESE IF WE WANT TO--LAST I CHECKED THIS WAS A FREE COUNTRY.
......
YOU'RE SUCH A LOSER, JIM. THIS IS TOTALLY MANGA! LOOK, SEE? CHIBIS!
UM, GUYS,... COME ON...
IT'S NOT! MANGA!
WHY NOT?!
BECAUSE SHE'S NOT JAPANESE!! MANGA IS A JAPANESE ARTFORM!
SO IF A NON-JAPANESE PERSON DRAWS IT, IT'S NOT MANGA?
EXACTLY! GET IT NOW??

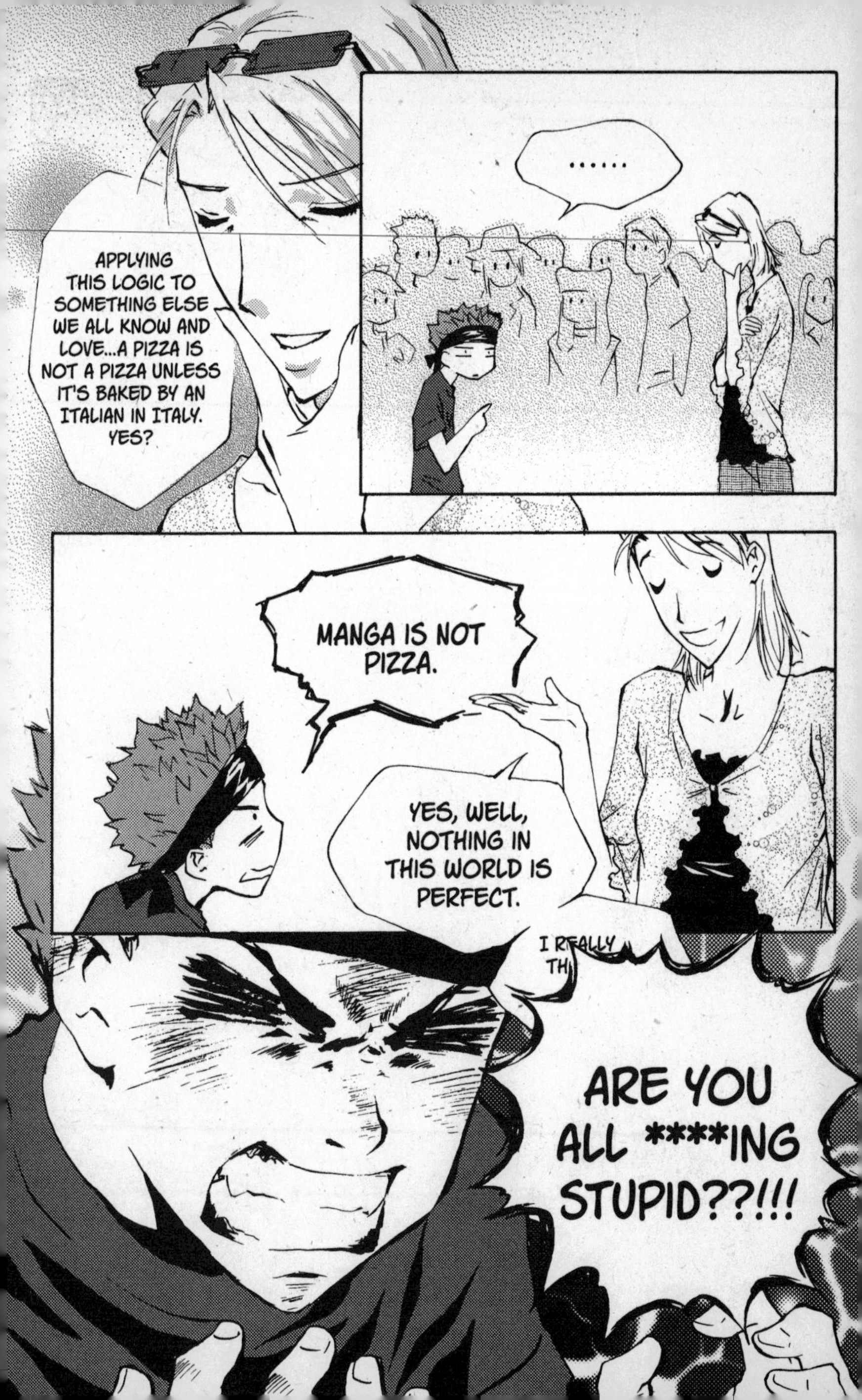
APPLYING THIS LOGIC TO SOMETHING ELSE WE ALL KNOW AND LOVE...A PIZZA IS NOT A PIZZA UNLESS IT'S BAKED BY AN ITALIAN IN ITALY. YES?
......
MANGA IS NOT PIZZA.
YES, WELL, NOTHING IN THIS WORLD IS PERFECT.
ARE YOU ALL ****ING STUPID??!!!

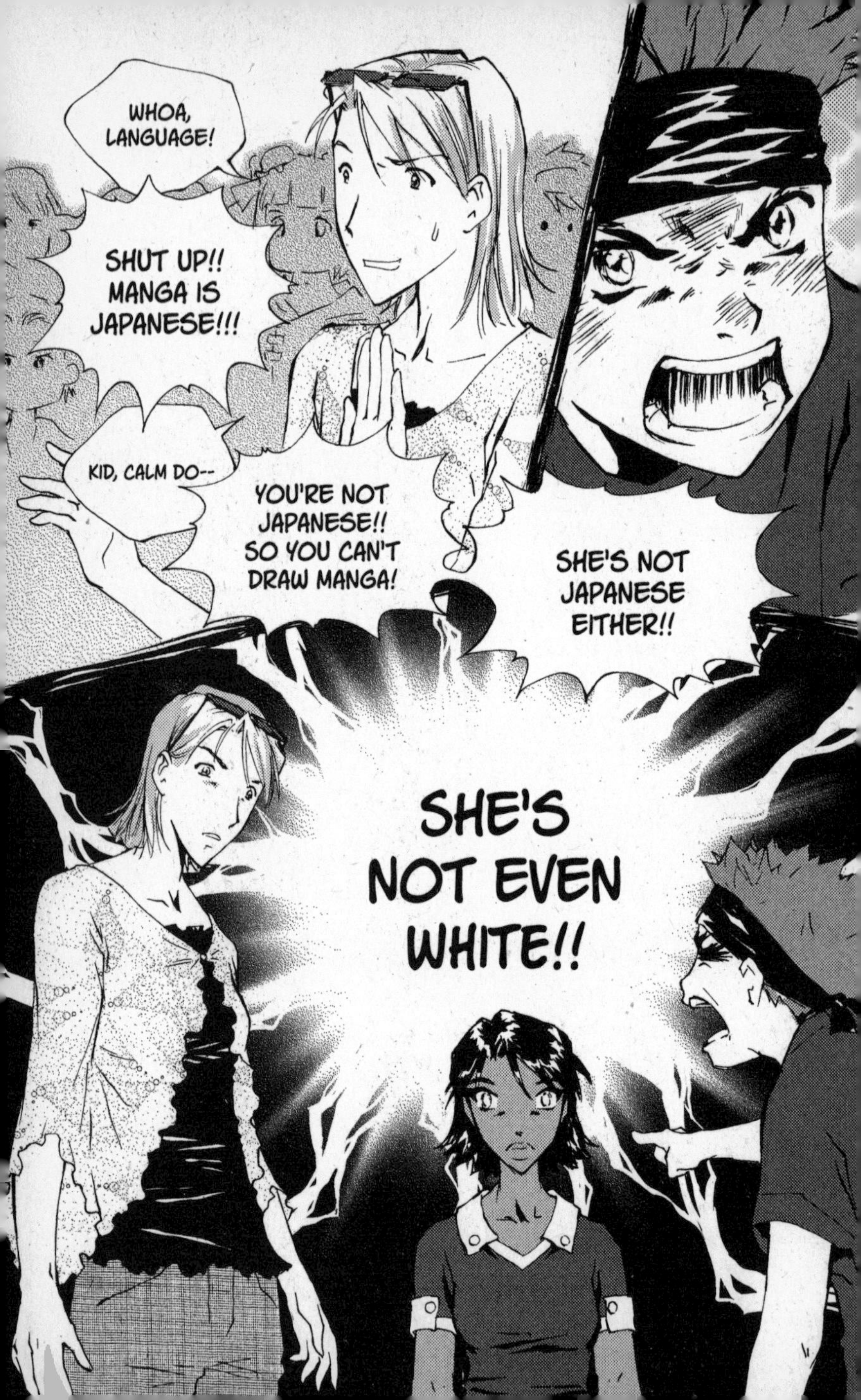
WHOA, LANGUAGE!
SHUT UP!! MANGA IS JAPANESE!!!
KID, CALM DO--
YOU'RE NOT JAPANESE!! SO YOU CAN'T DRAW MANGA!
SHE'S NOT JAPANESE EITHER!!
SHE'S NOT EVEN WHITE!!

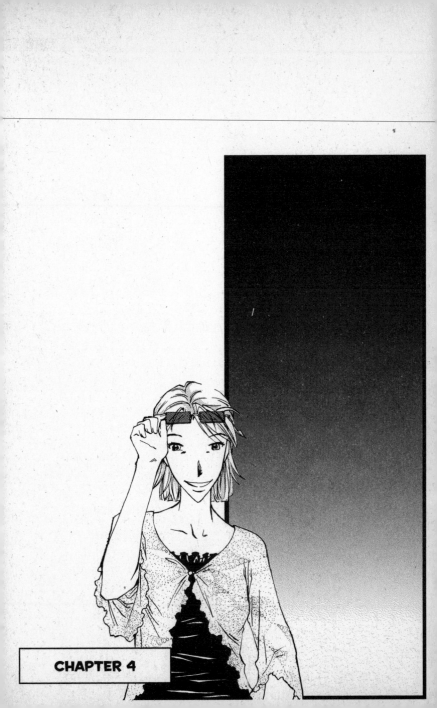

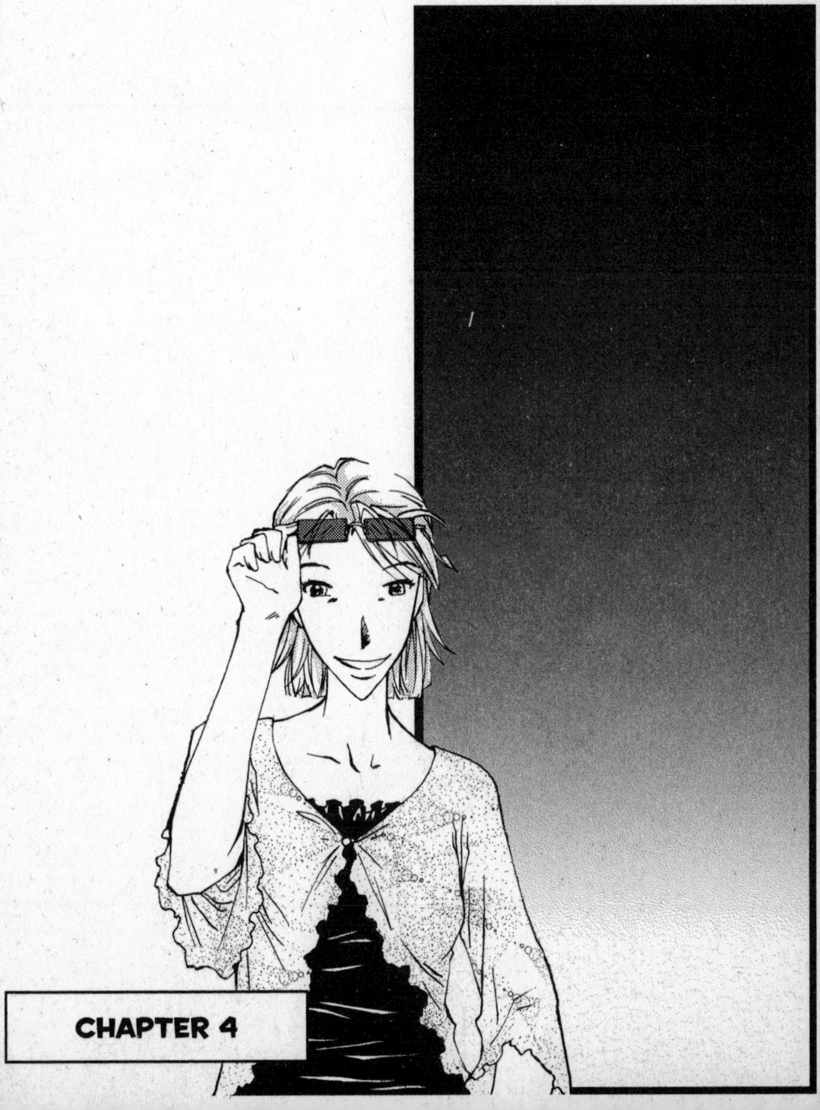
CHAPTER 4

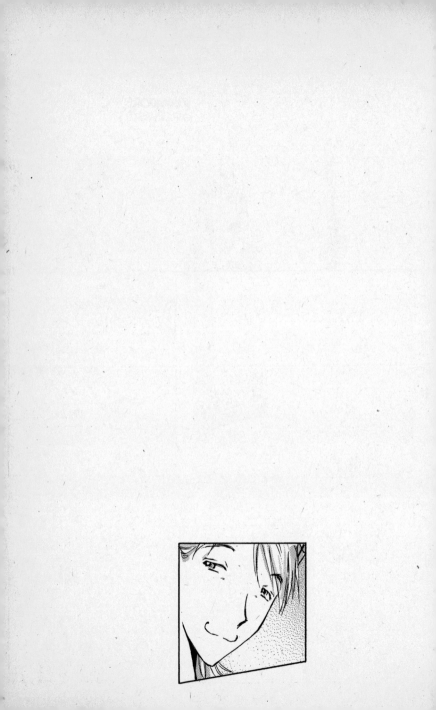

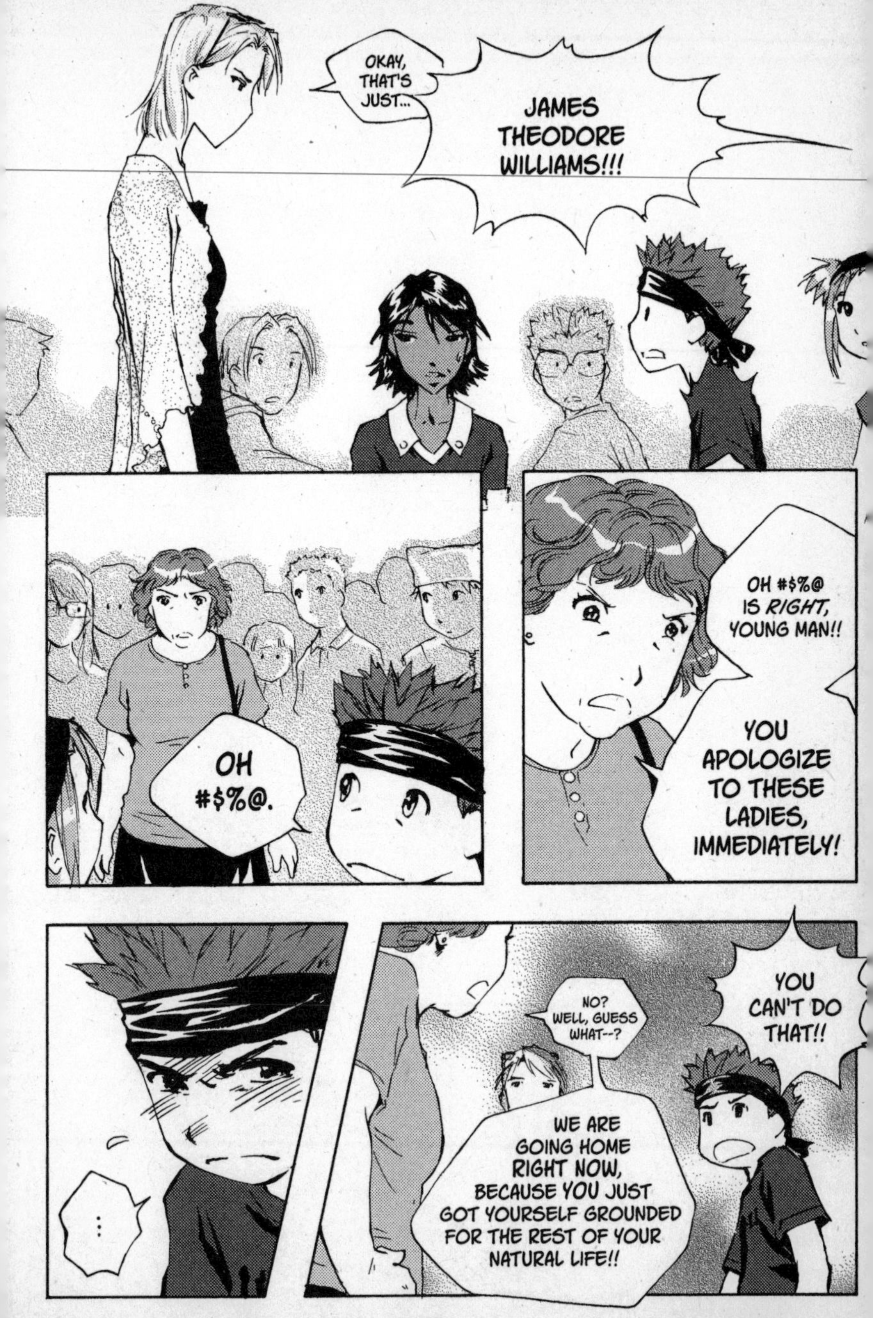

OKAY, THAT'S JUST...
JAMES THEODORE WILLIAMS!!!
OH #$%@.
OH #$%@ IS *RIGHT*, YOUNG MAN!!
YOU APOLOGIZE TO THESE LADIES, IMMEDIATELY!
...
NO? WELL, GUESS WHAT--?
WE ARE GOING HOME RIGHT NOW, BECAUSE YOU JUST GOT YOURSELF GROUNDED FOR THE REST OF YOUR NATURAL LIFE!!
YOU CAN'T DO THAT!!

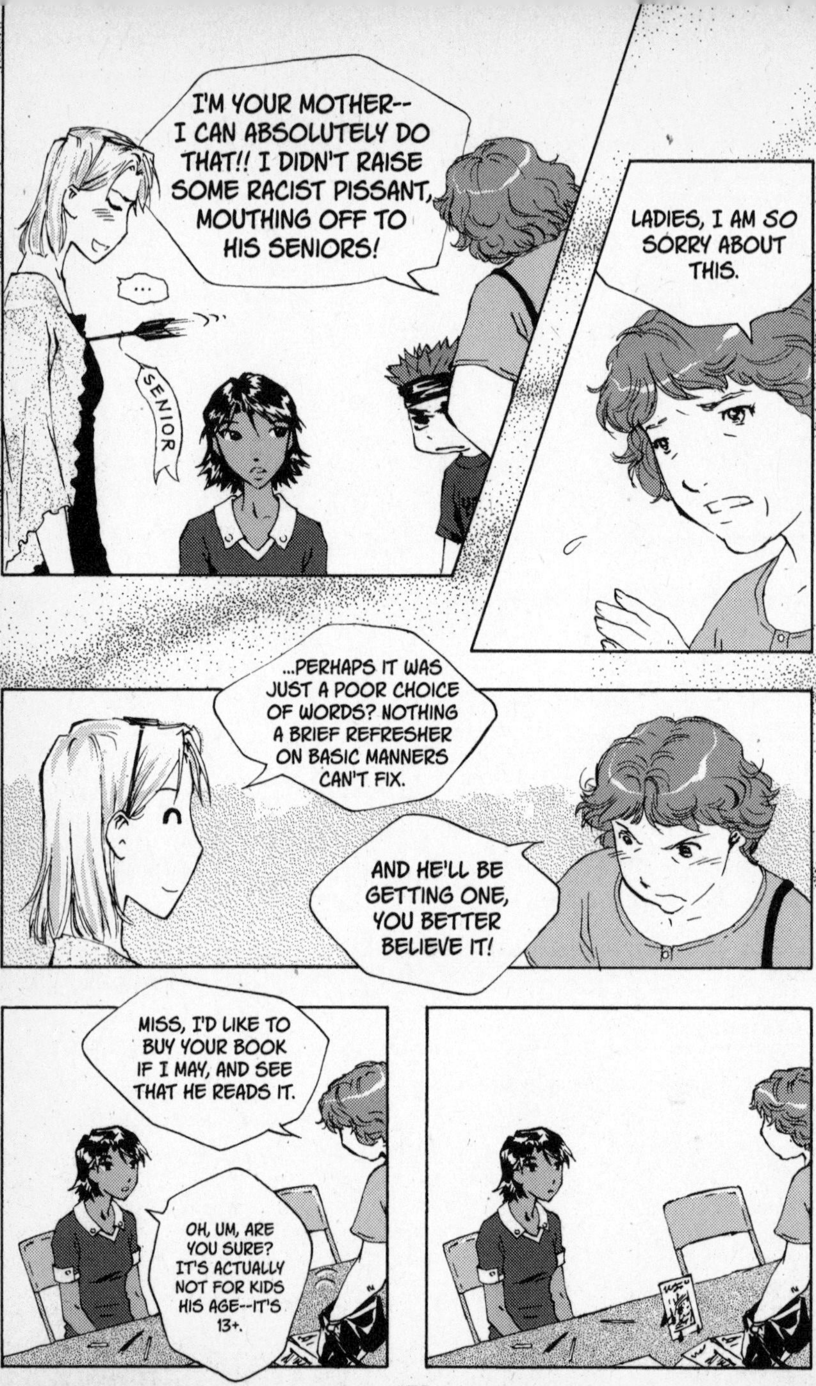
I'M YOUR MOTHER-- I CAN ABSOLUTELY DO THAT!! I DIDN'T RAISE SOME RACIST PISSANT, MOUTHING OFF TO HIS SENIORS!
...
SENIOR
LADIES, I AM SO SORRY ABOUT THIS.
...PERHAPS IT WAS JUST A POOR CHOICE OF WORDS? NOTHING A BRIEF REFRESHER ON BASIC MANNERS CAN'T FIX.
AND HE'LL BE GETTING ONE, YOU BETTER BELIEVE IT!
MISS, I'D LIKE TO BUY YOUR BOOK IF I MAY, AND SEE THAT HE READS IT.
OH, UM, ARE YOU SURE? IT'S ACTUALLY NOT FOR KIDS HIS AGE--IT'S 13+.

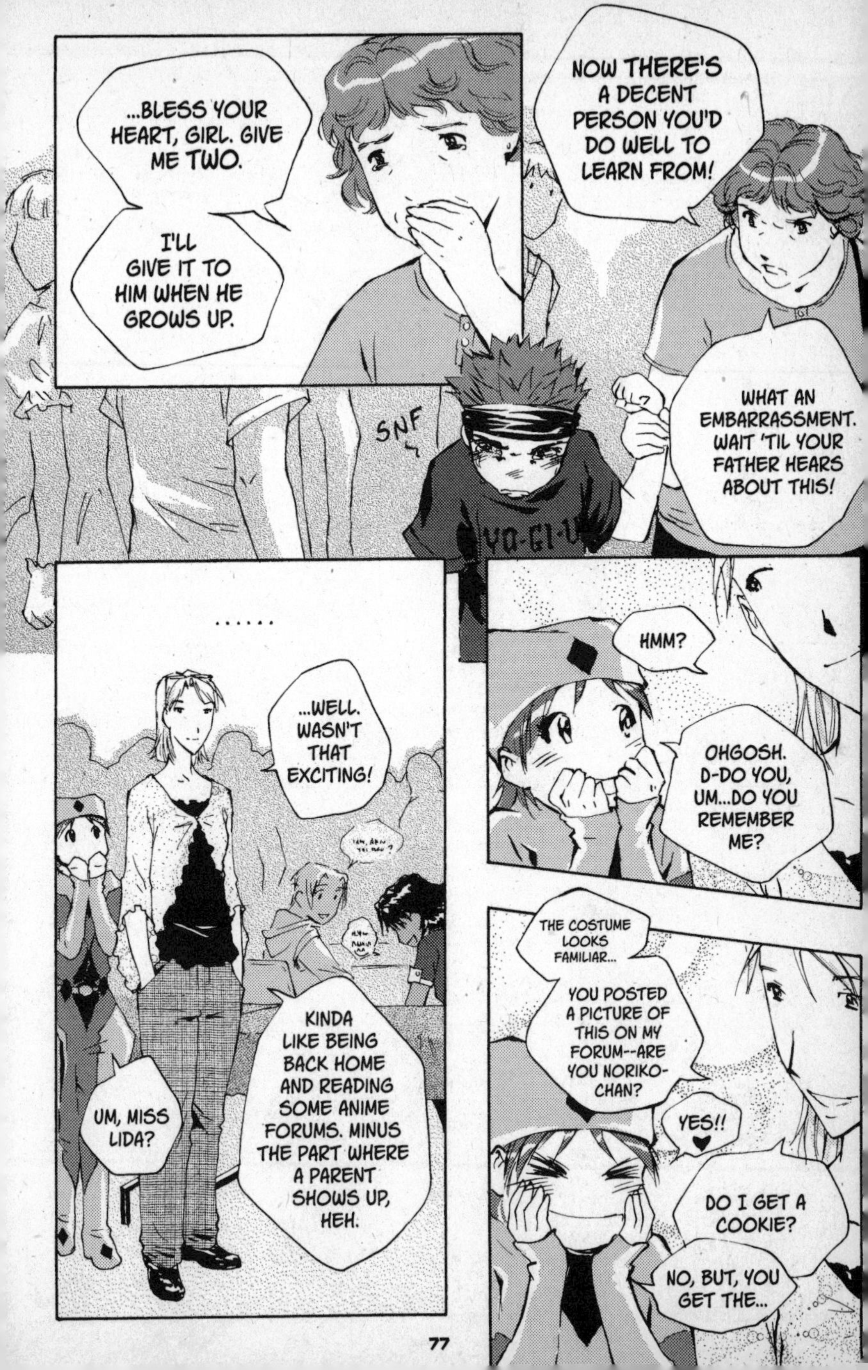
...BLESS YOUR HEART, GIRL. GIVE ME TWO.
I'LL GIVE IT TO HIM WHEN HE GROWS UP.
NOW THERE'S A DECENT PERSON YOU'D DO WELL TO LEARN FROM!
SNF
WHAT AN EMBARRASSMENT. WAIT 'TIL YOUR FATHER HEARS ABOUT THIS!
YU-GI-O
......
...WELL. WASN'T THAT EXCITING!
KINDA LIKE BEING BACK HOME AND READING SOME ANIME FORUMS. MINUS THE PART WHERE A PARENT SHOWS UP, HEH.
UM, MISS LIDA?
HMM?
OHGOSH. D-DO YOU, UM...DO YOU REMEMBER ME?
THE COSTUME LOOKS FAMILIAR...
YOU POSTED A PICTURE OF THIS ON MY FORUM--ARE YOU NORIKO-CHAN?
YES!!
DO I GET A COOKIE?
NO, BUT, YOU GET THE...

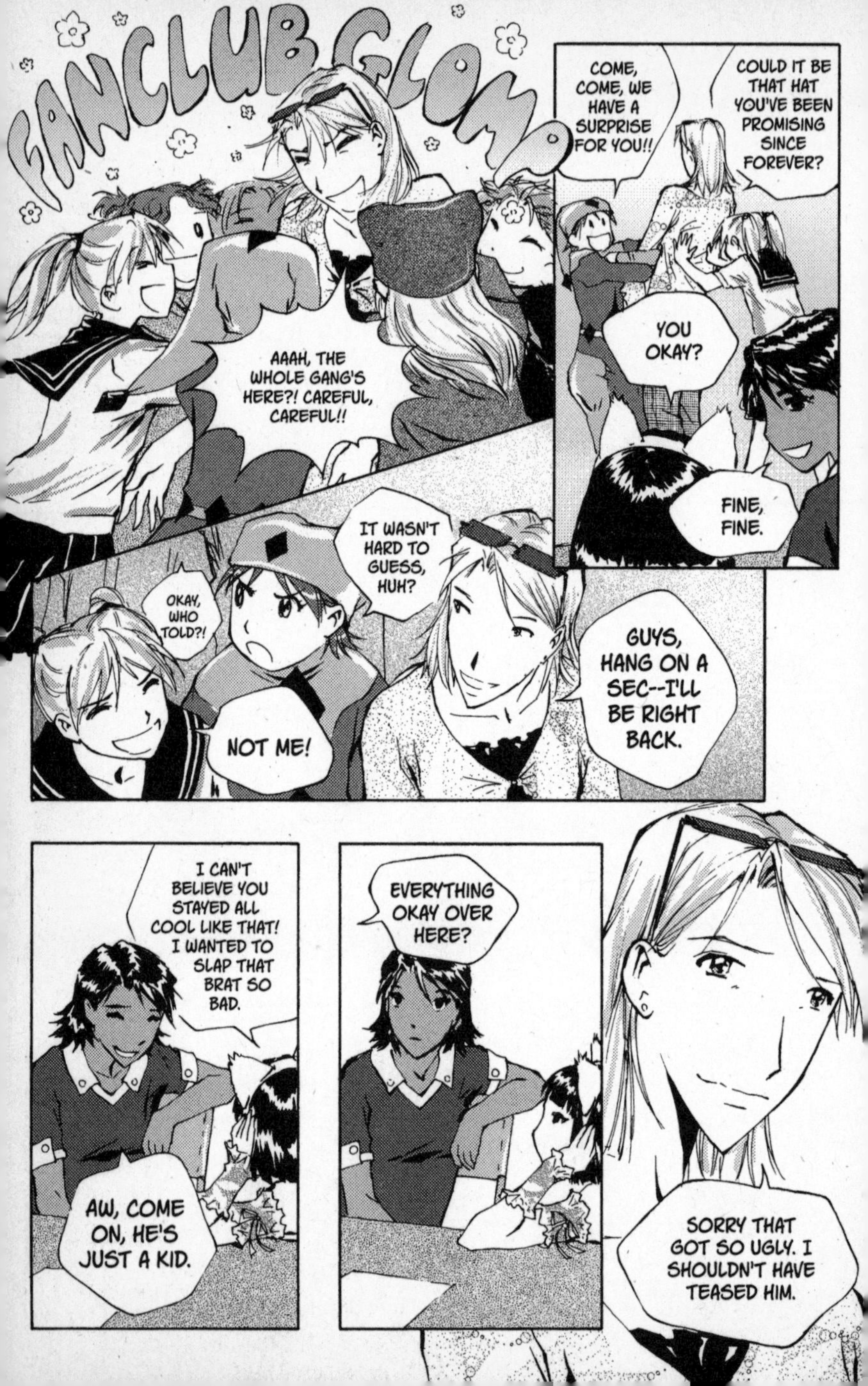
FANCLUB GLOMP
AAAH, THE WHOLE GANG'S HERE?! CAREFUL, CAREFUL!!
COME, COME, WE HAVE A SURPRISE FOR YOU!!
COULD IT BE THAT HAT YOU'VE BEEN PROMISING SINCE FOREVER?
YOU OKAY?
FINE, FINE.
OKAY, WHO TOLD?!
NOT ME!
IT WASN'T HARD TO GUESS, HUH?
GUYS, HANG ON A SEC--I'LL BE RIGHT BACK.
I CAN'T BELIEVE YOU STAYED ALL COOL LIKE THAT! I WANTED TO SLAP THAT BRAT SO BAD.
AW, COME ON, HE'S JUST A KID.
EVERYTHING OKAY OVER HERE?
SORRY THAT GOT SO UGLY. I SHOULDN'T HAVE TEASED HIM.

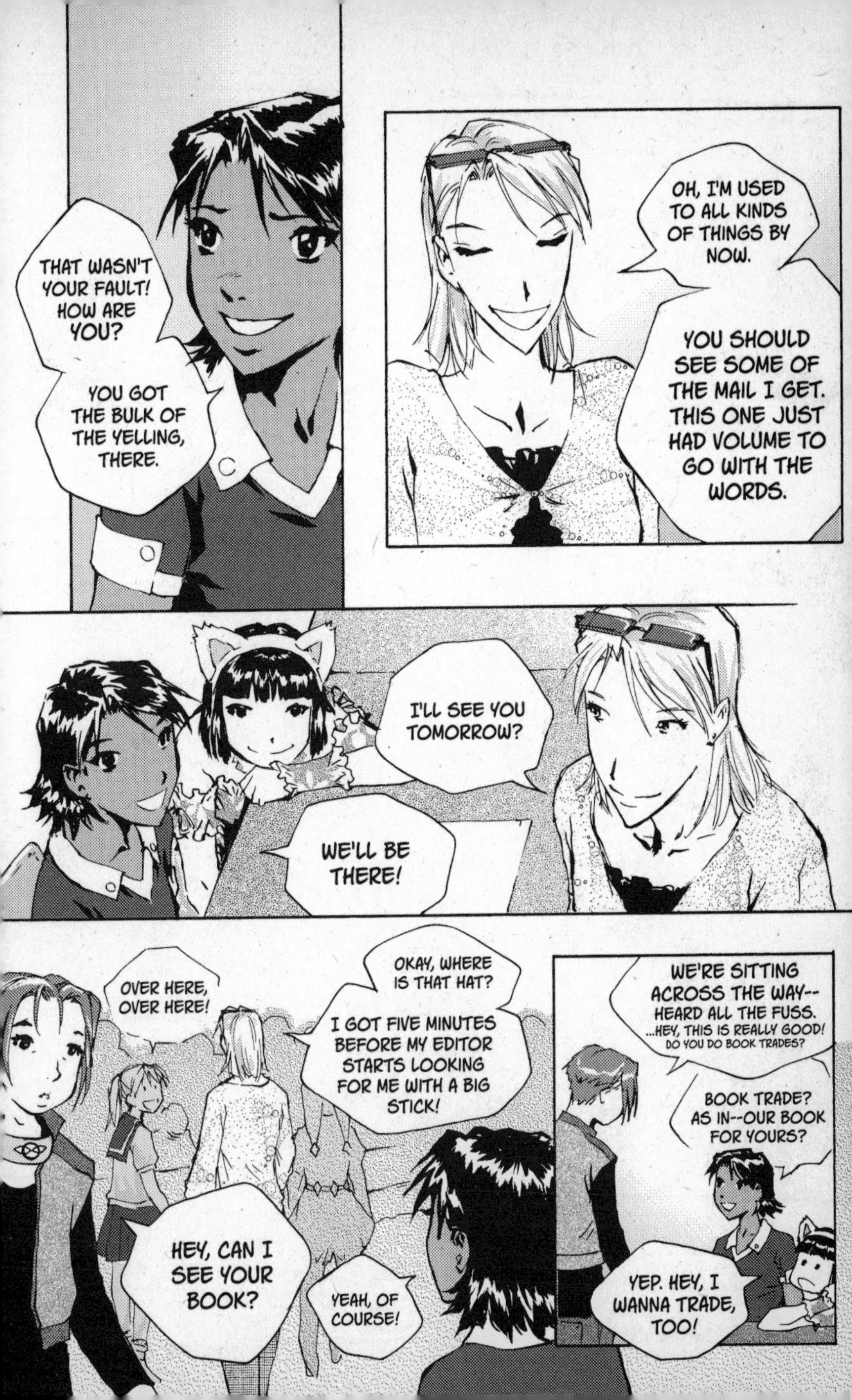
THAT WASN'T YOUR FAULT! HOW ARE YOU?
YOU GOT THE BULK OF THE YELLING, THERE.
OH, I'M USED TO ALL KINDS OF THINGS BY NOW.
YOU SHOULD SEE SOME OF THE MAIL I GET. THIS ONE JUST HAD VOLUME TO GO WITH THE WORDS.
I'LL SEE YOU TOMORROW?
WE'LL BE THERE!
OVER HERE, OVER HERE!
OKAY, WHERE IS THAT HAT?
I GOT FIVE MINUTES BEFORE MY EDITOR STARTS LOOKING FOR ME WITH A BIG STICK!
HEY, CAN I SEE YOUR BOOK?
YEAH, OF COURSE!
WE'RE SITTING ACROSS THE WAY-- HEARD ALL THE FUSS.
...HEY, THIS IS REALLY GOOD! DO YOU DO BOOK TRADES?
BOOK TRADE? AS IN--OUR BOOK FOR YOURS?
YEP. HEY, I WANNA TRADE, TOO!

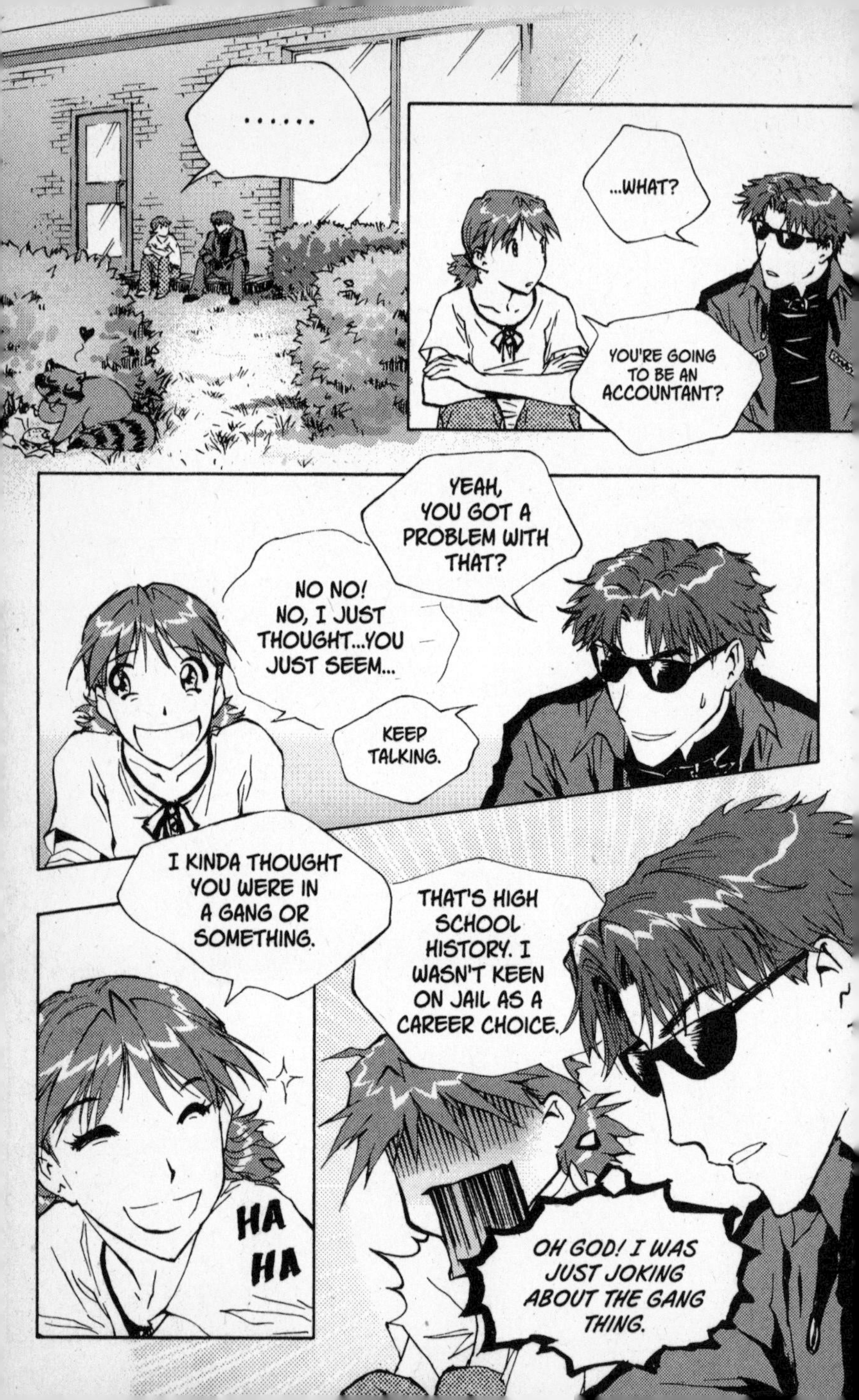
......
...WHAT?
YOU'RE GOING TO BE AN ACCOUNTANT?
YEAH, YOU GOT A PROBLEM WITH THAT?
NO NO! NO, I JUST THOUGHT...YOU JUST SEEM...
KEEP TALKING.
I KINDA THOUGHT YOU WERE IN A GANG OR SOMETHING.
HA HA
THAT'S HIGH SCHOOL HISTORY. I WASN'T KEEN ON JAIL AS A CAREER CHOICE.
OH GOD! I WAS JUST JOKING ABOUT THE GANG THING.

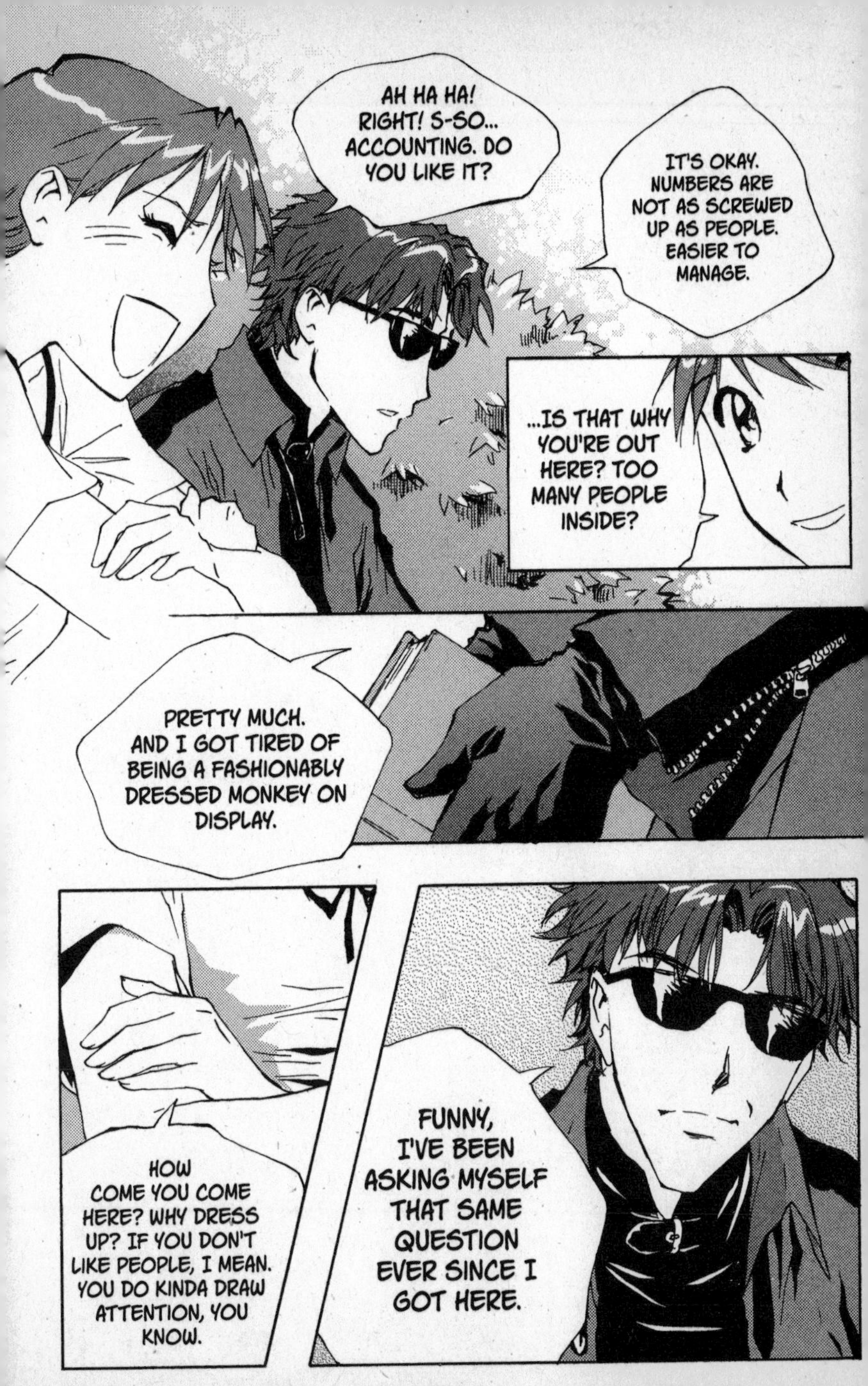
AH HA HA! RIGHT! S-SO... ACCOUNTING. DO YOU LIKE IT?
IT'S OKAY. NUMBERS ARE NOT AS SCREWED UP AS PEOPLE. EASIER TO MANAGE.
...IS THAT WHY YOU'RE OUT HERE? TOO MANY PEOPLE INSIDE?
PRETTY MUCH. AND I GOT TIRED OF BEING A FASHIONABLY DRESSED MONKEY ON DISPLAY.
HOW COME YOU COME HERE? WHY DRESS UP? IF YOU DON'T LIKE PEOPLE, I MEAN. YOU DO KINDA DRAW ATTENTION, YOU KNOW.
FUNNY, I'VE BEEN ASKING MYSELF THAT SAME QUESTION EVER SINCE I GOT HERE.

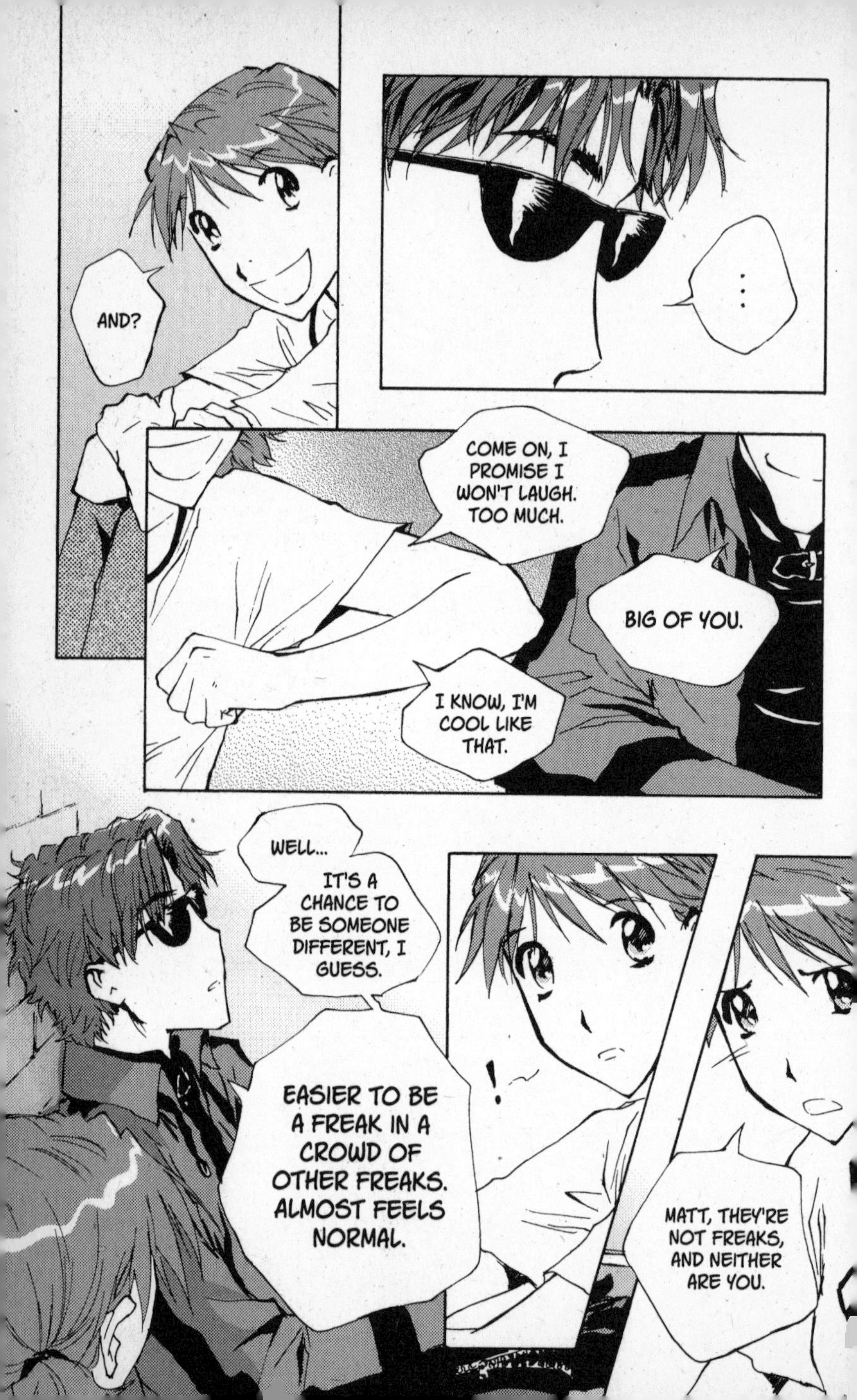
AND?
...
COME ON, I PROMISE I WON'T LAUGH. TOO MUCH.
BIG OF YOU.
I KNOW, I'M COOL LIKE THAT.
WELL...
IT'S A CHANCE TO BE SOMEONE DIFFERENT, I GUESS.
EASIER TO BE A FREAK IN A CROWD OF OTHER FREAKS. ALMOST FEELS NORMAL.
!
MATT, THEY'RE NOT FREAKS, AND NEITHER ARE YOU.

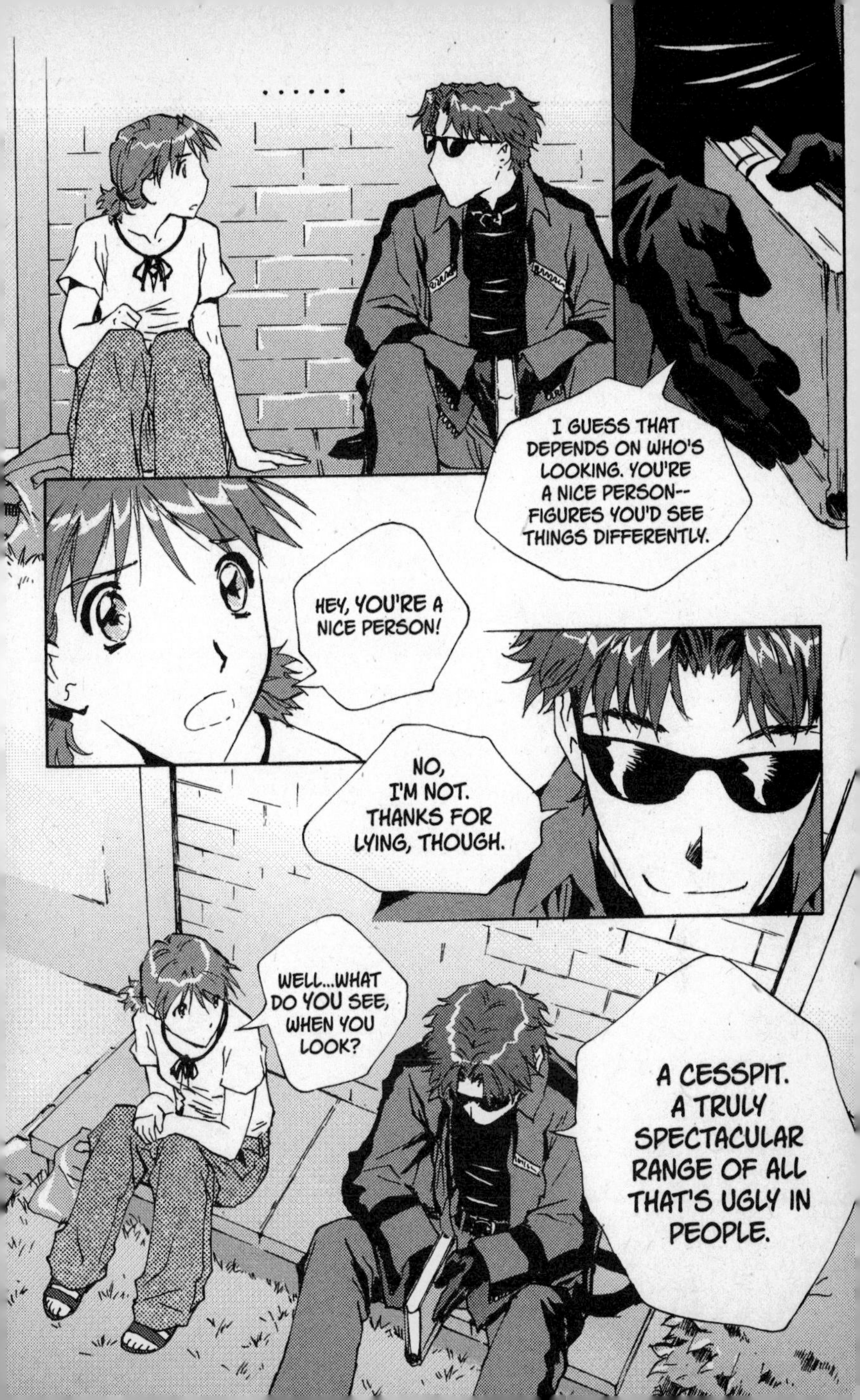
......
I GUESS THAT DEPENDS ON WHO'S LOOKING. YOU'RE A NICE PERSON-- FIGURES YOU'D SEE THINGS DIFFERENTLY.
HEY, YOU'RE A NICE PERSON!
NO, I'M NOT. THANKS FOR LYING, THOUGH.
WELL...WHAT DO YOU SEE, WHEN YOU LOOK?
A CESSPIT. A TRULY SPECTACULAR RANGE OF ALL THAT'S UGLY IN PEOPLE.

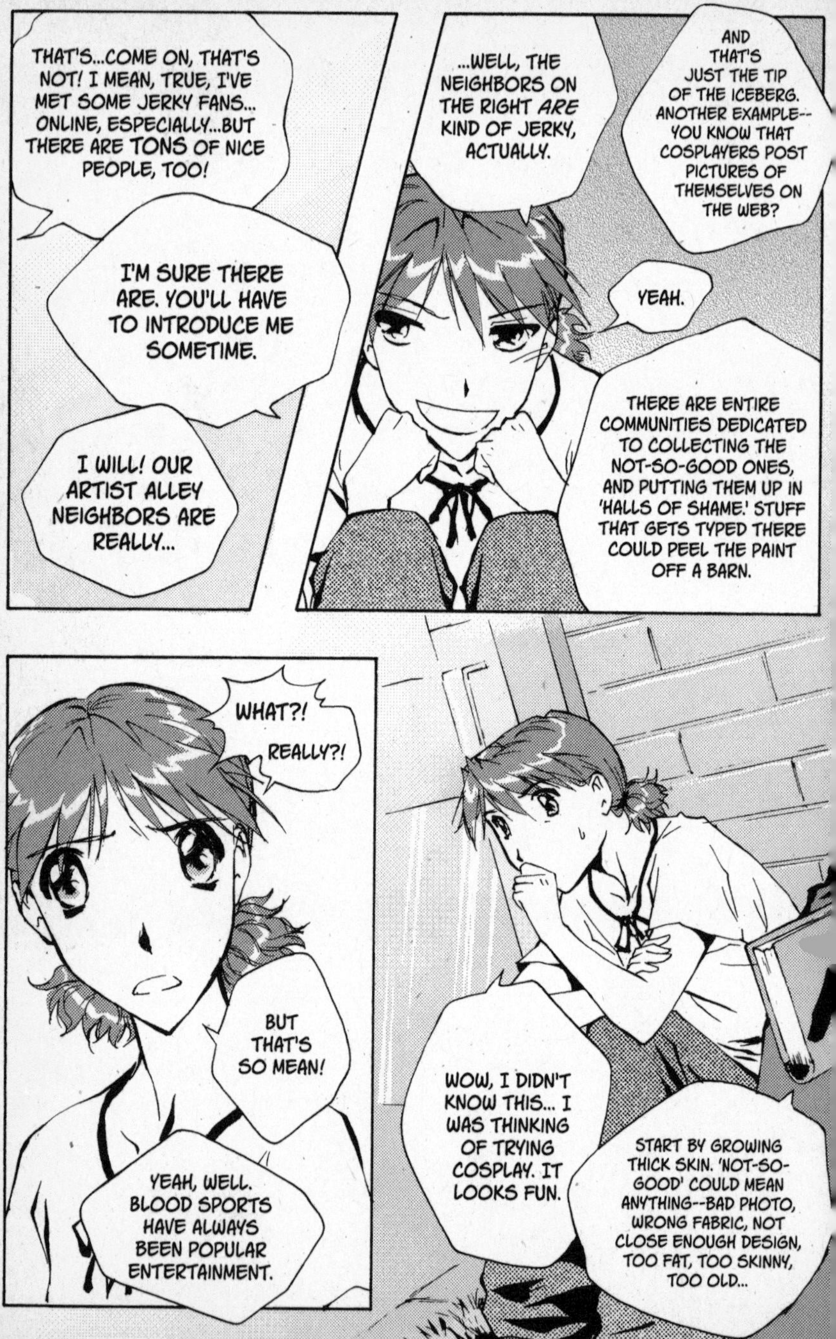
THAT'S...COME ON, THAT'S NOT! I MEAN, TRUE, I'VE MET SOME JERKY FANS... ONLINE, ESPECIALLY...BUT THERE ARE TONS OF NICE PEOPLE, TOO!
I'M SURE THERE ARE. YOU'LL HAVE TO INTRODUCE ME SOMETIME.
I WILL! OUR ARTIST ALLEY NEIGHBORS ARE REALLY...
...WELL, THE NEIGHBORS ON THE RIGHT *ARE* KIND OF JERKY, ACTUALLY.
AND THAT'S JUST THE TIP OF THE ICEBERG. ANOTHER EXAMPLE-- YOU KNOW THAT COSPLAYERS POST PICTURES OF THEMSELVES ON THE WEB?
YEAH.
THERE ARE ENTIRE COMMUNITIES DEDICATED TO COLLECTING THE NOT-SO-GOOD ONES, AND PUTTING THEM UP IN 'HALLS OF SHAME.' STUFF THAT GETS TYPED THERE COULD PEEL THE PAINT OFF A BARN.
WHAT?!
REALLY?!
BUT THAT'S SO MEAN!
YEAH, WELL. BLOOD SPORTS HAVE ALWAYS BEEN POPULAR ENTERTAINMENT.
WOW, I DIDN'T KNOW THIS... I WAS THINKING OF TRYING COSPLAY. IT LOOKS FUN.
START BY GROWING THICK SKIN. 'NOT-SO-GOOD' COULD MEAN ANYTHING--BAD PHOTO, WRONG FABRIC, NOT CLOSE ENOUGH DESIGN, TOO FAT, TOO SKINNY, TOO OLD...

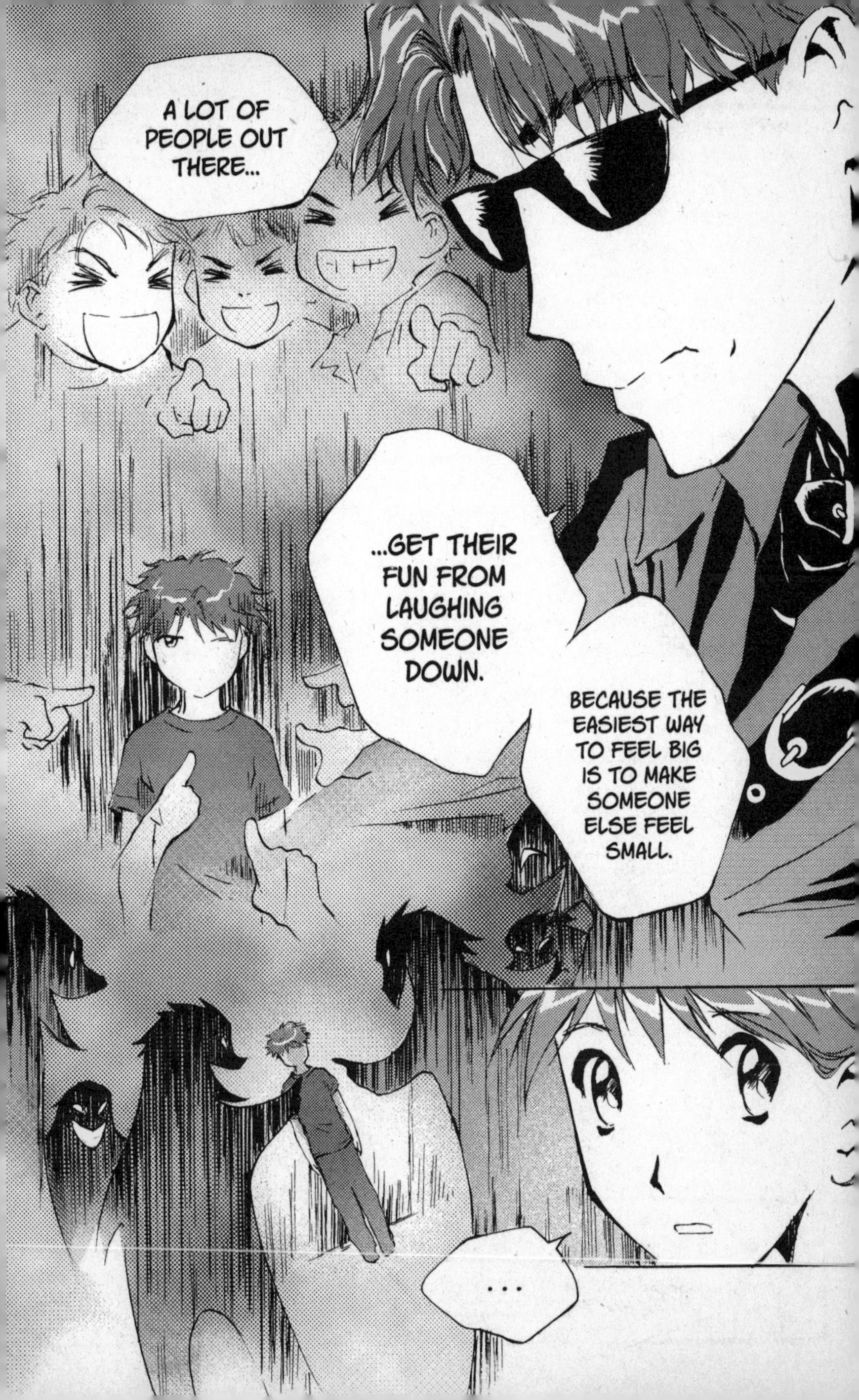
A LOT OF PEOPLE OUT THERE...
...GET THEIR FUN FROM LAUGHING SOMEONE DOWN.
BECAUSE THE EASIEST WAY TO FEEL BIG IS TO MAKE SOMEONE ELSE FEEL SMALL.
...

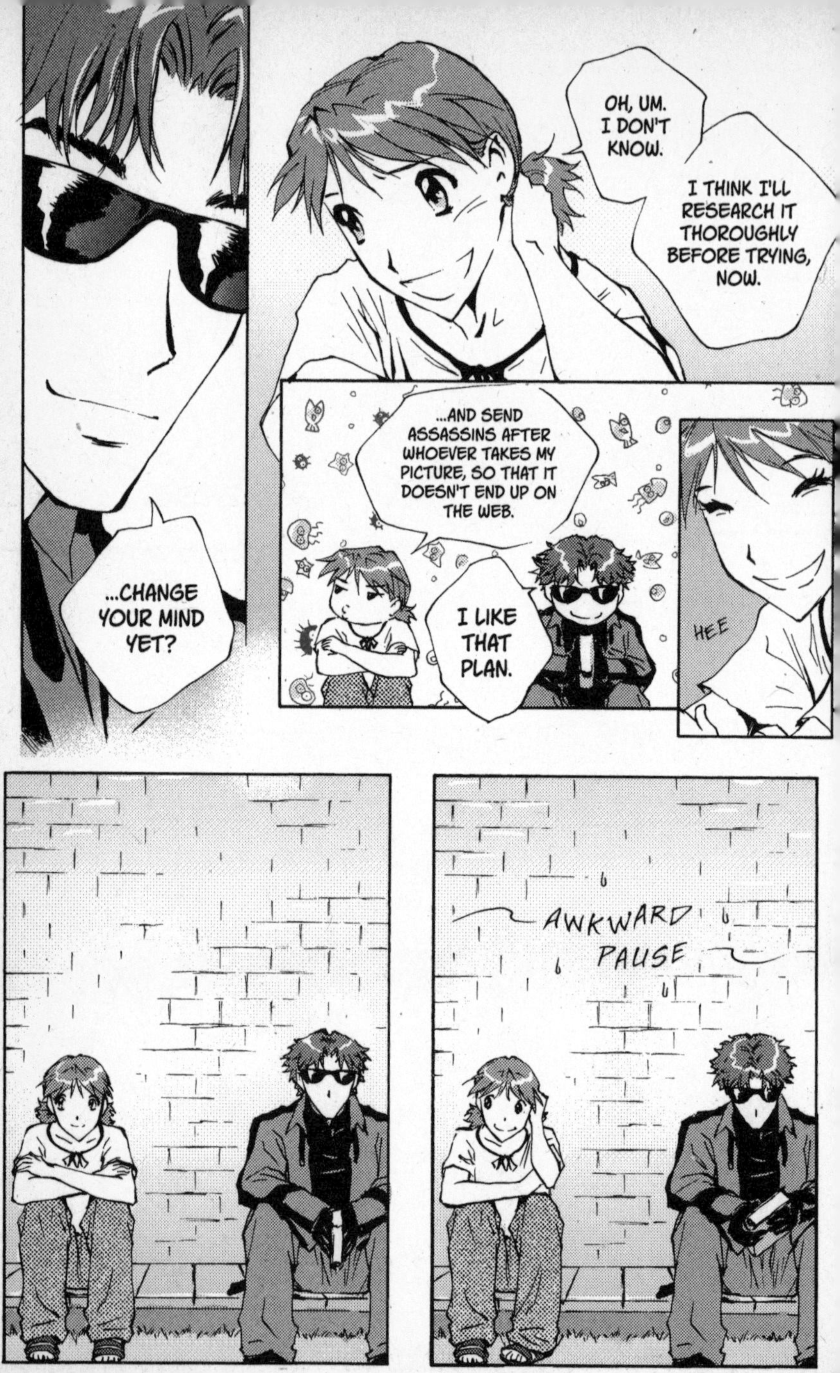
...CHANGE YOUR MIND YET?
OH, UM. I DON'T KNOW.
I THINK I'LL RESEARCH IT THOROUGHLY BEFORE TRYING, NOW.
...AND SEND ASSASSINS AFTER WHOEVER TAKES MY PICTURE, SO THAT IT DOESN'T END UP ON THE WEB.
I LIKE THAT PLAN.
HEE
AWKWARD PAUSE

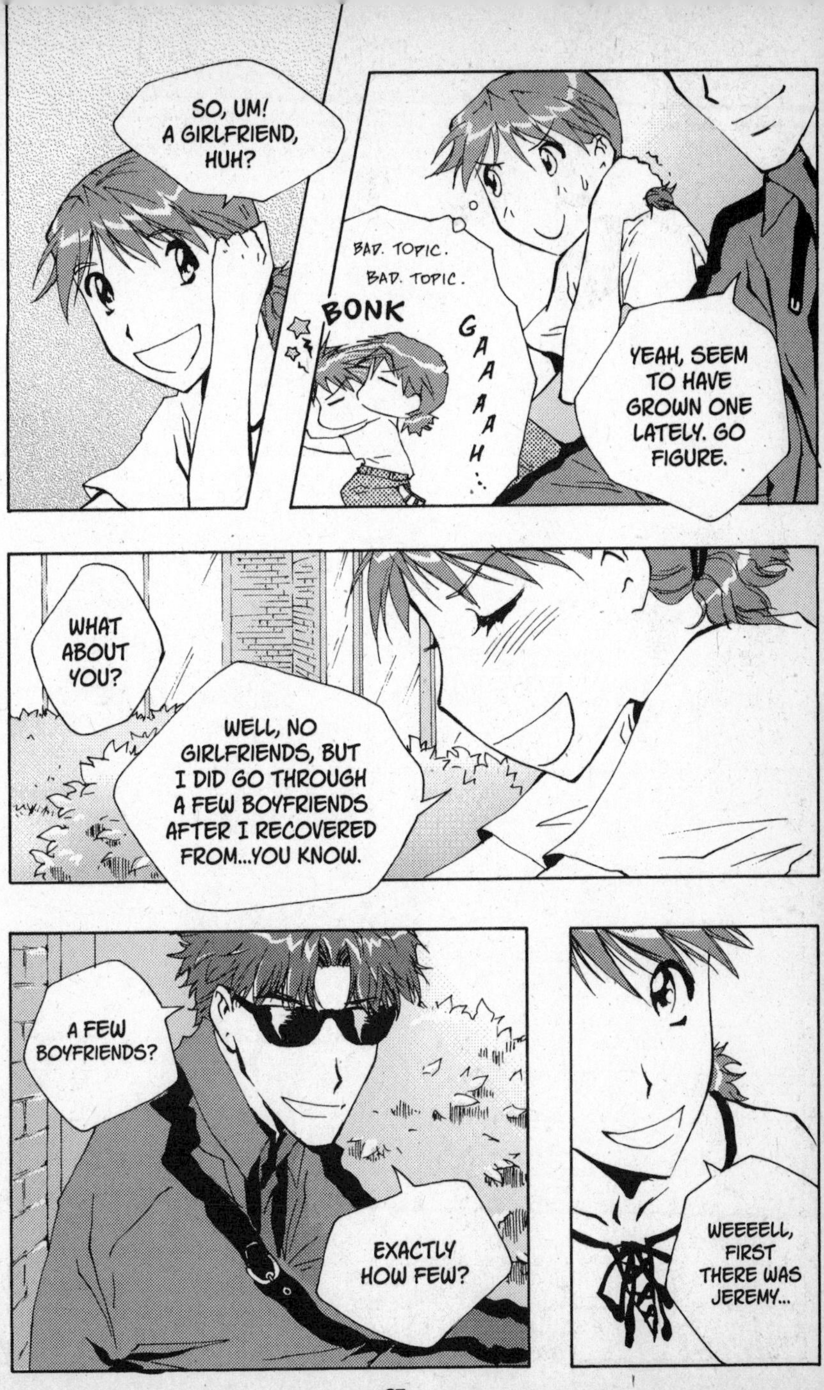
SO, UM! A GIRLFRIEND, HUH?
BAD. TOPIC. BAD. TOPIC.
BONK
GAAAAH...
YEAH, SEEM TO HAVE GROWN ONE LATELY. GO FIGURE.
WHAT ABOUT YOU?
WELL, NO GIRLFRIENDS, BUT I DID GO THROUGH A FEW BOYFRIENDS AFTER I RECOVERED FROM...YOU KNOW.
A FEW BOYFRIENDS?
EXACTLY HOW FEW?
WEEEELL, FIRST THERE WAS JEREMY...

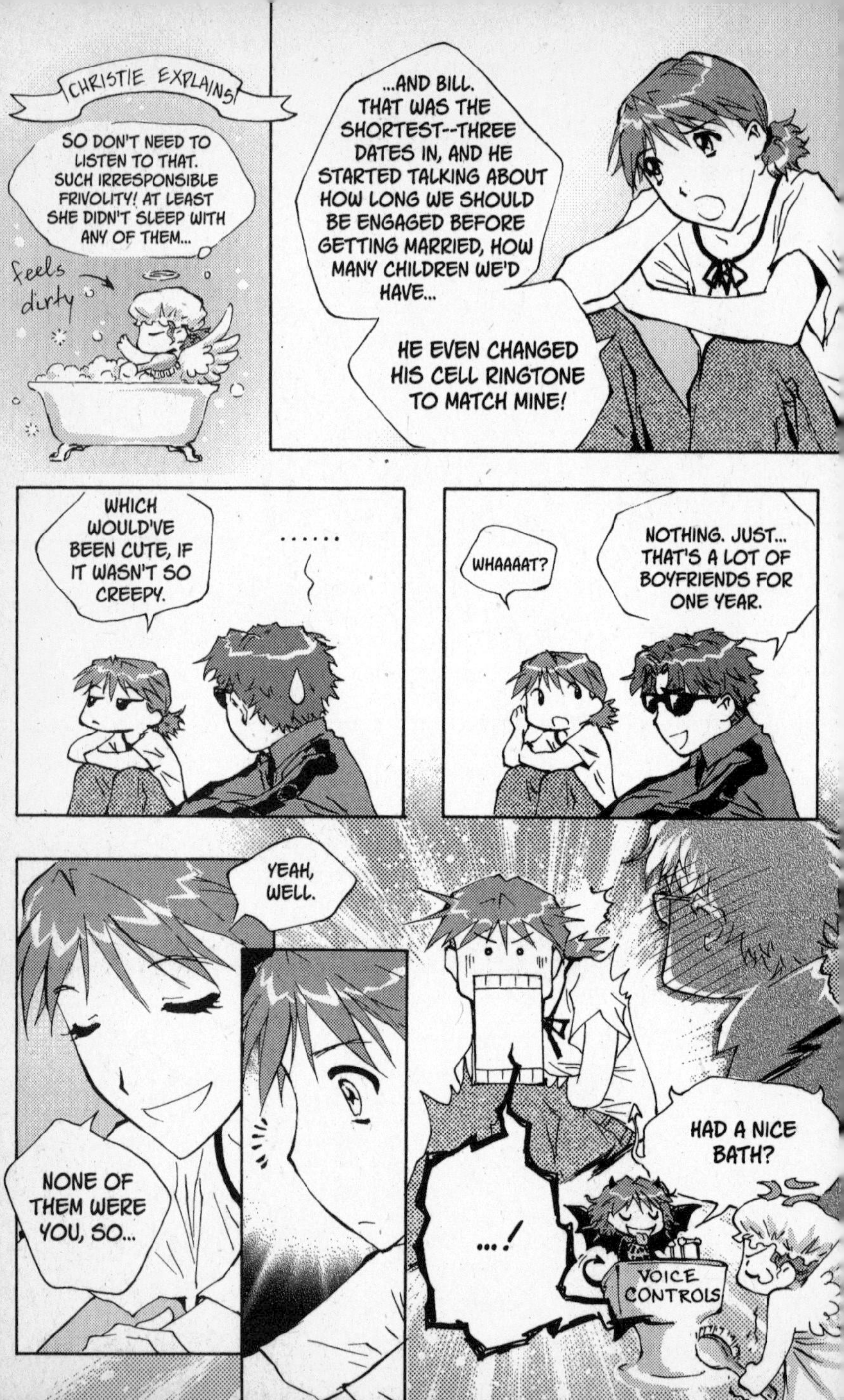
CHRISTIE EXPLAINS
SO DON'T NEED TO LISTEN TO THAT. SUCH IRRESPONSIBLE FRIVOLITY! AT LEAST SHE DIDN'T SLEEP WITH ANY OF THEM...
feels dirty
...AND BILL. THAT WAS THE SHORTEST--THREE DATES IN, AND HE STARTED TALKING ABOUT HOW LONG WE SHOULD BE ENGAGED BEFORE GETTING MARRIED, HOW MANY CHILDREN WE'D HAVE...
HE EVEN CHANGED HIS CELL RINGTONE TO MATCH MINE!
WHICH WOULD'VE BEEN CUTE, IF IT WASN'T SO CREEPY.
......
WHAAAAT?
NOTHING. JUST... THAT'S A LOT OF BOYFRIENDS FOR ONE YEAR.
YEAH, WELL.
NONE OF THEM WERE YOU, SO...
...!
HAD A NICE BATH?
VOICE CONTROLS

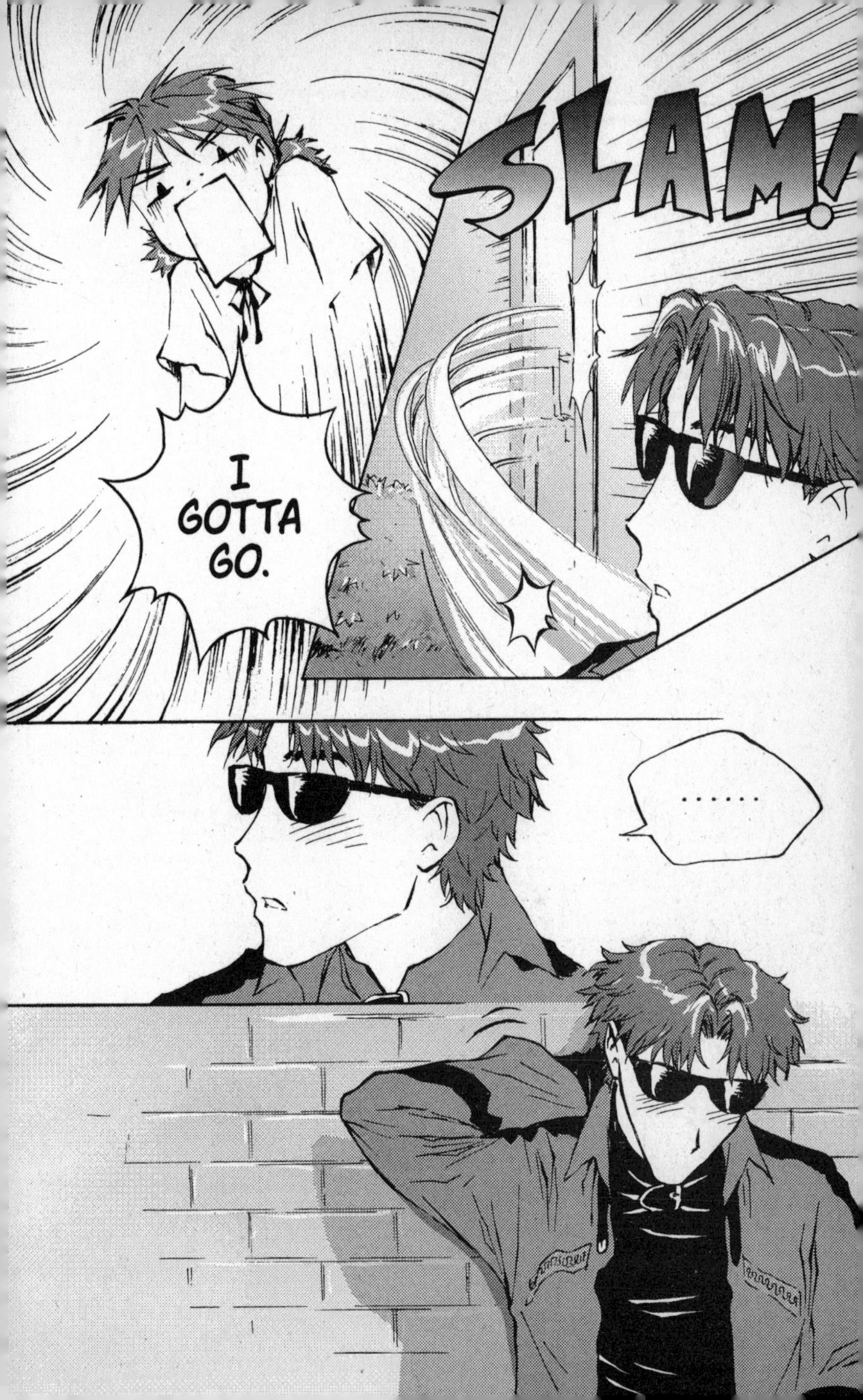
I GOTTA GO.
SLAM!
......

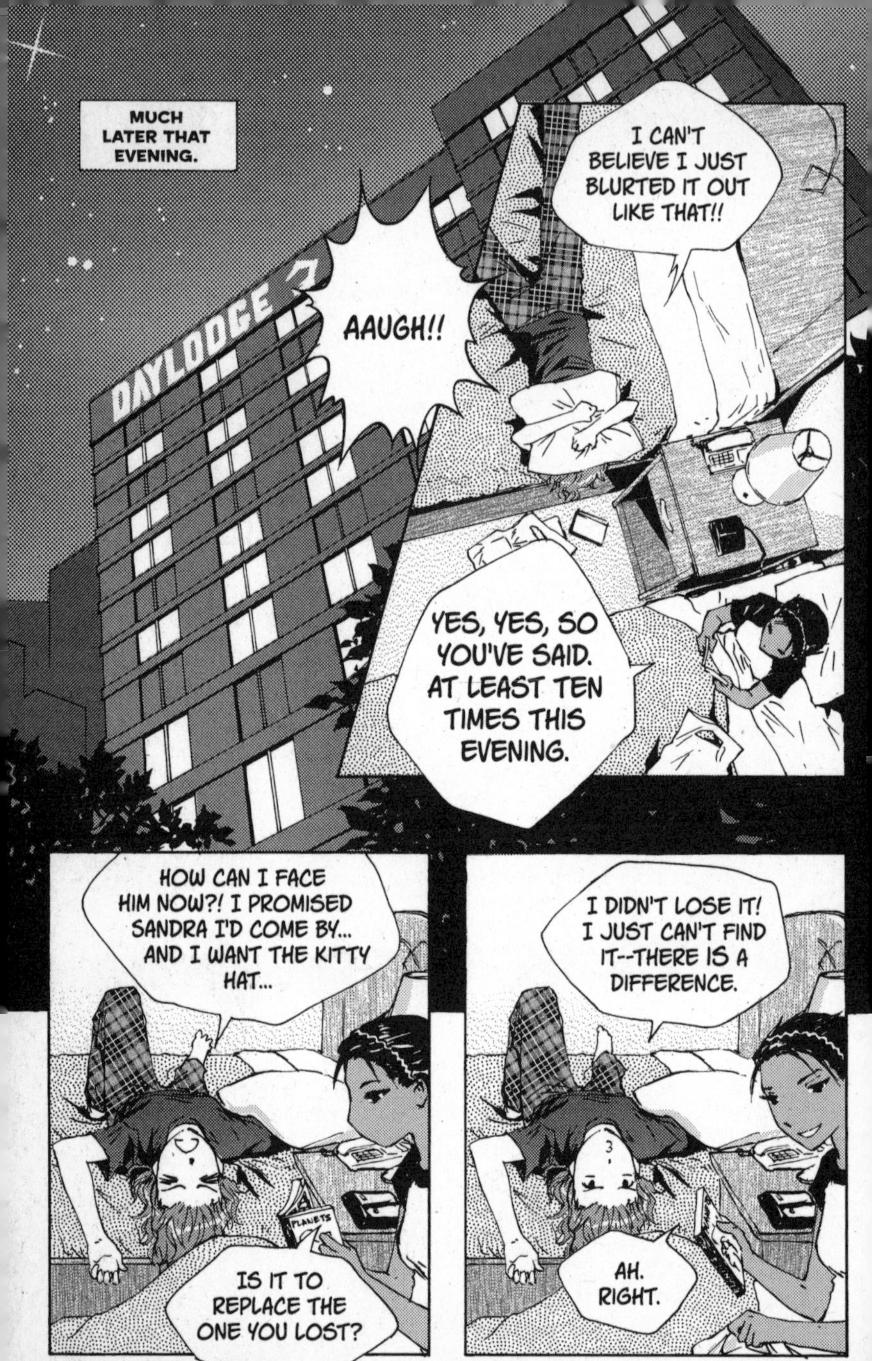
MUCH LATER THAT EVENING.
AAUGH!!
DAYLODGE
I CAN'T BELIEVE I JUST BLURTED IT OUT LIKE THAT!!
YES, YES, SO YOU'VE SAID. AT LEAST TEN TIMES THIS EVENING.
HOW CAN I FACE HIM NOW?! I PROMISED SANDRA I'D COME BY... AND I WANT THE KITTY HAT...
PLANETS
IS IT TO REPLACE THE ONE YOU LOST?
I DIDN'T LOSE IT! I JUST CAN'T FIND IT--THERE IS A DIFFERENCE.
AH. RIGHT.

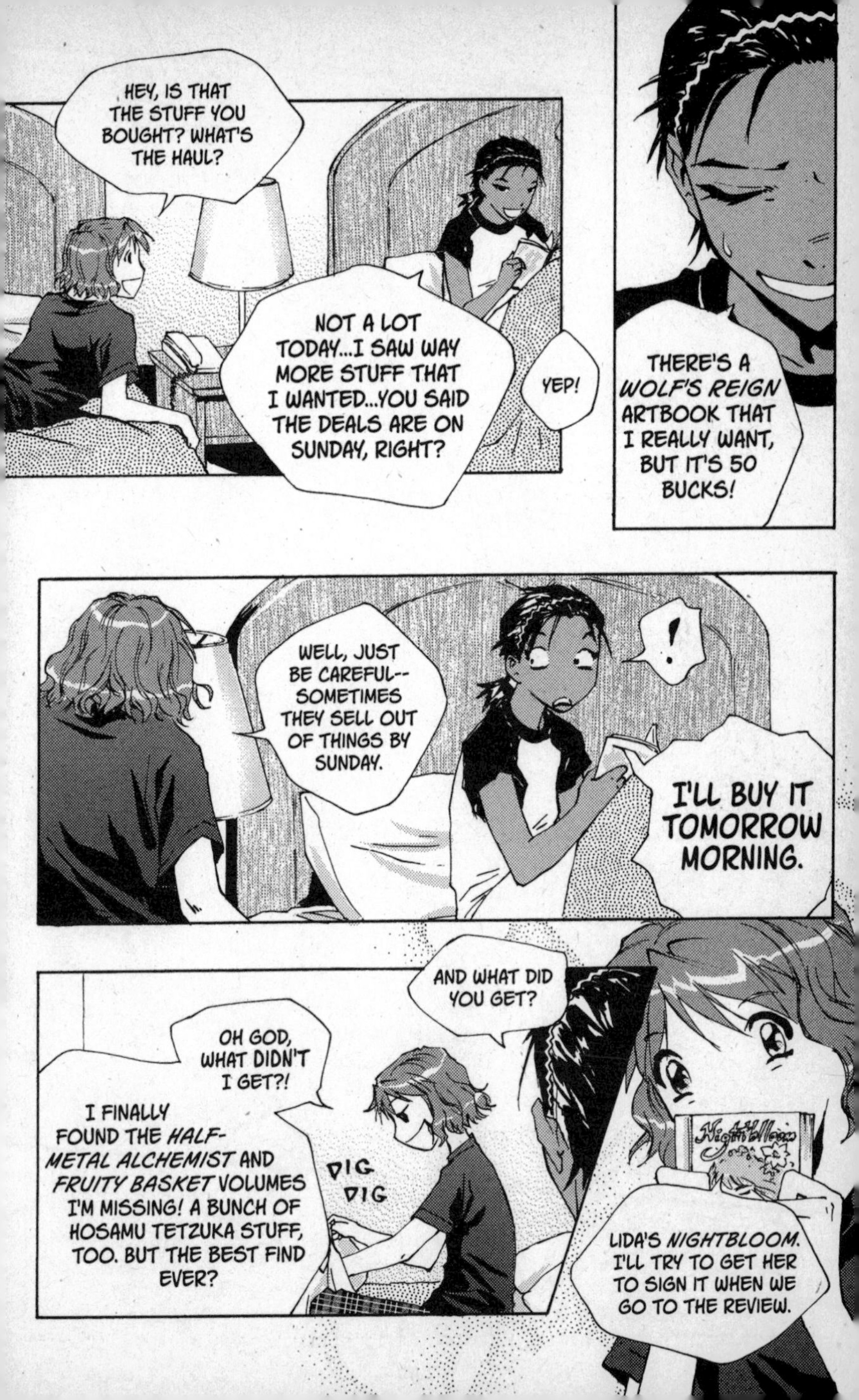
HEY, IS THAT THE STUFF YOU BOUGHT? WHAT'S THE HAUL?
NOT A LOT TODAY...I SAW WAY MORE STUFF THAT I WANTED...YOU SAID THE DEALS ARE ON SUNDAY, RIGHT?
YEP!
THERE'S A *WOLF'S REIGN* ARTBOOK THAT I REALLY WANT, BUT IT'S 50 BUCKS!
WELL, JUST BE CAREFUL-- SOMETIMES THEY SELL OUT OF THINGS BY SUNDAY.
!
I'LL BUY IT TOMORROW MORNING.
AND WHAT DID YOU GET?
OH GOD, WHAT DIDN'T I GET?!
I FINALLY FOUND THE *HALF-METAL ALCHEMIST* AND *FRUITY BASKET* VOLUMES I'M MISSING! A BUNCH OF HOSAMU TETZUKA STUFF, TOO. BUT THE BEST FIND EVER?
DIG DIG
LIDA'S *NIGHTBLOOM*. I'LL TRY TO GET HER TO SIGN IT WHEN WE GO TO THE REVIEW.

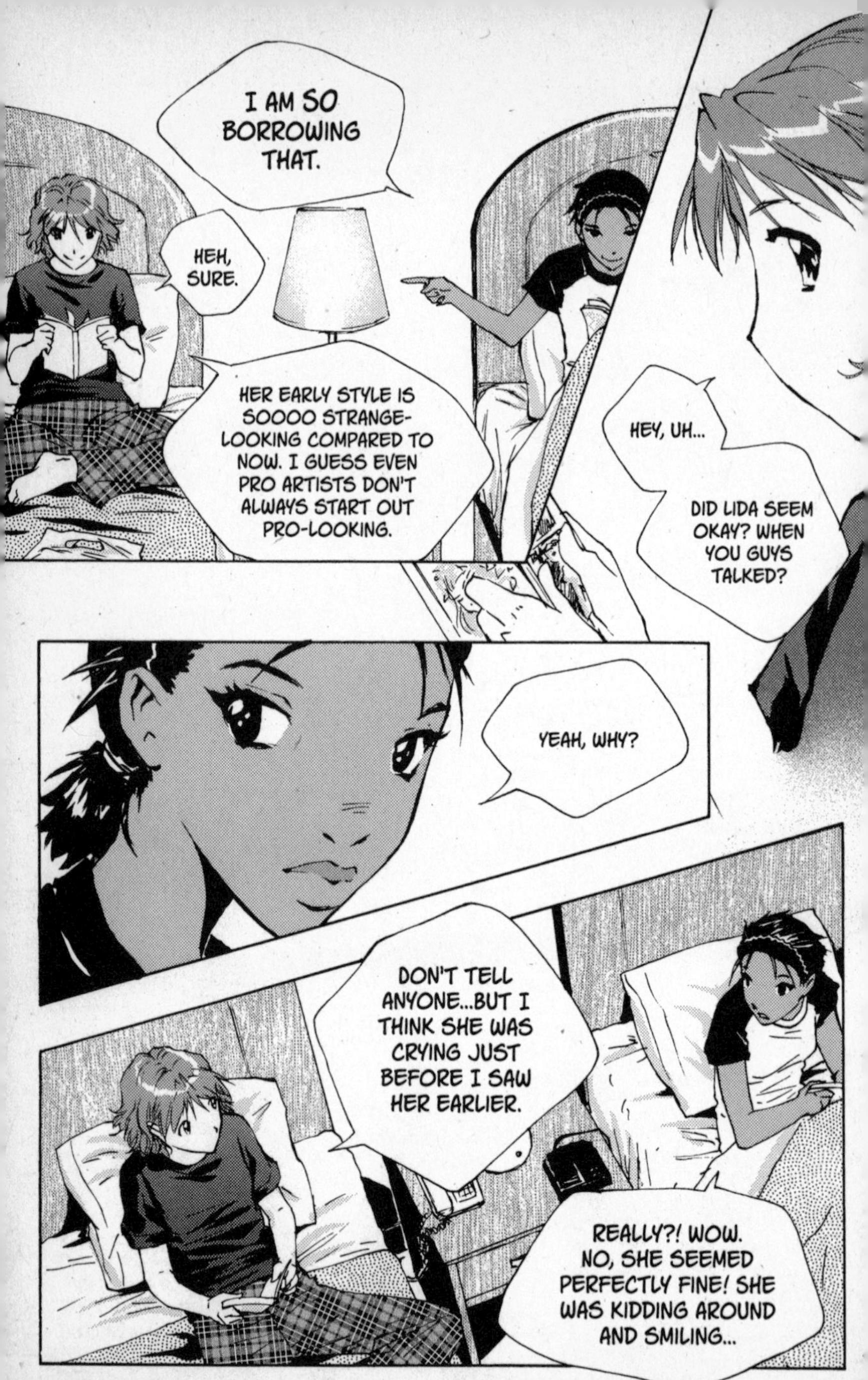
I AM SO BORROWING THAT.
HEH, SURE.
HER EARLY STYLE IS SOOOO STRANGE-LOOKING COMPARED TO NOW. I GUESS EVEN PRO ARTISTS DON'T ALWAYS START OUT PRO-LOOKING.
HEY, UH...
DID LIDA SEEM OKAY? WHEN YOU GUYS TALKED?
YEAH, WHY?
DON'T TELL ANYONE...BUT I THINK SHE WAS CRYING JUST BEFORE I SAW HER EARLIER.
REALLY?! WOW. NO, SHE SEEMED PERFECTLY FINE! SHE WAS KIDDING AROUND AND SMILING...

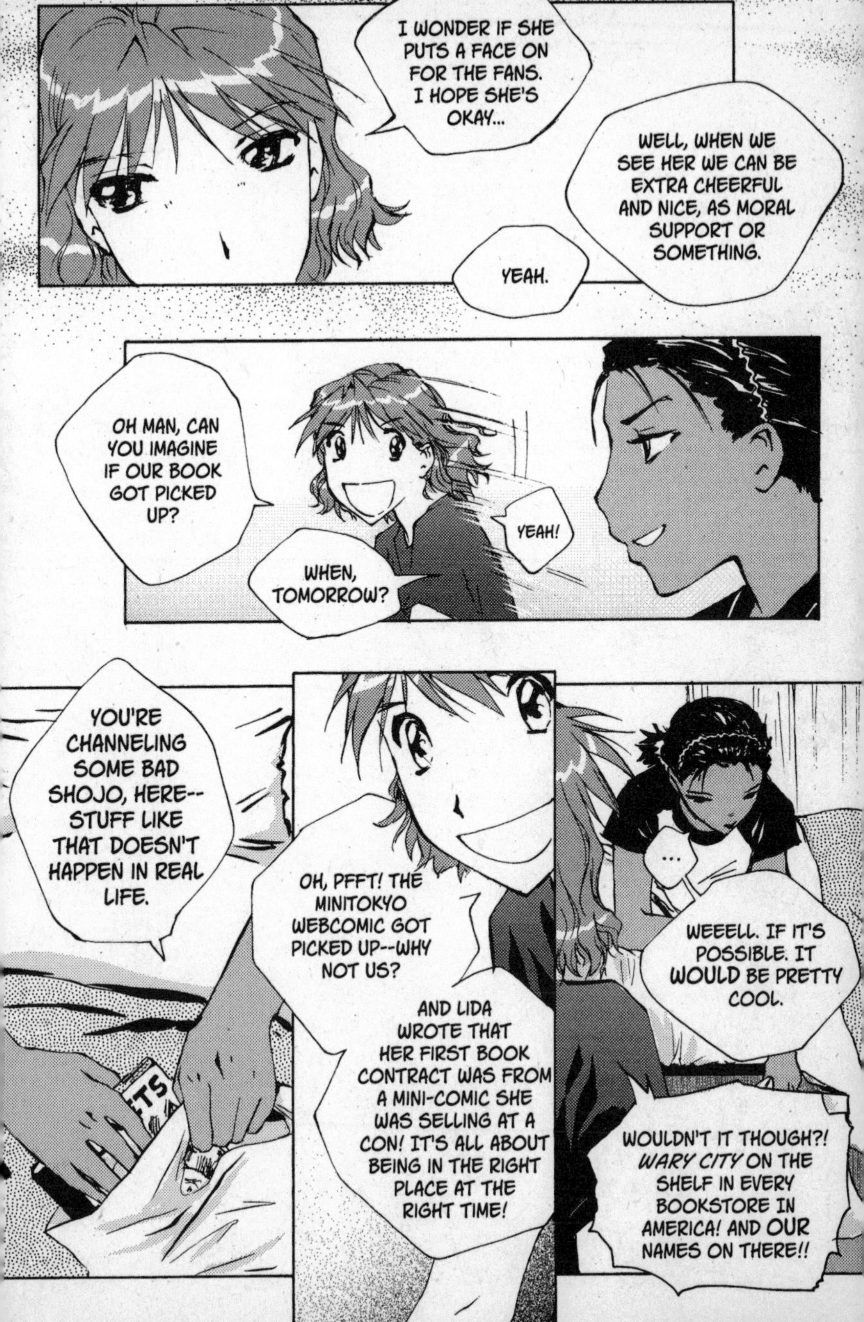
I WONDER IF SHE PUTS A FACE ON FOR THE FANS. I HOPE SHE'S OKAY...
WELL, WHEN WE SEE HER WE CAN BE EXTRA CHEERFUL AND NICE, AS MORAL SUPPORT OR SOMETHING.
YEAH.
OH MAN, CAN YOU IMAGINE IF OUR BOOK GOT PICKED UP?
YEAH!
WHEN, TOMORROW?
YOU'RE CHANNELING SOME BAD SHOJO, HERE-- STUFF LIKE THAT DOESN'T HAPPEN IN REAL LIFE.
OH, PFFT! THE MINITOKYO WEBCOMIC GOT PICKED UP--WHY NOT US?
AND LIDA WROTE THAT HER FIRST BOOK CONTRACT WAS FROM A MINI-COMIC SHE WAS SELLING AT A CON! IT'S ALL ABOUT BEING IN THE RIGHT PLACE AT THE RIGHT TIME!
...
WEEELL. IF IT'S POSSIBLE. IT WOULD BE PRETTY COOL.
WOULDN'T IT THOUGH?! *WARY CITY* ON THE SHELF IN EVERY BOOKSTORE IN AMERICA! AND OUR NAMES ON THERE!!

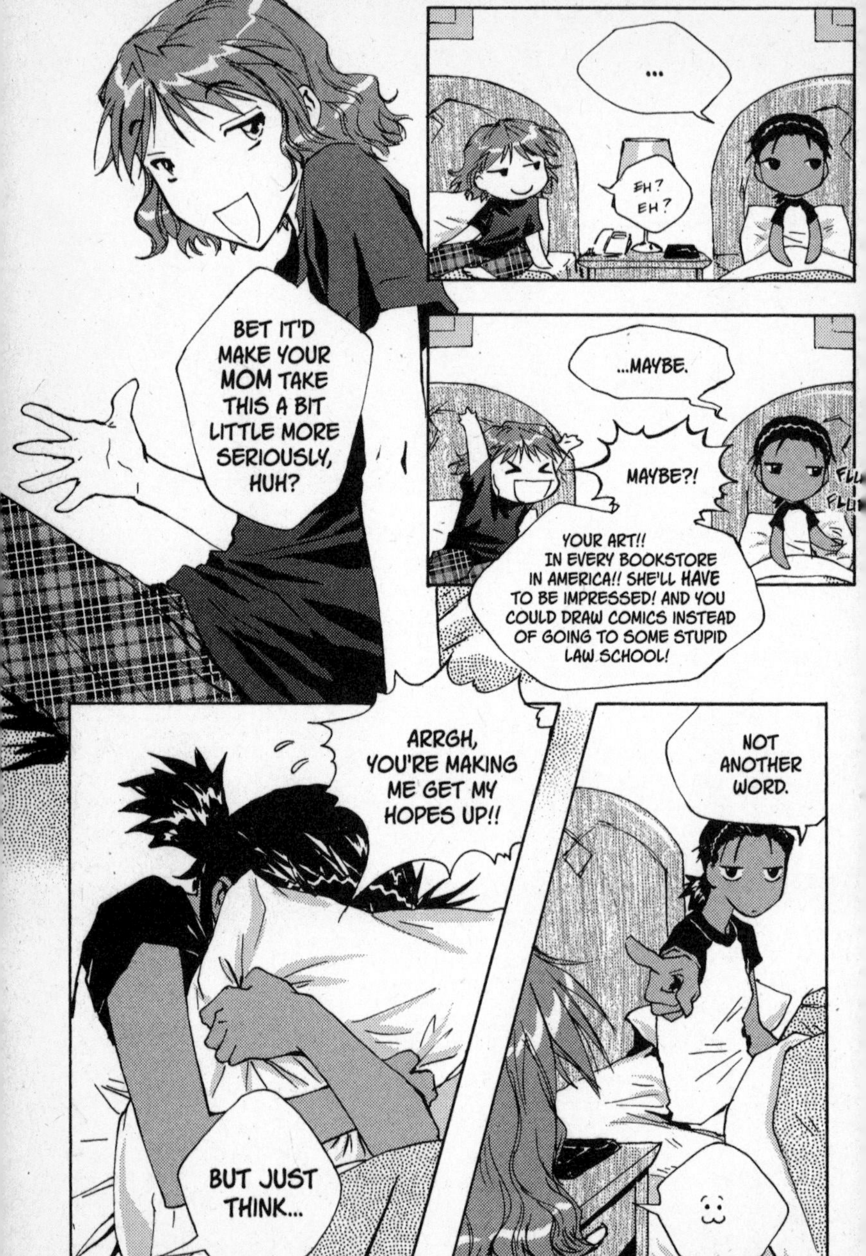
BET IT'D MAKE YOUR MOM TAKE THIS A BIT LITTLE MORE SERIOUSLY, HUH?
...
EH? EH?
...MAYBE.
MAYBE?!
YOUR ART!! IN EVERY BOOKSTORE IN AMERICA!! SHE'LL HAVE TO BE IMPRESSED! AND YOU COULD DRAW COMICS INSTEAD OF GOING TO SOME STUPID LAW SCHOOL!
ARRGH, YOU'RE MAKING ME GET MY HOPES UP!!
BUT JUST THINK...
NOT ANOTHER WORD.

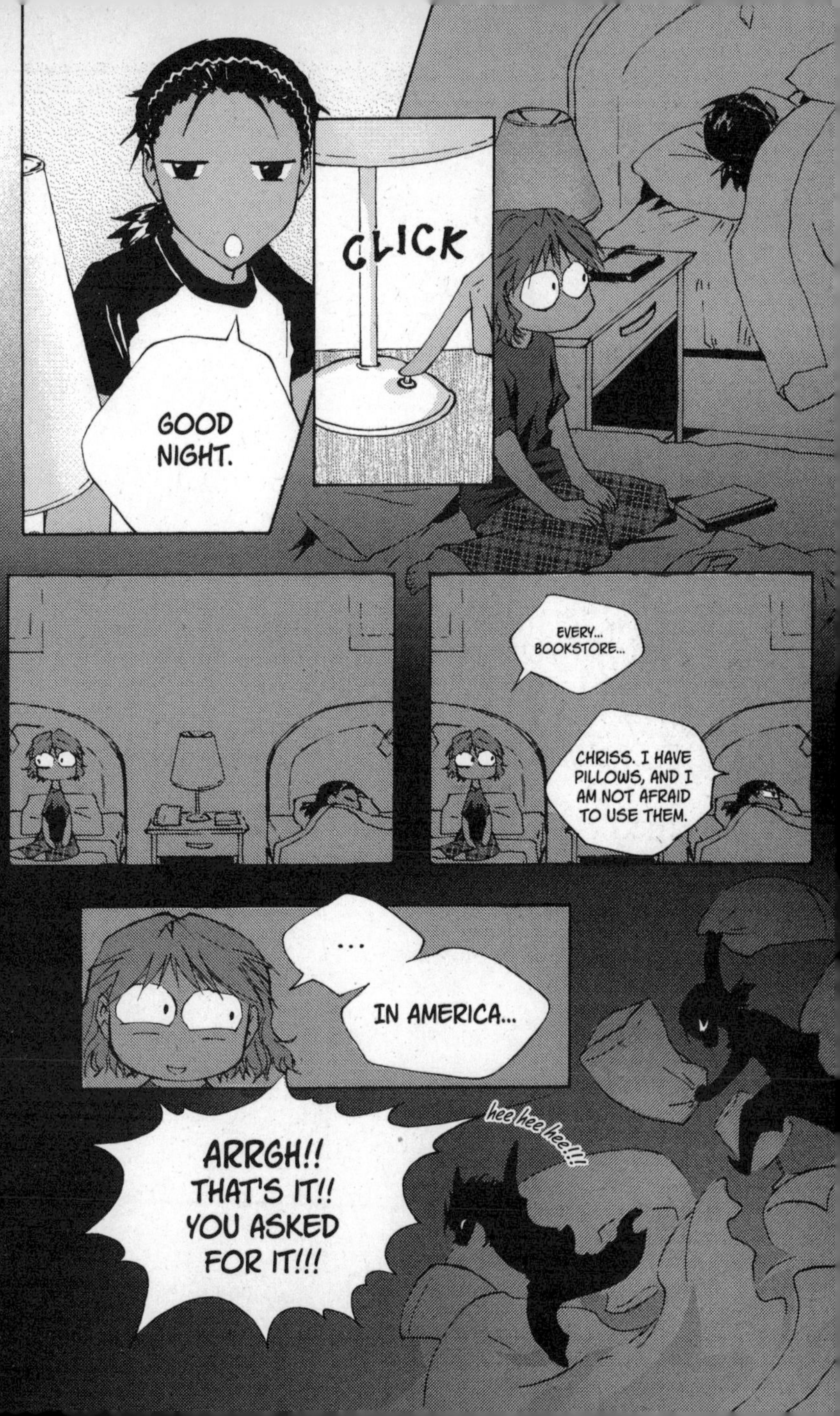
GOOD NIGHT.
CLICK
EVERY... BOOKSTORE...
CHRISS. I HAVE PILLOWS, AND I AM NOT AFRAID TO USE THEM.
...
IN AMERICA...
ARRGH!! THAT'S IT!! YOU ASKED FOR IT!!!
hee hee hee!!!

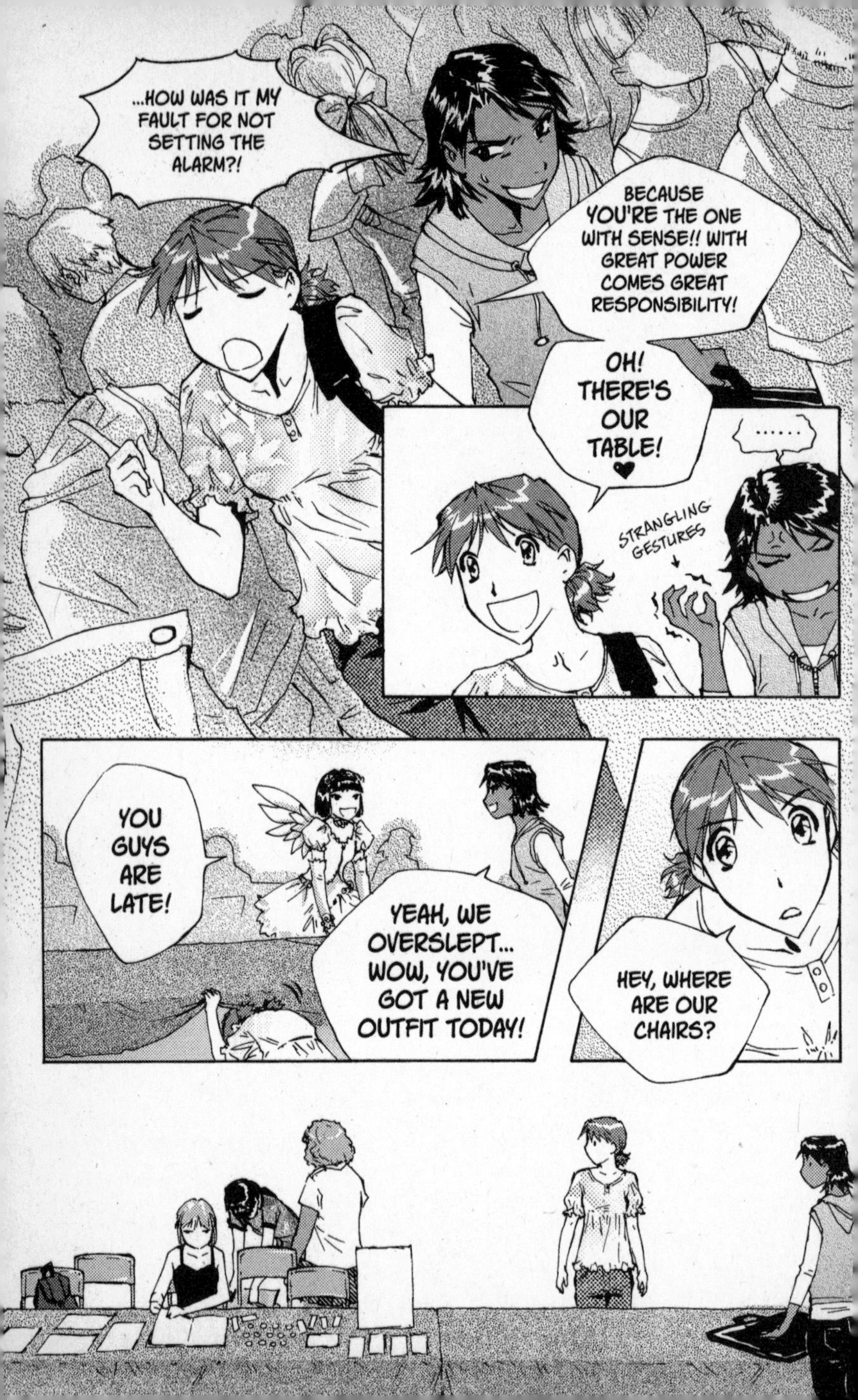
...HOW WAS IT MY FAULT FOR NOT SETTING THE ALARM?!
BECAUSE YOU'RE THE ONE WITH SENSE!! WITH GREAT POWER COMES GREAT RESPONSIBILITY!
OH! THERE'S OUR TABLE!
......
STRANGLING GESTURES
YOU GUYS ARE LATE!
YEAH, WE OVERSLEPT... WOW, YOU'VE GOT A NEW OUTFIT TODAY!
HEY, WHERE ARE OUR CHAIRS?

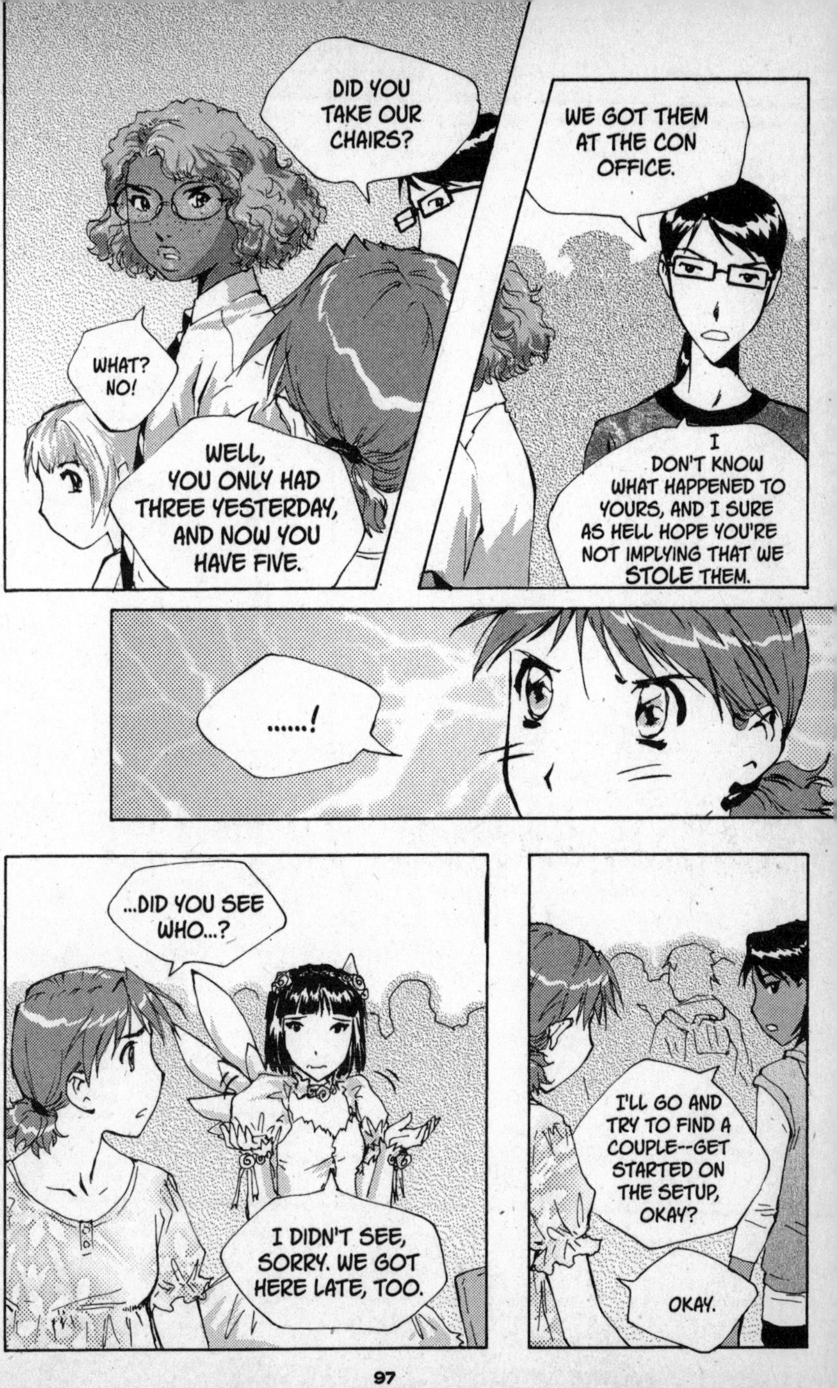
DID YOU TAKE OUR CHAIRS?
WHAT? NO!
WELL, YOU ONLY HAD THREE YESTERDAY, AND NOW YOU HAVE FIVE.
WE GOT THEM AT THE CON OFFICE.
I DON'T KNOW WHAT HAPPENED TO YOURS, AND I SURE AS HELL HOPE YOU'RE NOT IMPLYING THAT WE STOLE THEM.
......!
...DID YOU SEE WHO...?
I DIDN'T SEE, SORRY. WE GOT HERE LATE, TOO.
I'LL GO AND TRY TO FIND A COUPLE--GET STARTED ON THE SETUP, OKAY?
OKAY.

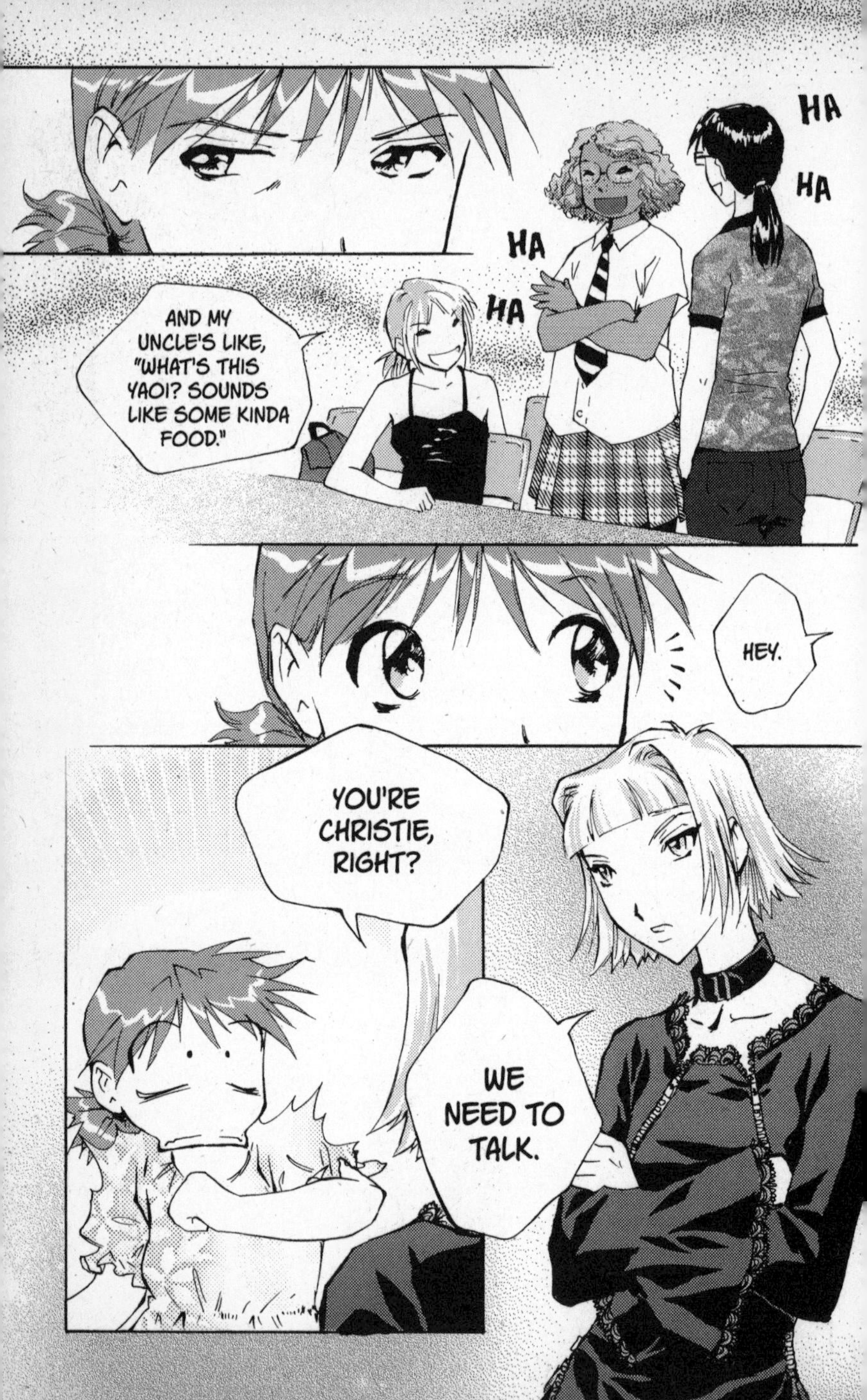
HA
HA
HA
HA
AND MY UNCLE'S LIKE, "WHAT'S THIS YAOI? SOUNDS LIKE SOME KINDA FOOD."
HEY.
YOU'RE CHRISTIE, RIGHT?
WE NEED TO TALK.

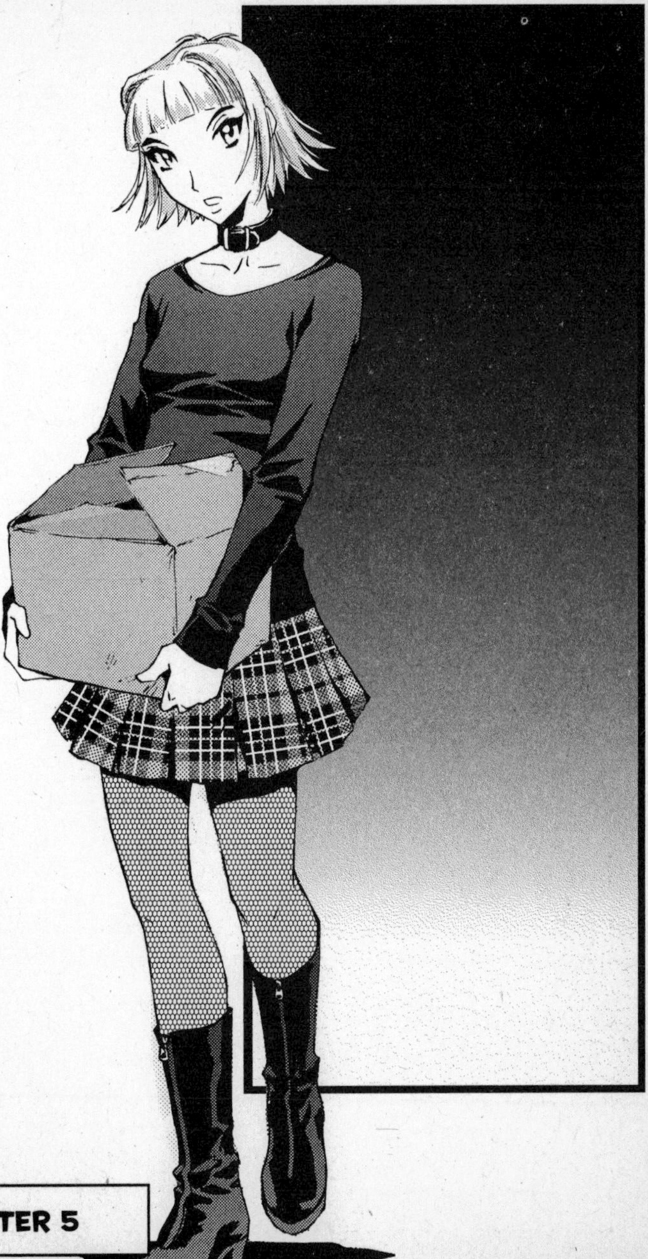

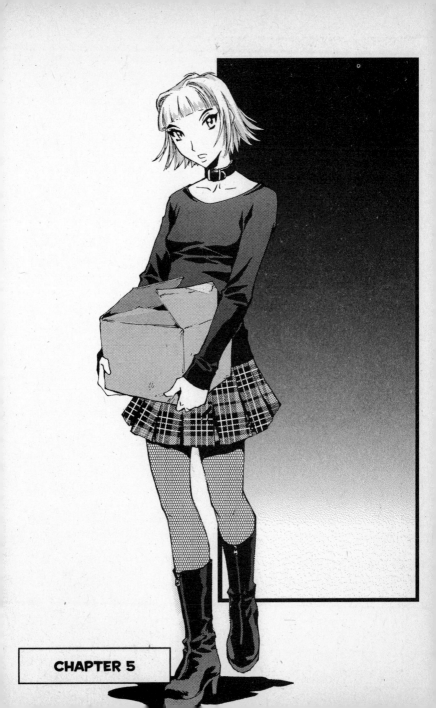

CHAPTER 5

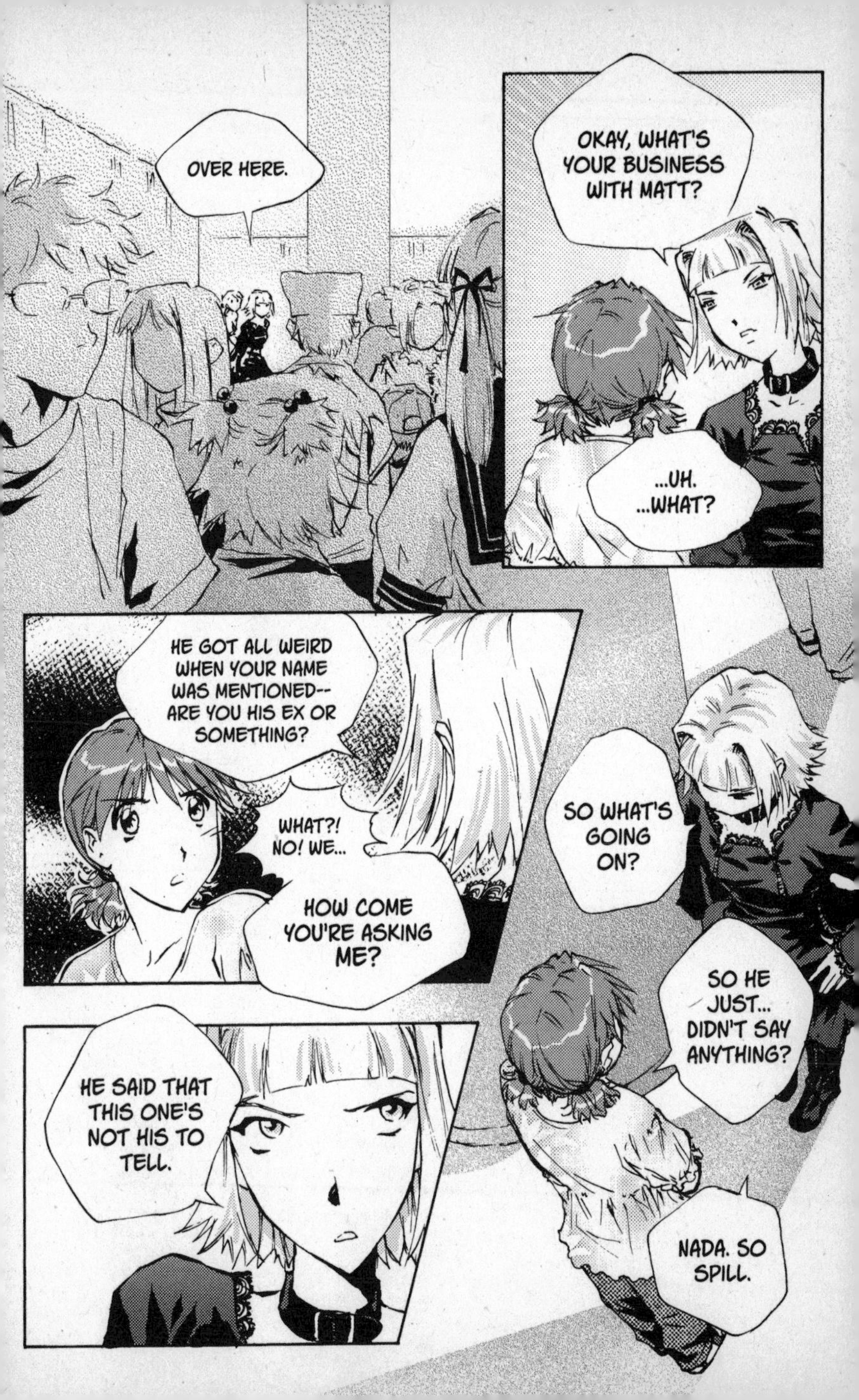
OVER HERE.
OKAY, WHAT'S YOUR BUSINESS WITH MATT?
...UH. ...WHAT?
HE GOT ALL WEIRD WHEN YOUR NAME WAS MENTIONED-- ARE YOU HIS EX OR SOMETHING?
WHAT?! NO! WE...
HOW COME YOU'RE ASKING ME?
HE SAID THAT THIS ONE'S NOT HIS TO TELL.
SO WHAT'S GOING ON?
SO HE JUST... DIDN'T SAY ANYTHING?
NADA. SO SPILL.

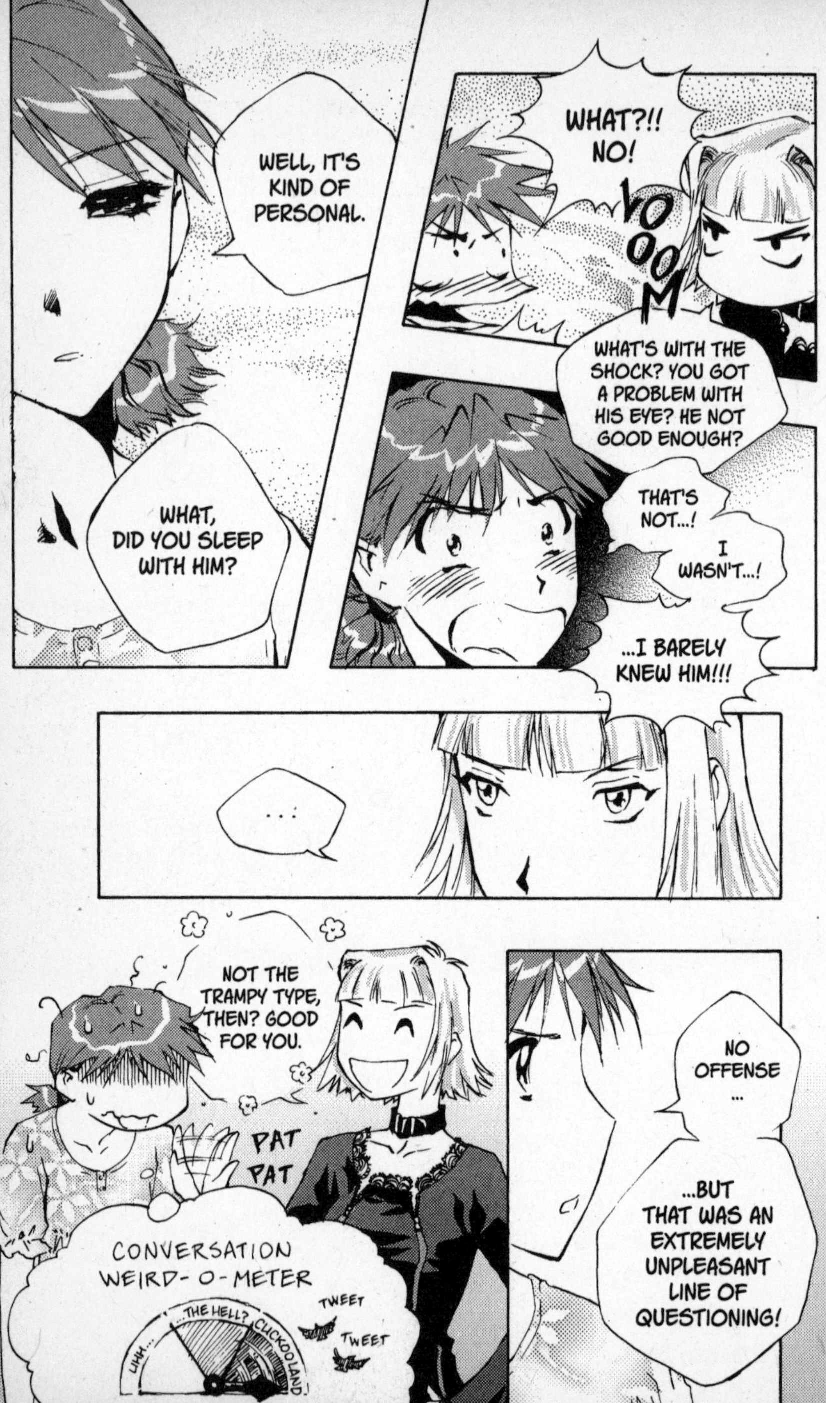
WELL, IT'S KIND OF PERSONAL.
WHAT, DID YOU SLEEP WITH HIM?
WHAT?!! NO!
VOOOM
WHAT'S WITH THE SHOCK? YOU GOT A PROBLEM WITH HIS EYE? HE NOT GOOD ENOUGH?
THAT'S NOT...!
I WASN'T...!
...I BARELY KNEW HIM!!!
...
NOT THE TRAMPY TYPE, THEN? GOOD FOR YOU.
PAT PAT
CONVERSATION WEIRD-O-METER
UHH...
...THE HELL?
CUCKOO LAND
TWEET
TWEET
NO OFFENSE ...
...BUT THAT WAS AN EXTREMELY UNPLEASANT LINE OF QUESTIONING!

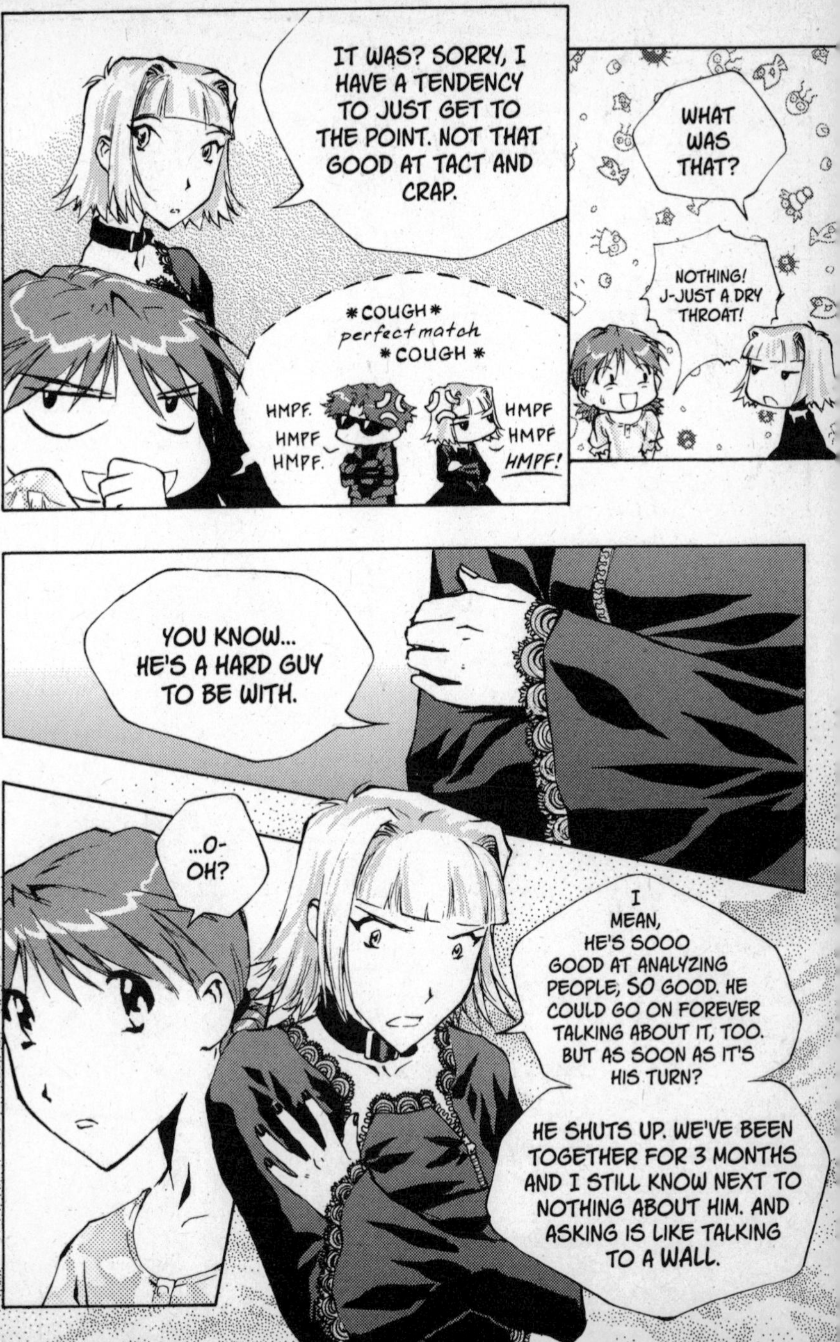
IT WAS? SORRY, I HAVE A TENDENCY TO JUST GET TO THE POINT. NOT THAT GOOD AT TACT AND CRAP.
COUGH perfect match *COUGH*
HMPF. HMPF HMPF.
HMPF HMPF HMPF!
WHAT WAS THAT?
NOTHING! J-JUST A DRY THROAT!
YOU KNOW... HE'S A HARD GUY TO BE WITH.
...O-OH?
I MEAN, HE'S SOOO GOOD AT ANALYZING PEOPLE, SO GOOD. HE COULD GO ON FOREVER TALKING ABOUT IT, TOO. BUT AS SOON AS IT'S HIS TURN?
HE SHUTS UP. WE'VE BEEN TOGETHER FOR 3 MONTHS AND I STILL KNOW NEXT TO NOTHING ABOUT HIM. AND ASKING IS LIKE TALKING TO A WALL.

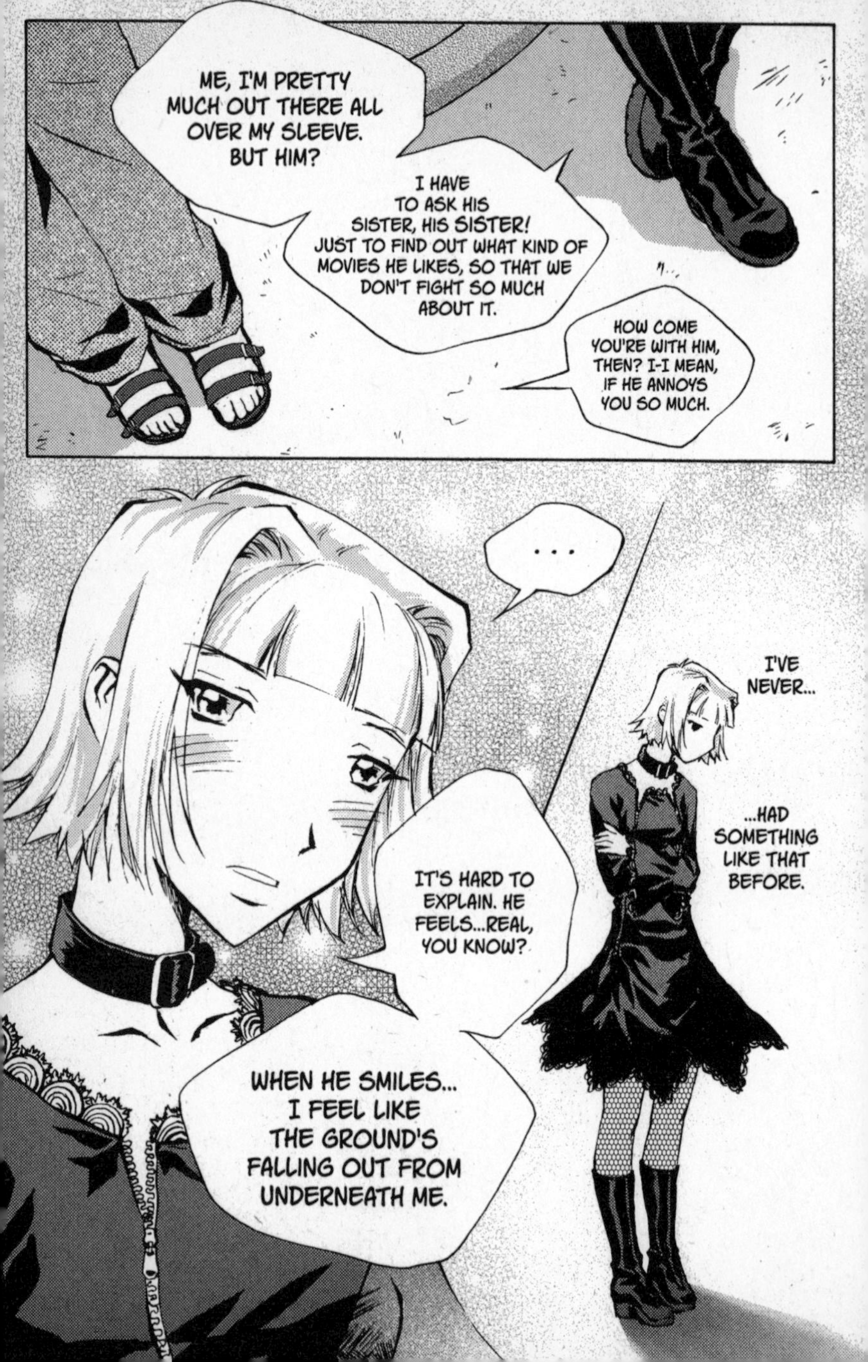
ME, I'M PRETTY MUCH OUT THERE ALL OVER MY SLEEVE. BUT HIM?
I HAVE TO ASK HIS SISTER, HIS SISTER! JUST TO FIND OUT WHAT KIND OF MOVIES HE LIKES, SO THAT WE DON'T FIGHT SO MUCH ABOUT IT.
HOW COME YOU'RE WITH HIM, THEN? I-I MEAN, IF HE ANNOYS YOU SO MUCH.
. . .
IT'S HARD TO EXPLAIN. HE FEELS...REAL, YOU KNOW?
WHEN HE SMILES... I FEEL LIKE THE GROUND'S FALLING OUT FROM UNDERNEATH ME.
I'VE NEVER...
...HAD SOMETHING LIKE THAT BEFORE.

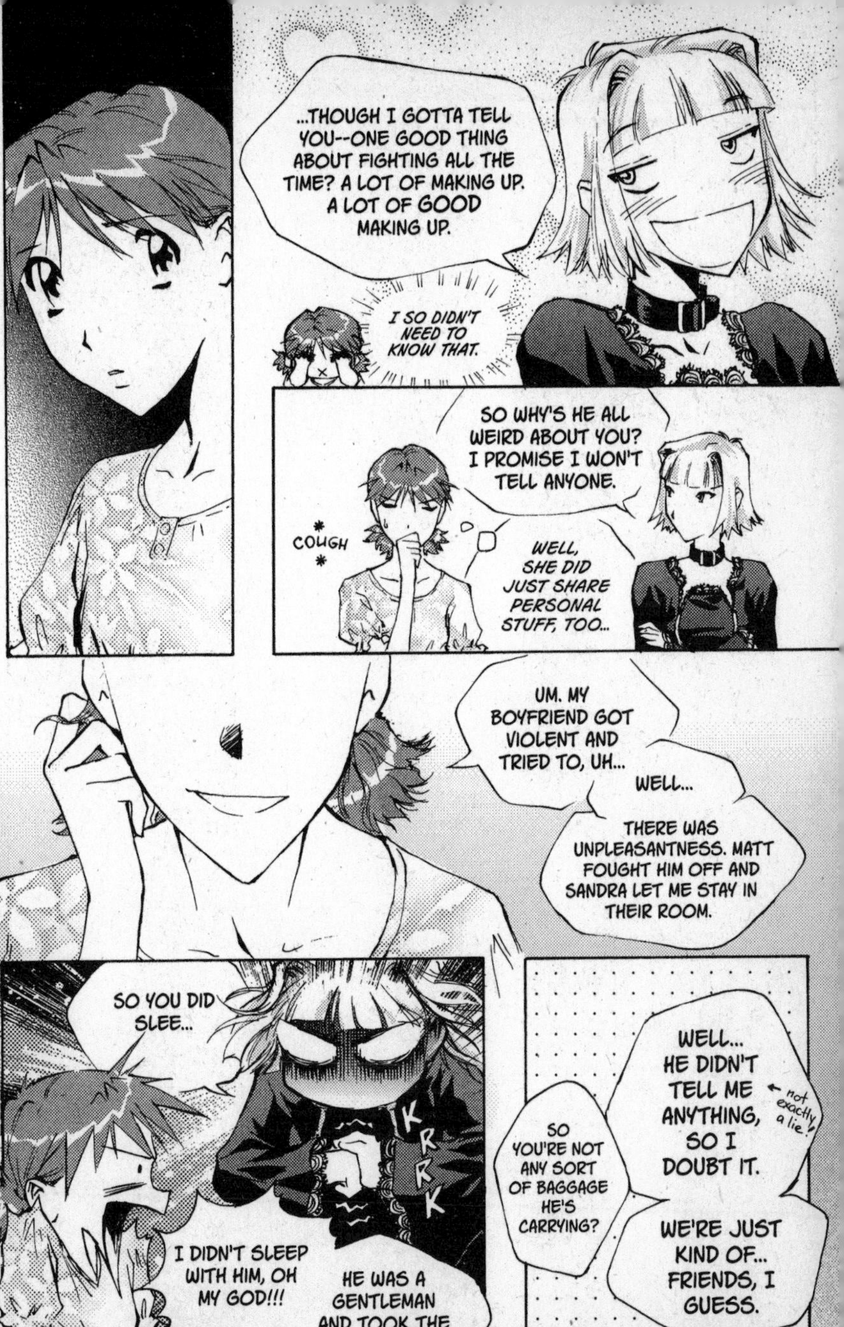
...THOUGH I GOTTA TELL YOU--ONE GOOD THING ABOUT FIGHTING ALL THE TIME? A LOT OF MAKING UP. A LOT OF GOOD MAKING UP.
I SO DIDN'T NEED TO KNOW THAT.
SO WHY'S HE ALL WEIRD ABOUT YOU? I PROMISE I WON'T TELL ANYONE.
COUGH
WELL, SHE DID JUST SHARE PERSONAL STUFF, TOO...
UM. MY BOYFRIEND GOT VIOLENT AND TRIED TO, UH...
WELL...
THERE WAS UNPLEASANTNESS. MATT FOUGHT HIM OFF AND SANDRA LET ME STAY IN THEIR ROOM.
SO YOU DID SLEE...
KRRK
I DIDN'T SLEEP WITH HIM, OH MY GOD!!!
HE WAS A GENTLEMAN AND TOOK THE FLOOR!
SO YOU'RE NOT ANY SORT OF BAGGAGE HE'S CARRYING?
WELL... HE DIDN'T TELL ME ANYTHING, SO I DOUBT IT.
not exactly a lie!
WE'RE JUST KIND OF... FRIENDS, I GUESS.

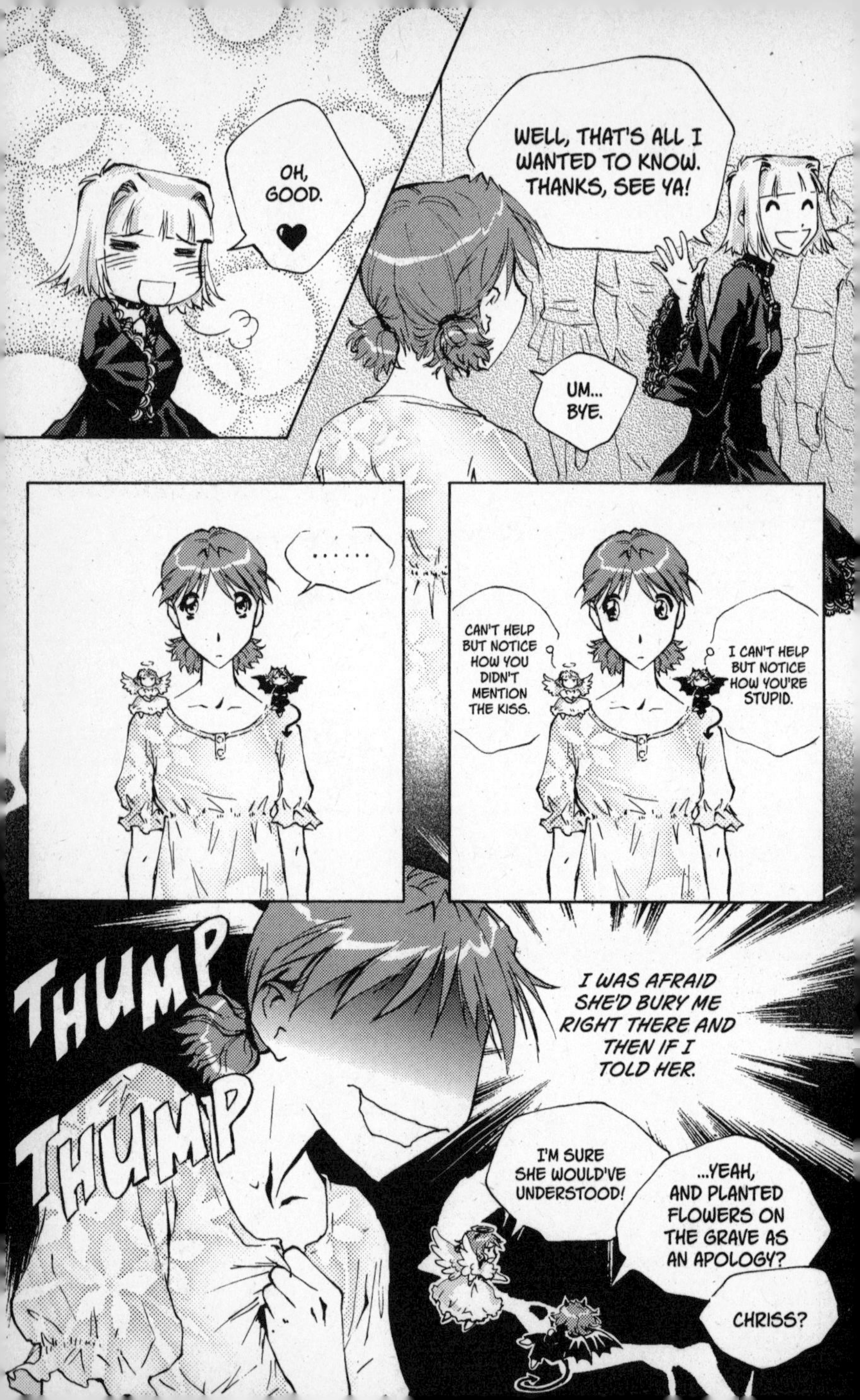
OH, GOOD.
WELL, THAT'S ALL I WANTED TO KNOW. THANKS, SEE YA!
UM... BYE.
......
CAN'T HELP BUT NOTICE HOW YOU DIDN'T MENTION THE KISS.
I CAN'T HELP BUT NOTICE HOW YOU'RE STUPID.
THUMP
THUMP
I WAS AFRAID SHE'D BURY ME RIGHT THERE AND THEN IF I TOLD HER.
I'M SURE SHE WOULD'VE UNDERSTOOD!
...YEAH, AND PLANTED FLOWERS ON THE GRAVE AS AN APOLOGY?
CHRISS?

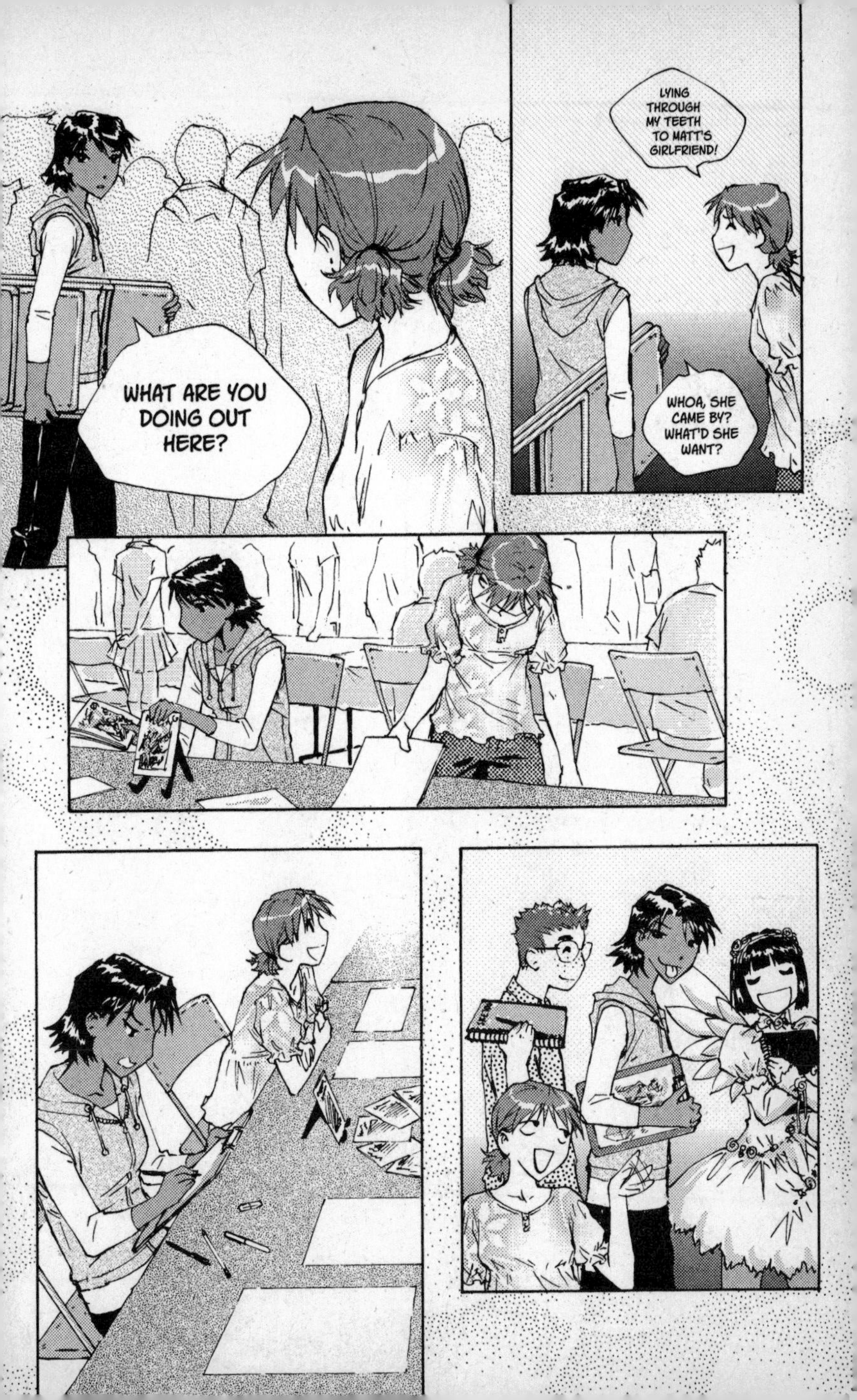
WHAT ARE YOU DOING OUT HERE?
LYING THROUGH MY TEETH TO MATT'S GIRLFRIEND!
WHOA, SHE CAME BY? WHAT'D SHE WANT?

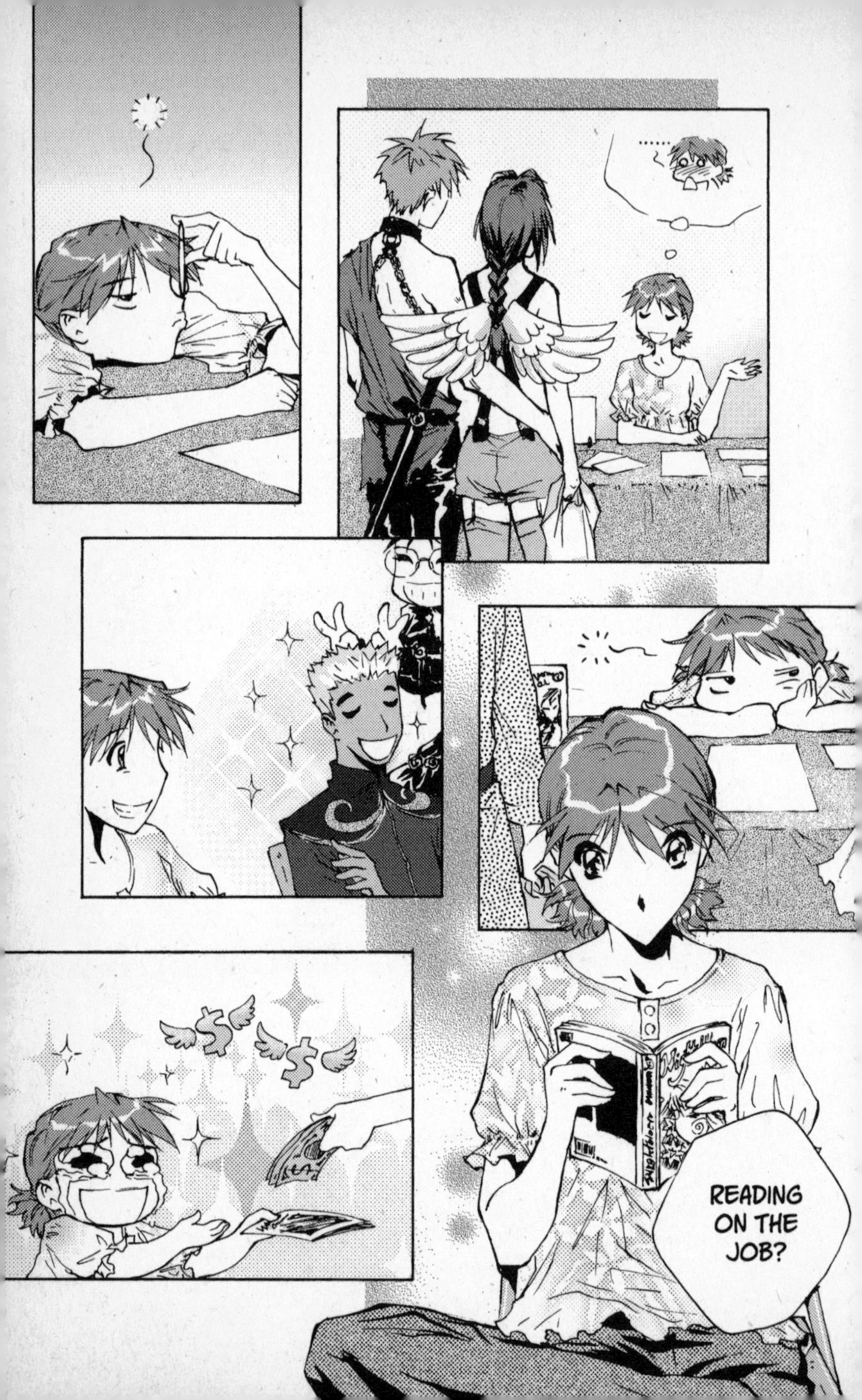
READING ON THE JOB?

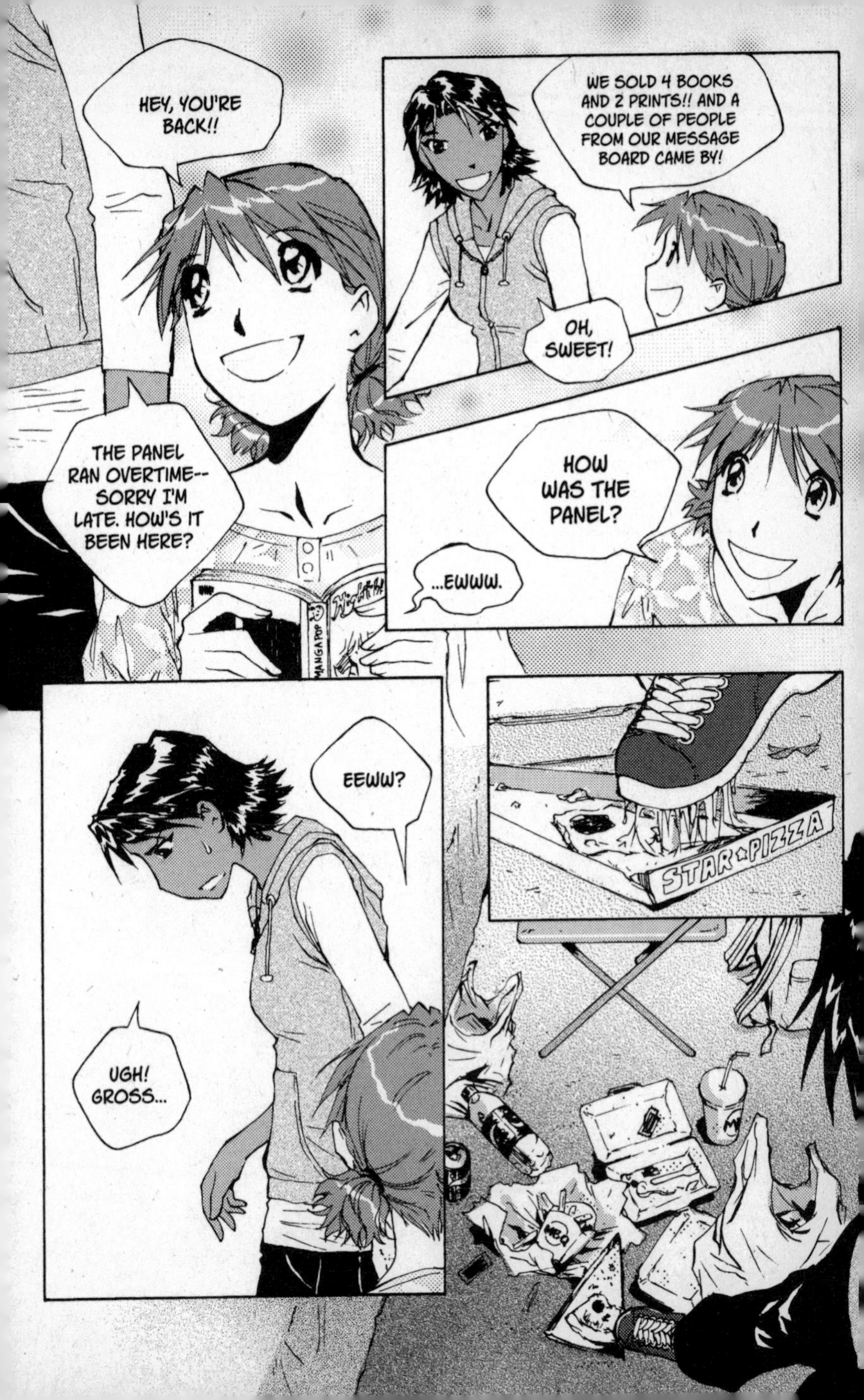
HEY, YOU'RE BACK!!
THE PANEL RAN OVERTIME-- SORRY I'M LATE. HOW'S IT BEEN HERE?
WE SOLD 4 BOOKS AND 2 PRINTS!! AND A COUPLE OF PEOPLE FROM OUR MESSAGE BOARD CAME BY!
OH, SWEET!
HOW WAS THE PANEL?
...EWWW.
EEWW?
UGH! GROSS...
STAR☆PIZZA

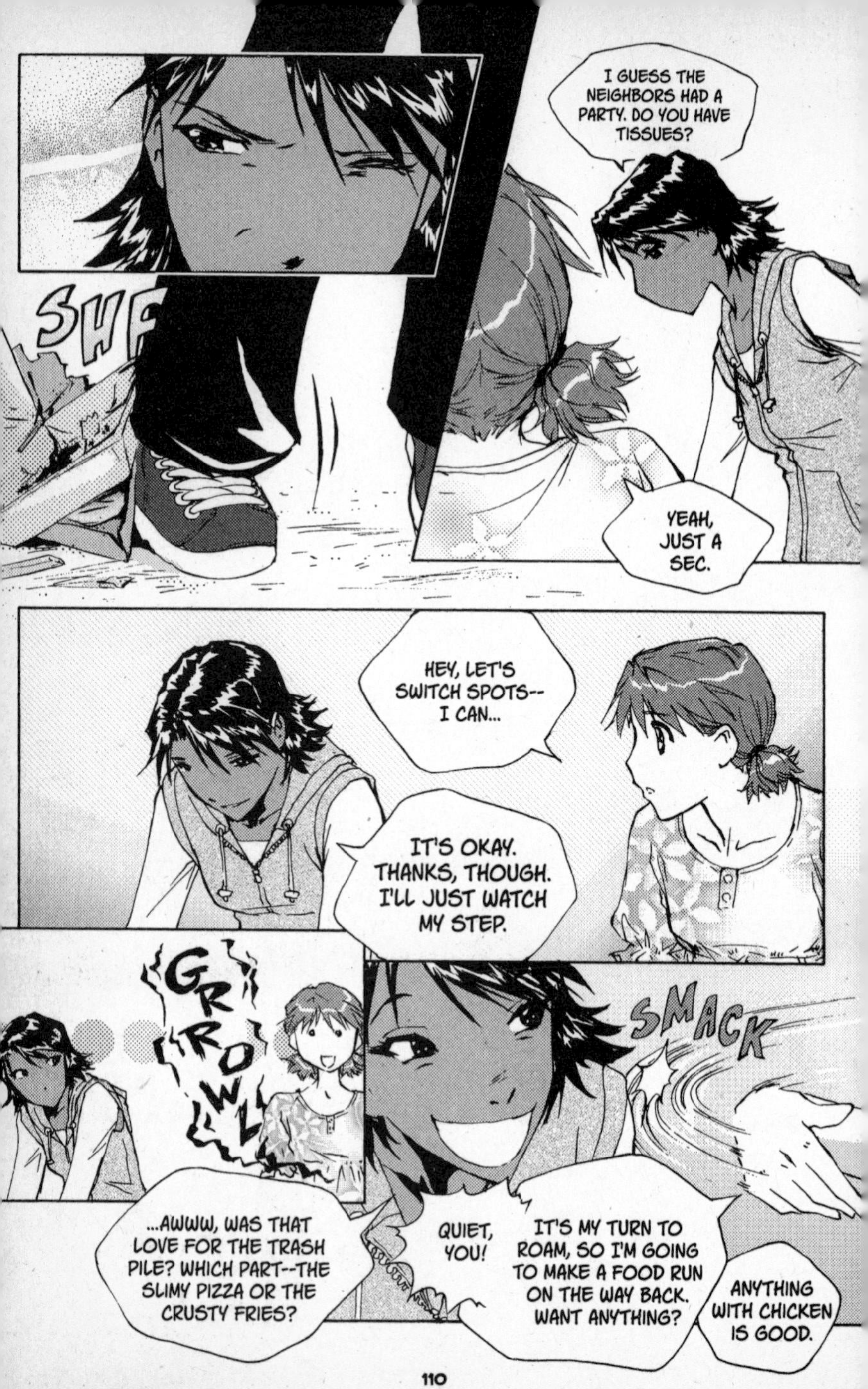
SHF
I GUESS THE NEIGHBORS HAD A PARTY. DO YOU HAVE TISSUES?
YEAH, JUST A SEC.
HEY, LET'S SWITCH SPOTS-- I CAN...
IT'S OKAY. THANKS, THOUGH. I'LL JUST WATCH MY STEP.
GROWL
...AWWW, WAS THAT LOVE FOR THE TRASH PILE? WHICH PART--THE SLIMY PIZZA OR THE CRUSTY FRIES?
SMACK
QUIET, YOU!
IT'S MY TURN TO ROAM, SO I'M GOING TO MAKE A FOOD RUN ON THE WAY BACK. WANT ANYTHING?
ANYTHING WITH CHICKEN IS GOOD.

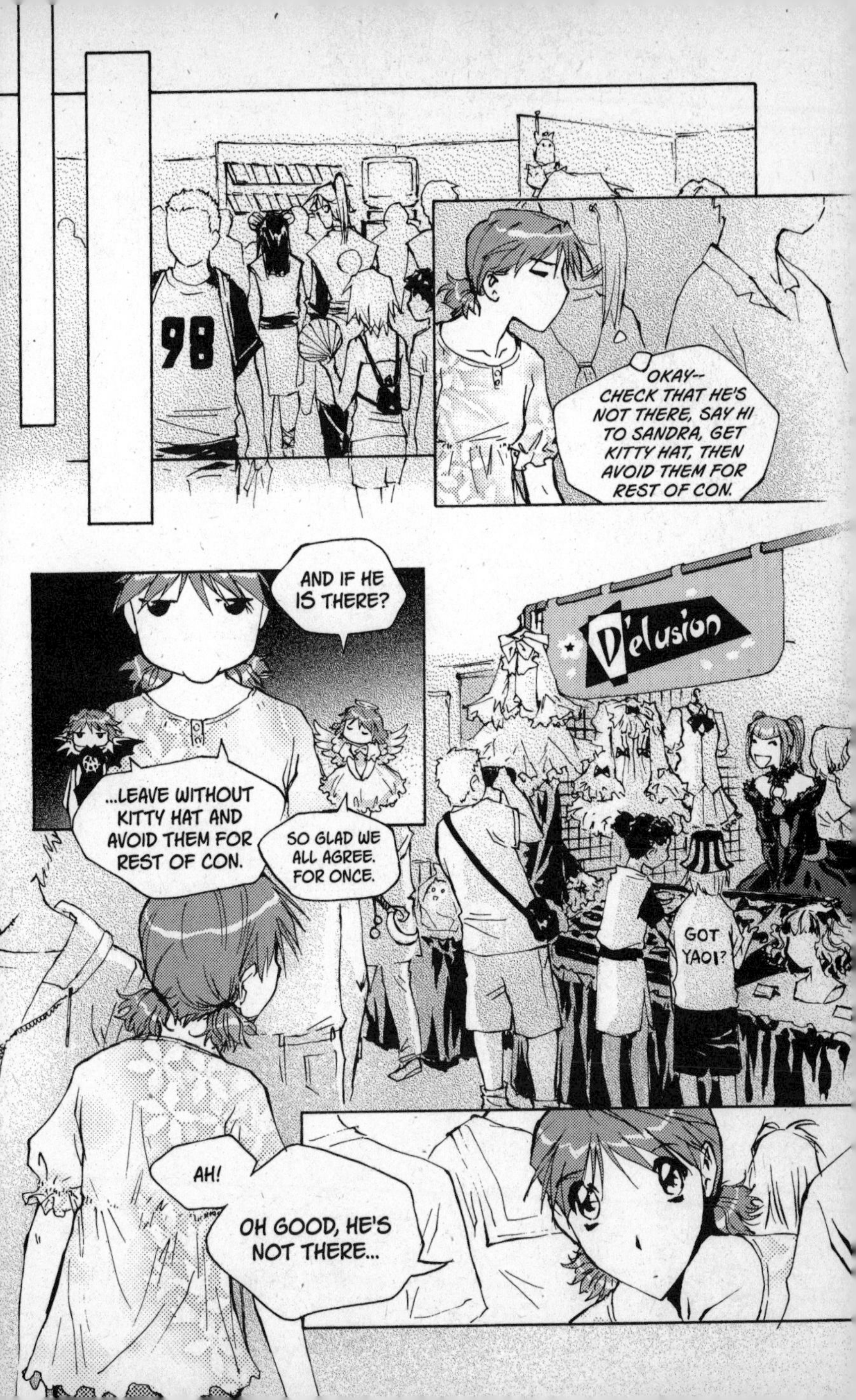
OKAY--
CHECK THAT HE'S NOT THERE, SAY HI TO SANDRA, GET KITTY HAT, THEN AVOID THEM FOR REST OF CON.
AND IF HE IS THERE?
...LEAVE WITHOUT KITTY HAT AND AVOID THEM FOR REST OF CON.
SO GLAD WE ALL AGREE. FOR ONCE.
D'elusion
GOT YAOI?
AH!
OH GOOD, HE'S NOT THERE...

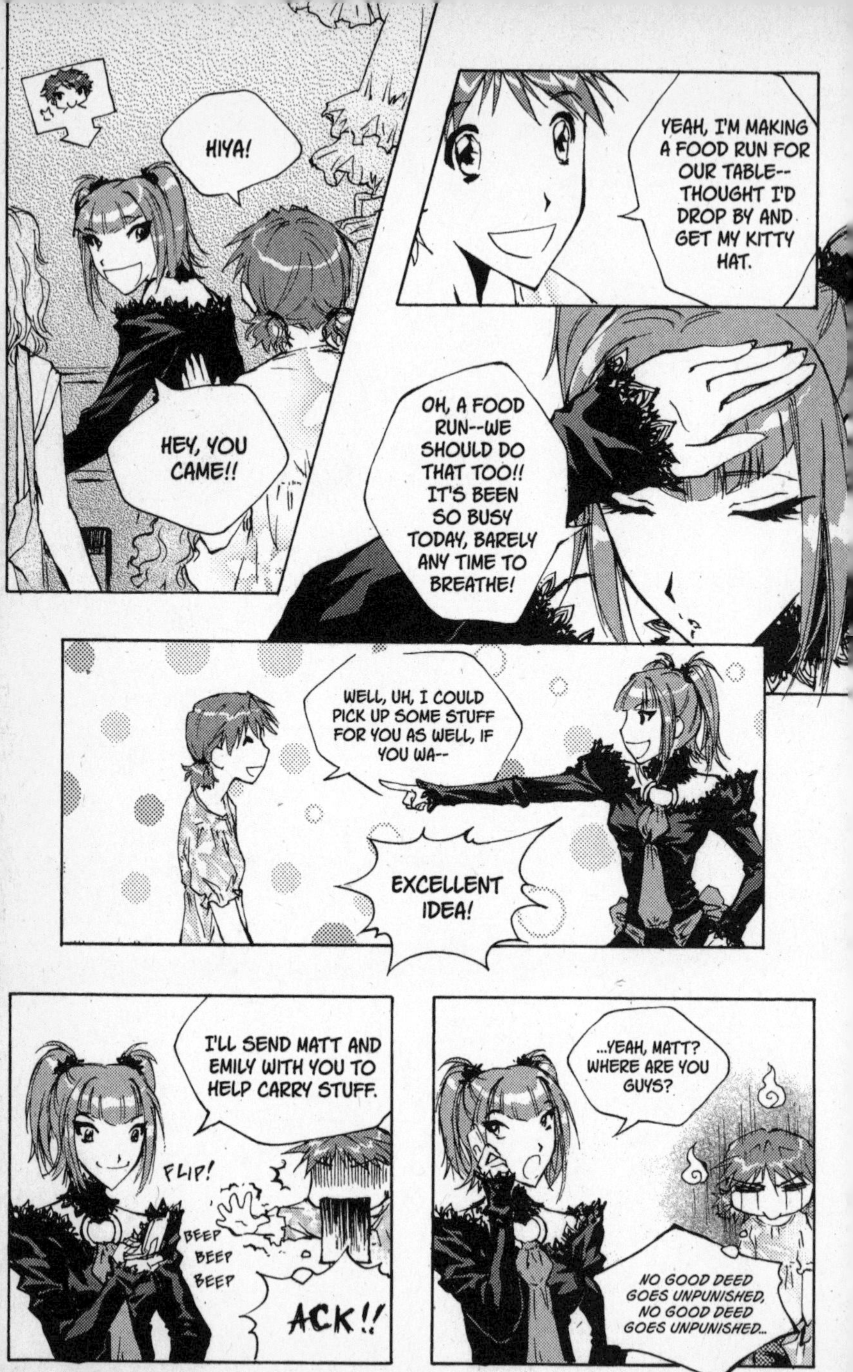
HIYA!
HEY, YOU CAME!!
YEAH, I'M MAKING A FOOD RUN FOR OUR TABLE-- THOUGHT I'D DROP BY AND GET MY KITTY HAT.
OH, A FOOD RUN--WE SHOULD DO THAT TOO!! IT'S BEEN SO BUSY TODAY, BARELY ANY TIME TO BREATHE!
WELL, UH, I COULD PICK UP SOME STUFF FOR YOU AS WELL, IF YOU WA--
EXCELLENT IDEA!
I'LL SEND MATT AND EMILY WITH YOU TO HELP CARRY STUFF.
FLIP!
BEEP BEEP BEEP
ACK!!
...YEAH, MATT? WHERE ARE YOU GUYS?
NO GOOD DEED GOES UNPUNISHED, NO GOOD DEED GOES UNPUNISHED...

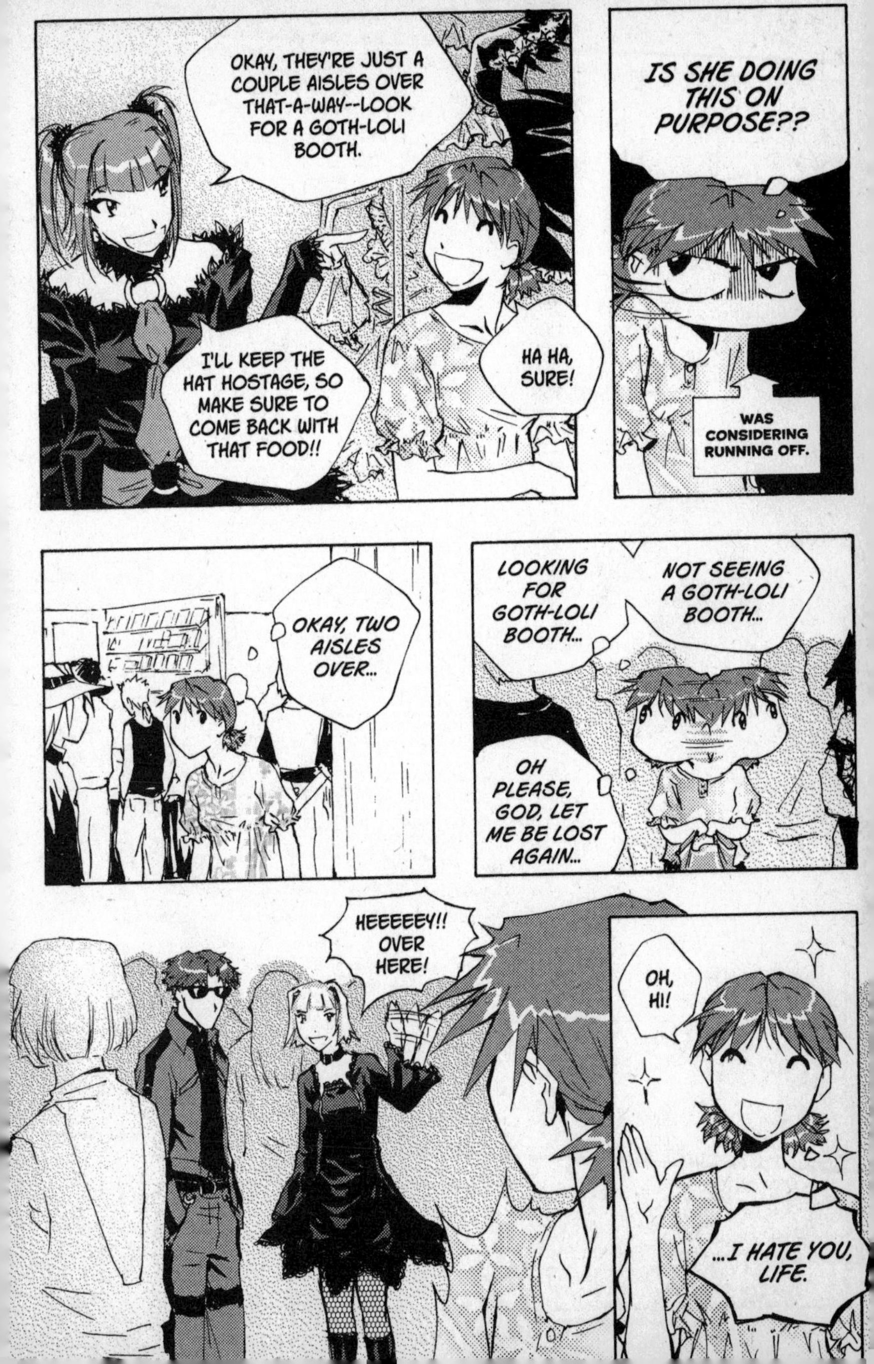
OKAY, THEY'RE JUST A COUPLE AISLES OVER THAT-A-WAY--LOOK FOR A GOTH-LOLI BOOTH.
I'LL KEEP THE HAT HOSTAGE, SO MAKE SURE TO COME BACK WITH THAT FOOD!!
HA HA, SURE!
IS SHE DOING THIS ON PURPOSE??
WAS CONSIDERING RUNNING OFF.
OKAY, TWO AISLES OVER...
LOOKING FOR GOTH-LOLI BOOTH...
NOT SEEING A GOTH-LOLI BOOTH...
OH PLEASE, GOD, LET ME BE LOST AGAIN...
HEEEEEY!! OVER HERE!
OH, HI!
...I HATE YOU, LIFE.

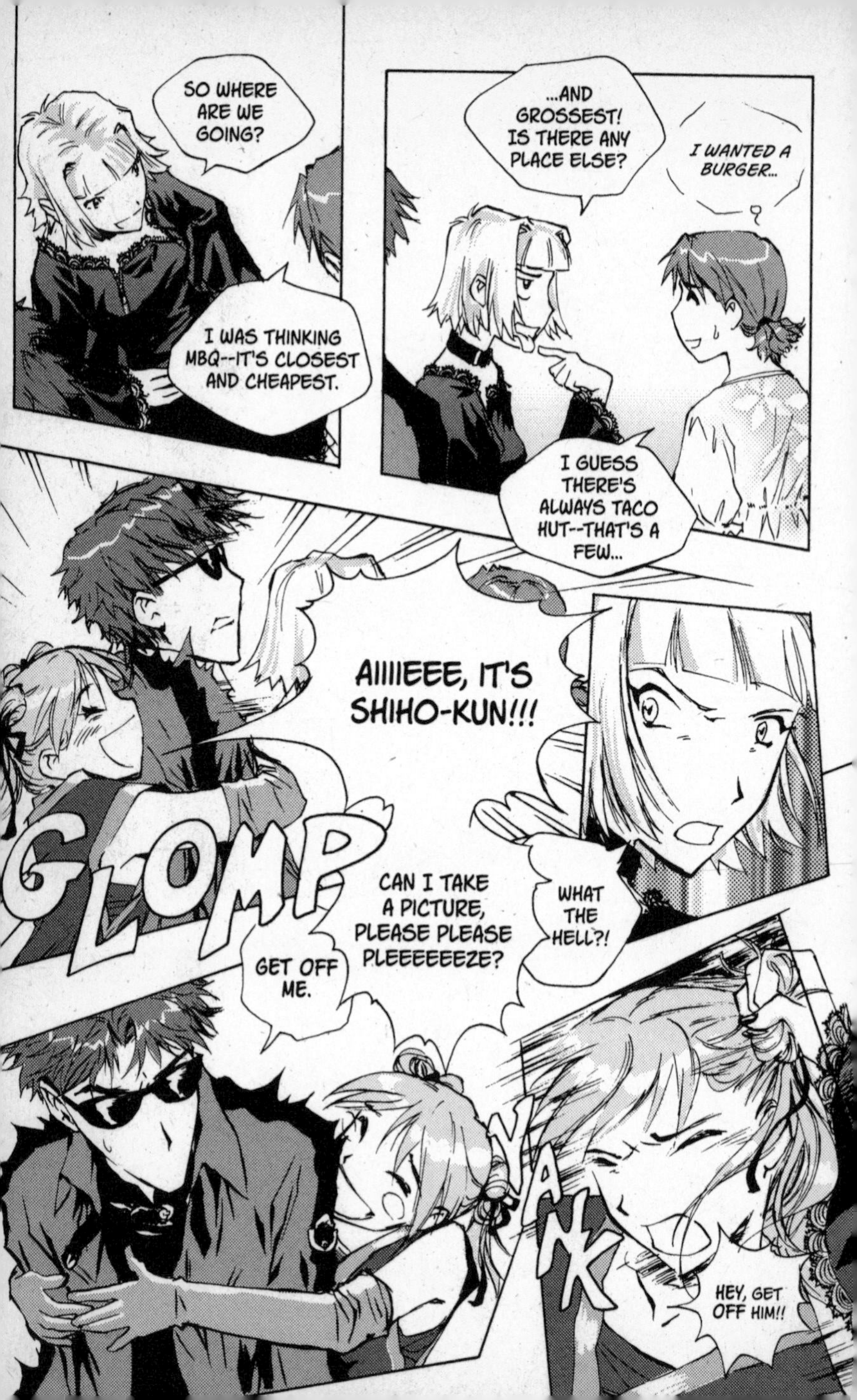
SO WHERE ARE WE GOING?
I WAS THINKING MBQ--IT'S CLOSEST AND CHEAPEST.
...AND GROSSEST! IS THERE ANY PLACE ELSE?
I WANTED A BURGER...
I GUESS THERE'S ALWAYS TACO HUT--THAT'S A FEW...
AIIIIEEE, IT'S SHIHO-KUN!!!
GLOMP
WHAT THE HELL?!
GET OFF ME.
CAN I TAKE A PICTURE, PLEASE PLEASE PLEEEEEEEZE?
YANK
HEY, GET OFF HIM!!

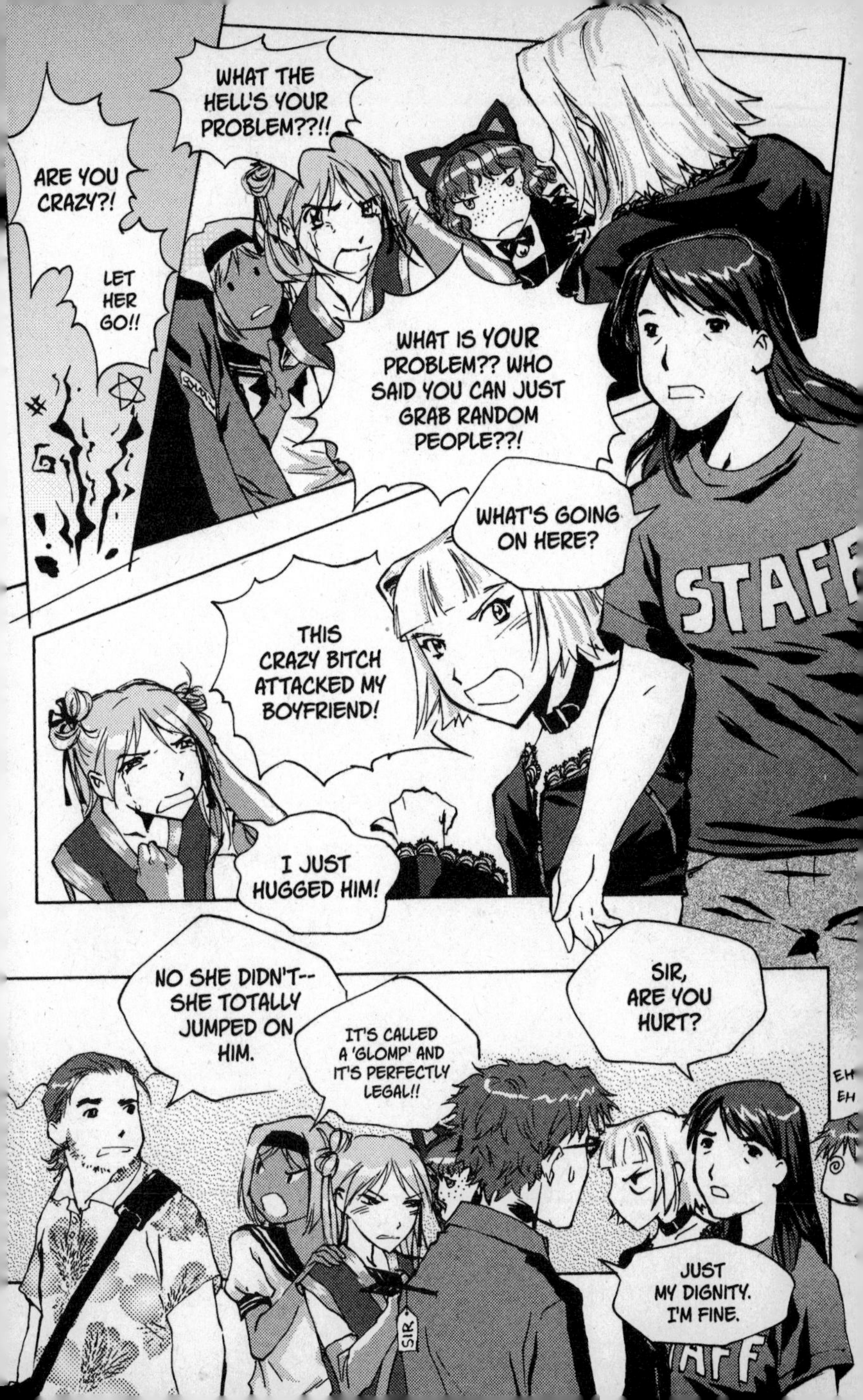
WHAT THE HELL'S YOUR PROBLEM??!!
ARE YOU CRAZY?!
LET HER GO!!
WHAT IS YOUR PROBLEM?? WHO SAID YOU CAN JUST GRAB RANDOM PEOPLE??!
WHAT'S GOING ON HERE?
STAFF
THIS CRAZY BITCH ATTACKED MY BOYFRIEND!
I JUST HUGGED HIM!
NO SHE DIDN'T--SHE TOTALLY JUMPED ON HIM.
IT'S CALLED A 'GLOMP' AND IT'S PERFECTLY LEGAL!!
SIR, ARE YOU HURT?
EH EH
SIR
JUST MY DIGNITY. I'M FINE.

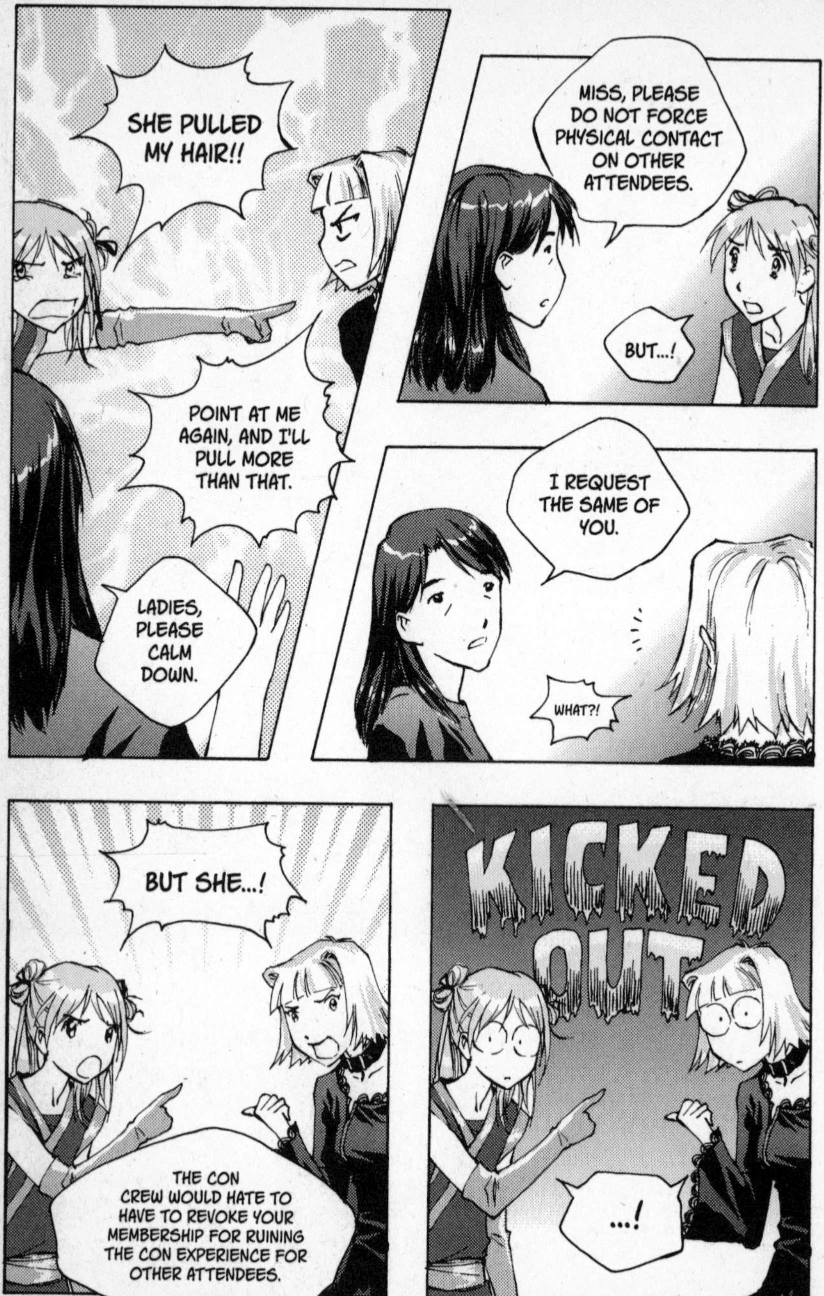
SHE PULLED MY HAIR!!
POINT AT ME AGAIN, AND I'LL PULL MORE THAN THAT.
LADIES, PLEASE CALM DOWN.
MISS, PLEASE DO NOT FORCE PHYSICAL CONTACT ON OTHER ATTENDEES.
BUT...!
I REQUEST THE SAME OF YOU.
WHAT?!
BUT SHE...!
THE CON CREW WOULD HATE TO HAVE TO REVOKE YOUR MEMBERSHIP FOR RUINING THE CON EXPERIENCE FOR OTHER ATTENDEES.
KICKED OUT
...!

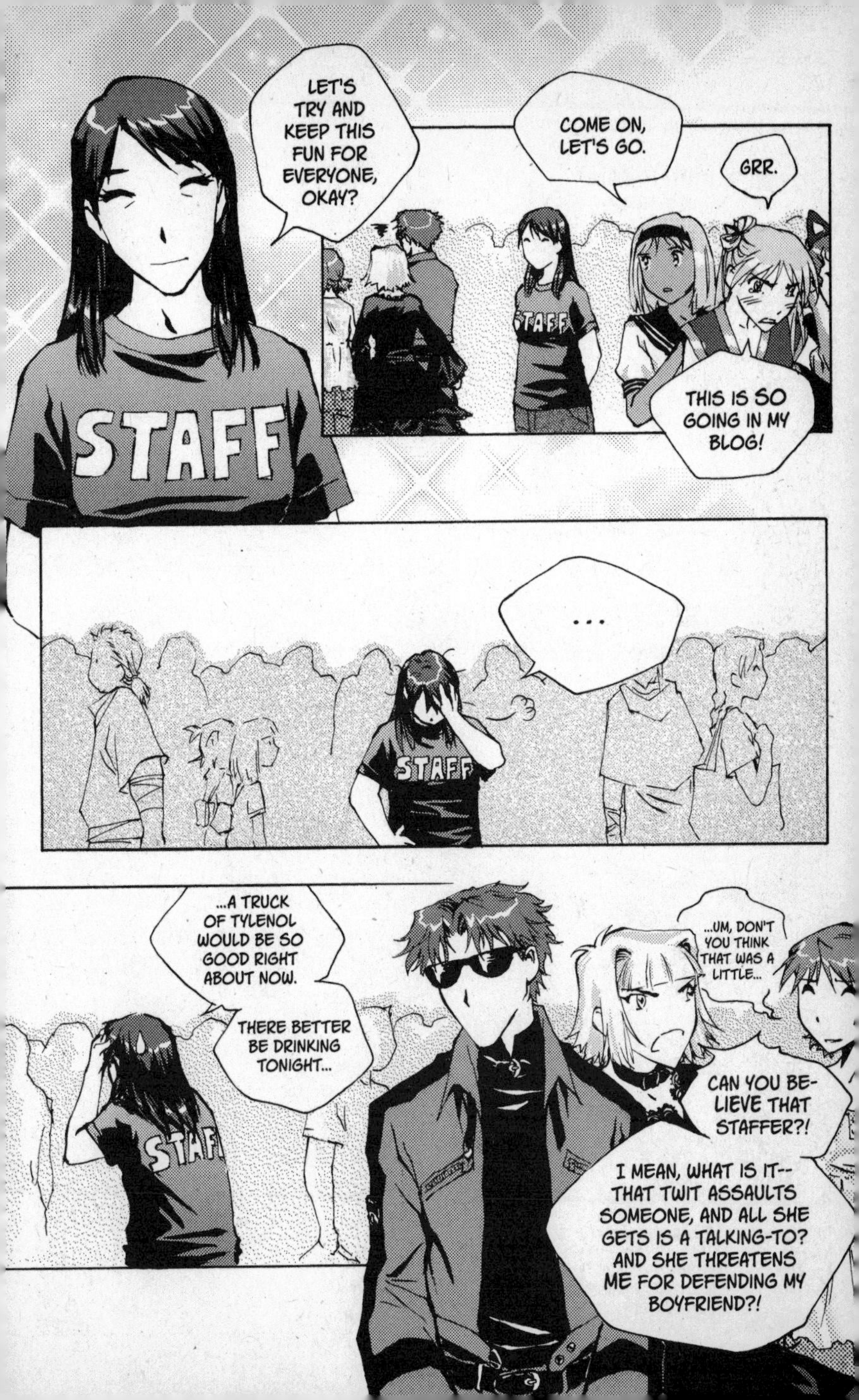
LET'S TRY AND KEEP THIS FUN FOR EVERYONE, OKAY?
COME ON, LET'S GO.
GRR.
THIS IS SO GOING IN MY BLOG!
...
...A TRUCK OF TYLENOL WOULD BE SO GOOD RIGHT ABOUT NOW.
THERE BETTER BE DRINKING TONIGHT...
...UM, DON'T YOU THINK THAT WAS A LITTLE...
CAN YOU BE-LIEVE THAT STAFFER?!
I MEAN, WHAT IS IT-- THAT TWIT ASSAULTS SOMEONE, AND ALL SHE GETS IS A TALKING-TO? AND SHE THREATENS ME FOR DEFENDING MY BOYFRIEND?!

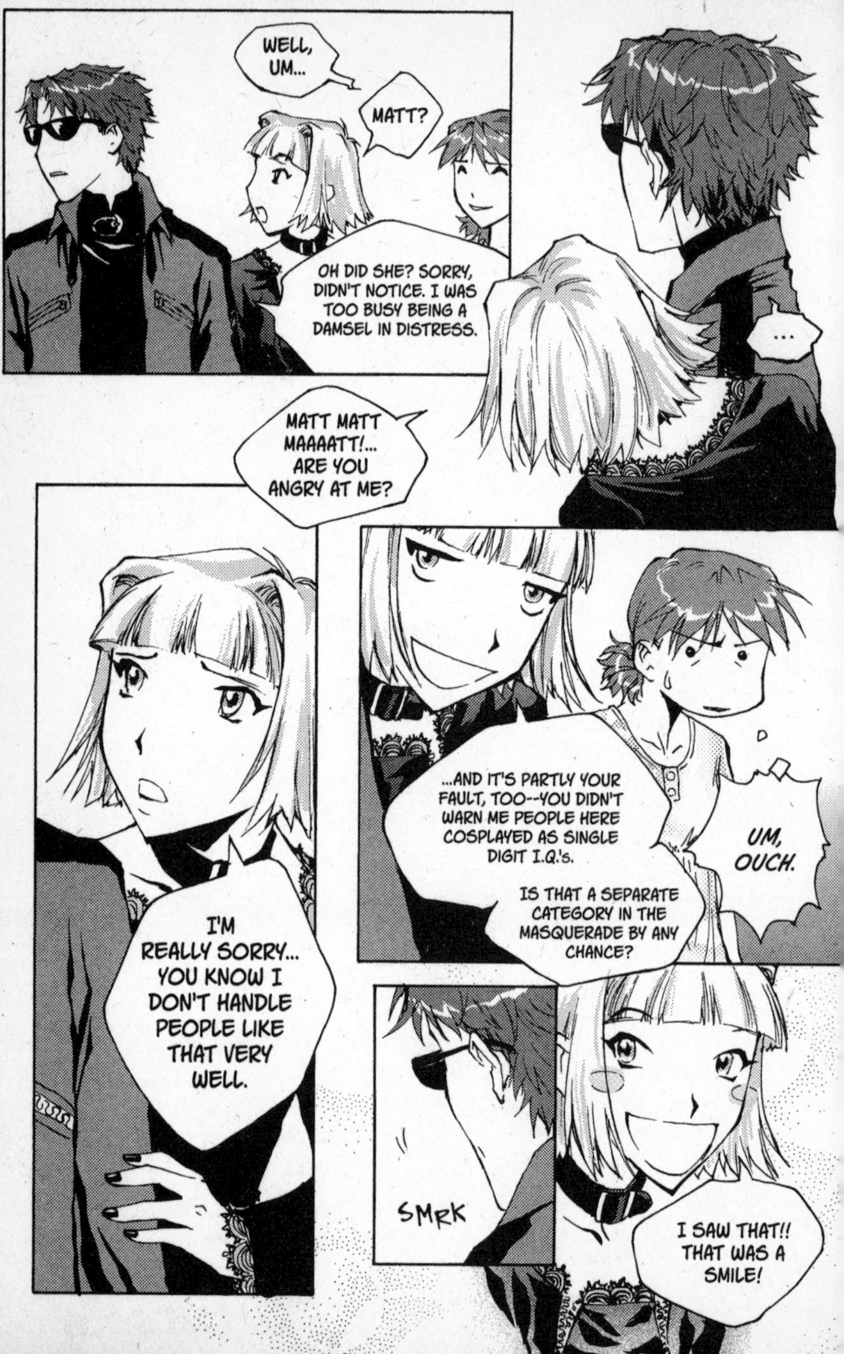
WELL, UM...
MATT?
OH DID SHE? SORRY, DIDN'T NOTICE. I WAS TOO BUSY BEING A DAMSEL IN DISTRESS.
...
MATT MATT MAAAATT!... ARE YOU ANGRY AT ME?
I'M REALLY SORRY... YOU KNOW I DON'T HANDLE PEOPLE LIKE THAT VERY WELL.
...AND IT'S PARTLY YOUR FAULT, TOO--YOU DIDN'T WARN ME PEOPLE HERE COSPLAYED AS SINGLE DIGIT I.Q.'s.
IS THAT A SEPARATE CATEGORY IN THE MASQUERADE BY ANY CHANCE?
UM, OUCH.
SMRK
I SAW THAT!! THAT WAS A SMILE!

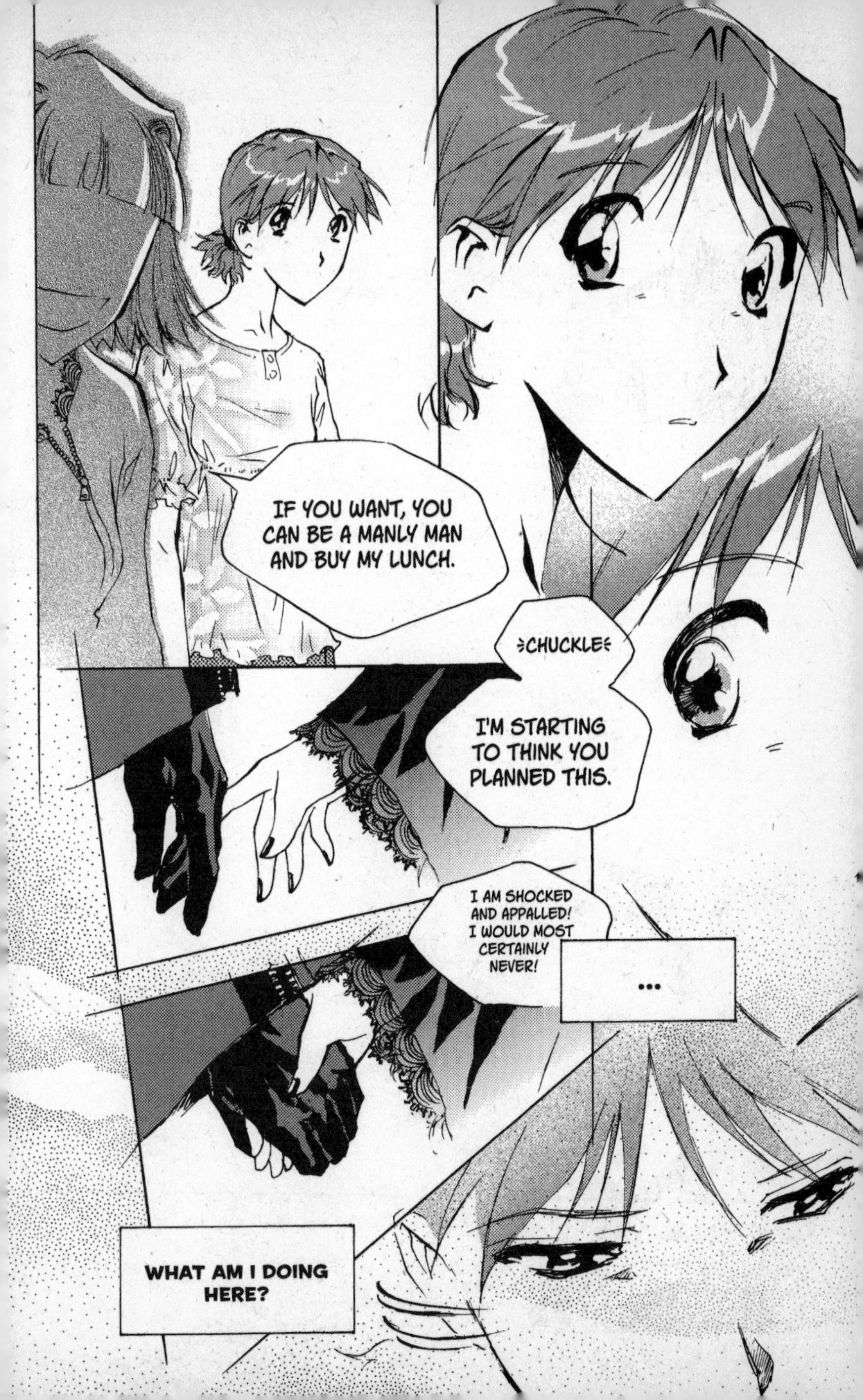
IF YOU WANT, YOU CAN BE A MANLY MAN AND BUY MY LUNCH.
CHUCKLE
I'M STARTING TO THINK YOU PLANNED THIS.
I AM SHOCKED AND APPALLED! I WOULD MOST CERTAINLY NEVER!
...
WHAT AM I DOING HERE?

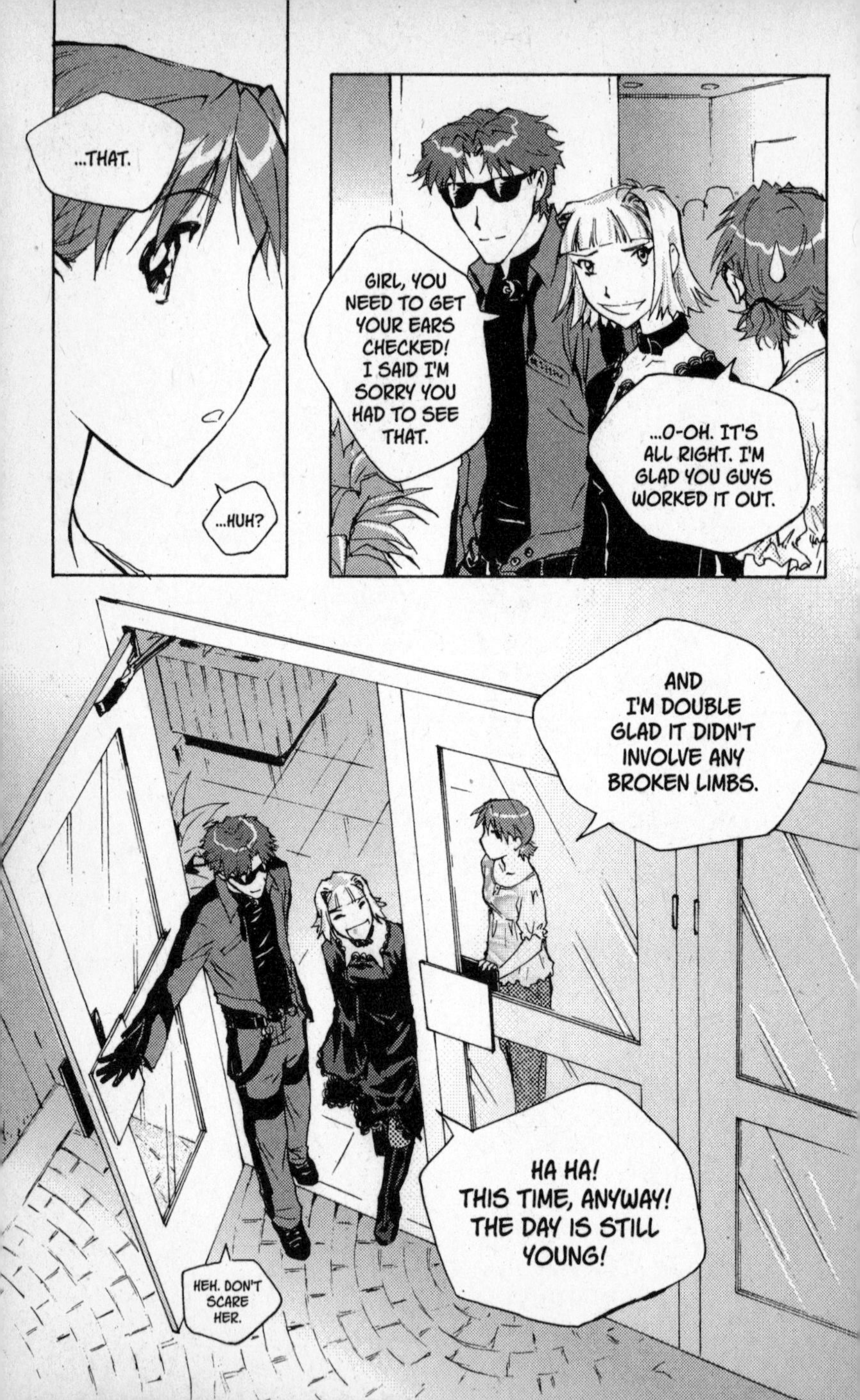
...THAT.
...HUH?
GIRL, YOU NEED TO GET YOUR EARS CHECKED! I SAID I'M SORRY YOU HAD TO SEE THAT.
...O-OH. IT'S ALL RIGHT. I'M GLAD YOU GUYS WORKED IT OUT.
AND I'M DOUBLE GLAD IT DIDN'T INVOLVE ANY BROKEN LIMBS.
HA HA! THIS TIME, ANYWAY! THE DAY IS STILL YOUNG!
HEH. DON'T SCARE HER.

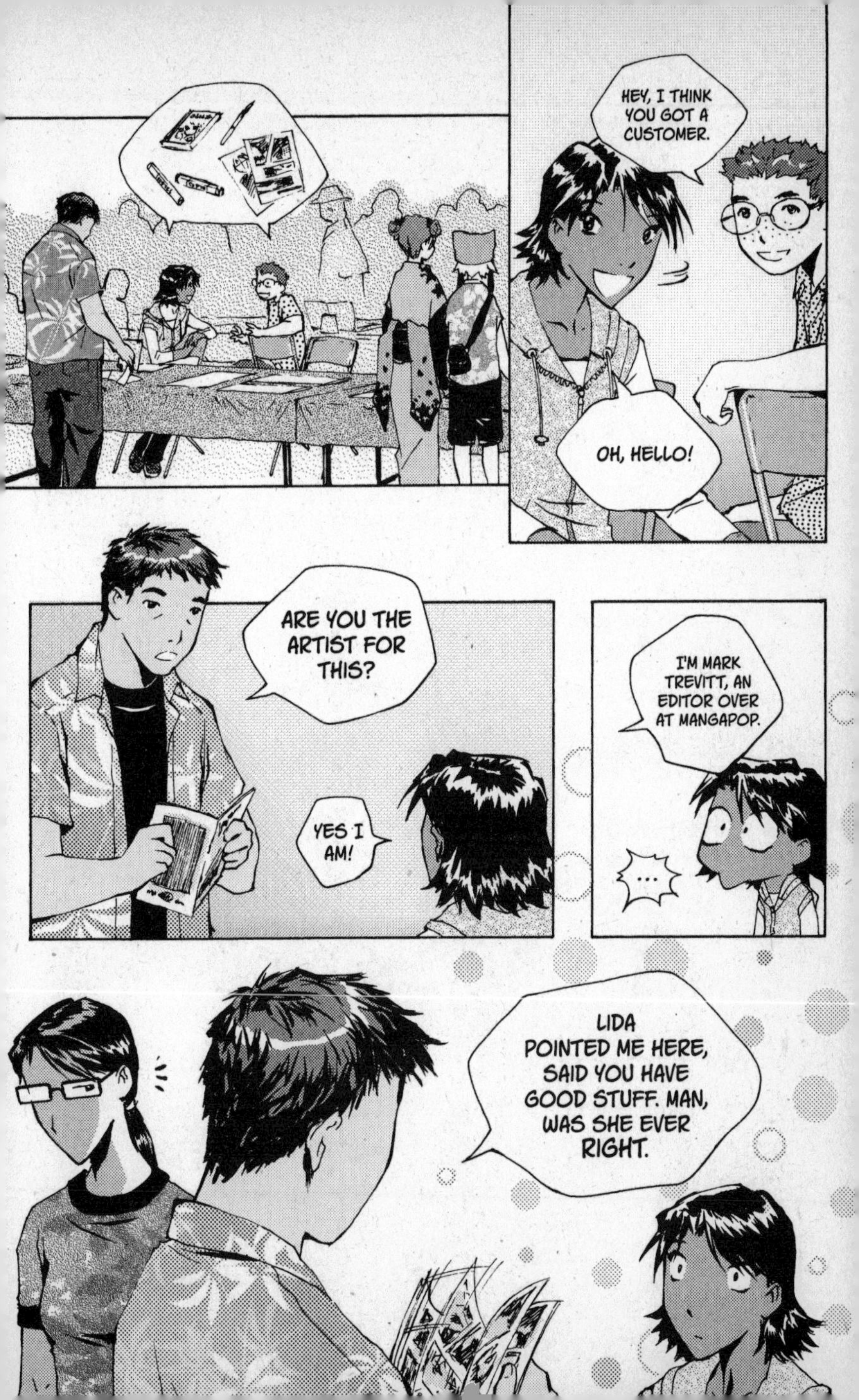
HEY, I THINK YOU GOT A CUSTOMER.
OH, HELLO!
ARE YOU THE ARTIST FOR THIS?
YES I AM!
I'M MARK TREVITT, AN EDITOR OVER AT MANGAPOP.
...
LIDA POINTED ME HERE, SAID YOU HAVE GOOD STUFF. MAN, WAS SHE EVER RIGHT.

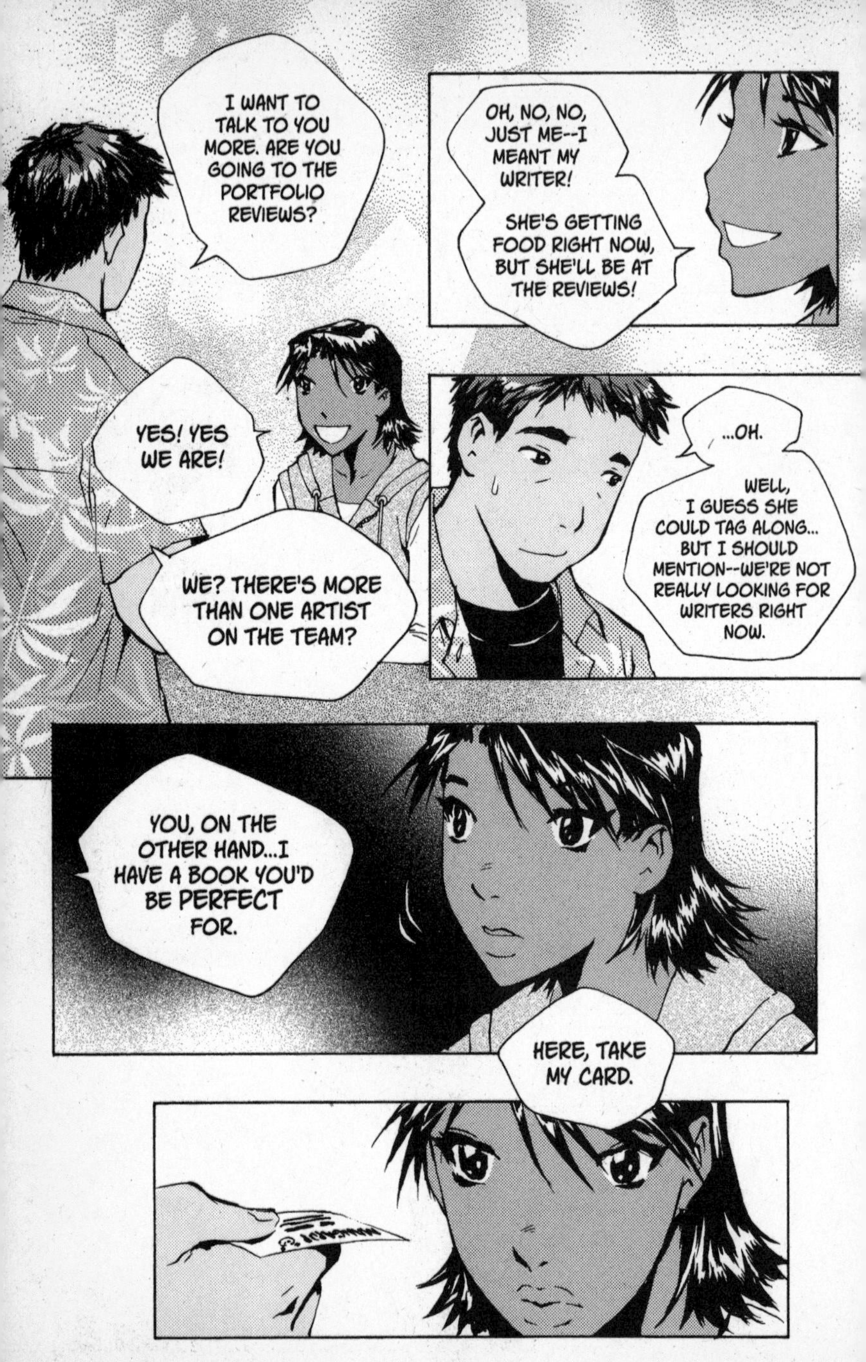
I WANT TO TALK TO YOU MORE. ARE YOU GOING TO THE PORTFOLIO REVIEWS?
YES! YES WE ARE!
WE? THERE'S MORE THAN ONE ARTIST ON THE TEAM?
OH, NO, NO, JUST ME--I MEANT MY WRITER!
SHE'S GETTING FOOD RIGHT NOW, BUT SHE'LL BE AT THE REVIEWS!
...OH.
WELL, I GUESS SHE COULD TAG ALONG... BUT I SHOULD MENTION--WE'RE NOT REALLY LOOKING FOR WRITERS RIGHT NOW.
YOU, ON THE OTHER HAND...I HAVE A BOOK YOU'D BE PERFECT FOR.
HERE, TAKE MY CARD.

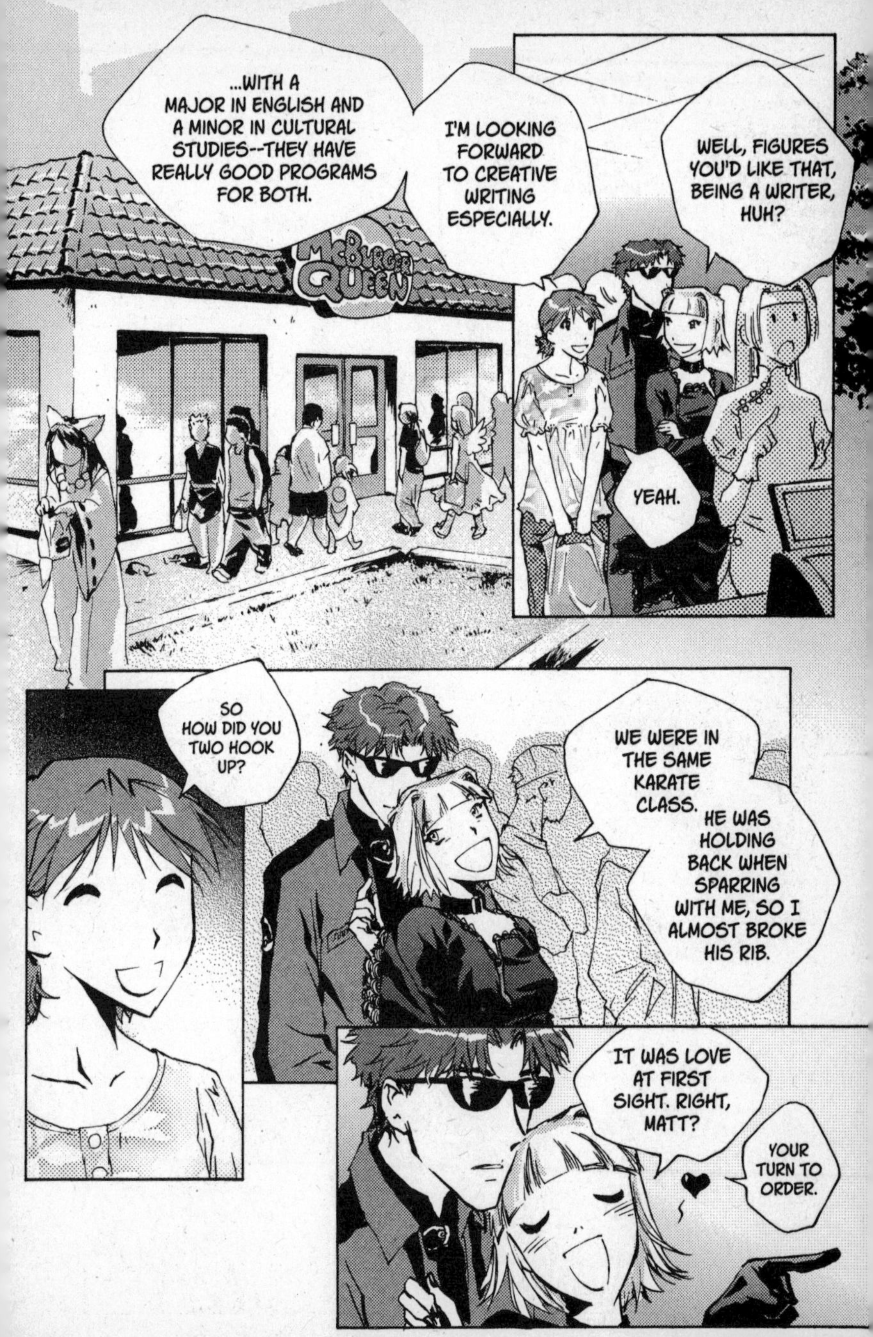

...WITH A MAJOR IN ENGLISH AND A MINOR IN CULTURAL STUDIES--THEY HAVE REALLY GOOD PROGRAMS FOR BOTH.
I'M LOOKING FORWARD TO CREATIVE WRITING ESPECIALLY.
McBURGER QUEEN
WELL, FIGURES YOU'D LIKE THAT, BEING A WRITER, HUH?
YEAH.
SO HOW DID YOU TWO HOOK UP?
WE WERE IN THE SAME KARATE CLASS.
HE WAS HOLDING BACK WHEN SPARRING WITH ME, SO I ALMOST BROKE HIS RIB.
IT WAS LOVE AT FIRST SIGHT. RIGHT, MATT?
YOUR TURN TO ORDER.

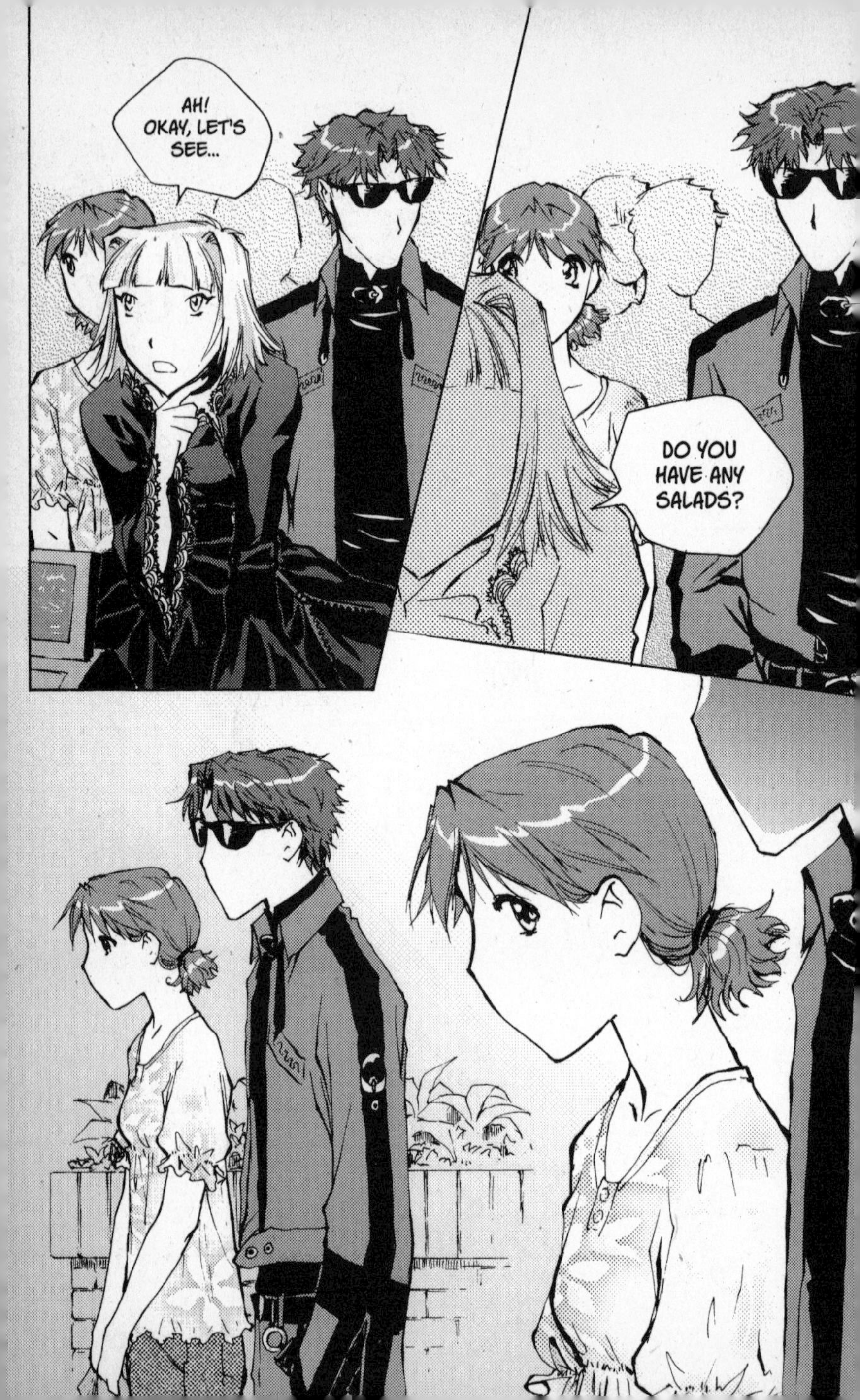
AH! OKAY, LET'S SEE...
DO YOU HAVE ANY SALADS?

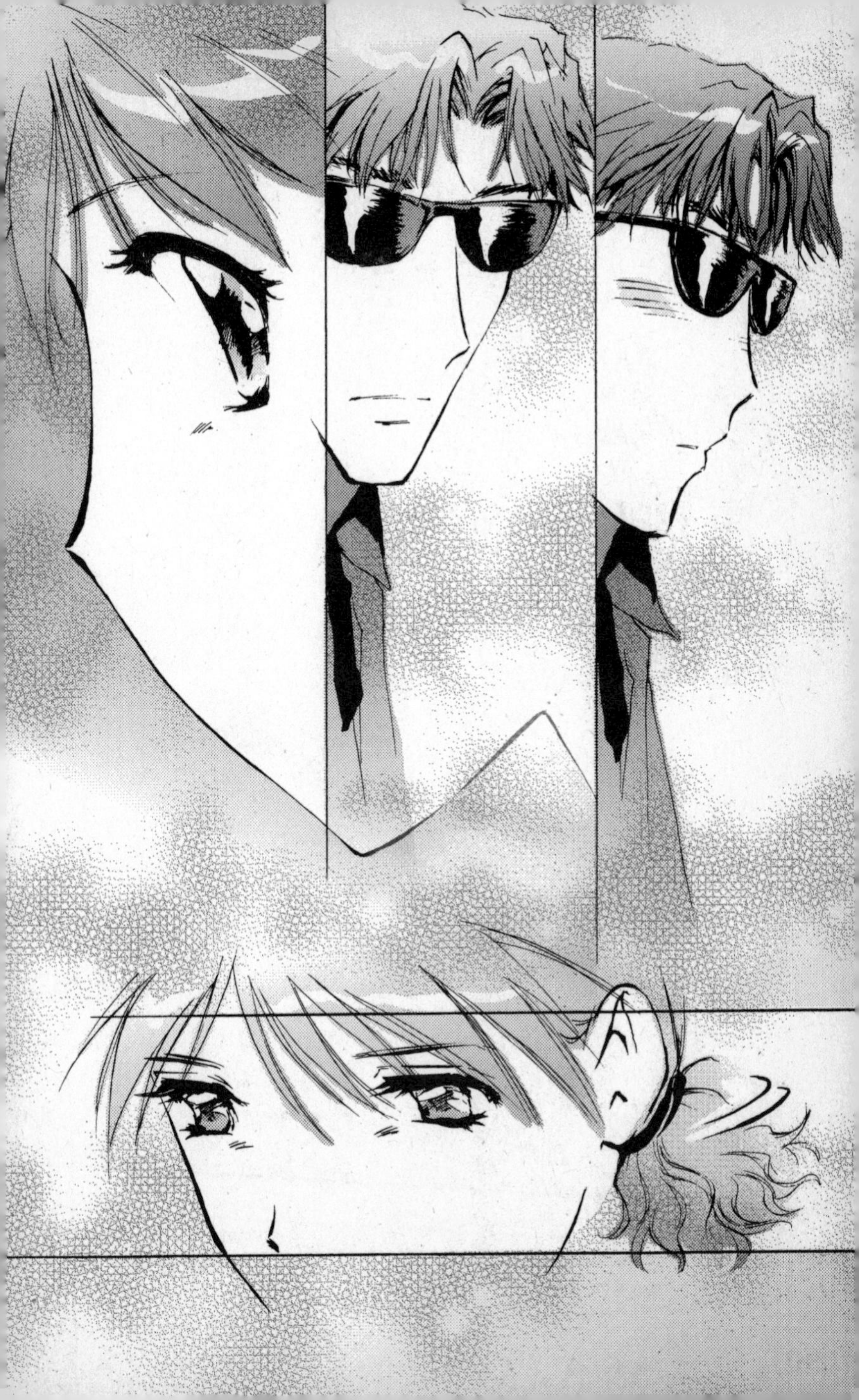

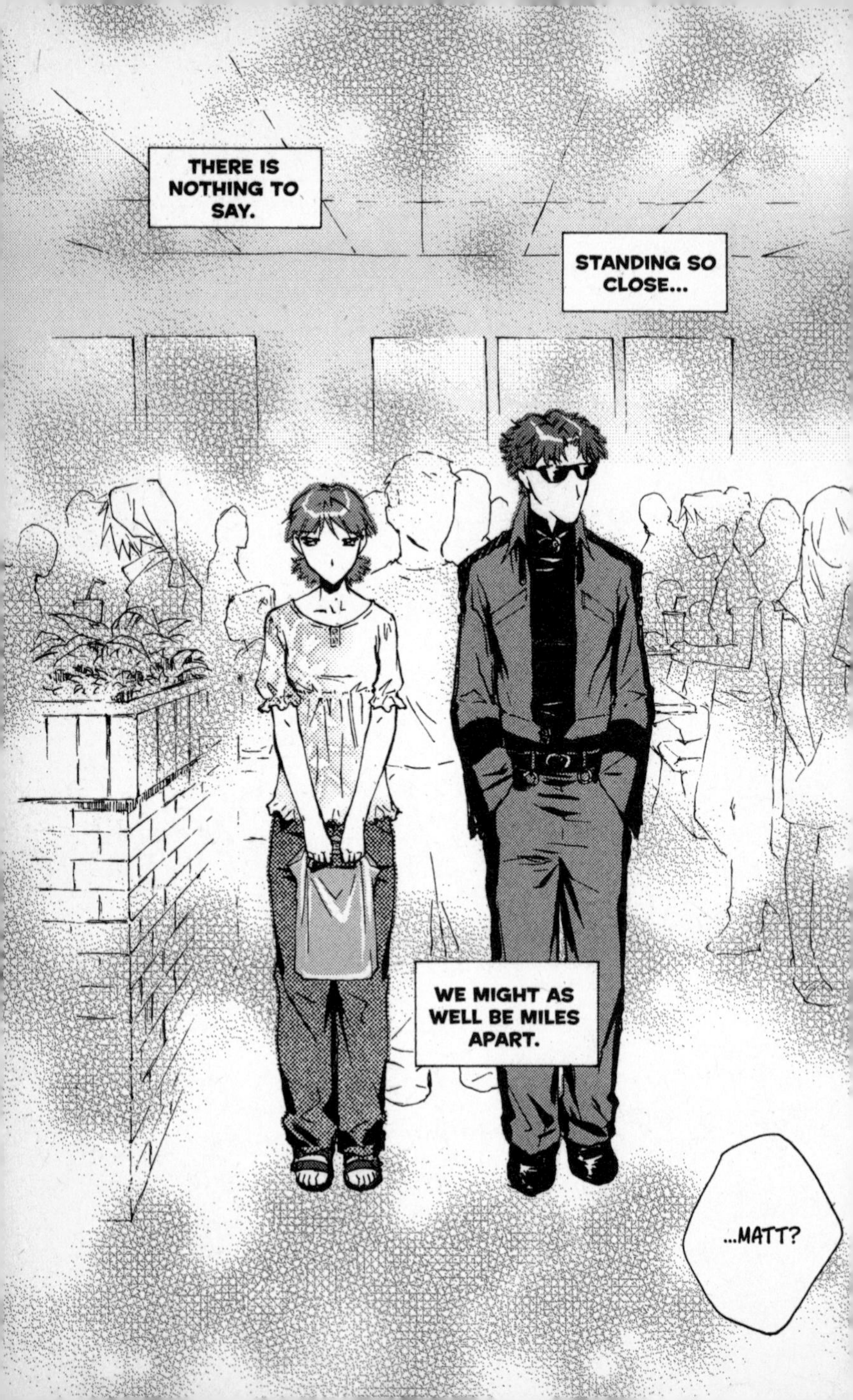
THERE IS NOTHING TO SAY.
STANDING SO CLOSE...
WE MIGHT AS WELL BE MILES APART.
...MATT?

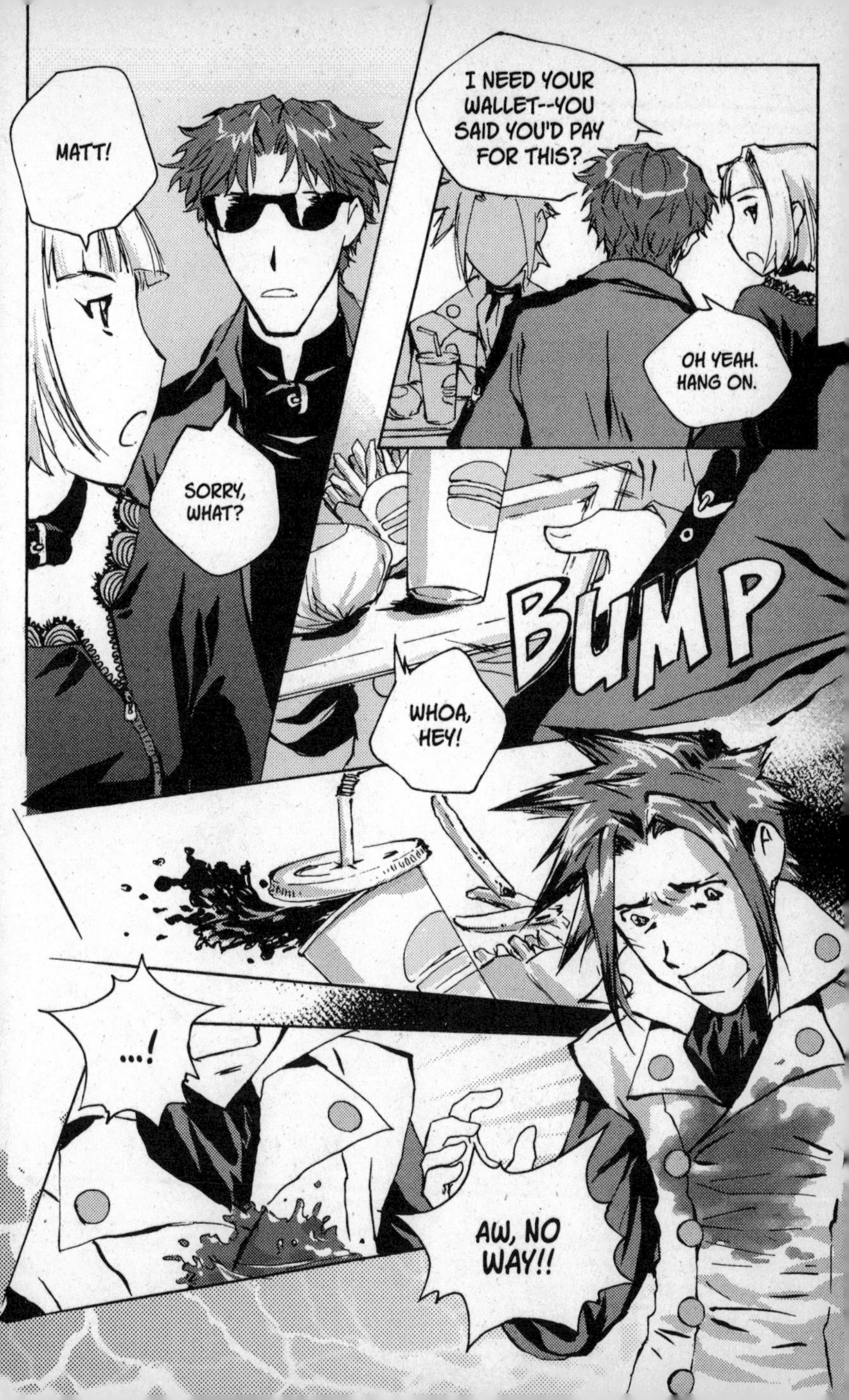
MATT!
SORRY, WHAT?
I NEED YOUR WALLET--YOU SAID YOU'D PAY FOR THIS?
OH YEAH. HANG ON.
BUMP
WHOA, HEY!
...!
AW, NO WAY!!

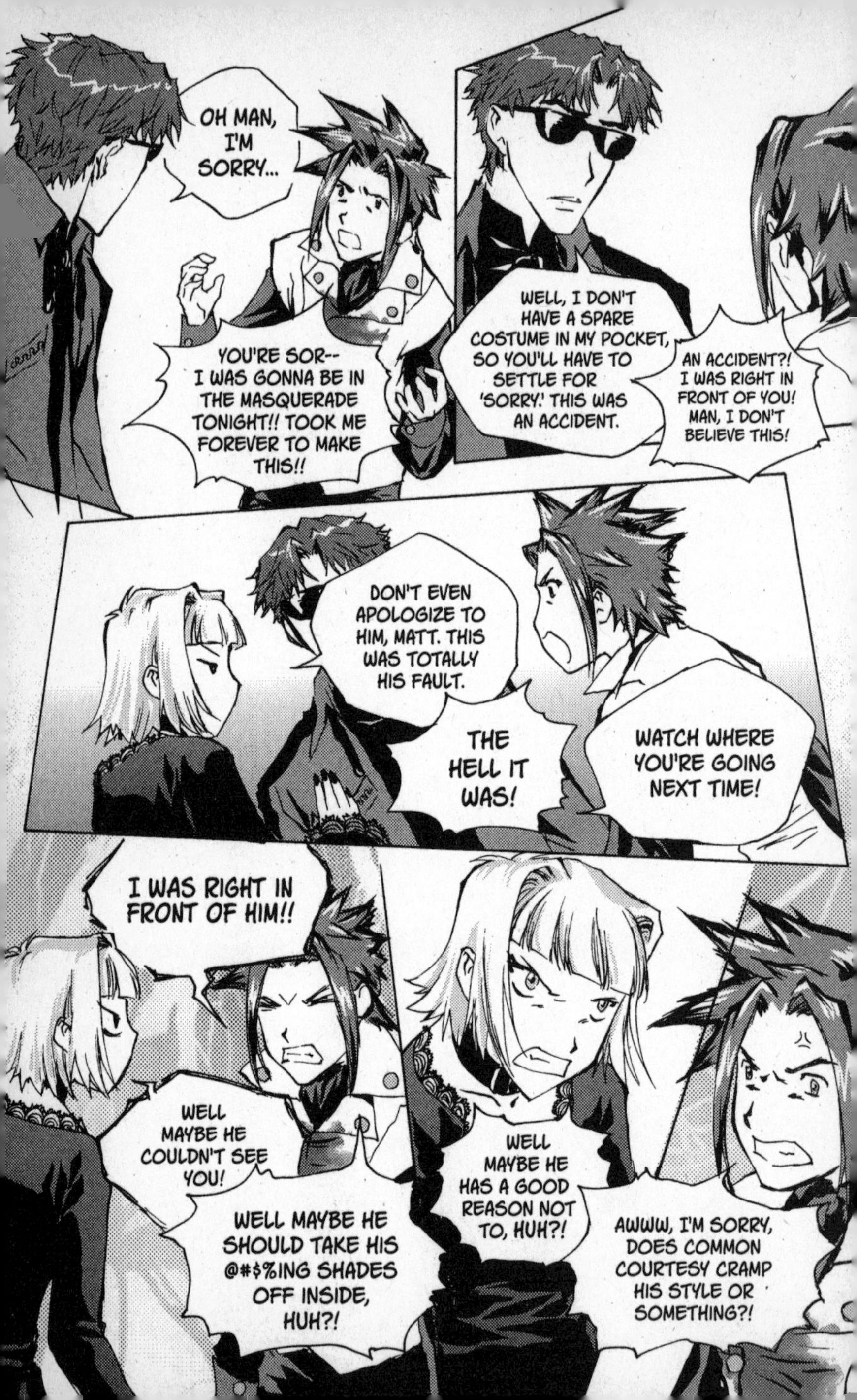
OH MAN, I'M SORRY...
YOU'RE SOR-- I WAS GONNA BE IN THE MASQUERADE TONIGHT!! TOOK ME FOREVER TO MAKE THIS!!
WELL, I DON'T HAVE A SPARE COSTUME IN MY POCKET, SO YOU'LL HAVE TO SETTLE FOR 'SORRY.' THIS WAS AN ACCIDENT.
AN ACCIDENT?! I WAS RIGHT IN FRONT OF YOU! MAN, I DON'T BELIEVE THIS!
DON'T EVEN APOLOGIZE TO HIM, MATT. THIS WAS TOTALLY HIS FAULT.
THE HELL IT WAS!
WATCH WHERE YOU'RE GOING NEXT TIME!
I WAS RIGHT IN FRONT OF HIM!!
WELL MAYBE HE COULDN'T SEE YOU!
WELL MAYBE HE SHOULD TAKE HIS @#$%ING SHADES OFF INSIDE, HUH?!
WELL MAYBE HE HAS A GOOD REASON NOT TO, HUH?!
AWWW, I'M SORRY, DOES COMMON COURTESY CRAMP HIS STYLE OR SOMETHING?!

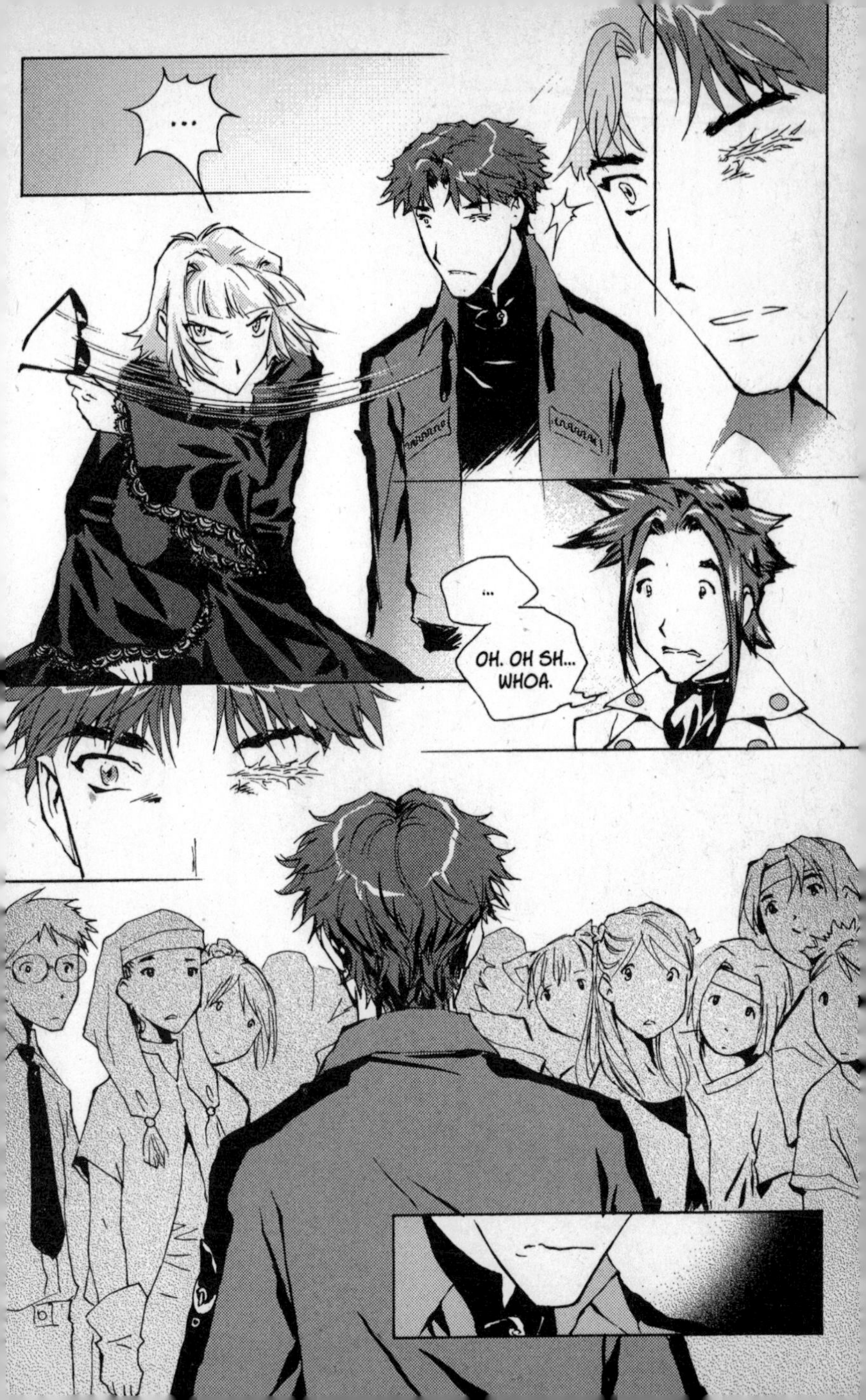
...
...
OH. OH SH... WHOA.

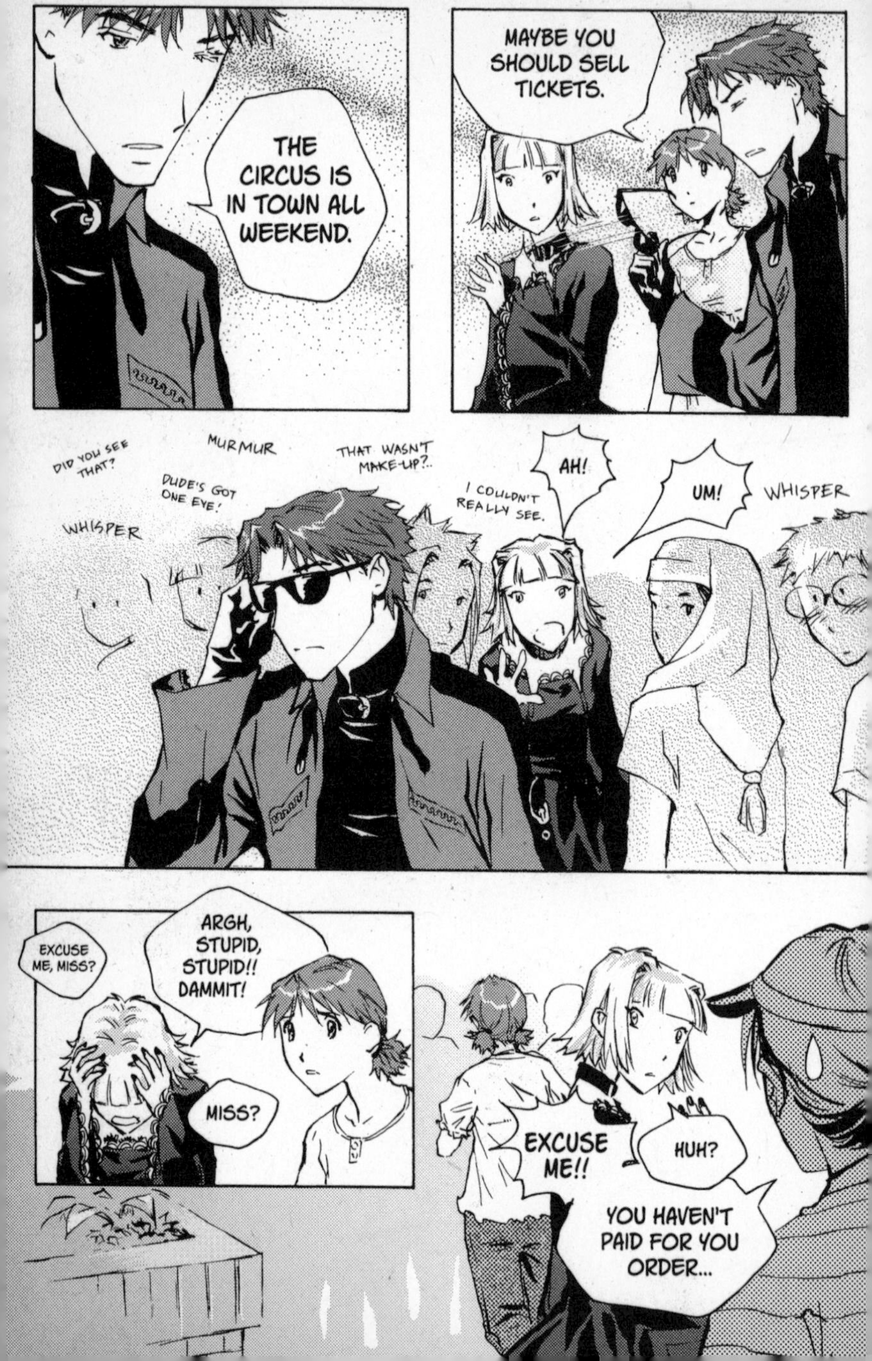
THE CIRCUS IS IN TOWN ALL WEEKEND.
MAYBE YOU SHOULD SELL TICKETS.
DID YOU SEE THAT?
WHISPER
DUDE'S GOT ONE EYE!
MURMUR
THAT WASN'T MAKE-UP?..
I COULDN'T REALLY SEE.
AH!
UM!
WHISPER
EXCUSE ME, MISS?
ARGH, STUPID, STUPID!! DAMMIT!
MISS?
EXCUSE ME!!
HUH?
YOU HAVEN'T PAID FOR YOU ORDER...

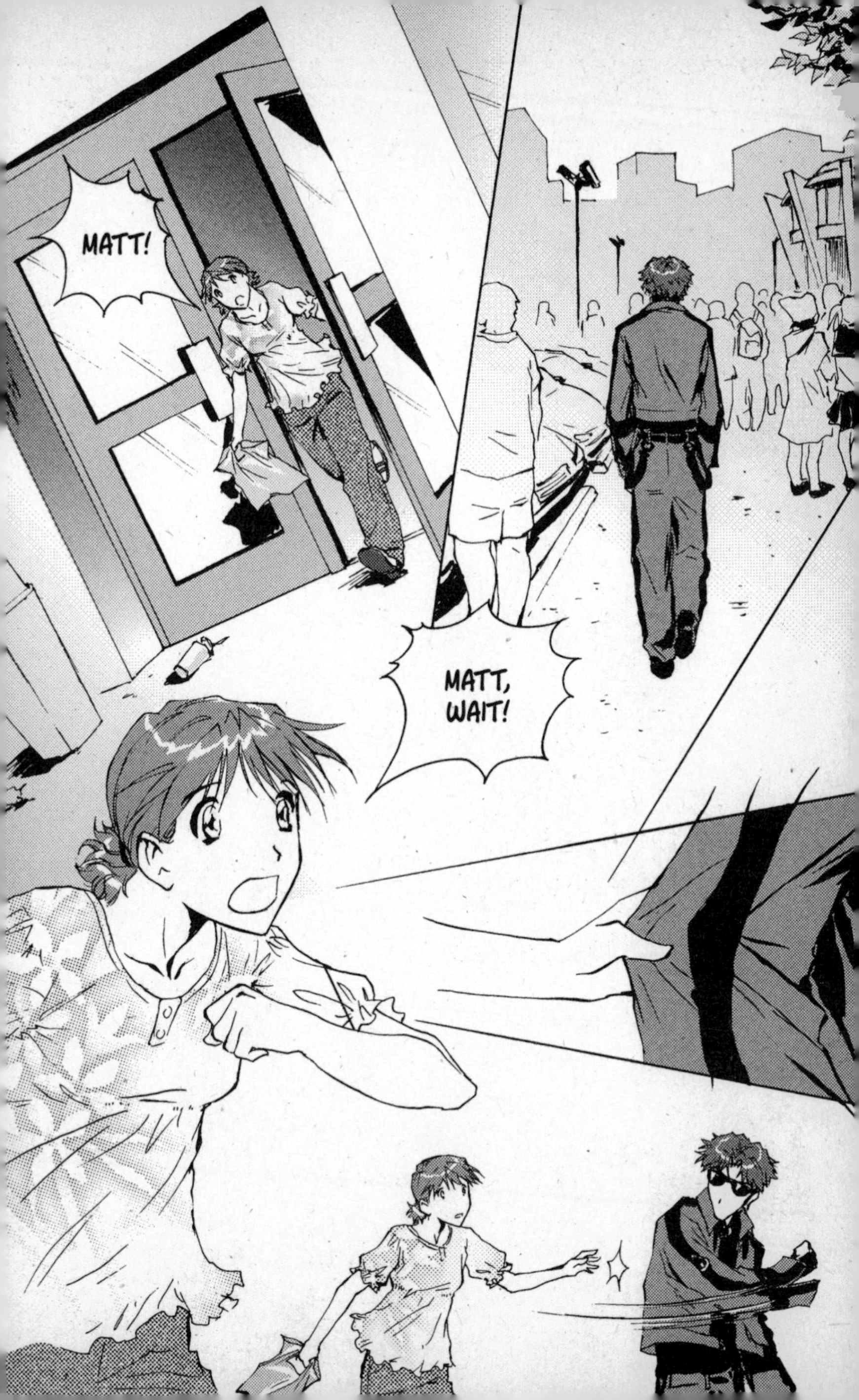
MATT!
MATT, WAIT!

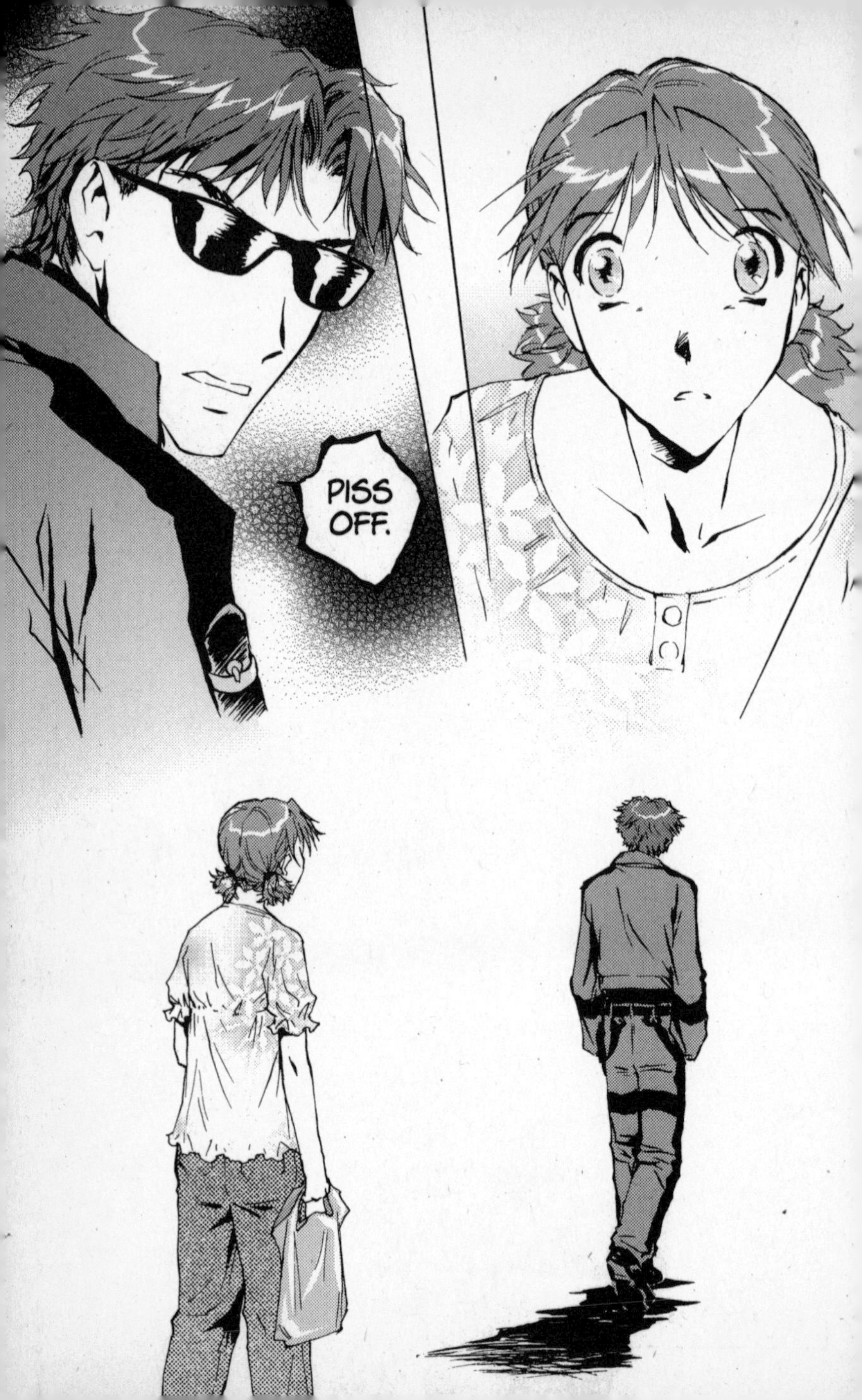
PISS OFF.

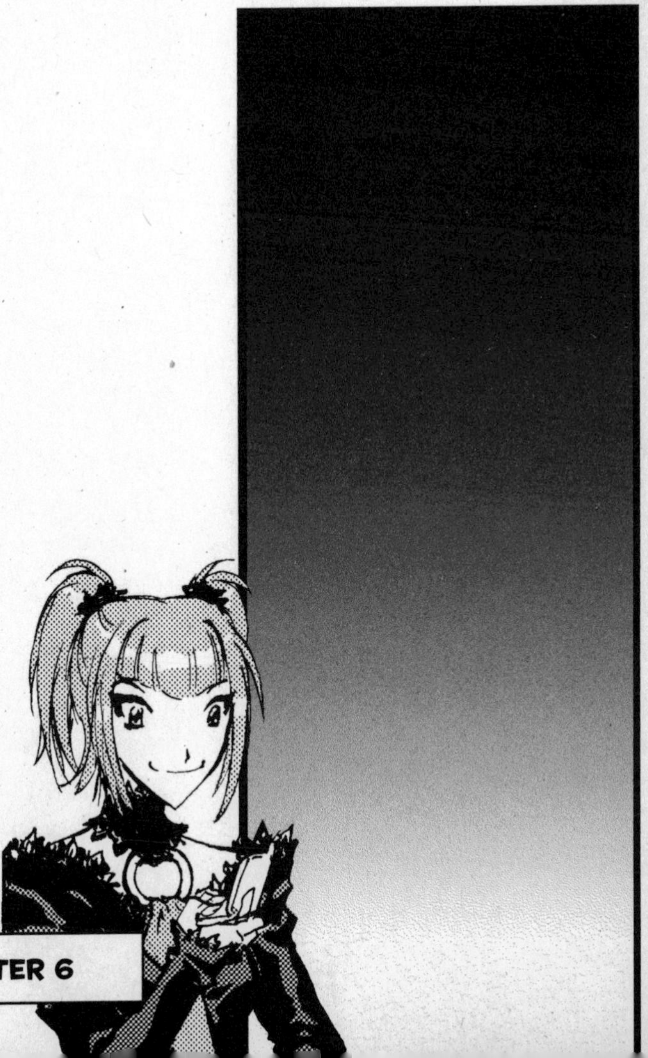

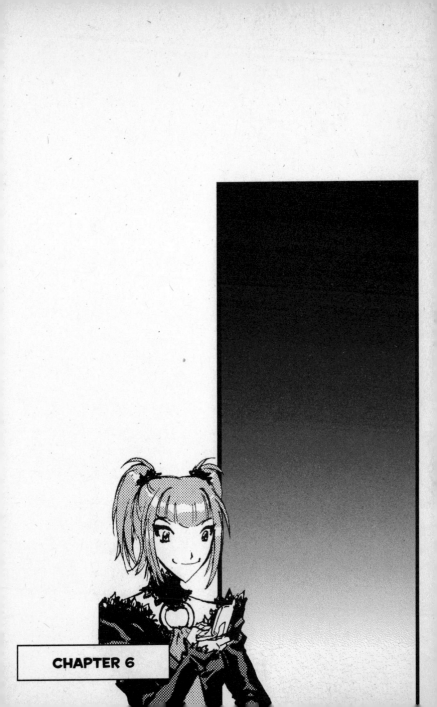

CHAPTER 6

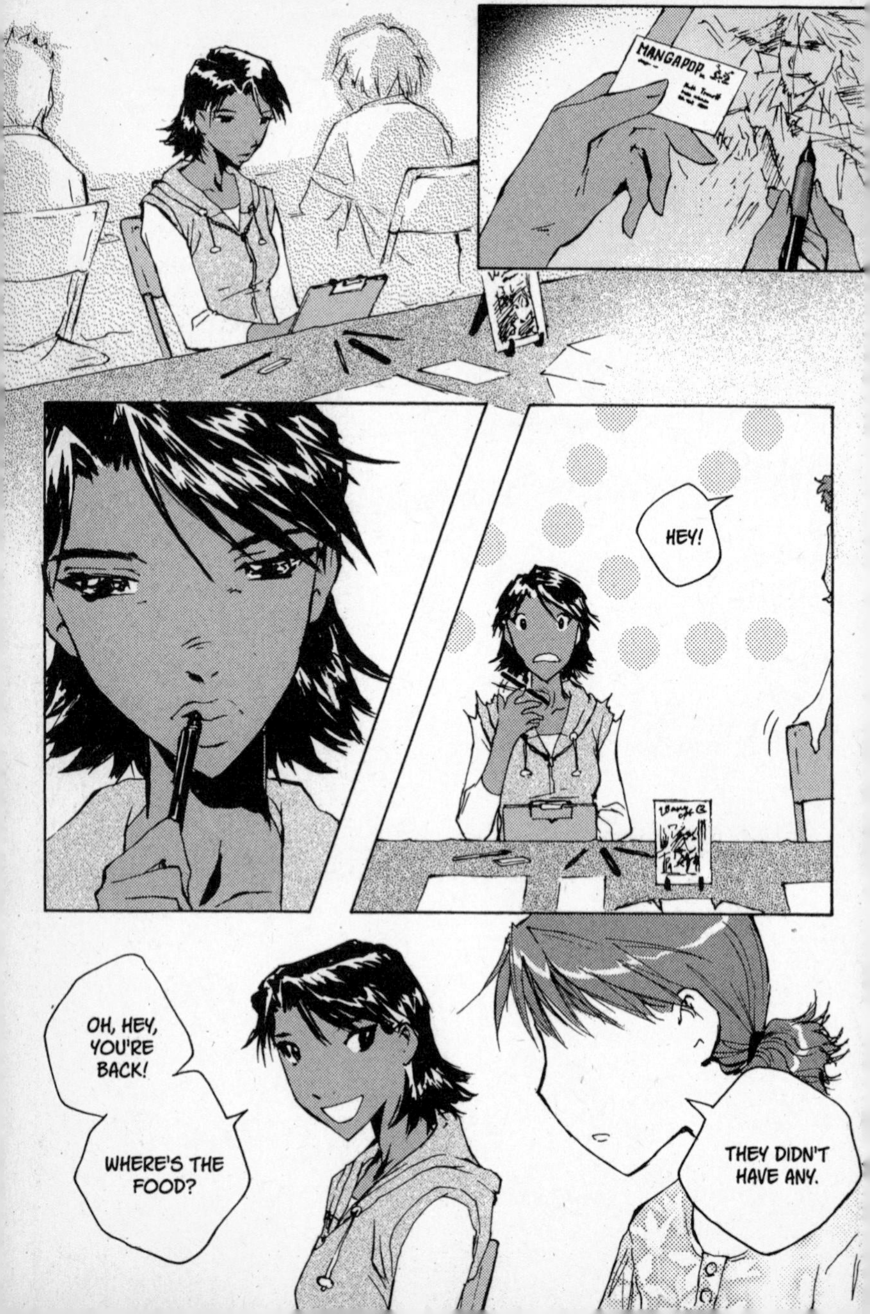
MANGAPOP
HEY!
OH, HEY, YOU'RE BACK!
WHERE'S THE FOOD?
THEY DIDN'T HAVE ANY.

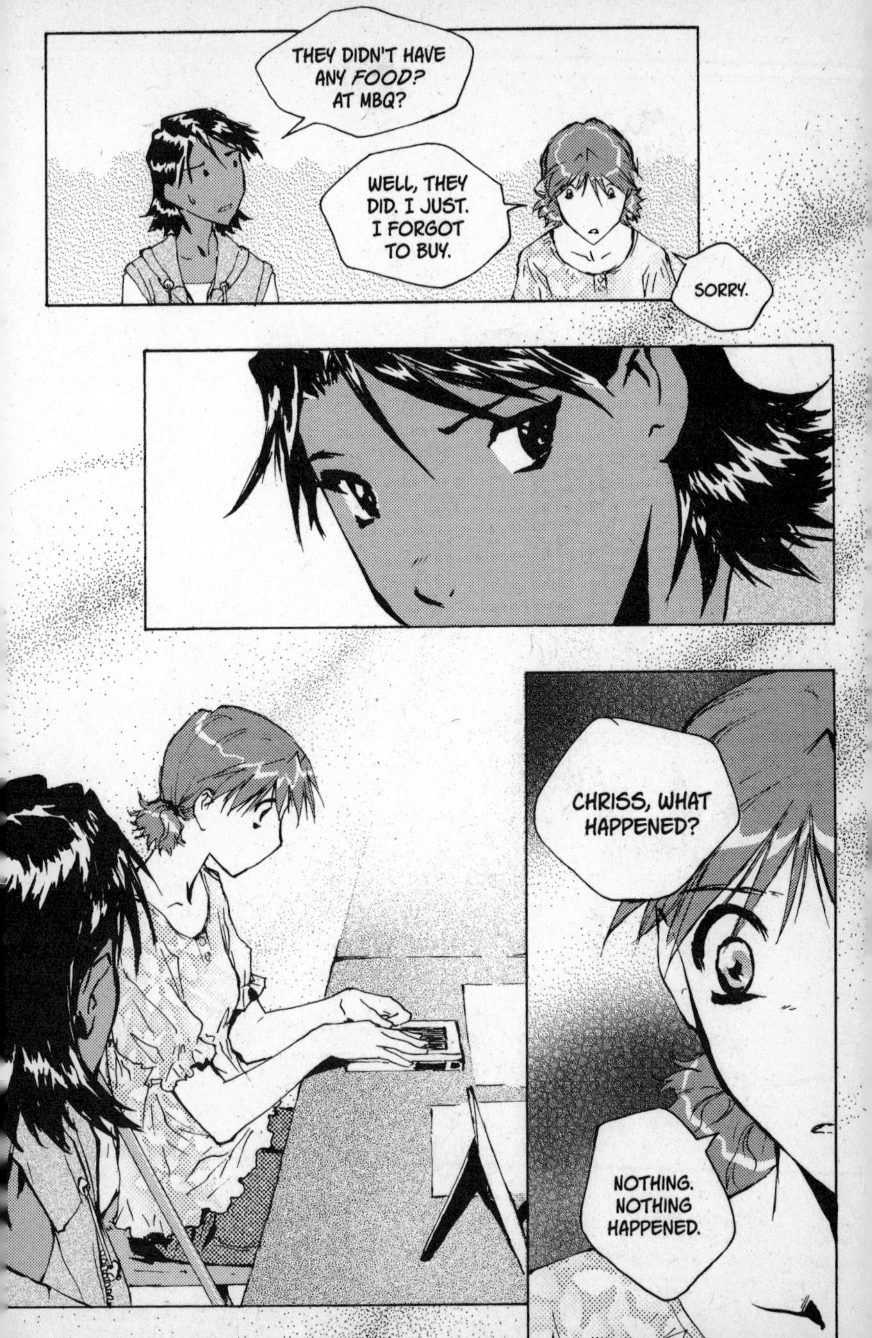
THEY DIDN'T HAVE ANY *FOOD?* AT MBQ?
WELL, THEY DID. I JUST. I FORGOT TO BUY.
SORRY.
CHRISS, WHAT HAPPENED?
NOTHING. NOTHING HAPPENED.

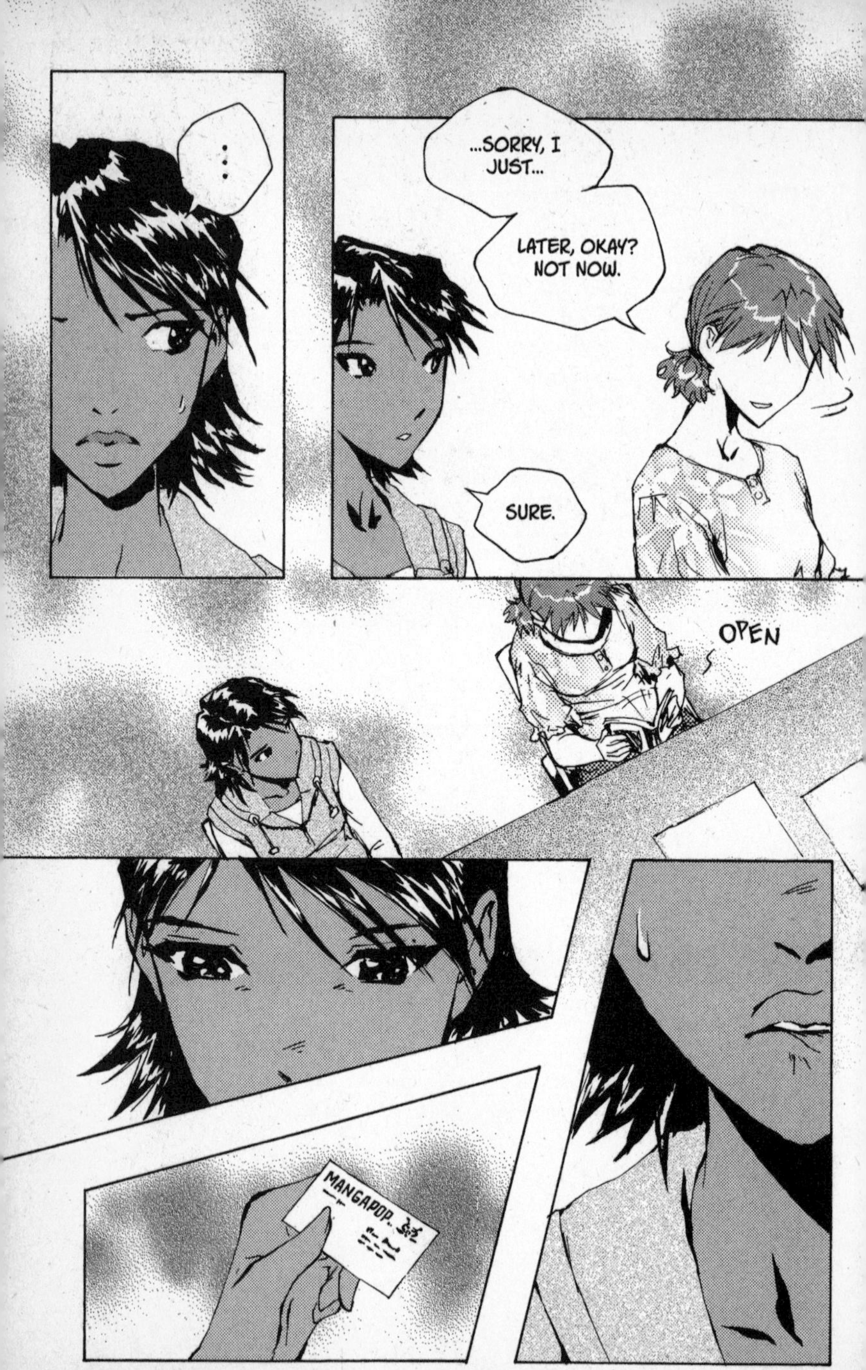
...
...SORRY, I JUST...
LATER, OKAY? NOT NOW.
SURE.
OPEN
MANGAPOP.

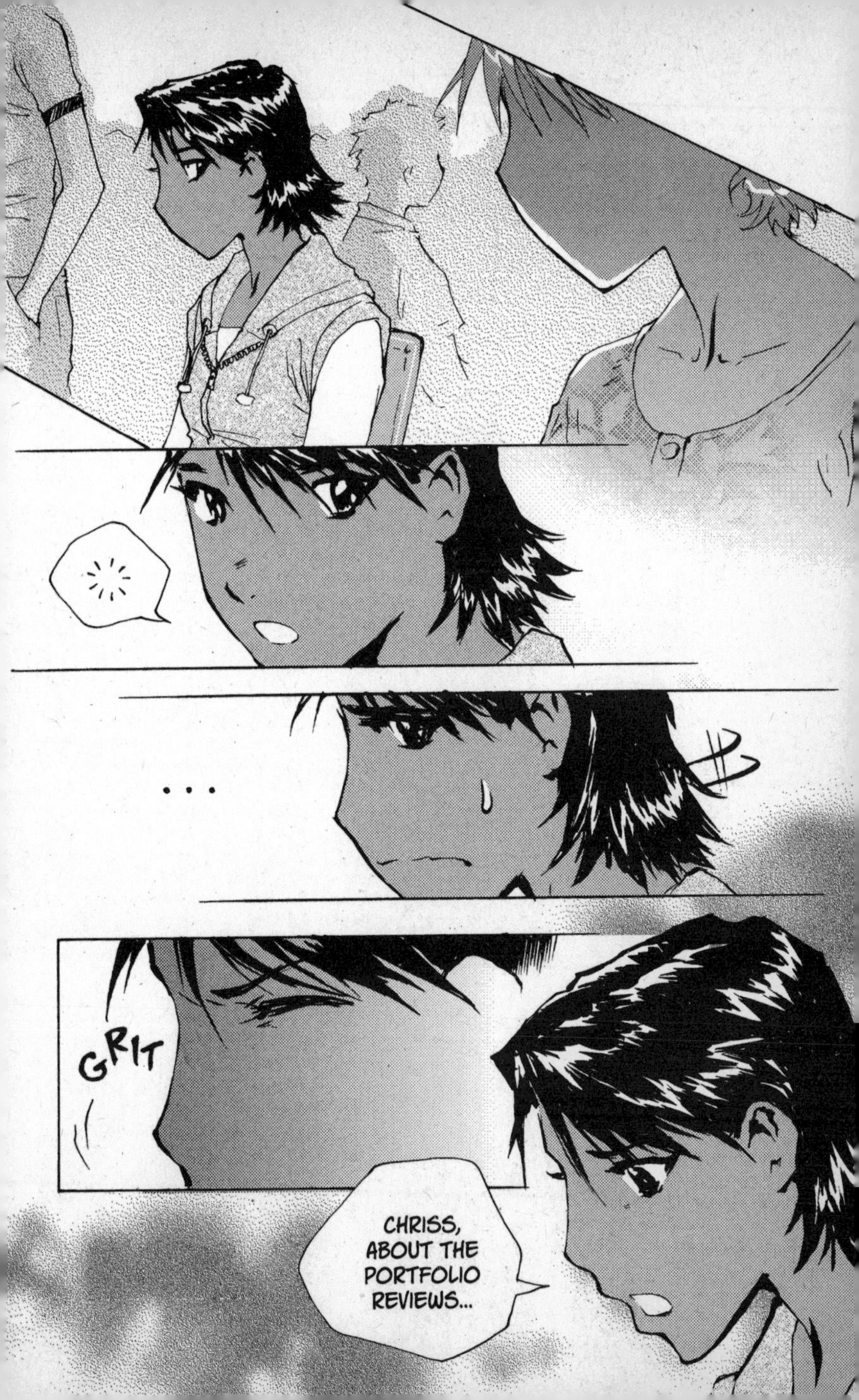
...
GRIT
CHRISS, ABOUT THE PORTFOLIO REVIEWS...

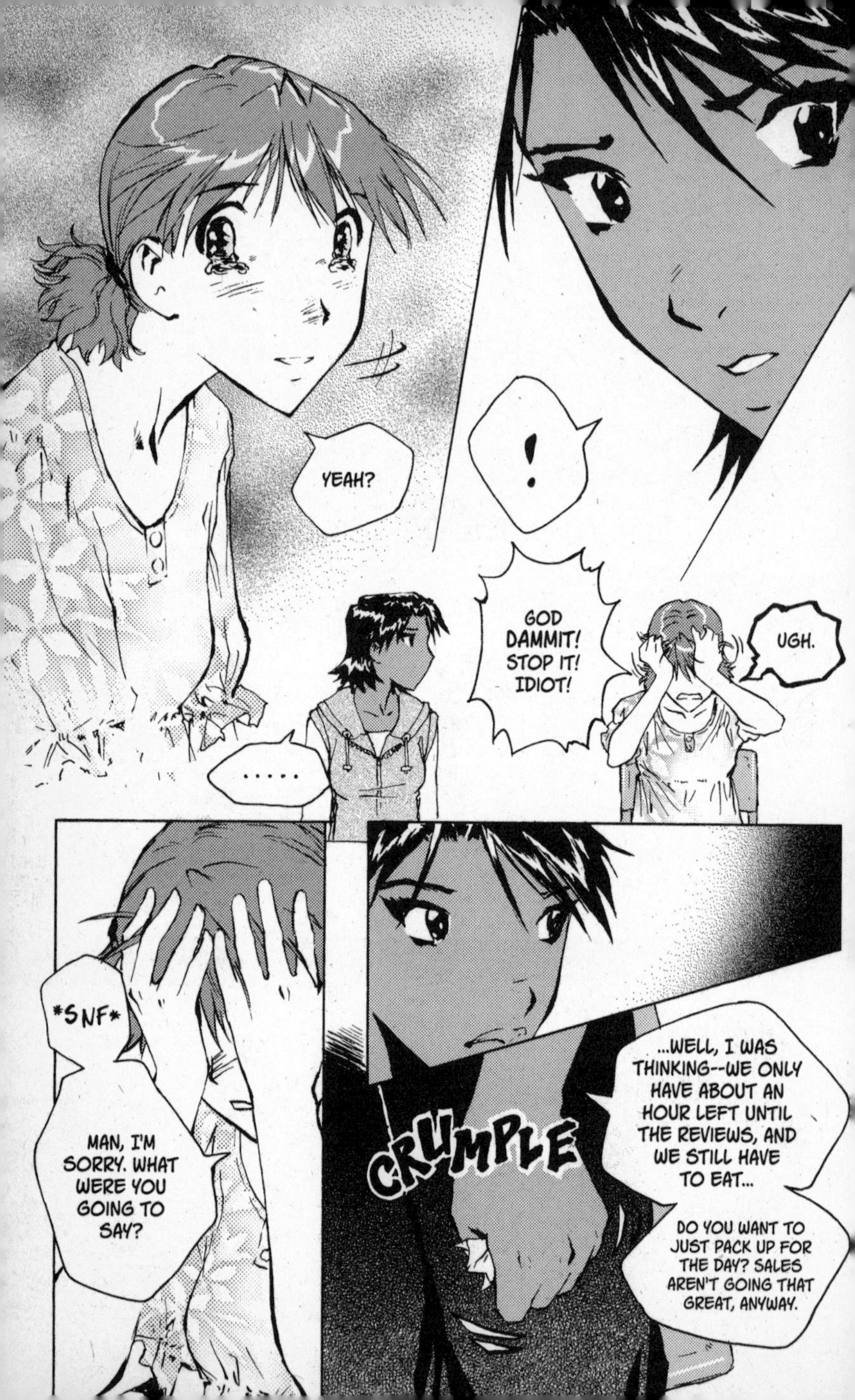
YEAH?
!
GOD DAMMIT! STOP IT! IDIOT!
UGH.
......
SNF
MAN, I'M SORRY. WHAT WERE YOU GOING TO SAY?
CRUMPLE
...WELL, I WAS THINKING--WE ONLY HAVE ABOUT AN HOUR LEFT UNTIL THE REVIEWS, AND WE STILL HAVE TO EAT...
DO YOU WANT TO JUST PACK UP FOR THE DAY? SALES AREN'T GOING THAT GREAT, ANYWAY.

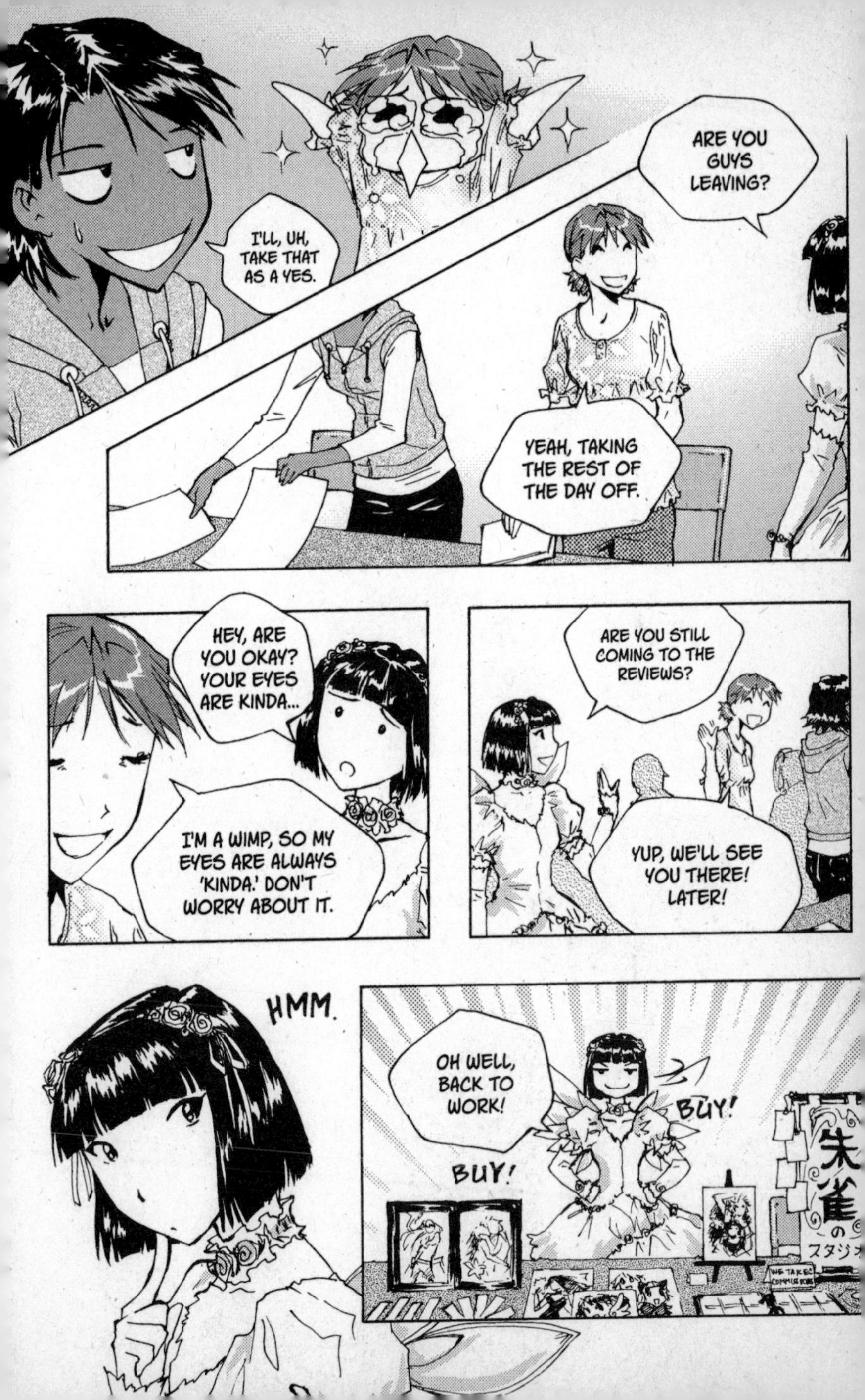
I'LL, UH, TAKE THAT AS A YES.
ARE YOU GUYS LEAVING?
YEAH, TAKING THE REST OF THE DAY OFF.
HEY, ARE YOU OKAY? YOUR EYES ARE KINDA...
I'M A WIMP, SO MY EYES ARE ALWAYS 'KINDA.' DON'T WORRY ABOUT IT.
ARE YOU STILL COMING TO THE REVIEWS?
YUP, WE'LL SEE YOU THERE! LATER!
HMM.
OH WELL, BACK TO WORK!
BUY!
BUY!

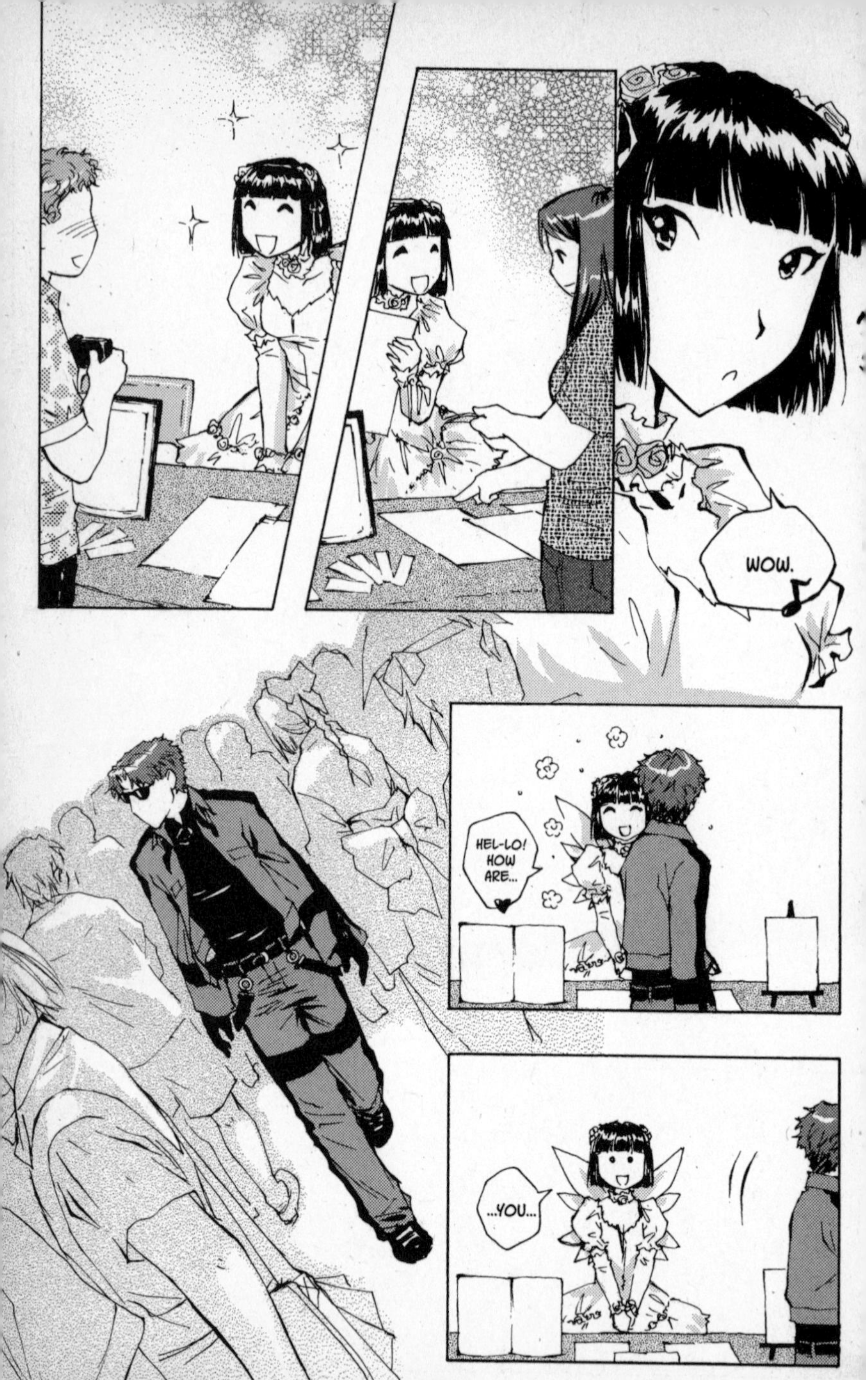
WOW.
HEL-LO! HOW ARE...
...YOU...

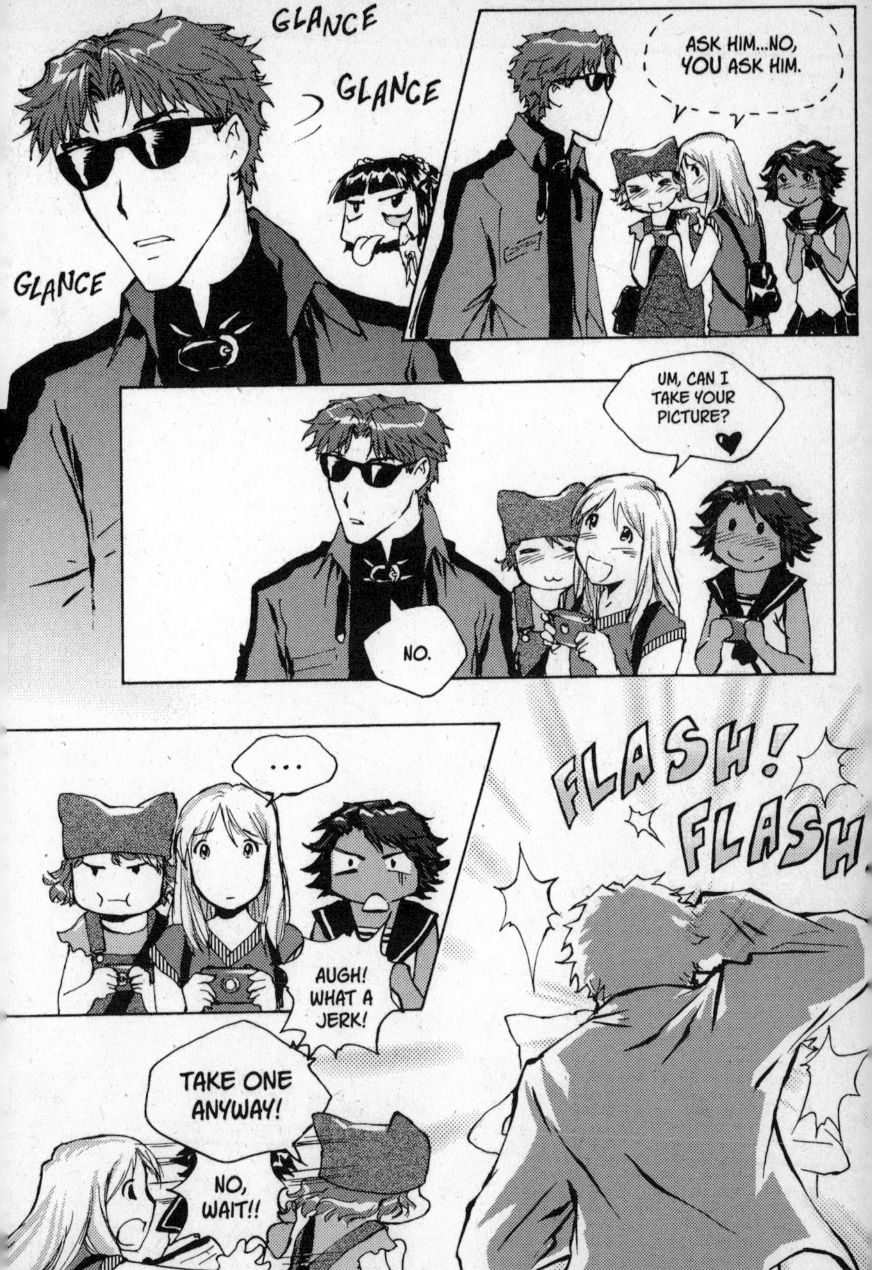
GLANCE
GLANCE
GLANCE
ASK HIM...NO, YOU ASK HIM.
UM, CAN I TAKE YOUR PICTURE? ♥
NO.
...
AUGH! WHAT A JERK!
TAKE ONE ANYWAY!
NO, WAIT!!
FLASH!
FLASH

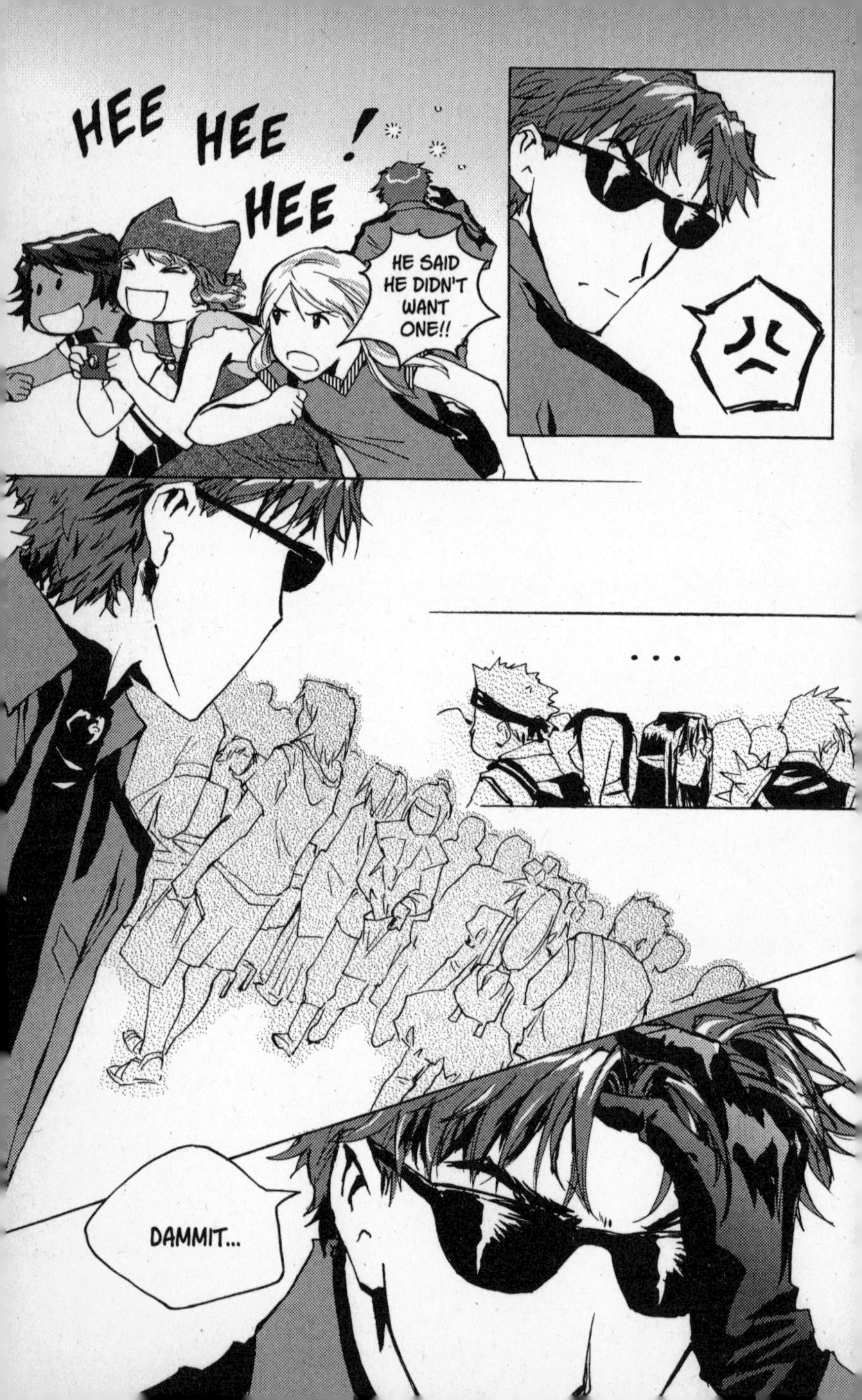
HEE HEE HEE
!
HE SAID HE DIDN'T WANT ONE!!
...
DAMMIT...

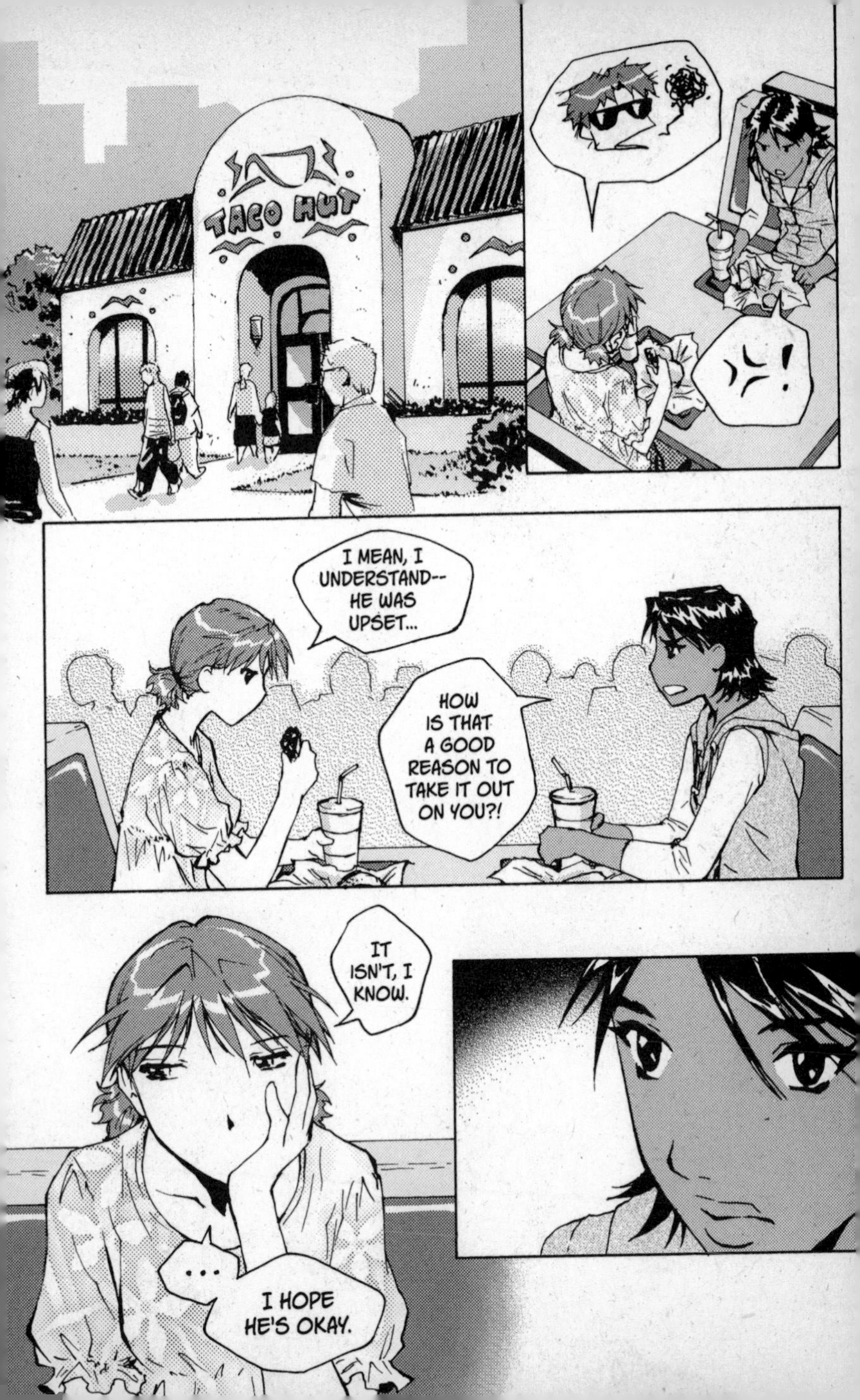
TACO HUT
!
I MEAN, I UNDERSTAND-- HE WAS UPSET...
HOW IS THAT A GOOD REASON TO TAKE IT OUT ON YOU?!
IT ISN'T, I KNOW.
...
I HOPE HE'S OKAY.

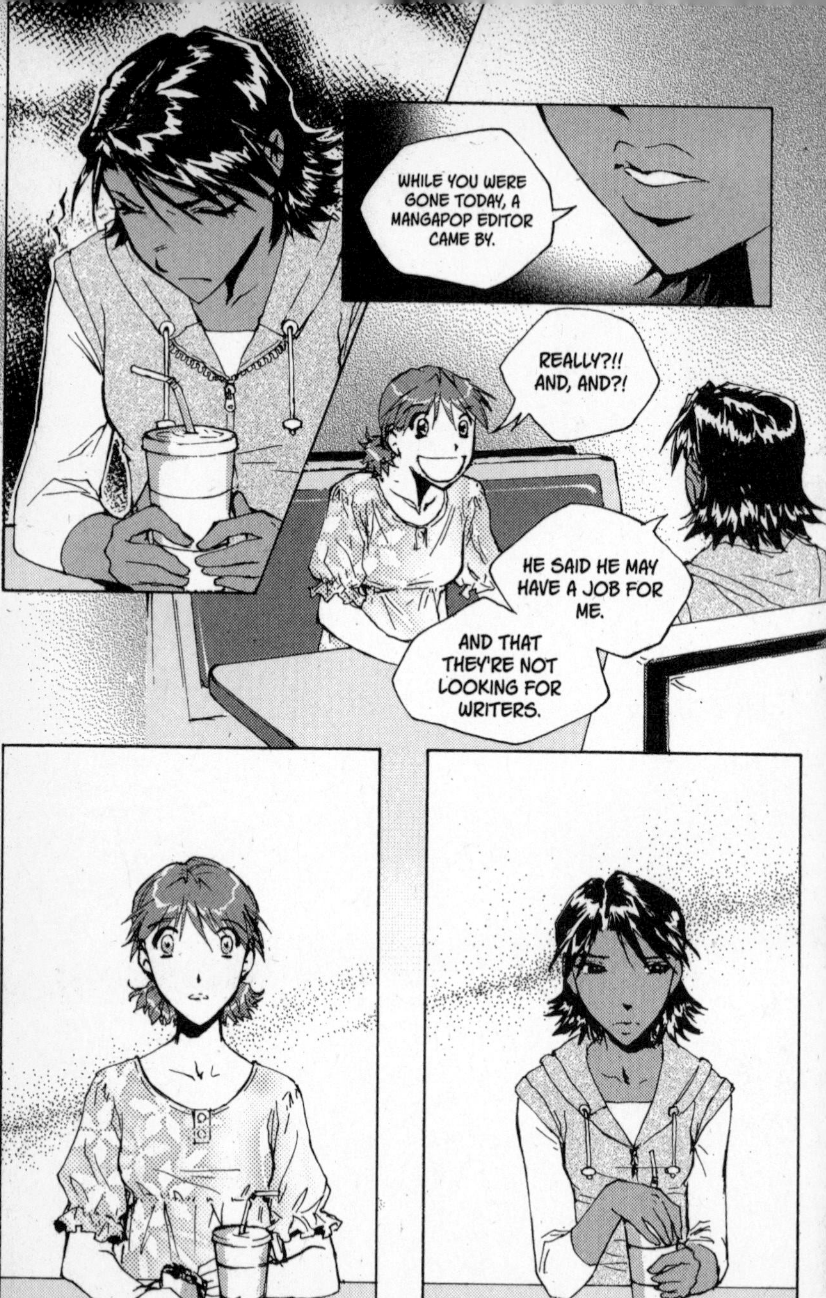
WHILE YOU WERE GONE TODAY, A MANGAPOP EDITOR CAME BY.
REALLY?!! AND, AND?!
HE SAID HE MAY HAVE A JOB FOR ME.
AND THAT THEY'RE NOT LOOKING FOR WRITERS.

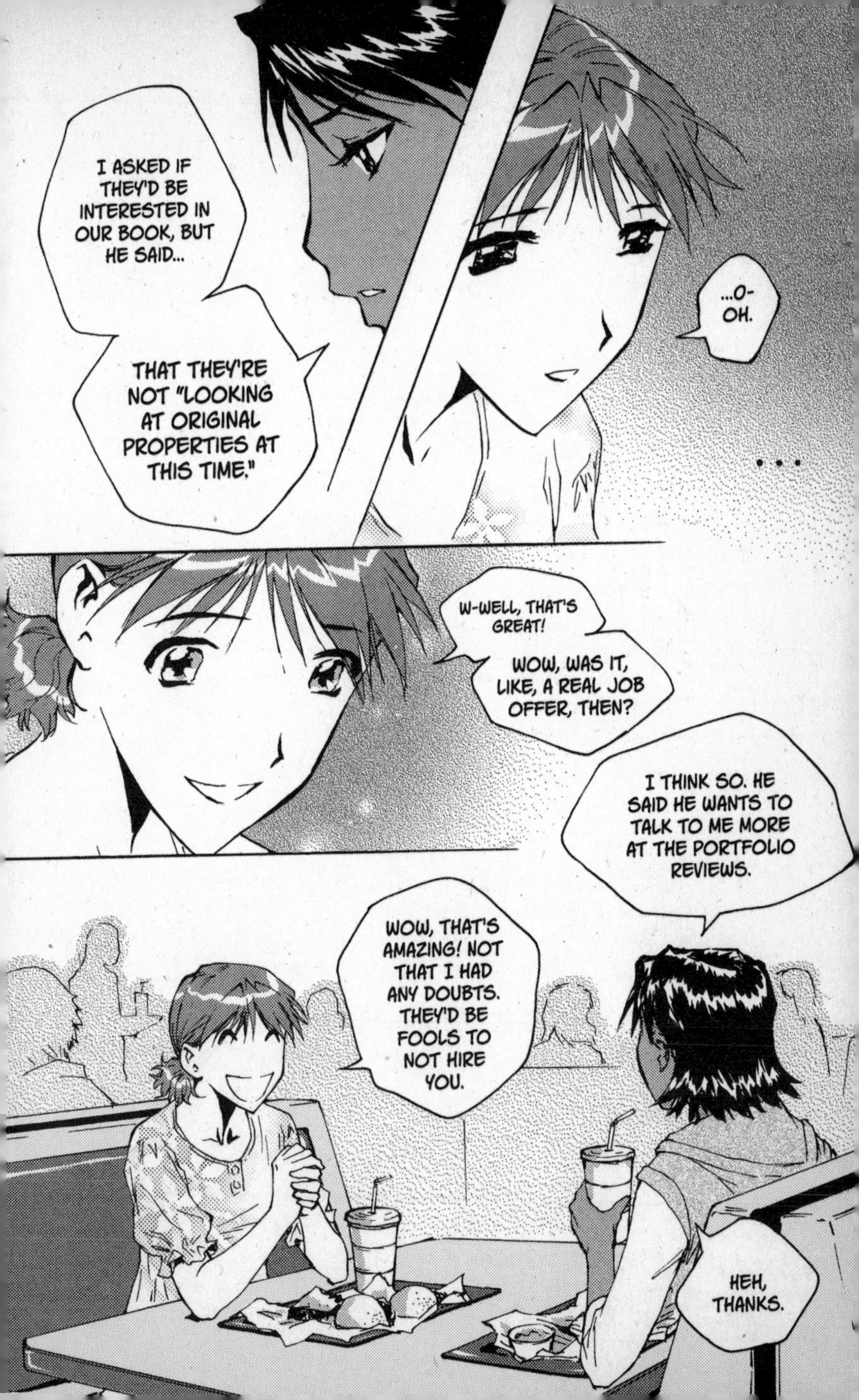
I ASKED IF THEY'D BE INTERESTED IN OUR BOOK, BUT HE SAID...
THAT THEY'RE NOT "LOOKING AT ORIGINAL PROPERTIES AT THIS TIME."
...O-OH.
...
W-WELL, THAT'S GREAT!
WOW, WAS IT, LIKE, A REAL JOB OFFER, THEN?
I THINK SO. HE SAID HE WANTS TO TALK TO ME MORE AT THE PORTFOLIO REVIEWS.
WOW, THAT'S AMAZING! NOT THAT I HAD ANY DOUBTS. THEY'D BE FOOLS TO NOT HIRE YOU.
HEH, THANKS.

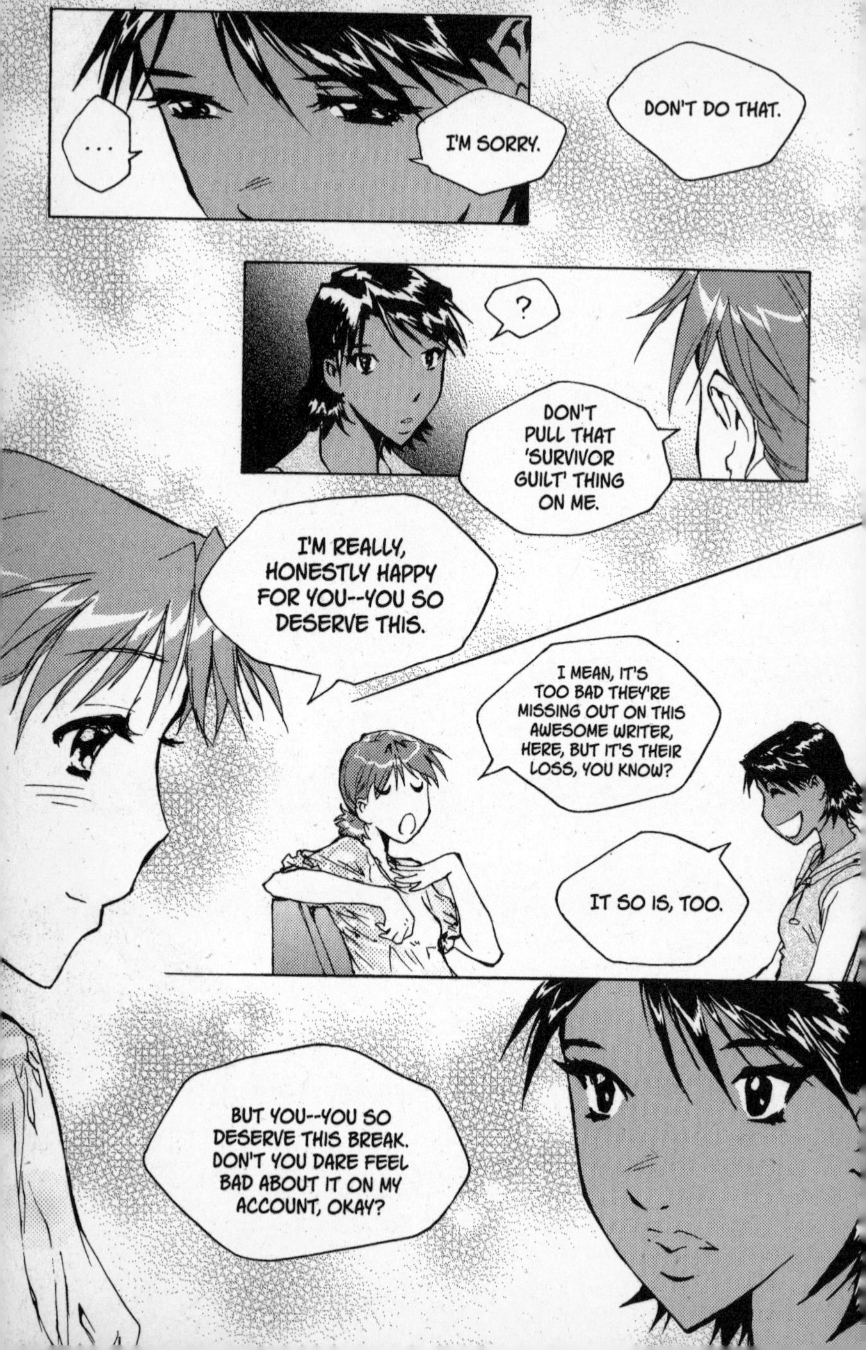
...
I'M SORRY.
DON'T DO THAT.
?
DON'T PULL THAT 'SURVIVOR GUILT' THING ON ME.
I'M REALLY, HONESTLY HAPPY FOR YOU--YOU SO DESERVE THIS.
I MEAN, IT'S TOO BAD THEY'RE MISSING OUT ON THIS AWESOME WRITER, HERE, BUT IT'S THEIR LOSS, YOU KNOW?
IT SO IS, TOO.
BUT YOU--YOU SO DESERVE THIS BREAK. DON'T YOU DARE FEEL BAD ABOUT IT ON MY ACCOUNT, OKAY?

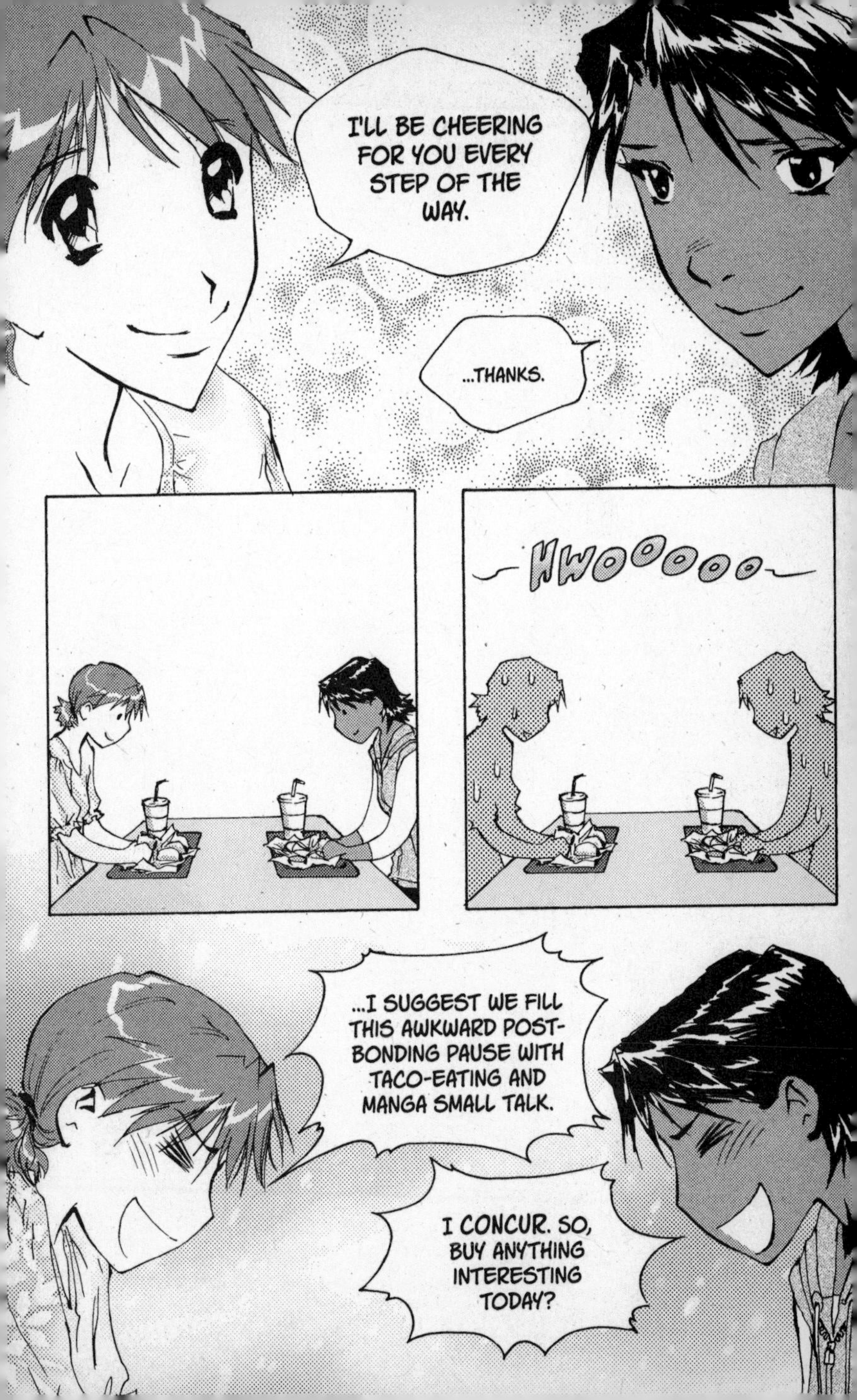
I'LL BE CHEERING FOR YOU EVERY STEP OF THE WAY.
...THANKS.
HWOOOOOO
...I SUGGEST WE FILL THIS AWKWARD POST-BONDING PAUSE WITH TACO-EATING AND MANGA SMALL TALK.
I CONCUR. SO, BUY ANYTHING INTERESTING TODAY?

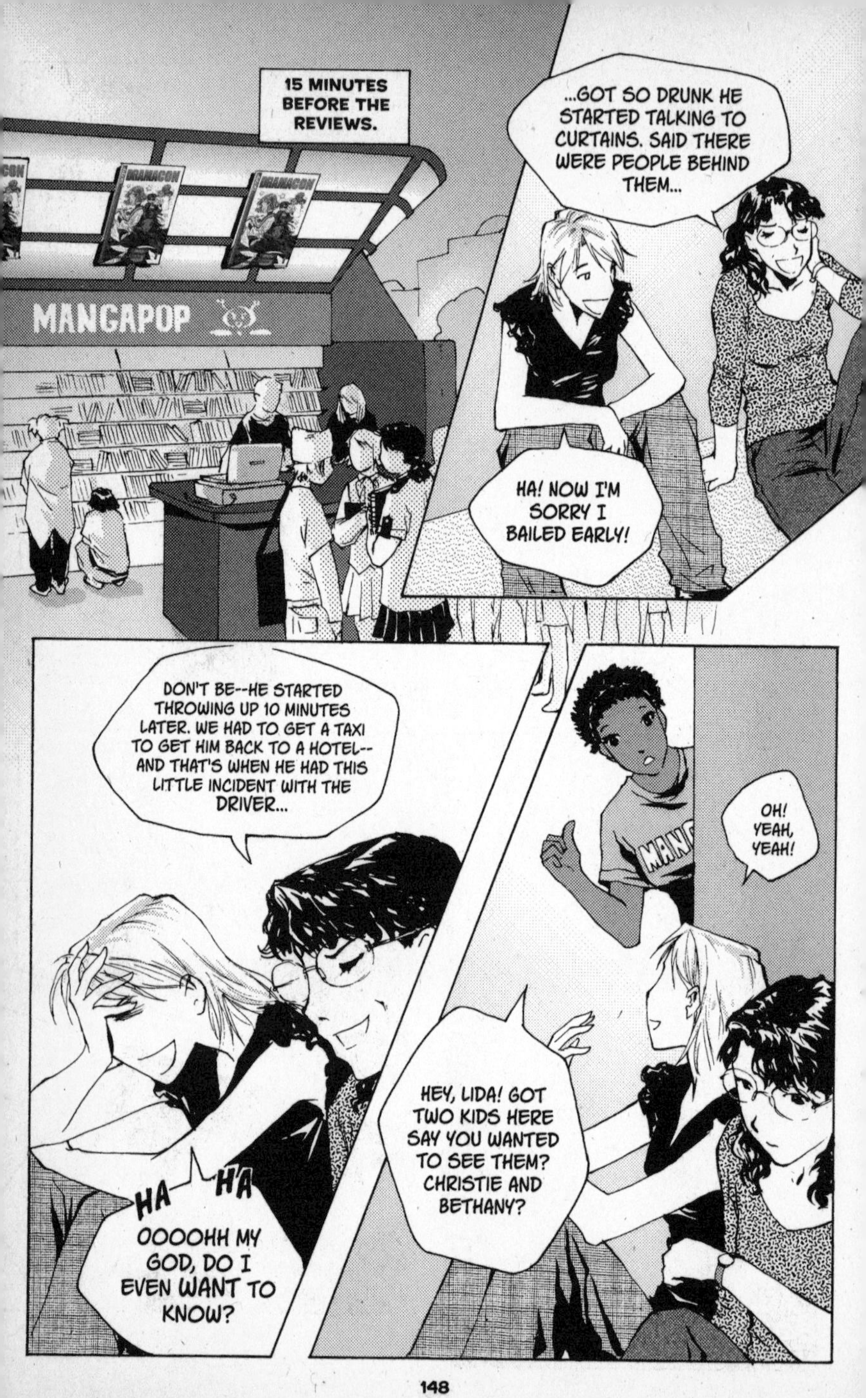
15 MINUTES BEFORE THE REVIEWS.
MANGAPOP
...GOT SO DRUNK HE STARTED TALKING TO CURTAINS. SAID THERE WERE PEOPLE BEHIND THEM...
HA! NOW I'M SORRY I BAILED EARLY!
DON'T BE--HE STARTED THROWING UP 10 MINUTES LATER. WE HAD TO GET A TAXI TO GET HIM BACK TO A HOTEL--AND THAT'S WHEN HE HAD THIS LITTLE INCIDENT WITH THE DRIVER...
HA HA
OOOOHH MY GOD, DO I EVEN WANT TO KNOW?
OH! YEAH, YEAH!
HEY, LIDA! GOT TWO KIDS HERE SAY YOU WANTED TO SEE THEM? CHRISTIE AND BETHANY?

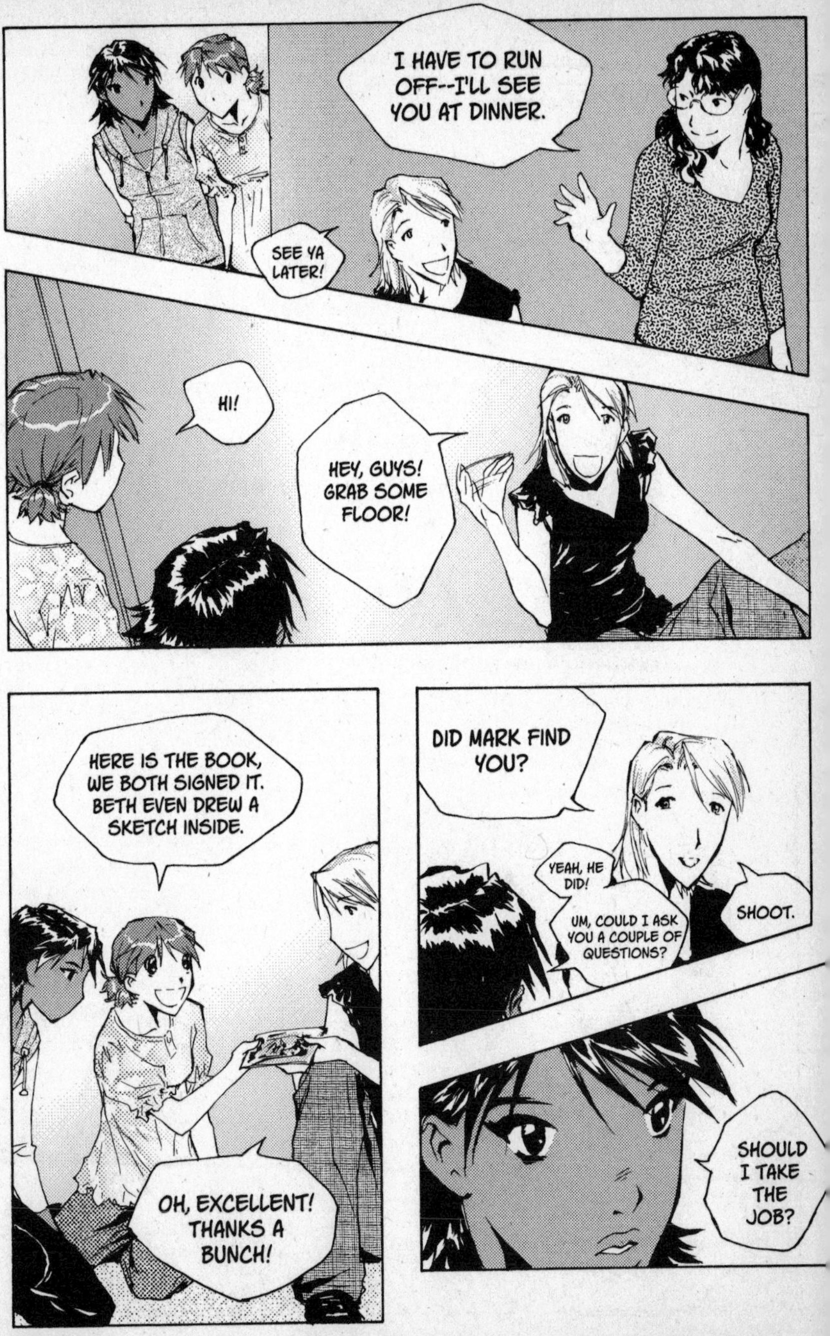
I HAVE TO RUN OFF--I'LL SEE YOU AT DINNER.
SEE YA LATER!
HI!
HEY, GUYS! GRAB SOME FLOOR!
HERE IS THE BOOK, WE BOTH SIGNED IT. BETH EVEN DREW A SKETCH INSIDE.
OH, EXCELLENT! THANKS A BUNCH!
DID MARK FIND YOU?
YEAH, HE DID!
UM, COULD I ASK YOU A COUPLE OF QUESTIONS?
SHOOT.
SHOULD I TAKE THE JOB?

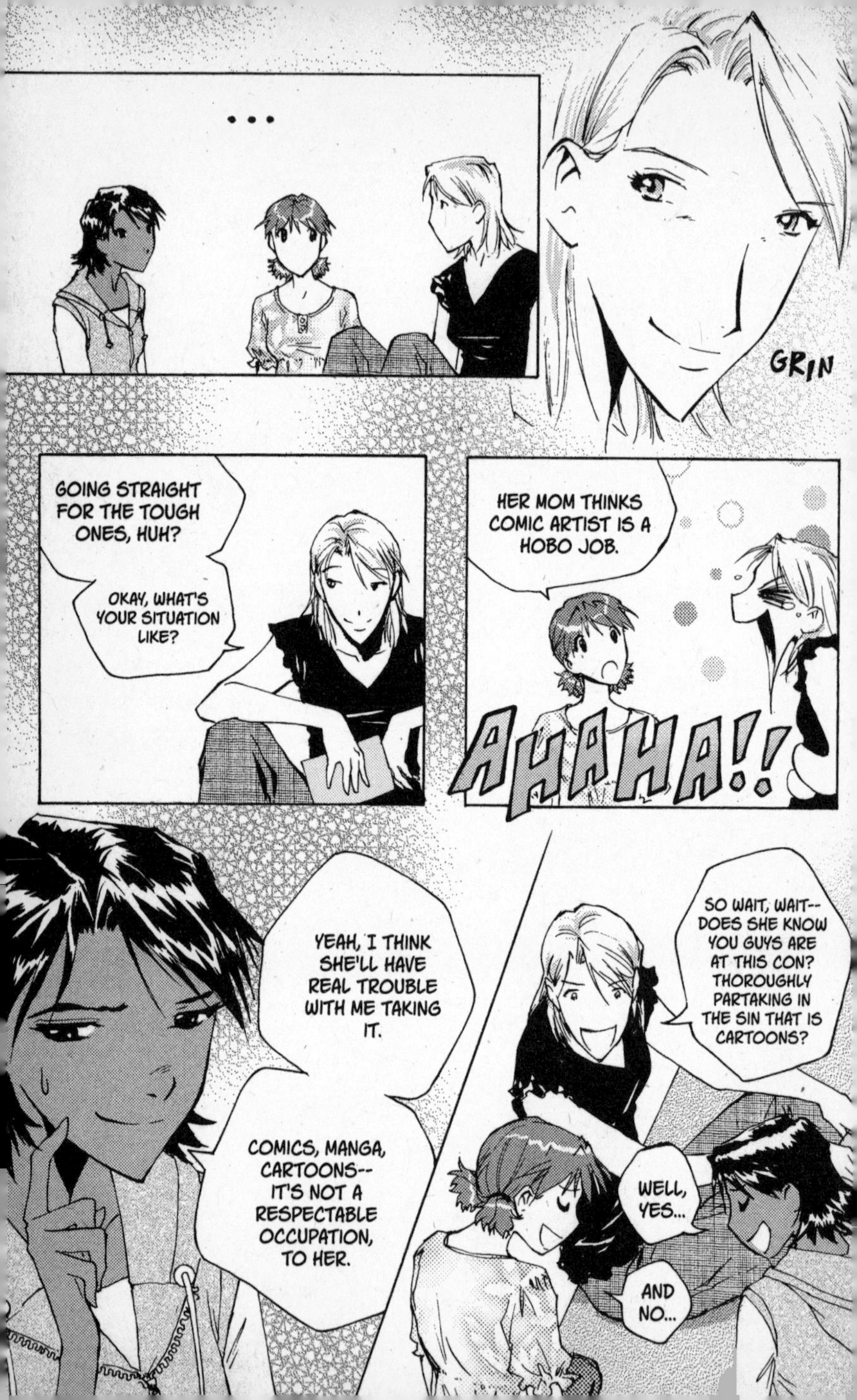
. . .
GRIN
GOING STRAIGHT FOR THE TOUGH ONES, HUH?
OKAY, WHAT'S YOUR SITUATION LIKE?
HER MOM THINKS COMIC ARTIST IS A HOBO JOB.
AHAHA!!
YEAH, I THINK SHE'LL HAVE REAL TROUBLE WITH ME TAKING IT.
COMICS, MANGA, CARTOONS-- IT'S NOT A RESPECTABLE OCCUPATION, TO HER.
SO WAIT, WAIT-- DOES SHE KNOW YOU GUYS ARE AT THIS CON? THOROUGHLY PARTAKING IN THE SIN THAT IS CARTOONS?
WELL, YES...
AND NO...

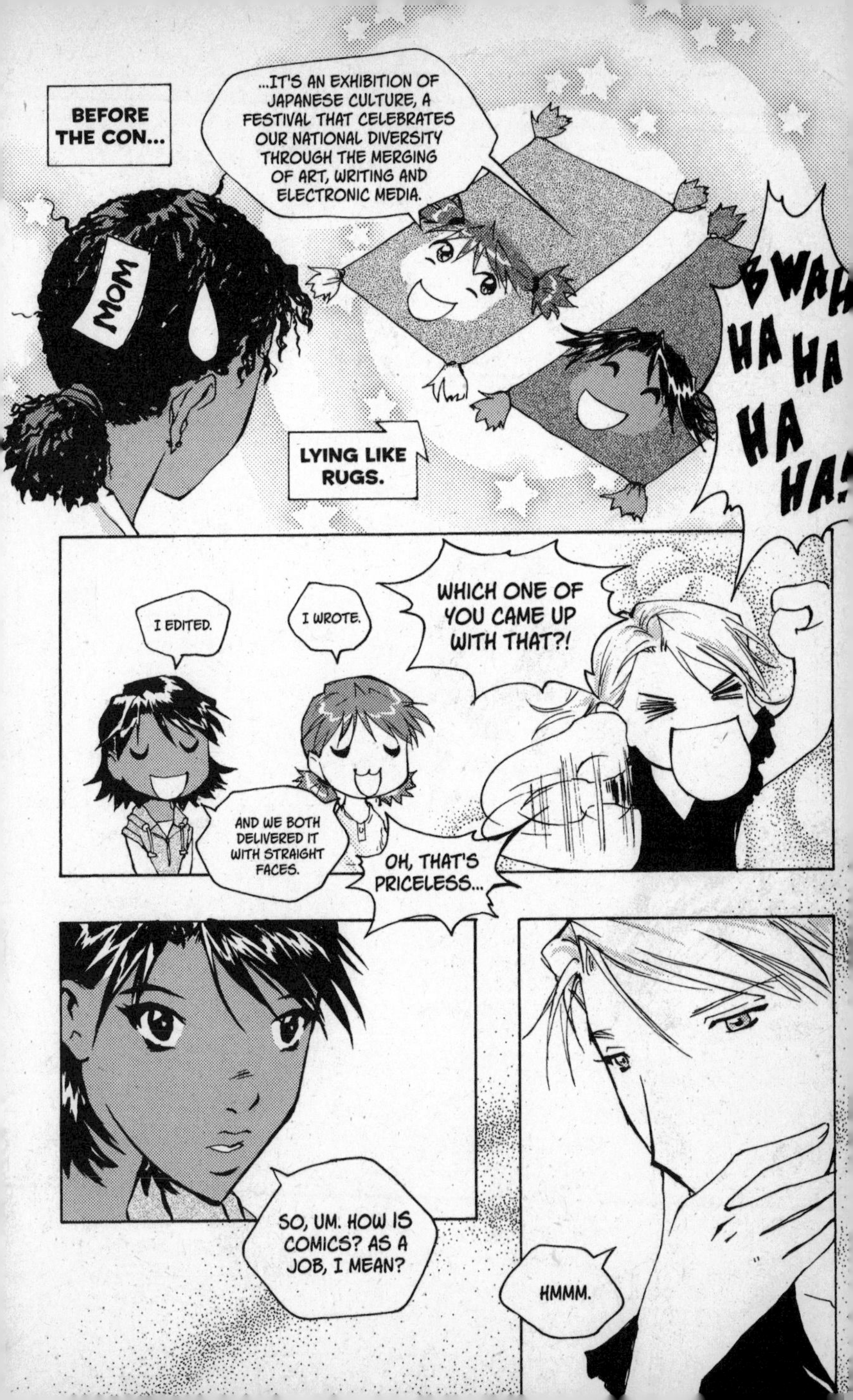
BEFORE THE CON...
...IT'S AN EXHIBITION OF JAPANESE CULTURE, A FESTIVAL THAT CELEBRATES OUR NATIONAL DIVERSITY THROUGH THE MERGING OF ART, WRITING AND ELECTRONIC MEDIA.
MOM
LYING LIKE RUGS.
BWAH HA HA HA HA HA!
I EDITED.
I WROTE.
WHICH ONE OF YOU CAME UP WITH THAT?!
AND WE BOTH DELIVERED IT WITH STRAIGHT FACES.
OH, THAT'S PRICELESS...
SO, UM. HOW IS COMICS? AS A JOB, I MEAN?
HMMM.

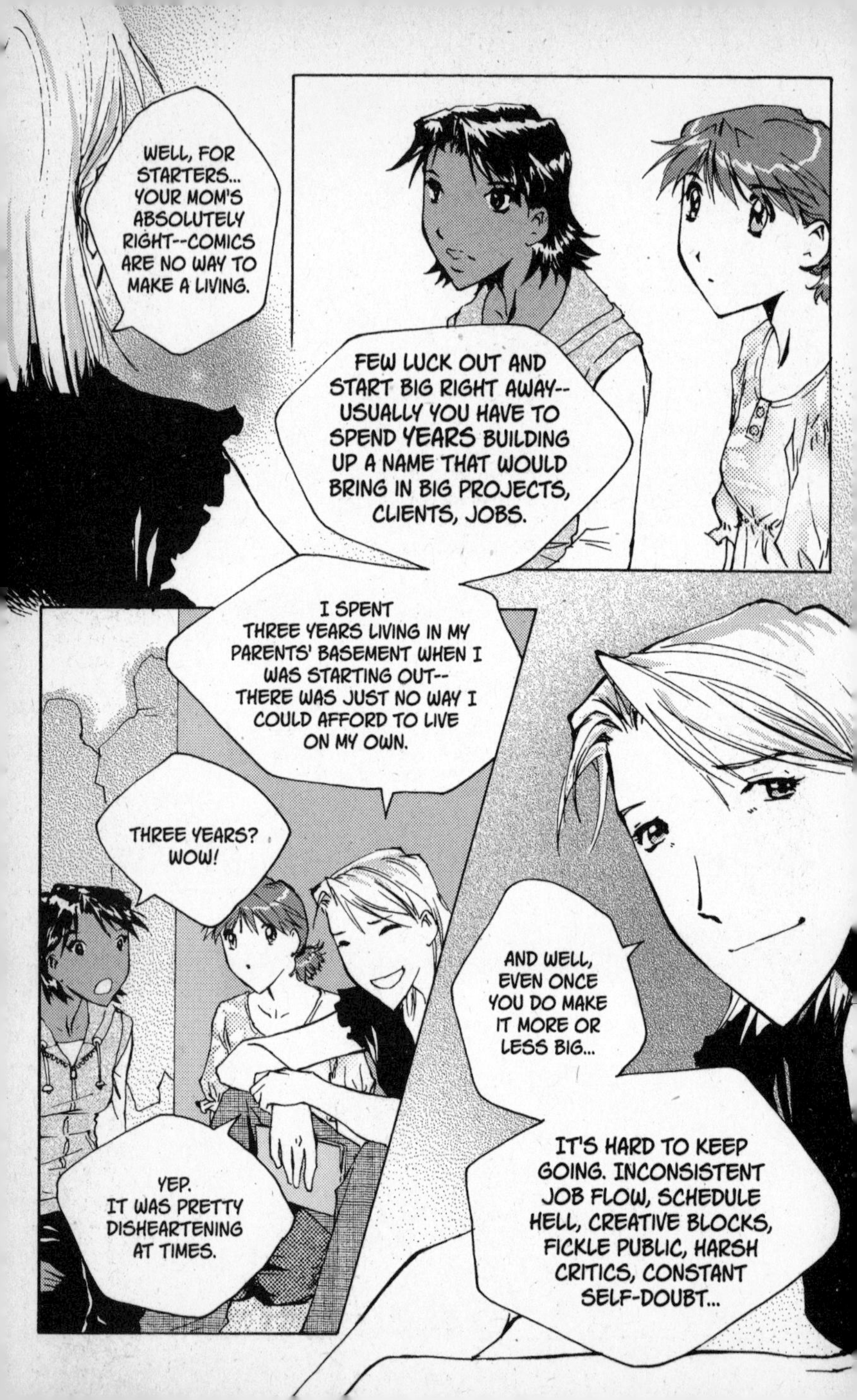
WELL, FOR STARTERS... YOUR MOM'S ABSOLUTELY RIGHT--COMICS ARE NO WAY TO MAKE A LIVING.
FEW LUCK OUT AND START BIG RIGHT AWAY--USUALLY YOU HAVE TO SPEND YEARS BUILDING UP A NAME THAT WOULD BRING IN BIG PROJECTS, CLIENTS, JOBS.
I SPENT THREE YEARS LIVING IN MY PARENTS' BASEMENT WHEN I WAS STARTING OUT--THERE WAS JUST NO WAY I COULD AFFORD TO LIVE ON MY OWN.
THREE YEARS? WOW!
YEP. IT WAS PRETTY DISHEARTENING AT TIMES.
AND WELL, EVEN ONCE YOU DO MAKE IT MORE OR LESS BIG...
IT'S HARD TO KEEP GOING. INCONSISTENT JOB FLOW, SCHEDULE HELL, CREATIVE BLOCKS, FICKLE PUBLIC, HARSH CRITICS, CONSTANT SELF-DOUBT...

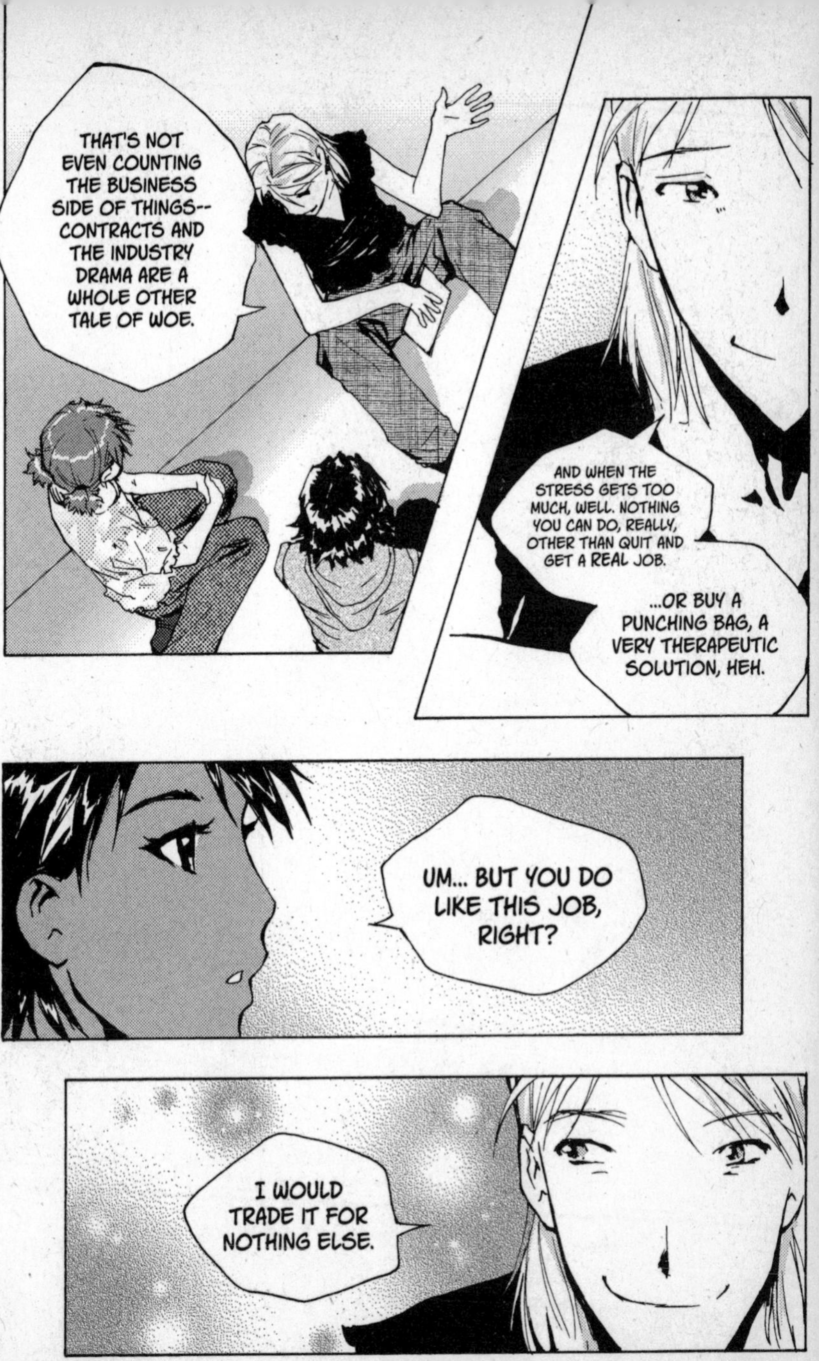
THAT'S NOT EVEN COUNTING THE BUSINESS SIDE OF THINGS-- CONTRACTS AND THE INDUSTRY DRAMA ARE A WHOLE OTHER TALE OF WOE.
AND WHEN THE STRESS GETS TOO MUCH, WELL. NOTHING YOU CAN DO, REALLY, OTHER THAN QUIT AND GET A REAL JOB.
...OR BUY A PUNCHING BAG, A VERY THERAPEUTIC SOLUTION, HEH.
UM... BUT YOU DO LIKE THIS JOB, RIGHT?
I WOULD TRADE IT FOR NOTHING ELSE.

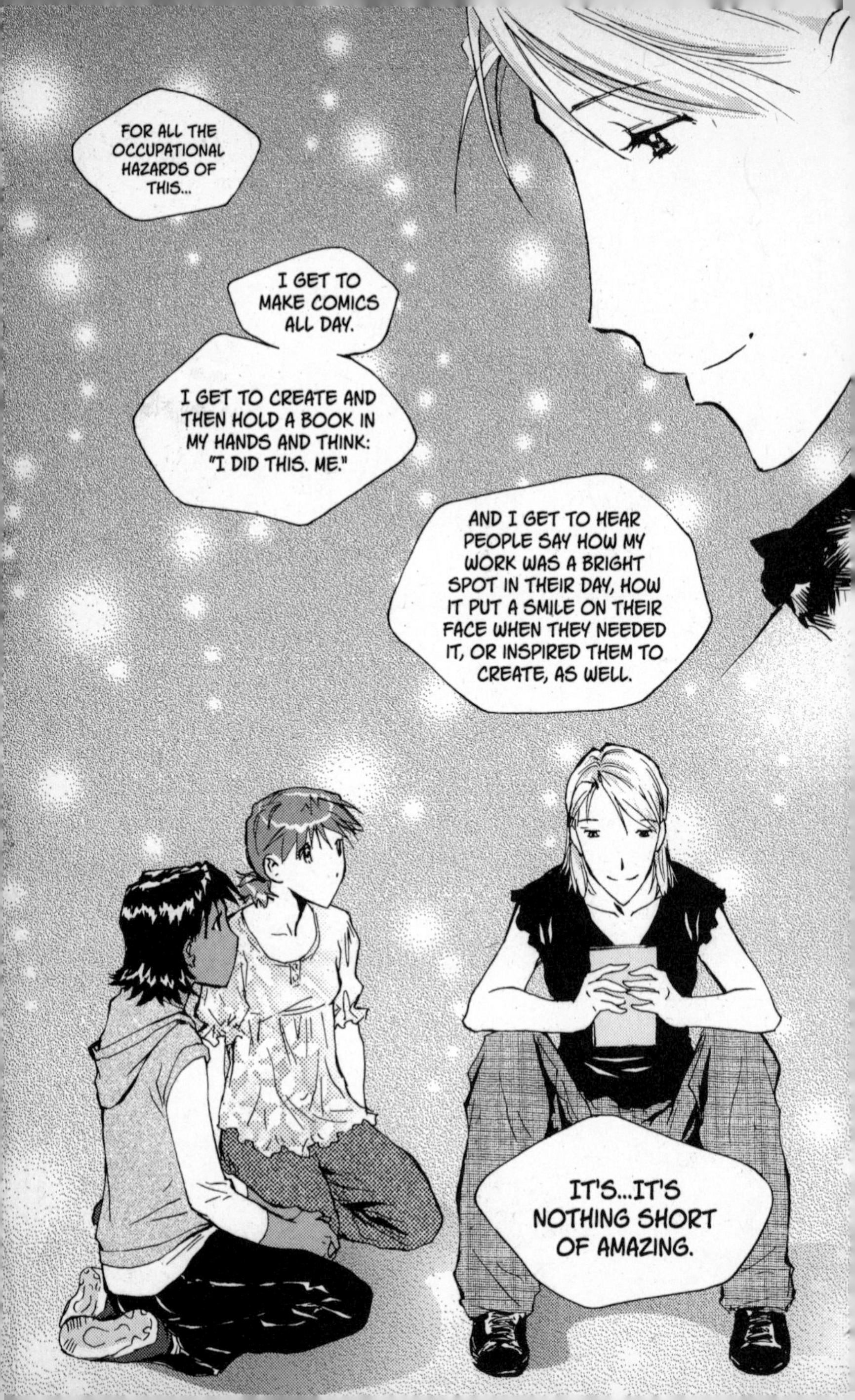
FOR ALL THE OCCUPATIONAL HAZARDS OF THIS...
I GET TO MAKE COMICS ALL DAY.
I GET TO CREATE AND THEN HOLD A BOOK IN MY HANDS AND THINK: "I DID THIS. ME."
AND I GET TO HEAR PEOPLE SAY HOW MY WORK WAS A BRIGHT SPOT IN THEIR DAY, HOW IT PUT A SMILE ON THEIR FACE WHEN THEY NEEDED IT, OR INSPIRED THEM TO CREATE, AS WELL.
IT'S...IT'S NOTHING SHORT OF AMAZING.

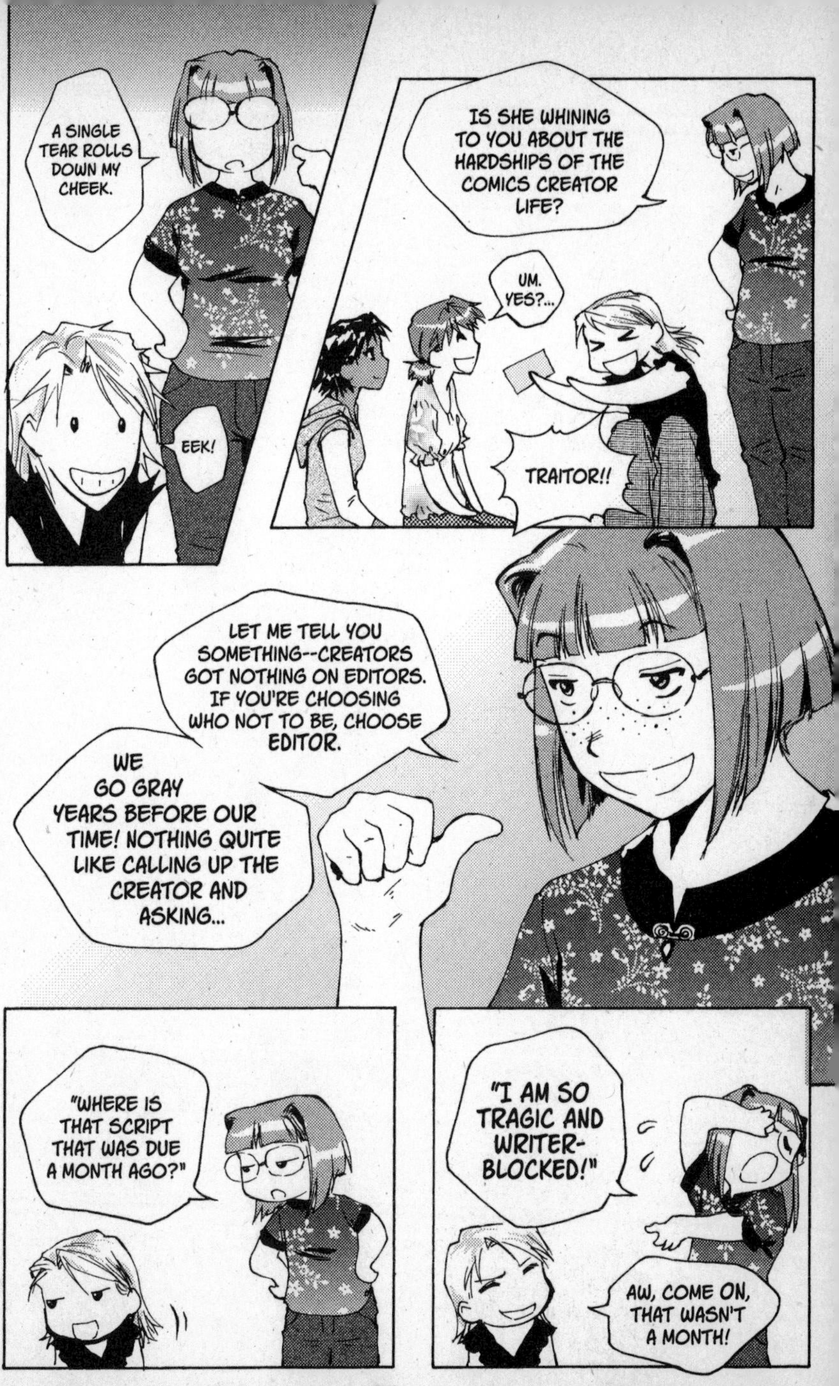
A SINGLE TEAR ROLLS DOWN MY CHEEK.
EEK!
IS SHE WHINING TO YOU ABOUT THE HARDSHIPS OF THE COMICS CREATOR LIFE?
UM. YES?...
TRAITOR!!
LET ME TELL YOU SOMETHING--CREATORS GOT NOTHING ON EDITORS. IF YOU'RE CHOOSING WHO NOT TO BE, CHOOSE EDITOR.
WE GO GRAY YEARS BEFORE OUR TIME! NOTHING QUITE LIKE CALLING UP THE CREATOR AND ASKING...
"WHERE IS THAT SCRIPT THAT WAS DUE A MONTH AGO?"
"I AM SO TRAGIC AND WRITER-BLOCKED!"
AW, COME ON, THAT WASN'T A MONTH!

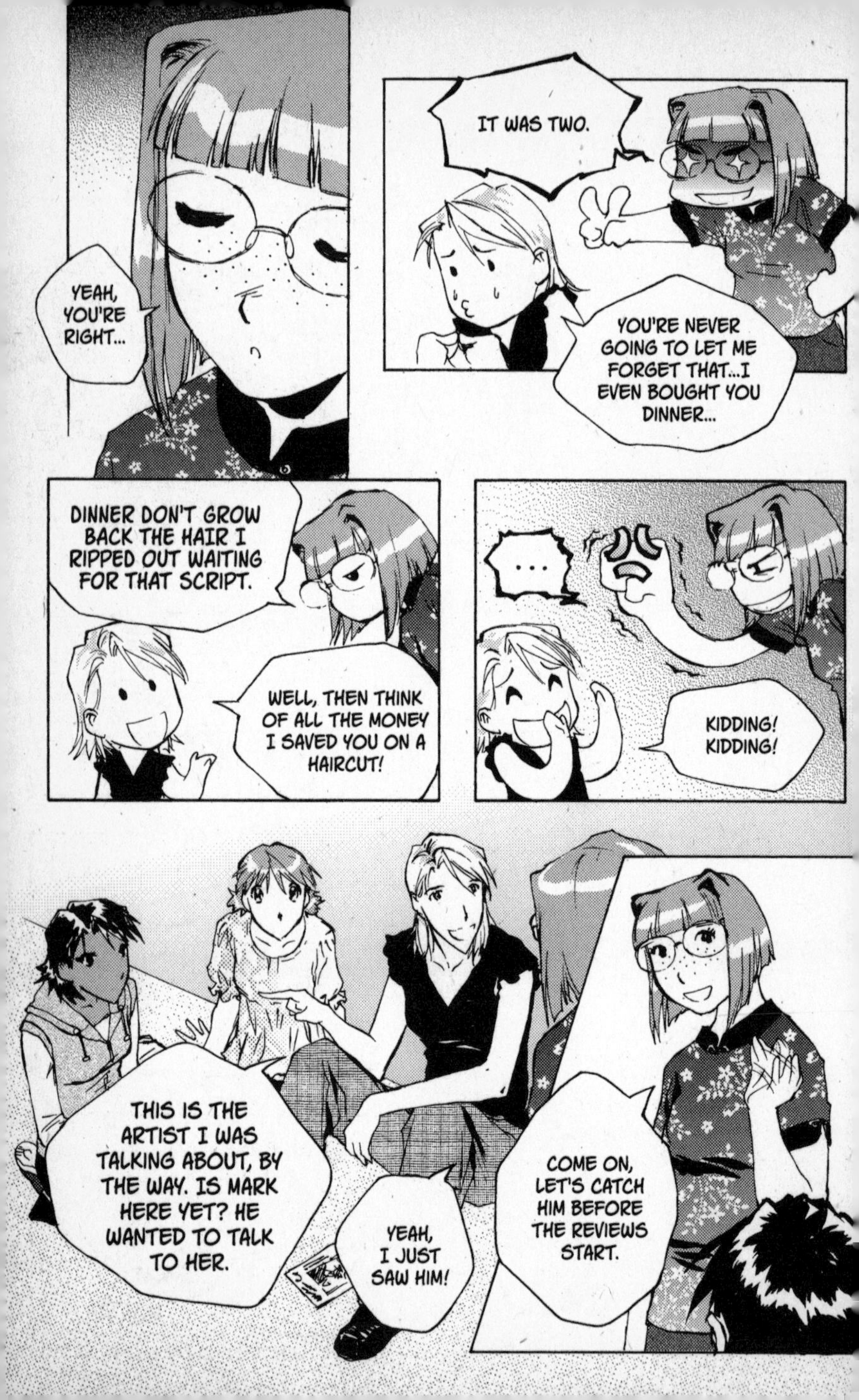

YEAH, YOU'RE RIGHT...
IT WAS TWO.
YOU'RE NEVER GOING TO LET ME FORGET THAT...I EVEN BOUGHT YOU DINNER...
DINNER DON'T GROW BACK THE HAIR I RIPPED OUT WAITING FOR THAT SCRIPT.
WELL, THEN THINK OF ALL THE MONEY I SAVED YOU ON A HAIRCUT!
...
KIDDING! KIDDING!
THIS IS THE ARTIST I WAS TALKING ABOUT, BY THE WAY. IS MARK HERE YET? HE WANTED TO TALK TO HER.
YEAH, I JUST SAW HIM!
COME ON, LET'S CATCH HIM BEFORE THE REVIEWS START.

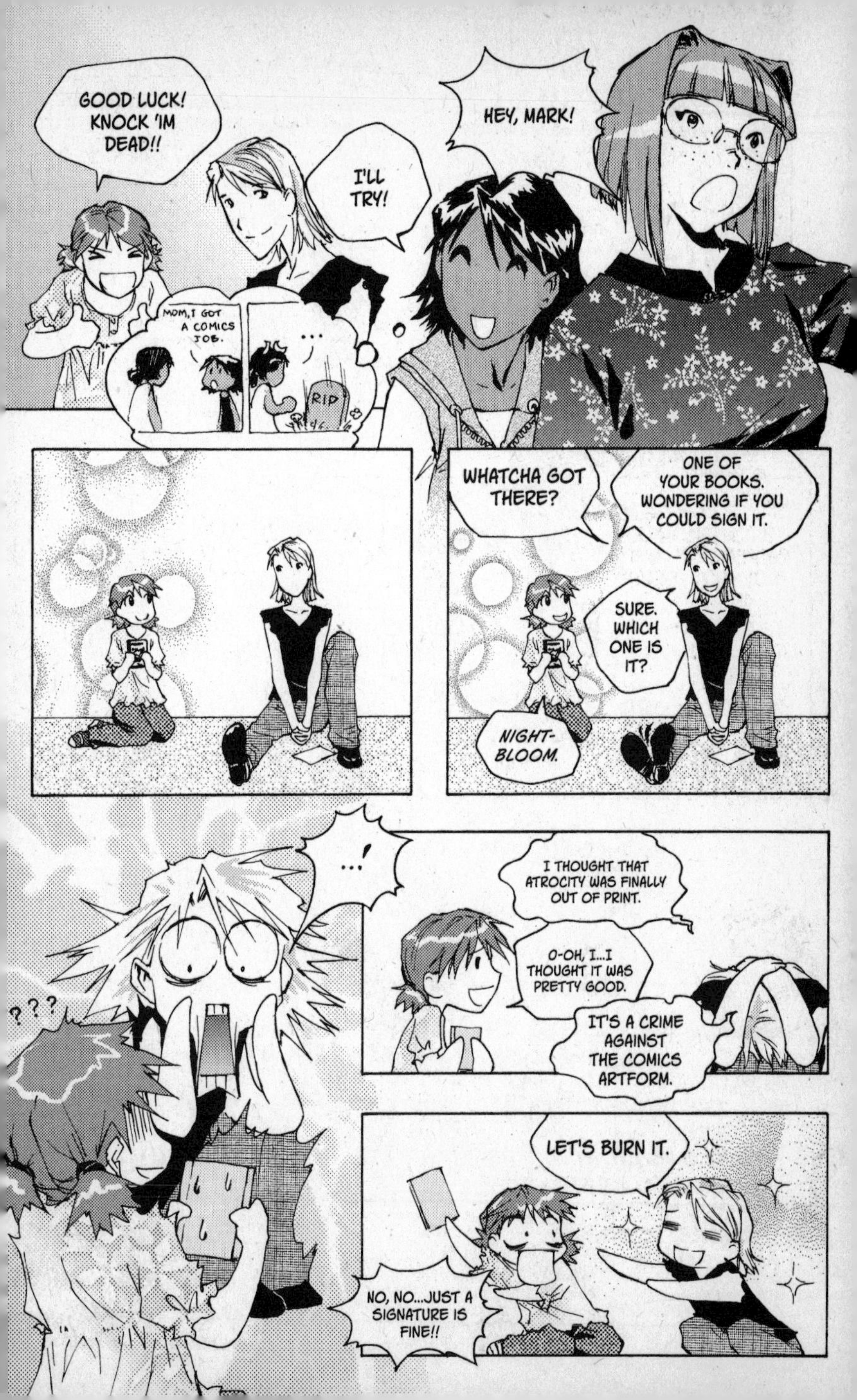
GOOD LUCK! KNOCK 'IM DEAD!!
I'LL TRY!
MOM, I GOT A COMICS JOB.
...
RIP
HEY, MARK!
WHATCHA GOT THERE?
ONE OF YOUR BOOKS. WONDERING IF YOU COULD SIGN IT.
SURE. WHICH ONE IS IT?
NIGHT-BLOOM.
...!
???
I THOUGHT THAT ATROCITY WAS FINALLY OUT OF PRINT.
O-OH, I...I THOUGHT IT WAS PRETTY GOOD.
IT'S A CRIME AGAINST THE COMICS ARTFORM.
LET'S BURN IT.
NO, NO...JUST A SIGNATURE IS FINE!!

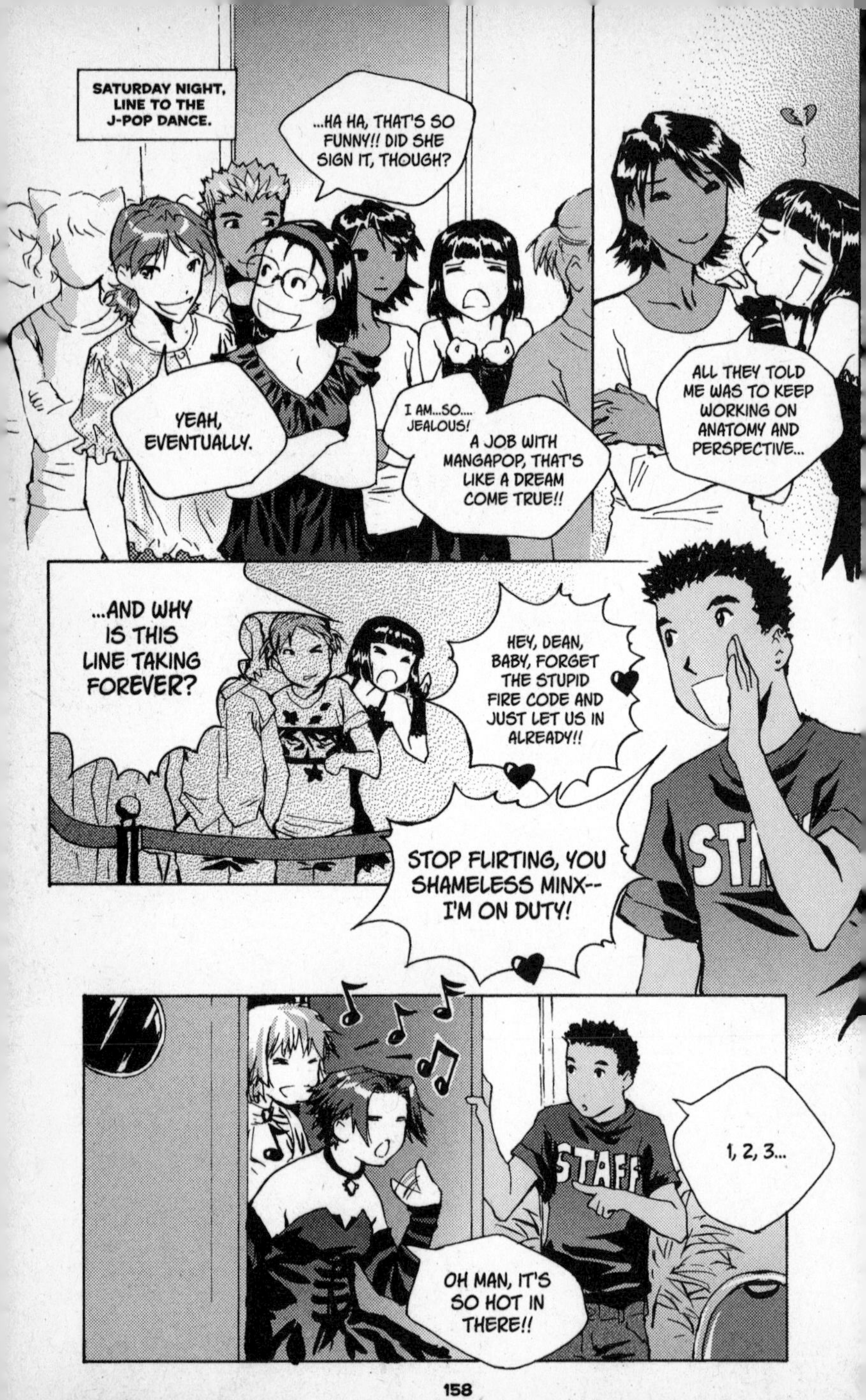
SATURDAY NIGHT, LINE TO THE J-POP DANCE.
...HA HA, THAT'S SO FUNNY!! DID SHE SIGN IT, THOUGH?
YEAH, EVENTUALLY.
I AM...SO... JEALOUS!
A JOB WITH MANGAPOP, THAT'S LIKE A DREAM COME TRUE!!
ALL THEY TOLD ME WAS TO KEEP WORKING ON ANATOMY AND PERSPECTIVE...
...AND WHY IS THIS LINE TAKING FOREVER?
HEY, DEAN, BABY, FORGET THE STUPID FIRE CODE AND JUST LET US IN ALREADY!!
STAFF
STOP FLIRTING, YOU SHAMELESS MINX-- I'M ON DUTY!
STAFF
OH MAN, IT'S SO HOT IN THERE!!
1, 2, 3...

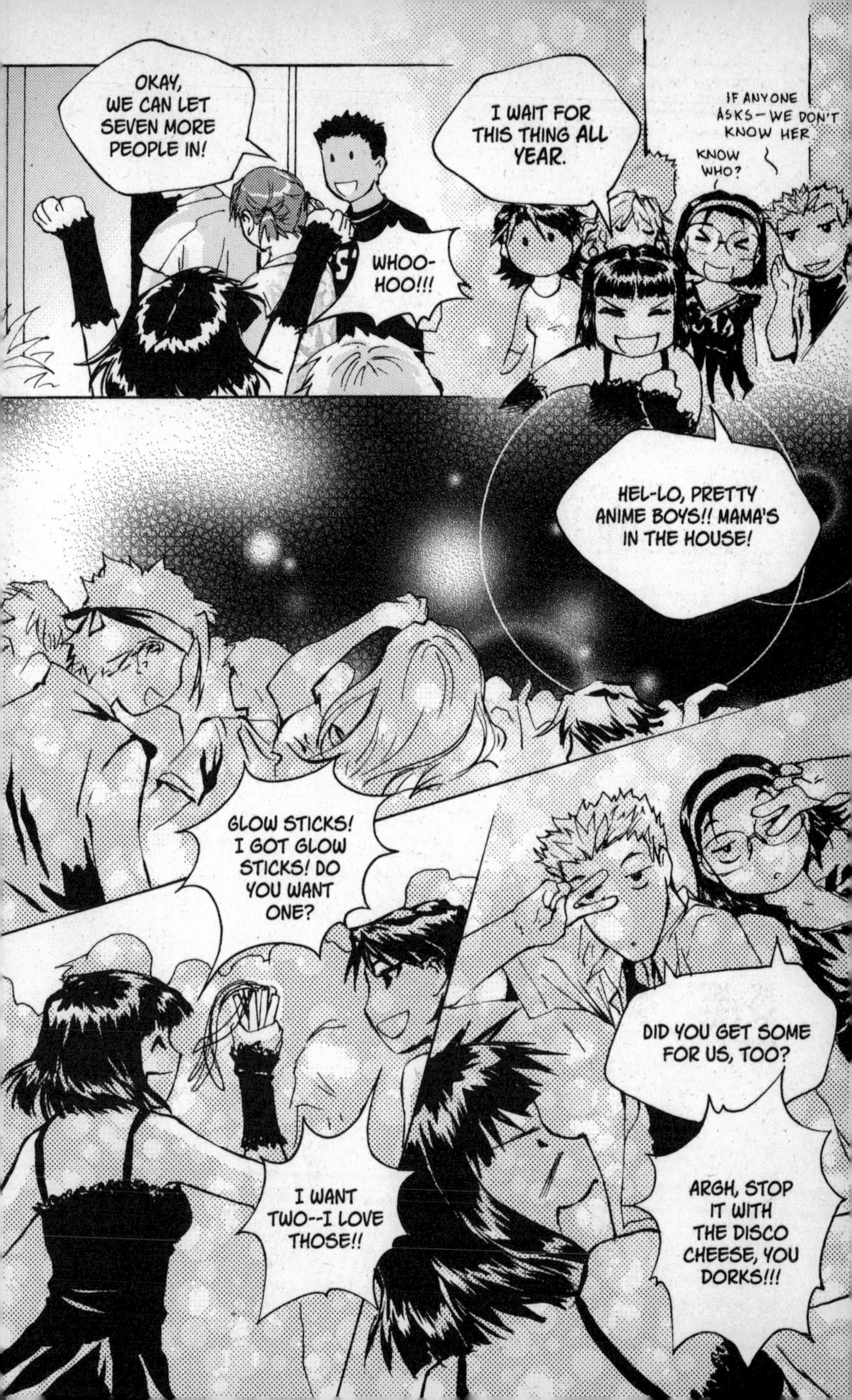
OKAY, WE CAN LET SEVEN MORE PEOPLE IN!
WHOO-HOO!!!
I WAIT FOR THIS THING ALL YEAR.
IF ANYONE ASKS—WE DON'T KNOW HER
KNOW WHO?
HEL-LO, PRETTY ANIME BOYS!! MAMA'S IN THE HOUSE!
GLOW STICKS! I GOT GLOW STICKS! DO YOU WANT ONE?
I WANT TWO--I LOVE THOSE!!
DID YOU GET SOME FOR US, TOO?
ARGH, STOP IT WITH THE DISCO CHEESE, YOU DORKS!!!

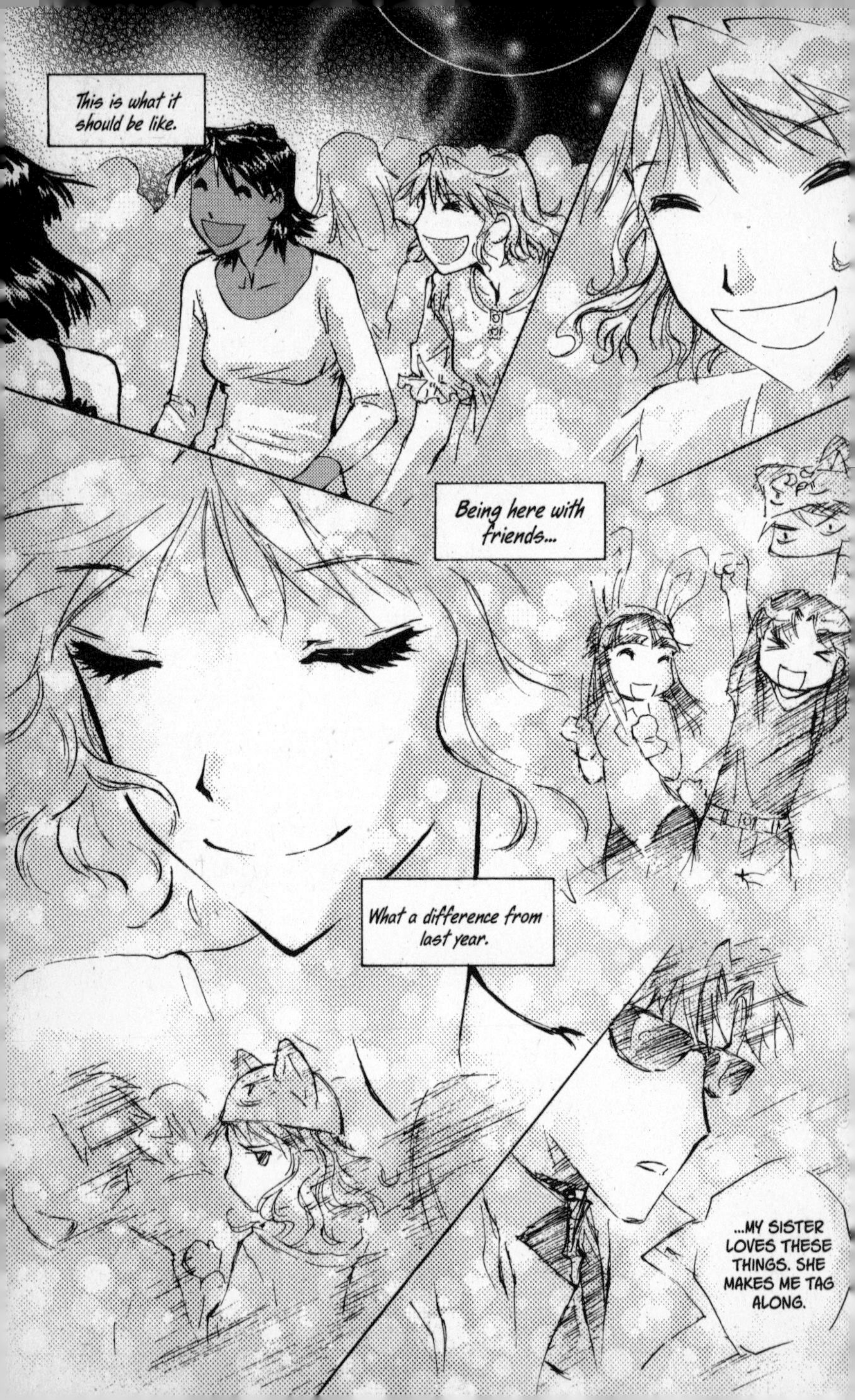
This is what it should be like.
Being here with friends...
What a difference from last year.
...MY SISTER LOVES THESE THINGS. SHE MAKES ME TAG ALONG.

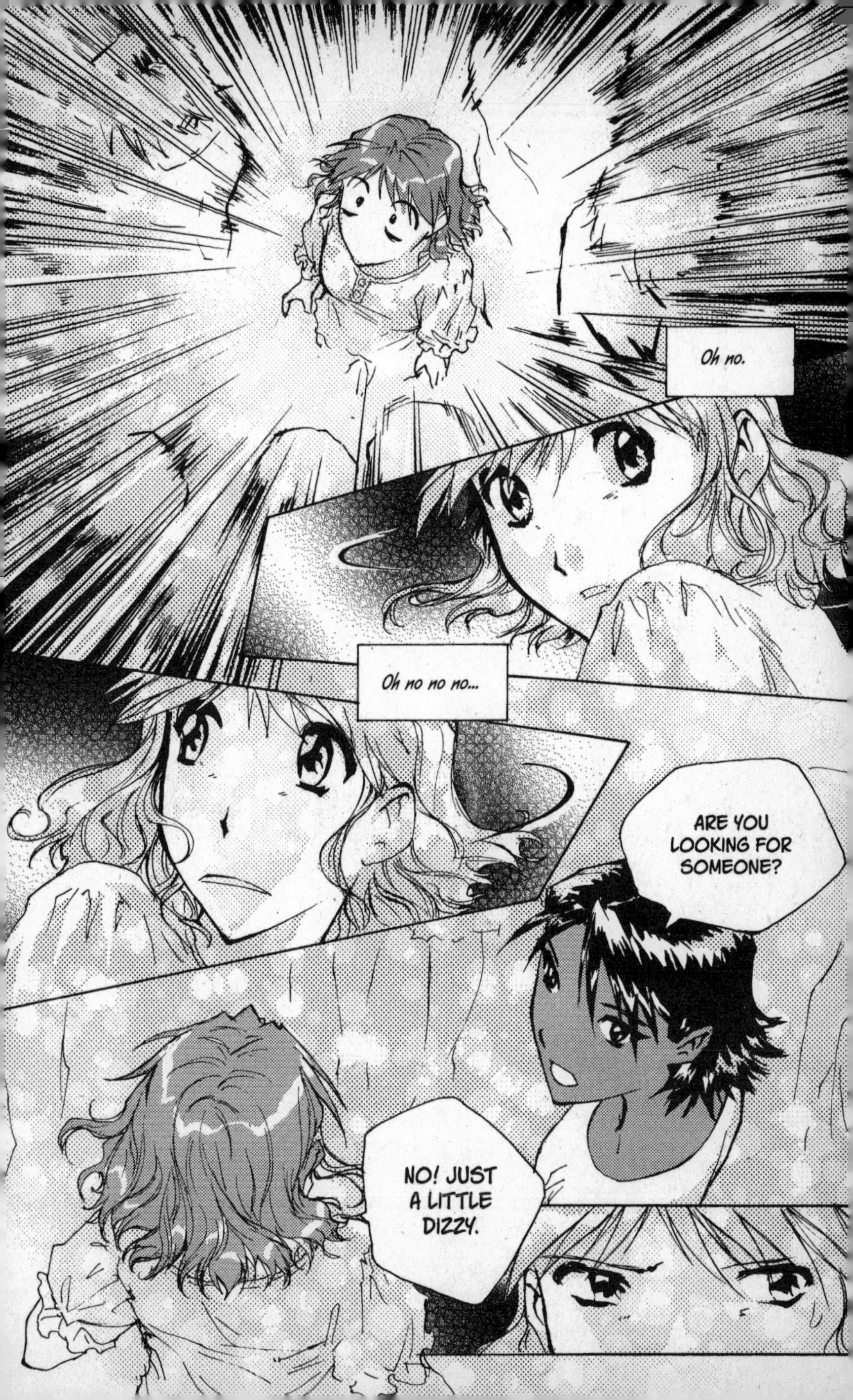
Oh no.
Oh no no no...
ARE YOU LOOKING FOR SOMEONE?
NO! JUST A LITTLE DIZZY.

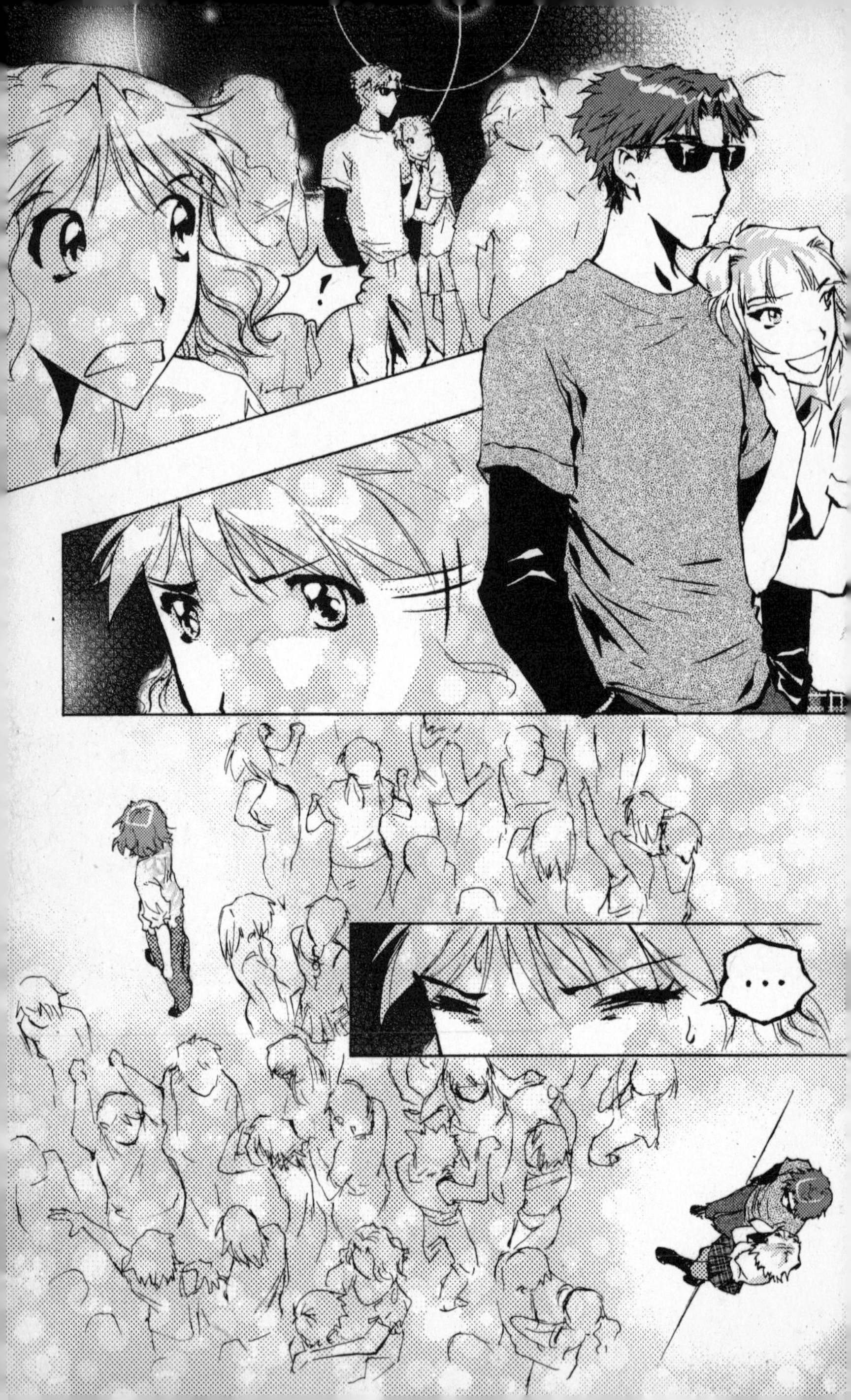
!
...

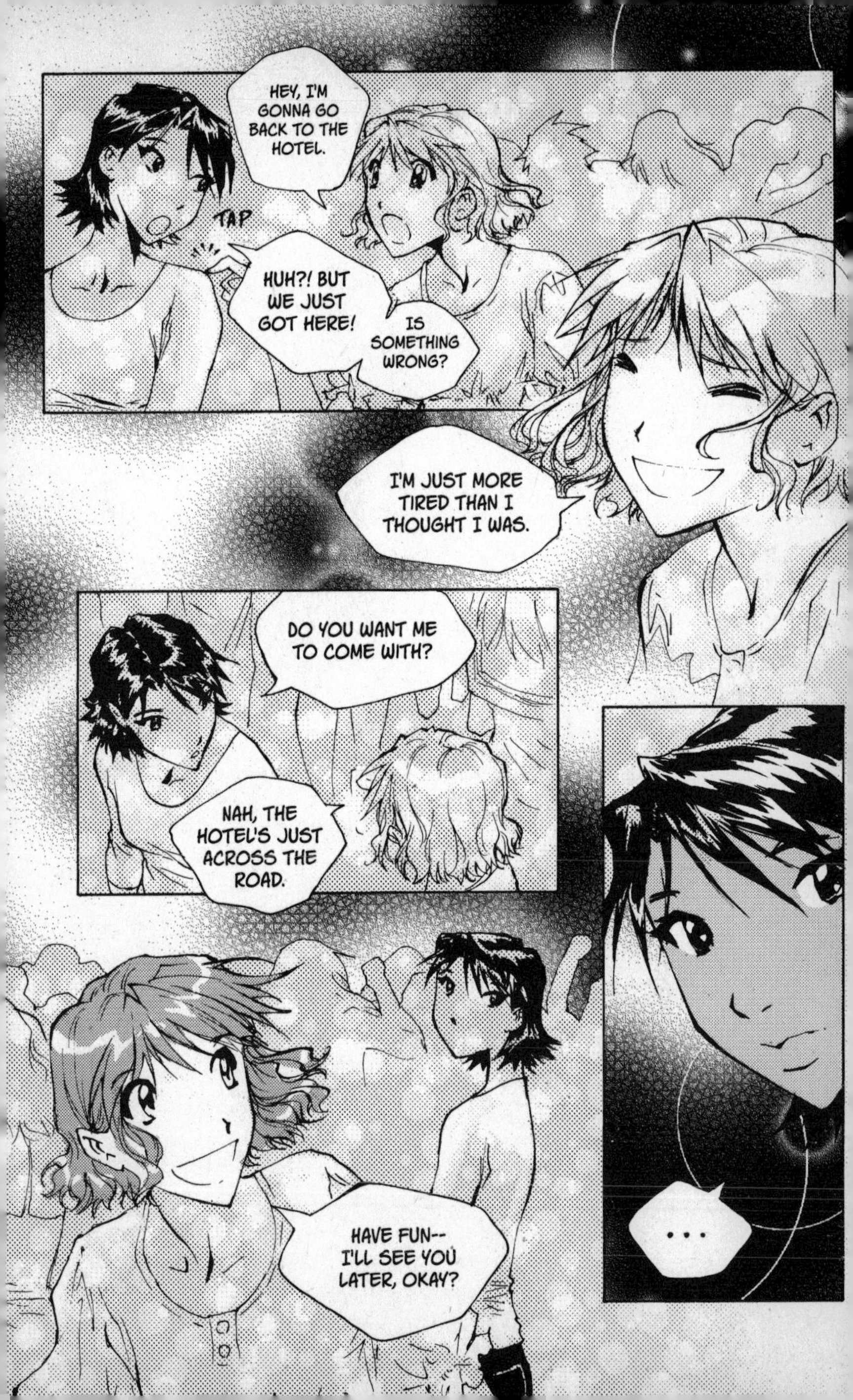
HEY, I'M GONNA GO BACK TO THE HOTEL.
TAP
HUH?! BUT WE JUST GOT HERE!
IS SOMETHING WRONG?
I'M JUST MORE TIRED THAN I THOUGHT I WAS.
DO YOU WANT ME TO COME WITH?
NAH, THE HOTEL'S JUST ACROSS THE ROAD.
HAVE FUN-- I'LL SEE YOU LATER, OKAY?
...

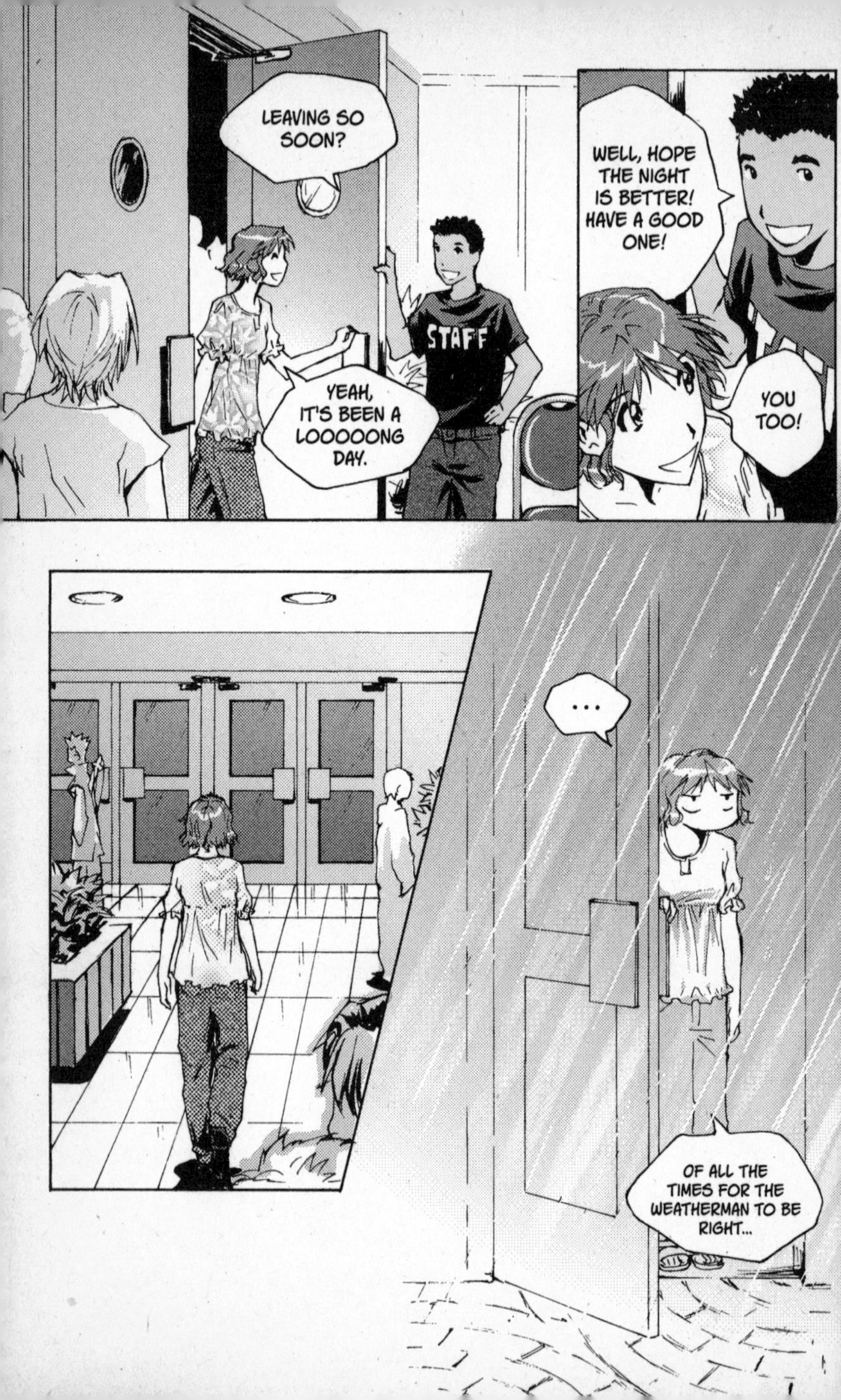
LEAVING SO SOON?
YEAH, IT'S BEEN A LOOOOONG DAY.
WELL, HOPE THE NIGHT IS BETTER! HAVE A GOOD ONE!
YOU TOO!
...
OF ALL THE TIMES FOR THE WEATHERMAN TO BE RIGHT...

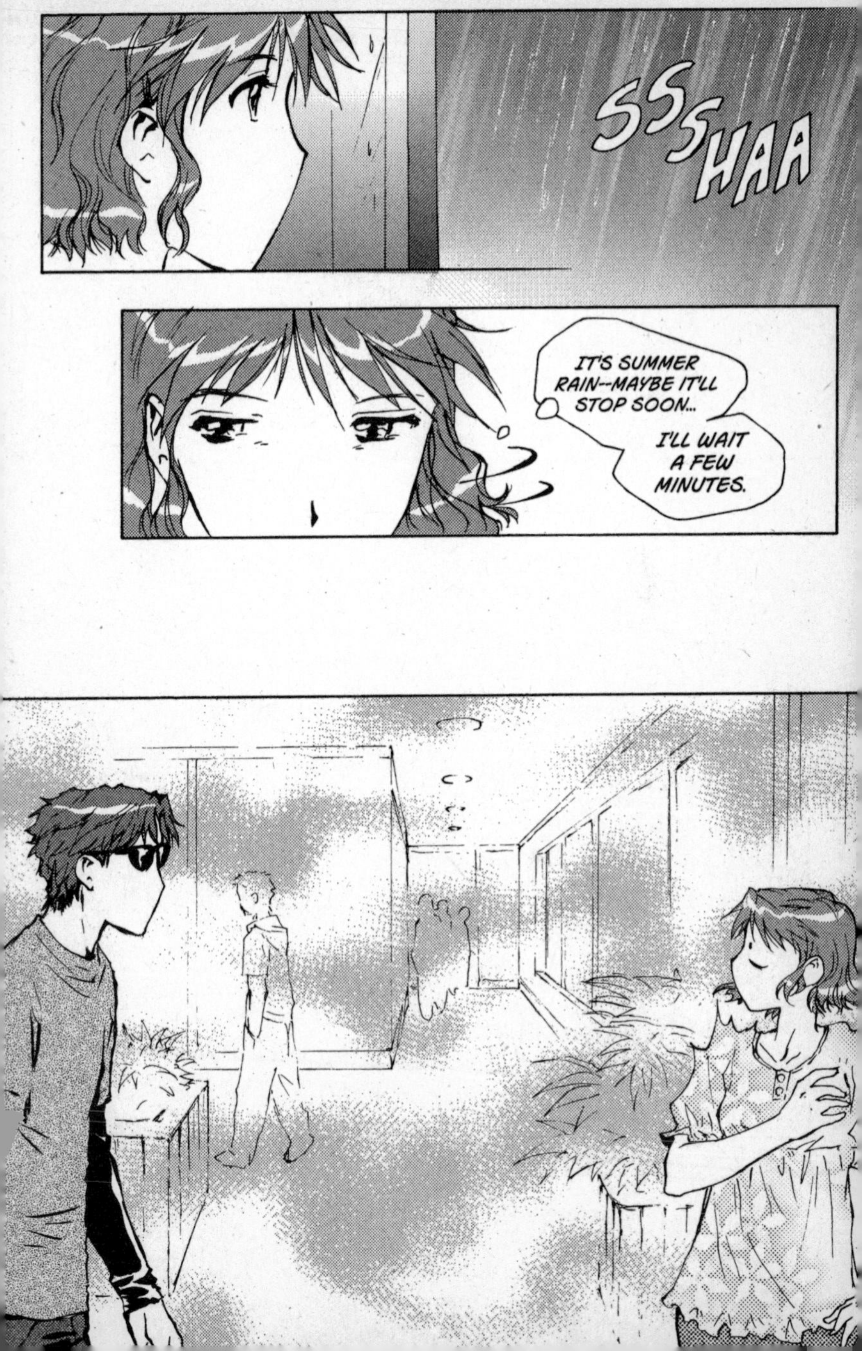
SSSHAA
IT'S SUMMER RAIN--MAYBE IT'LL STOP SOON...
I'LL WAIT A FEW MINUTES.

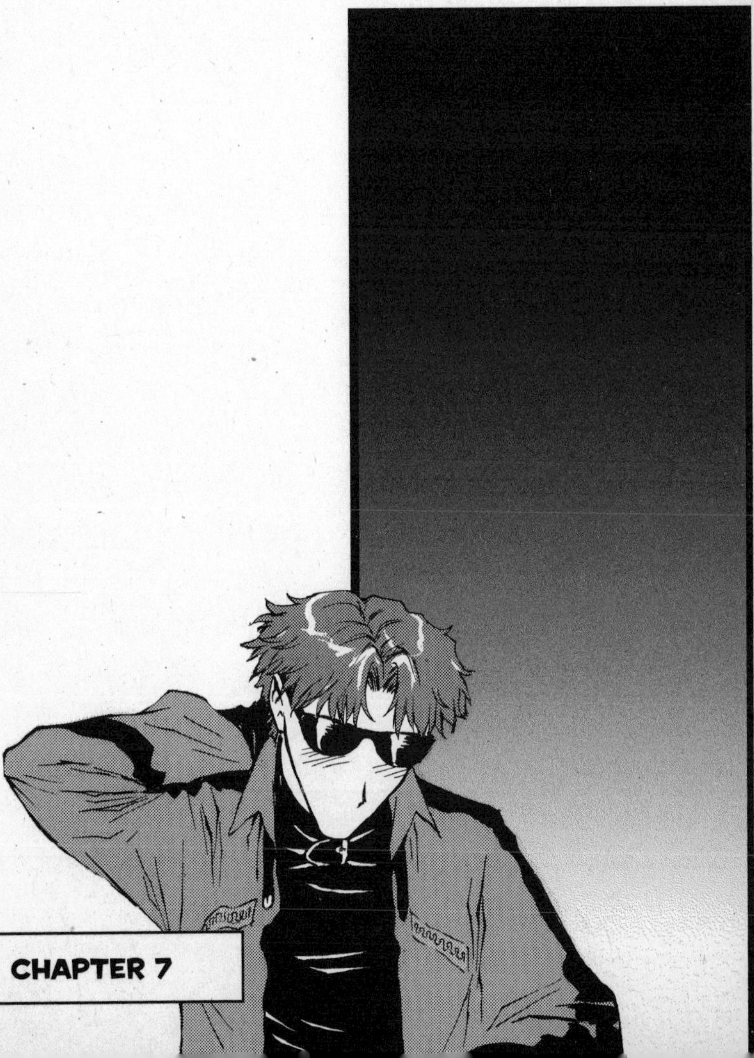

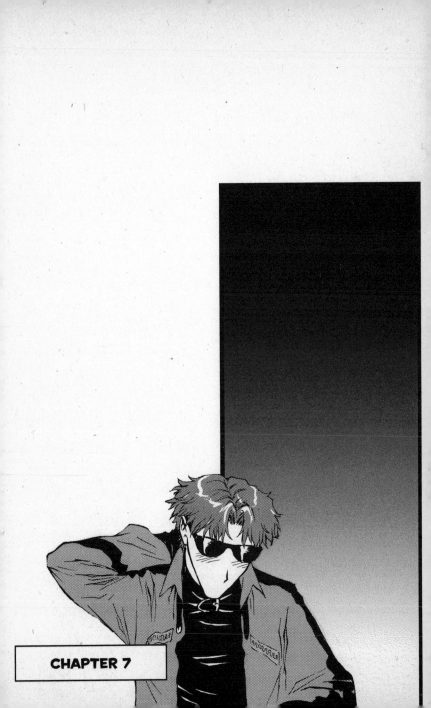

CHAPTER 7

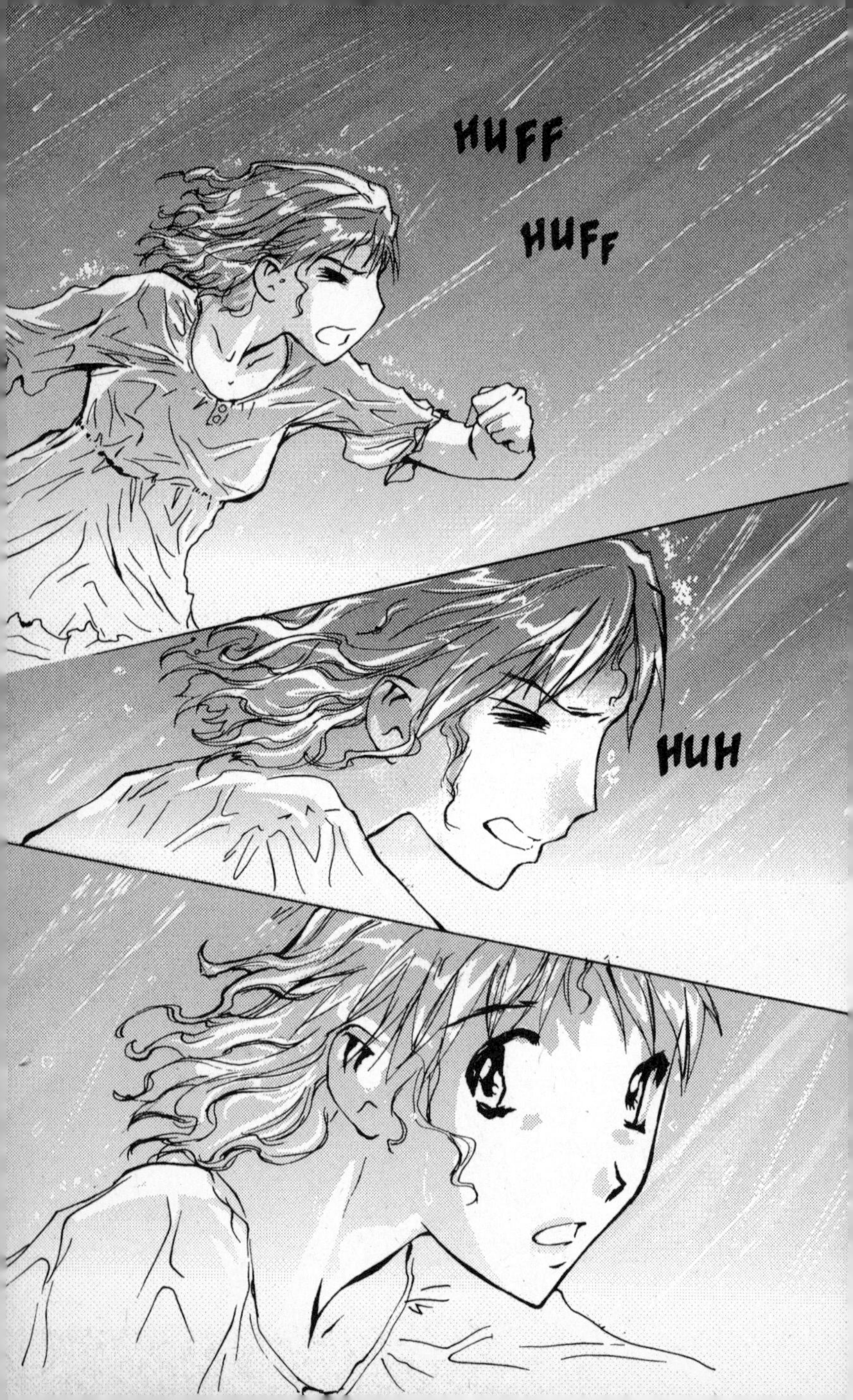
HUFF
HUFF
HUH

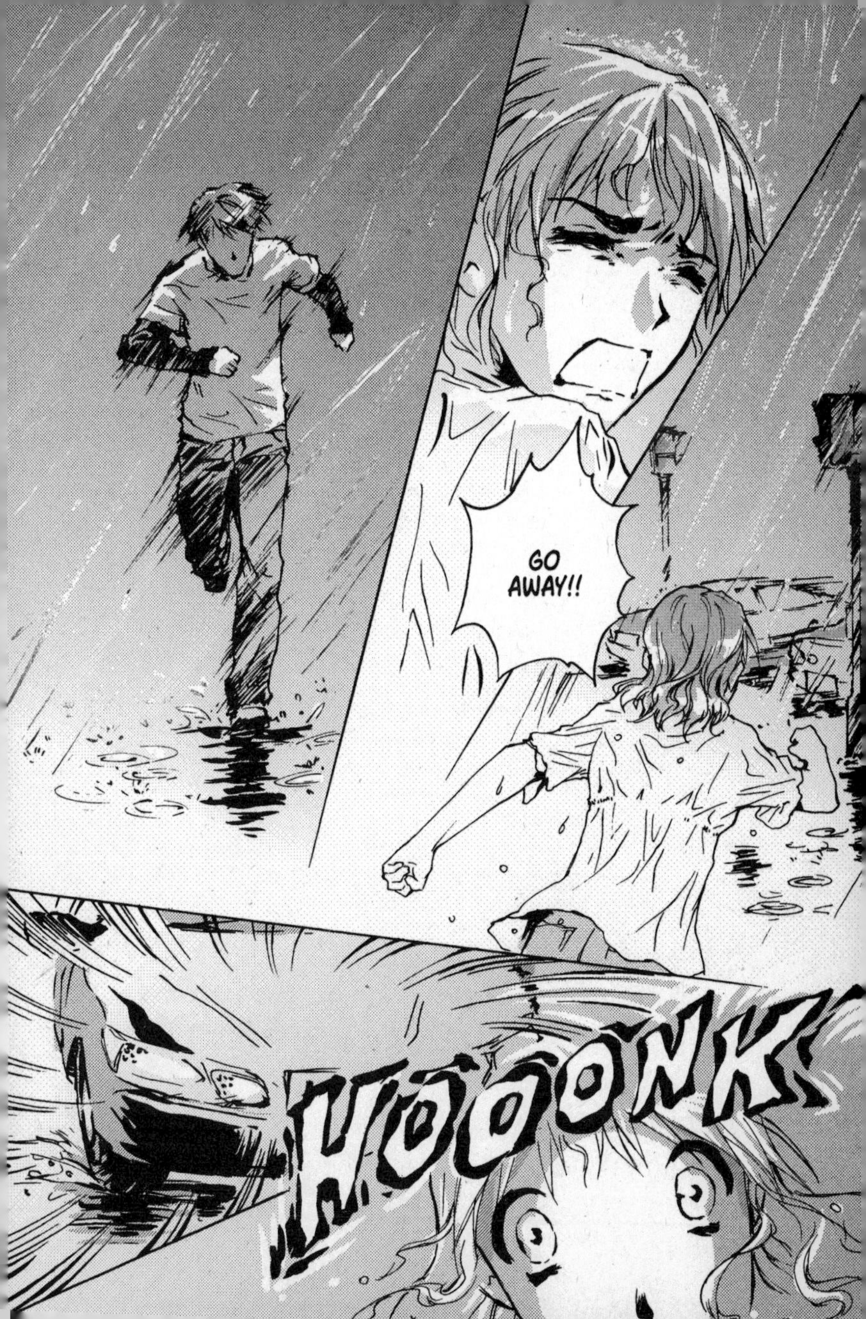
GO AWAY!!
HOOOONK

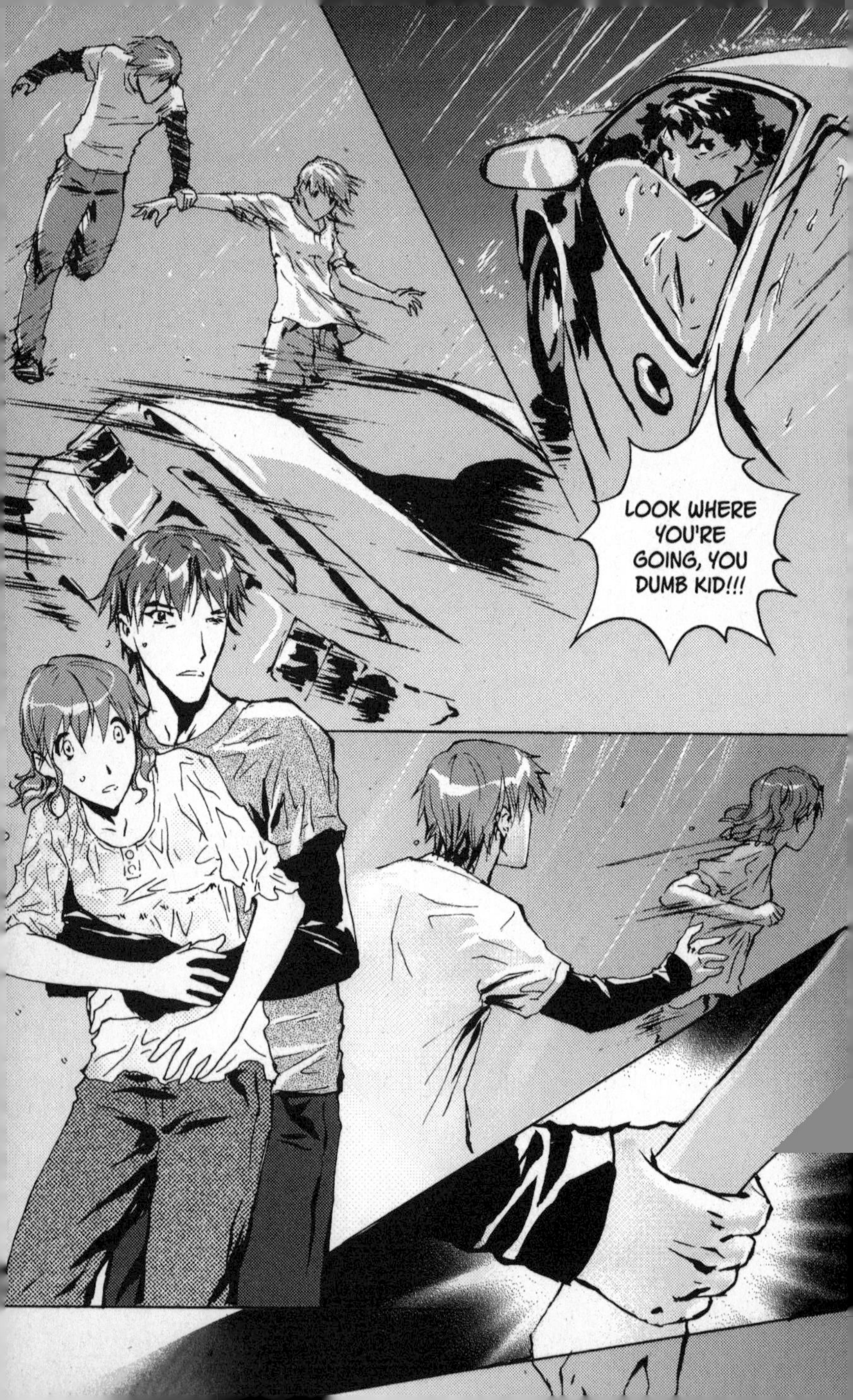
LOOK WHERE YOU'RE GOING, YOU DUMB KID!!!

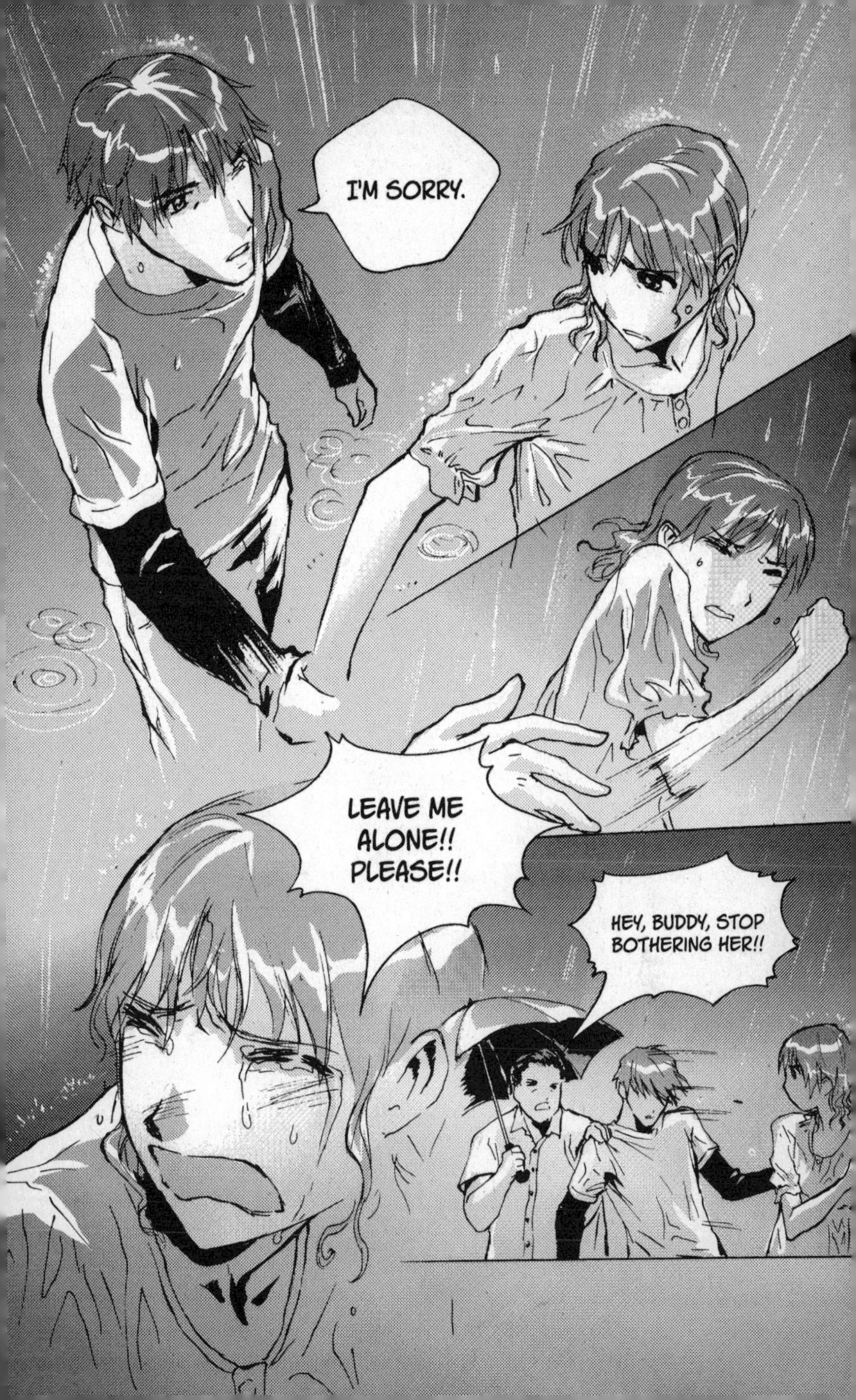
I'M SORRY.
LEAVE ME ALONE!! PLEASE!!
HEY, BUDDY, STOP BOTHERING HER!!

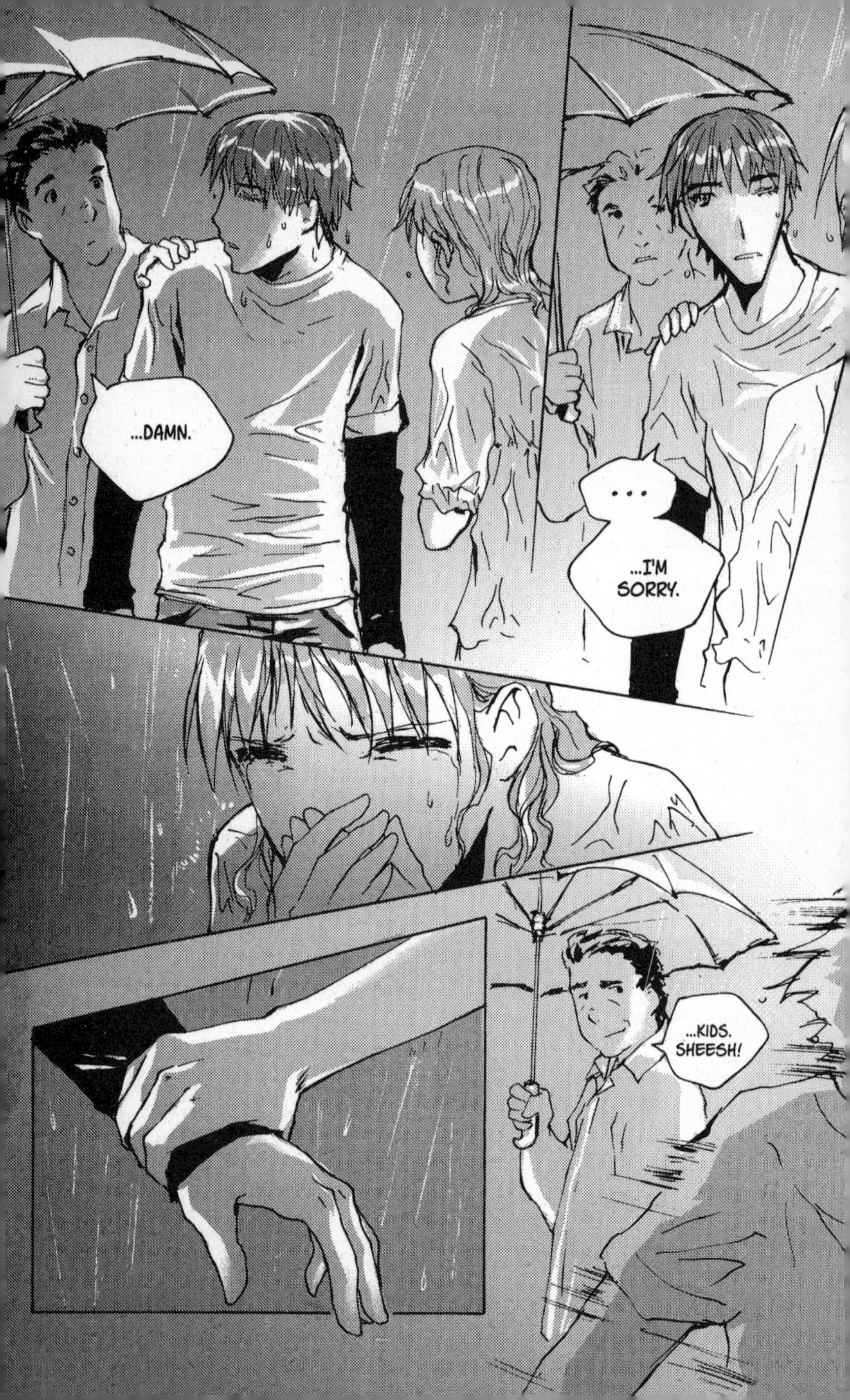
...DAMN.
...
...I'M SORRY.
...KIDS. SHEESH!

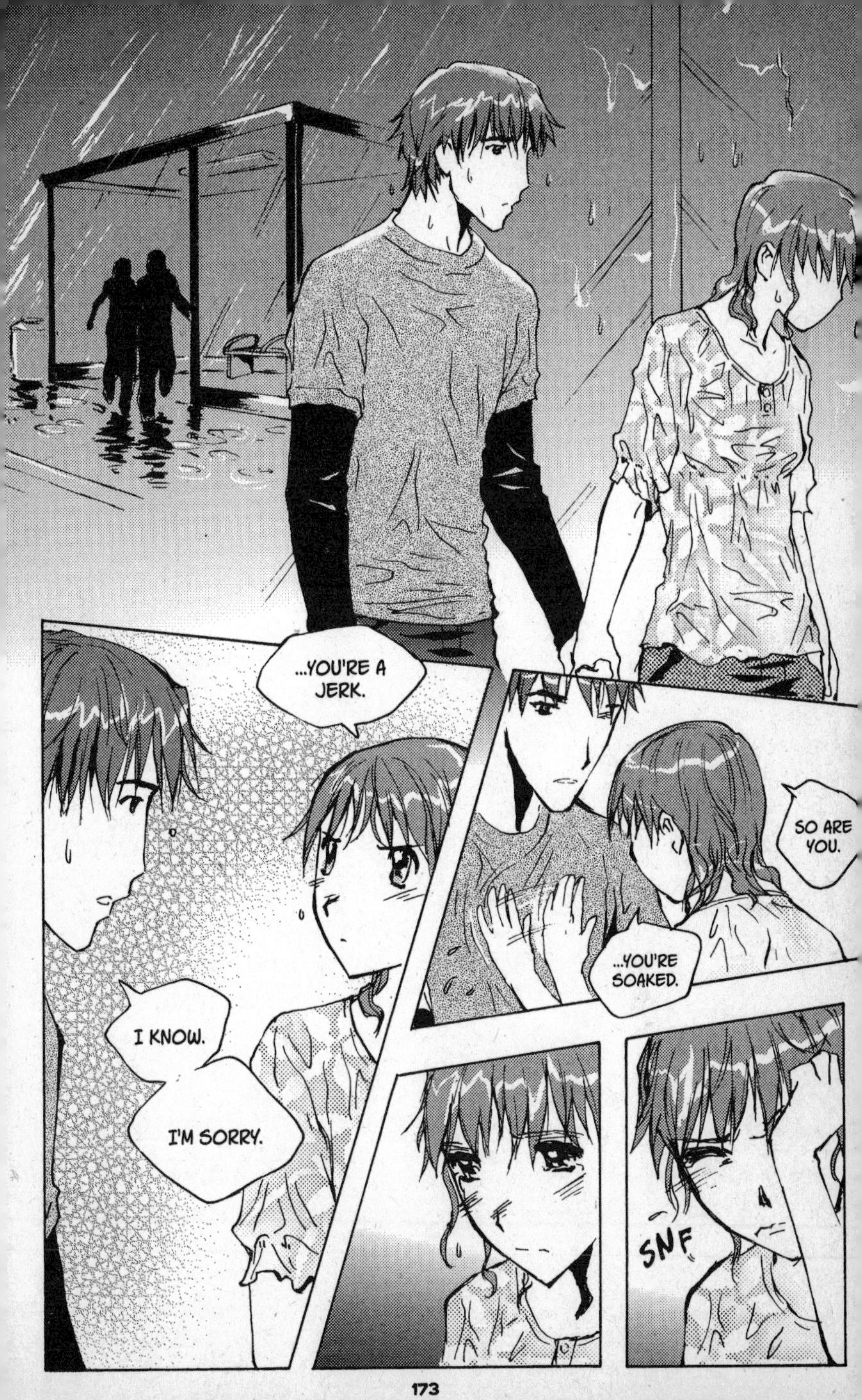
...YOU'RE A JERK.
I KNOW.
I'M SORRY.
SO ARE YOU.
...YOU'RE SOAKED.
SNF

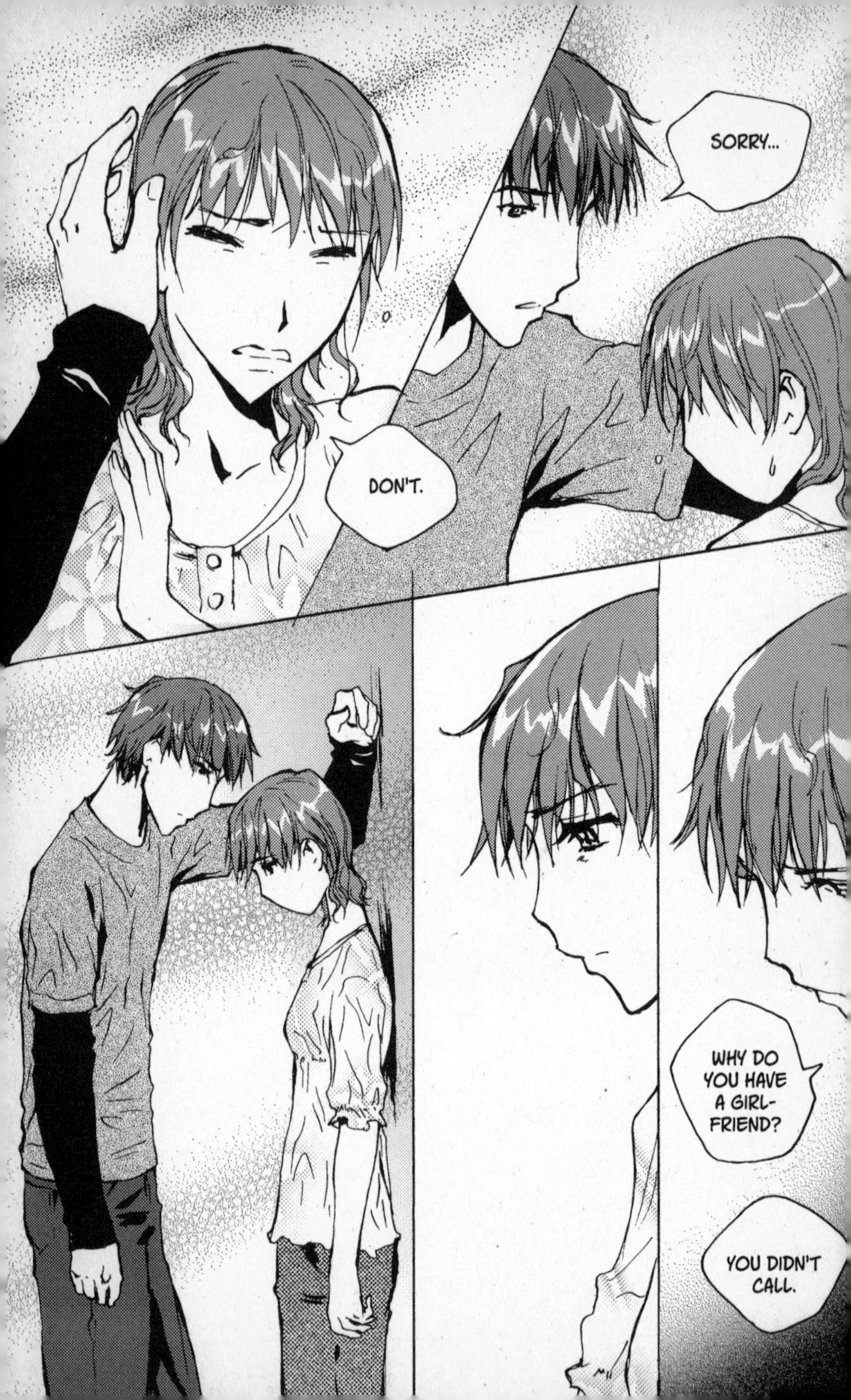
DON'T.
SORRY...
WHY DO YOU HAVE A GIRL- FRIEND?
YOU DIDN'T CALL.

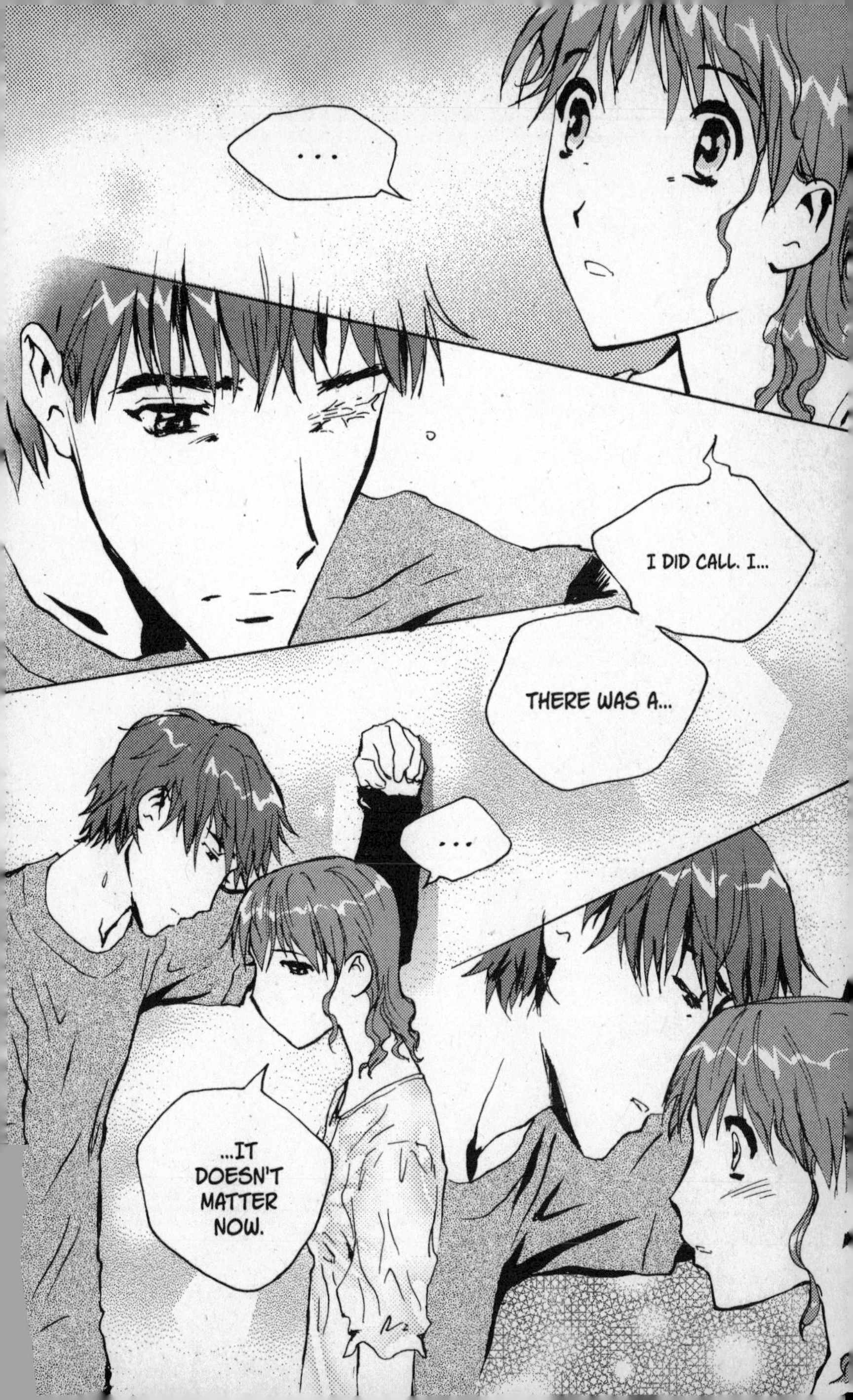
...
I DID CALL. I...
THERE WAS A...
...
...IT DOESN'T MATTER NOW.

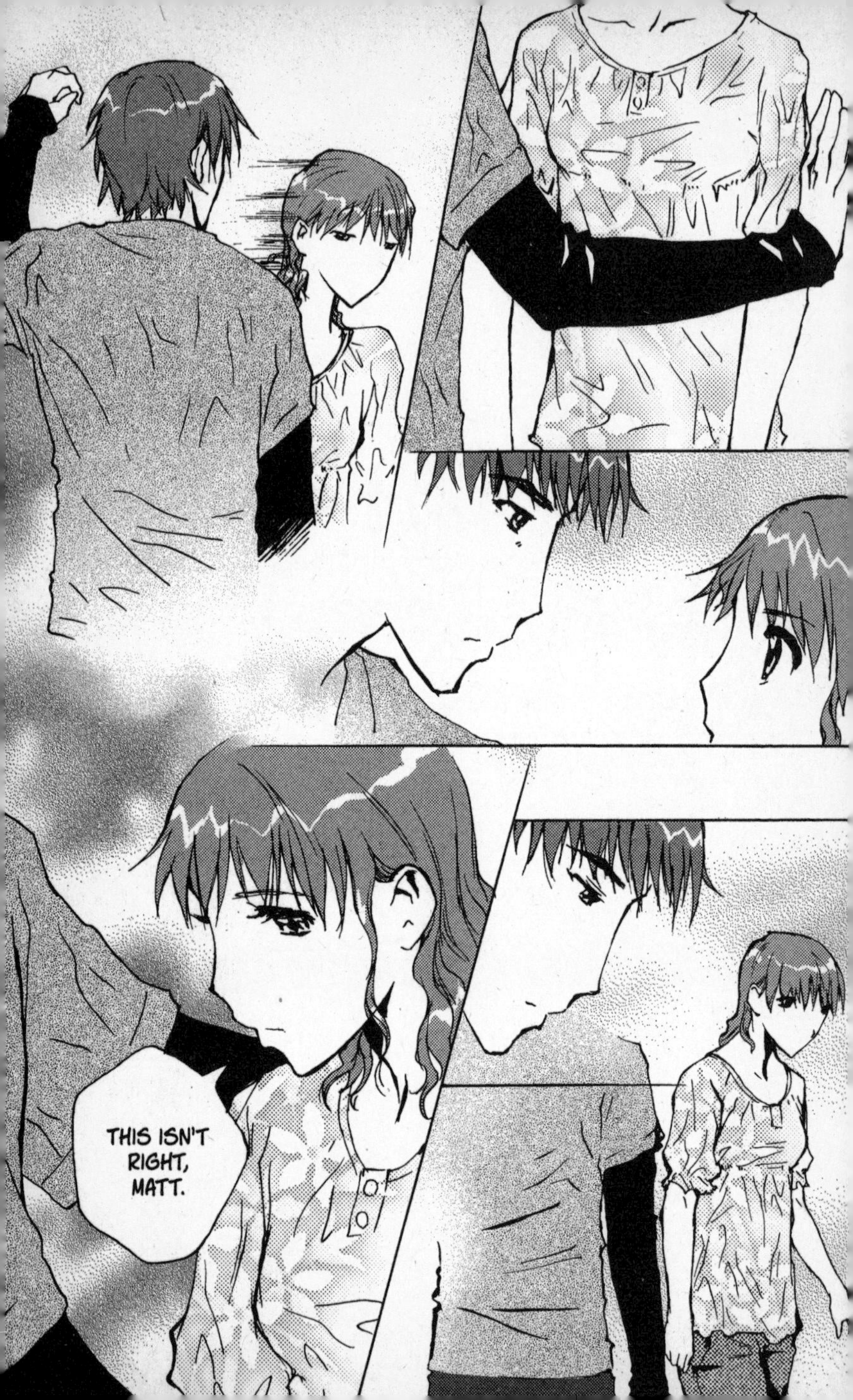
THIS ISN'T RIGHT, MATT.

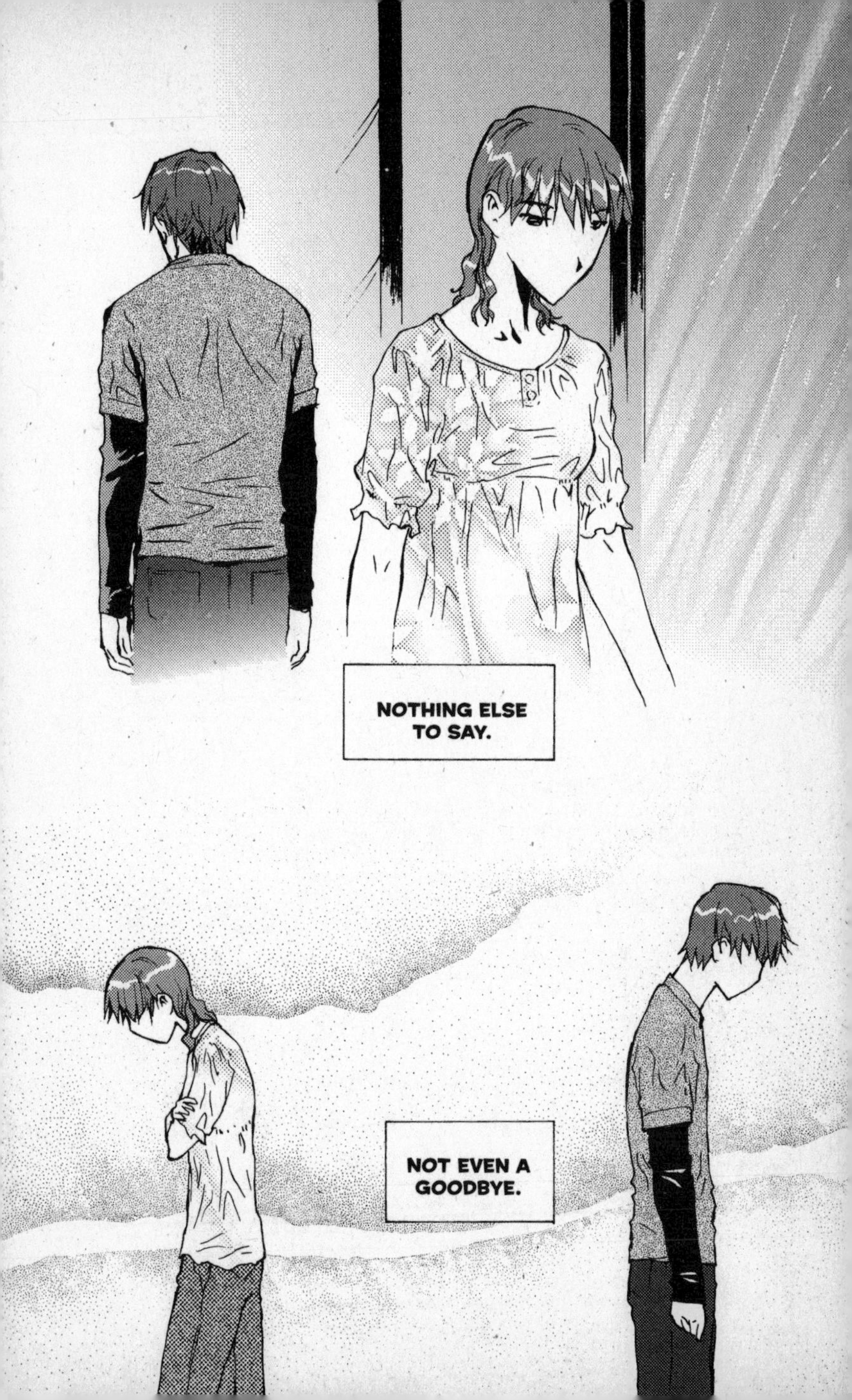
NOTHING ELSE TO SAY.
NOT EVEN A GOODBYE.

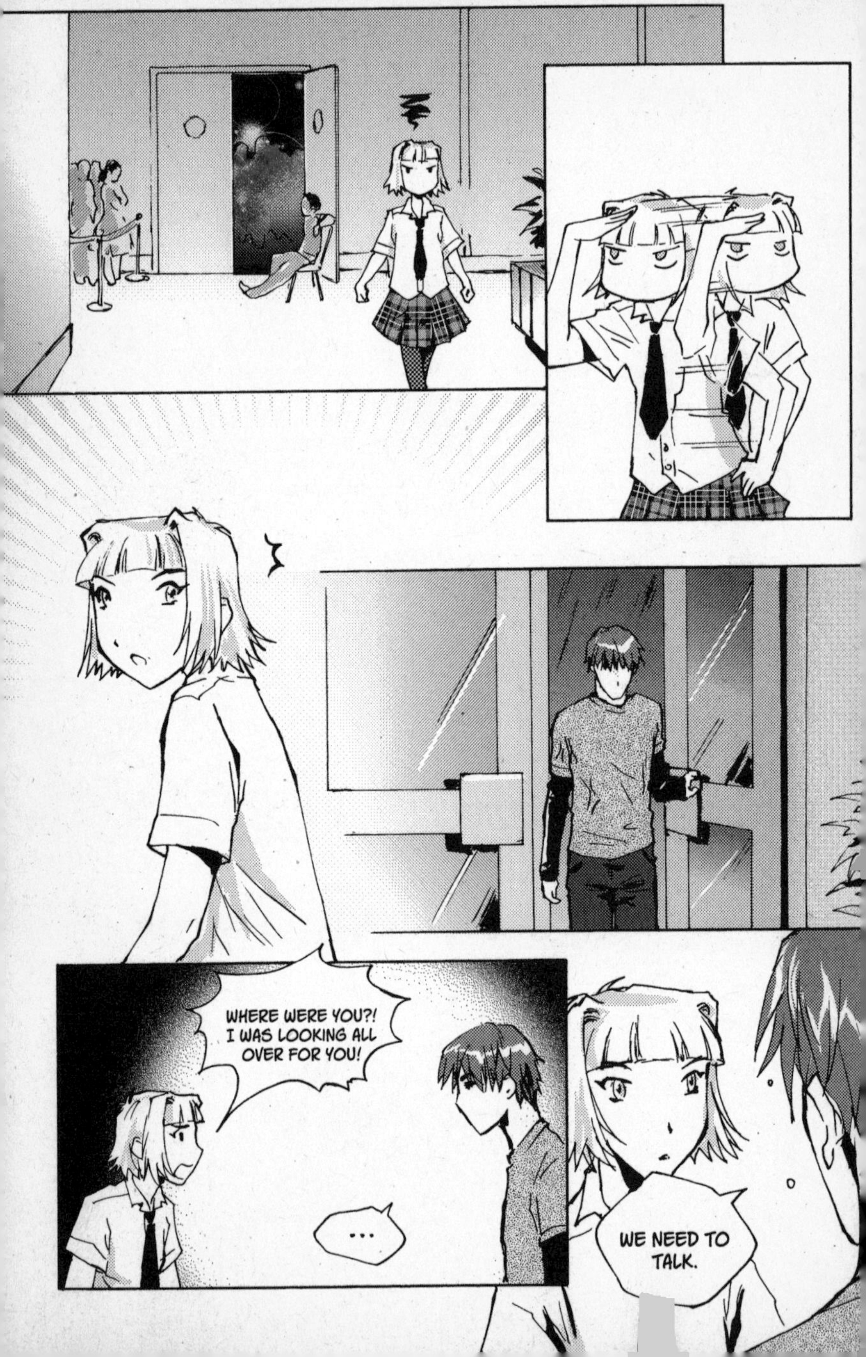
WHERE WERE YOU?! I WAS LOOKING ALL OVER FOR YOU!
...
WE NEED TO TALK.

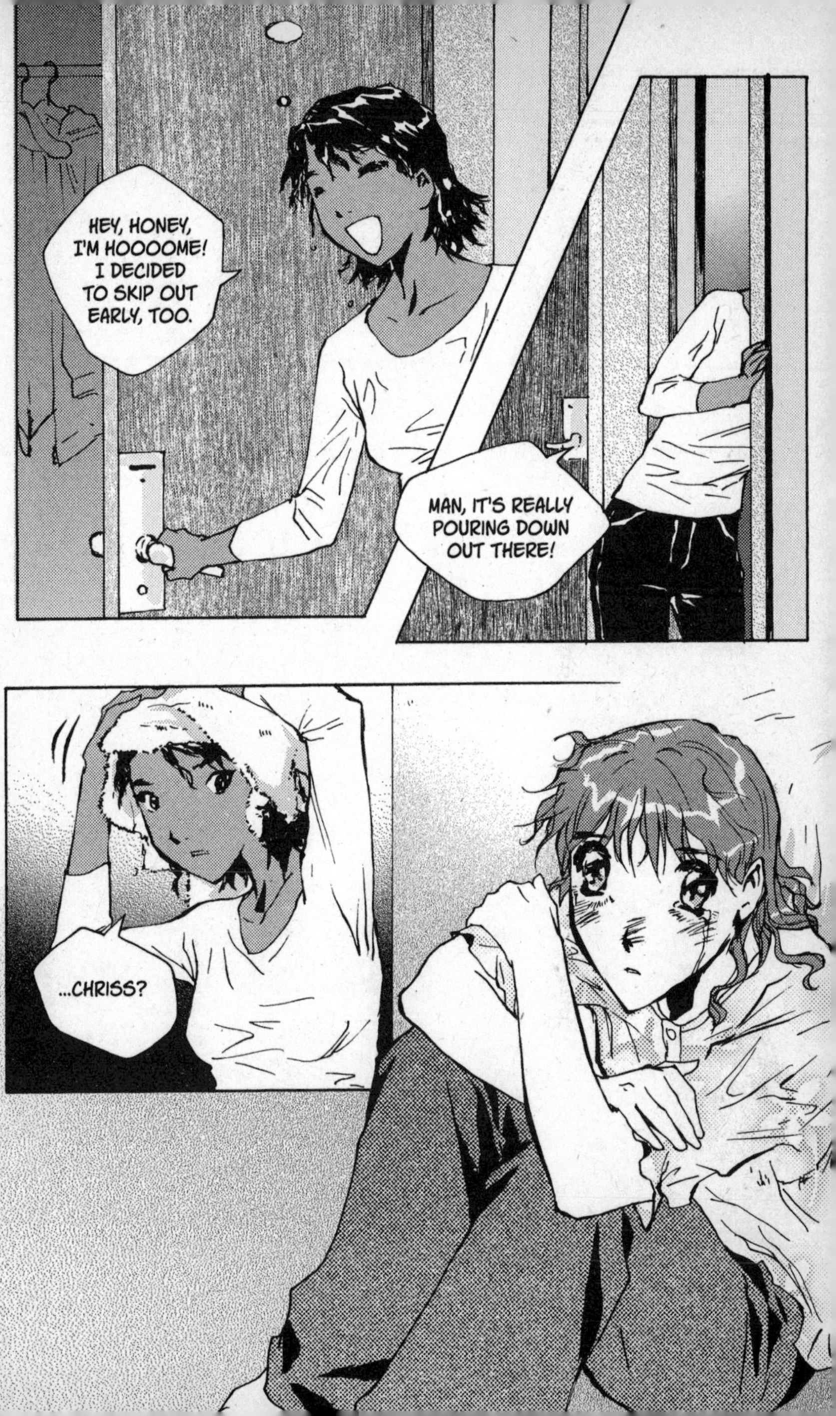
HEY, HONEY, I'M HOOOOME! I DECIDED TO SKIP OUT EARLY, TOO.
MAN, IT'S REALLY POURING DOWN OUT THERE!
...CHRISS?

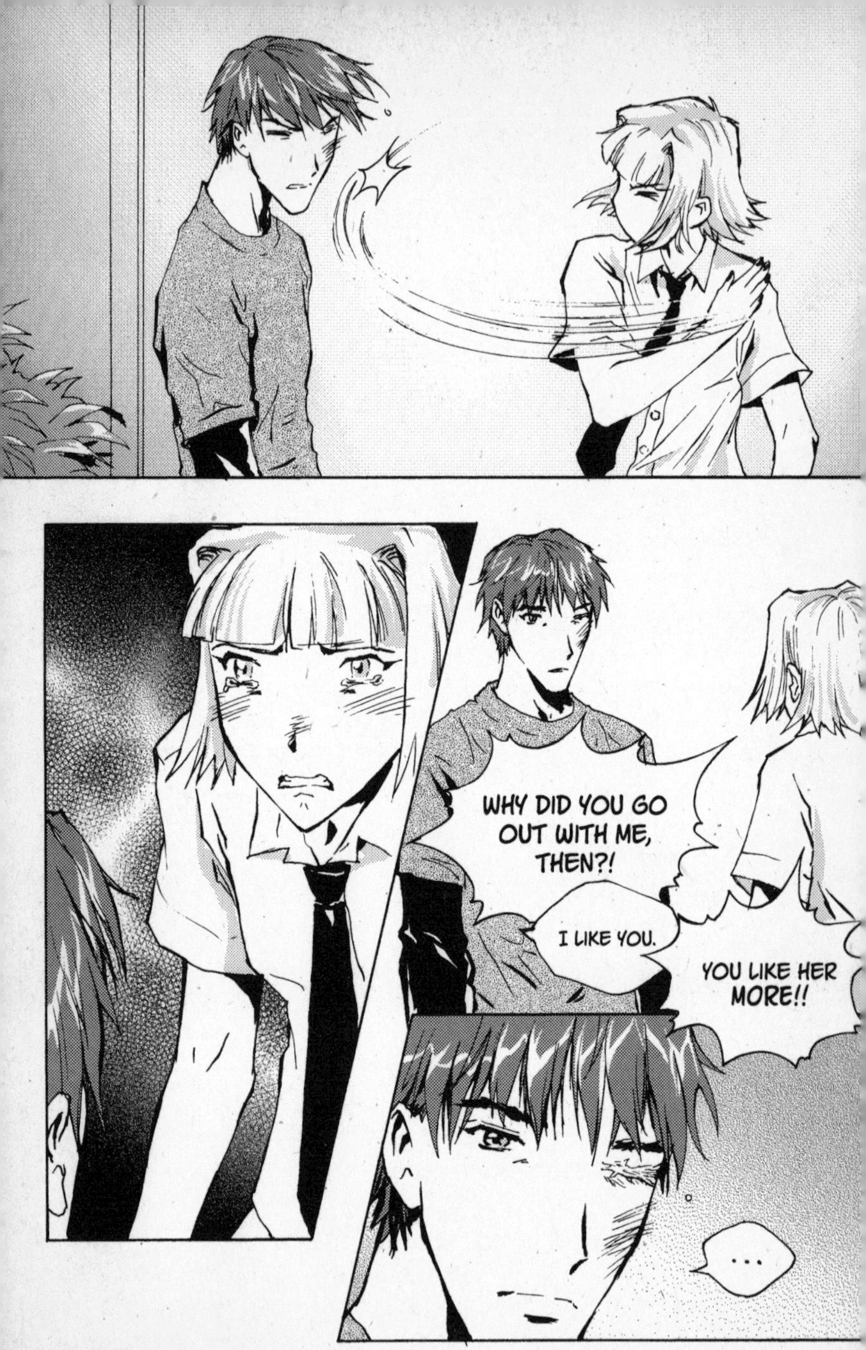
WHY DID YOU GO OUT WITH ME, THEN?!
I LIKE YOU.
YOU LIKE HER MORE!!
...

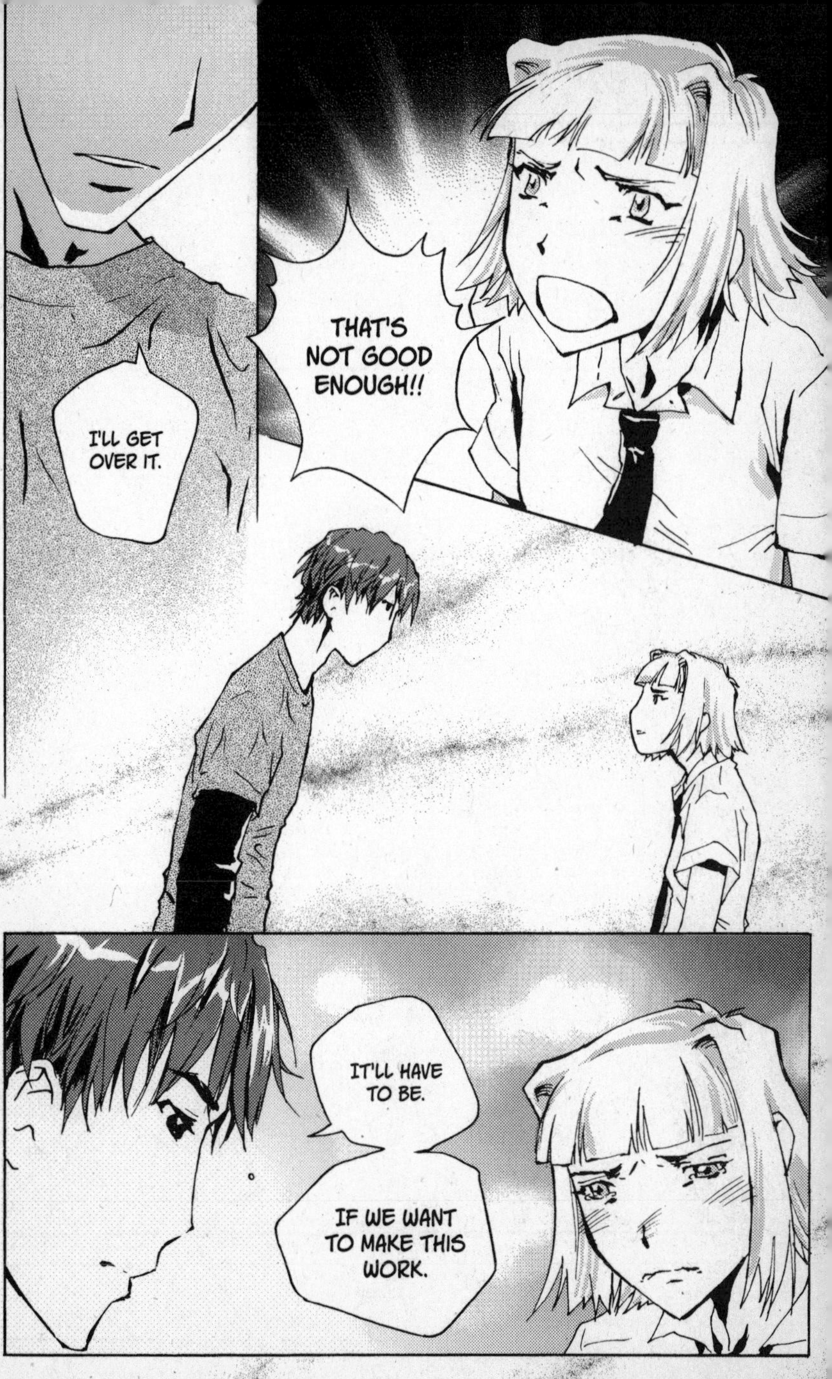
I'LL GET OVER IT.
THAT'S NOT GOOD ENOUGH!!
IT'LL HAVE TO BE.
IF WE WANT TO MAKE THIS WORK.

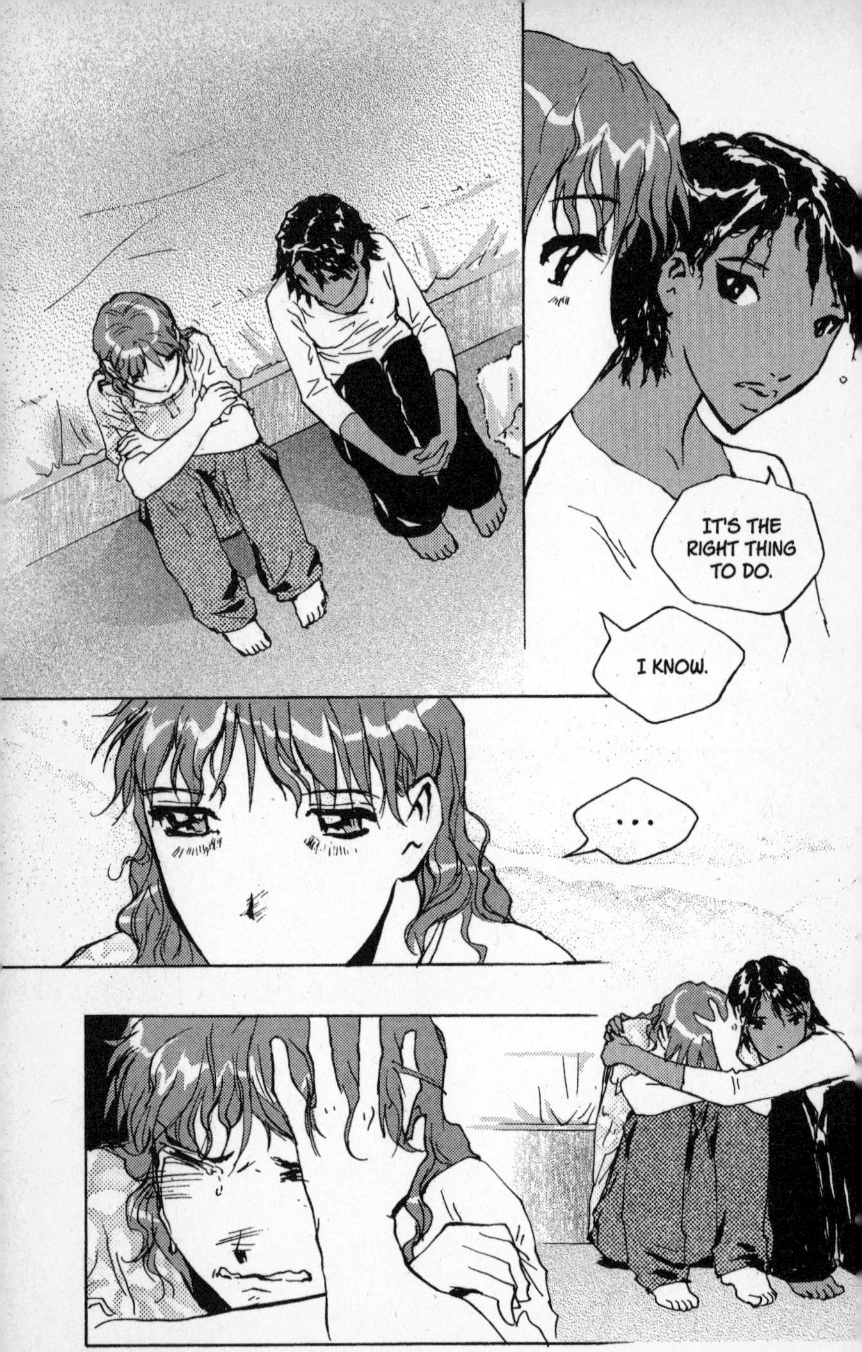
IT'S THE RIGHT THING TO DO.
I KNOW.
...

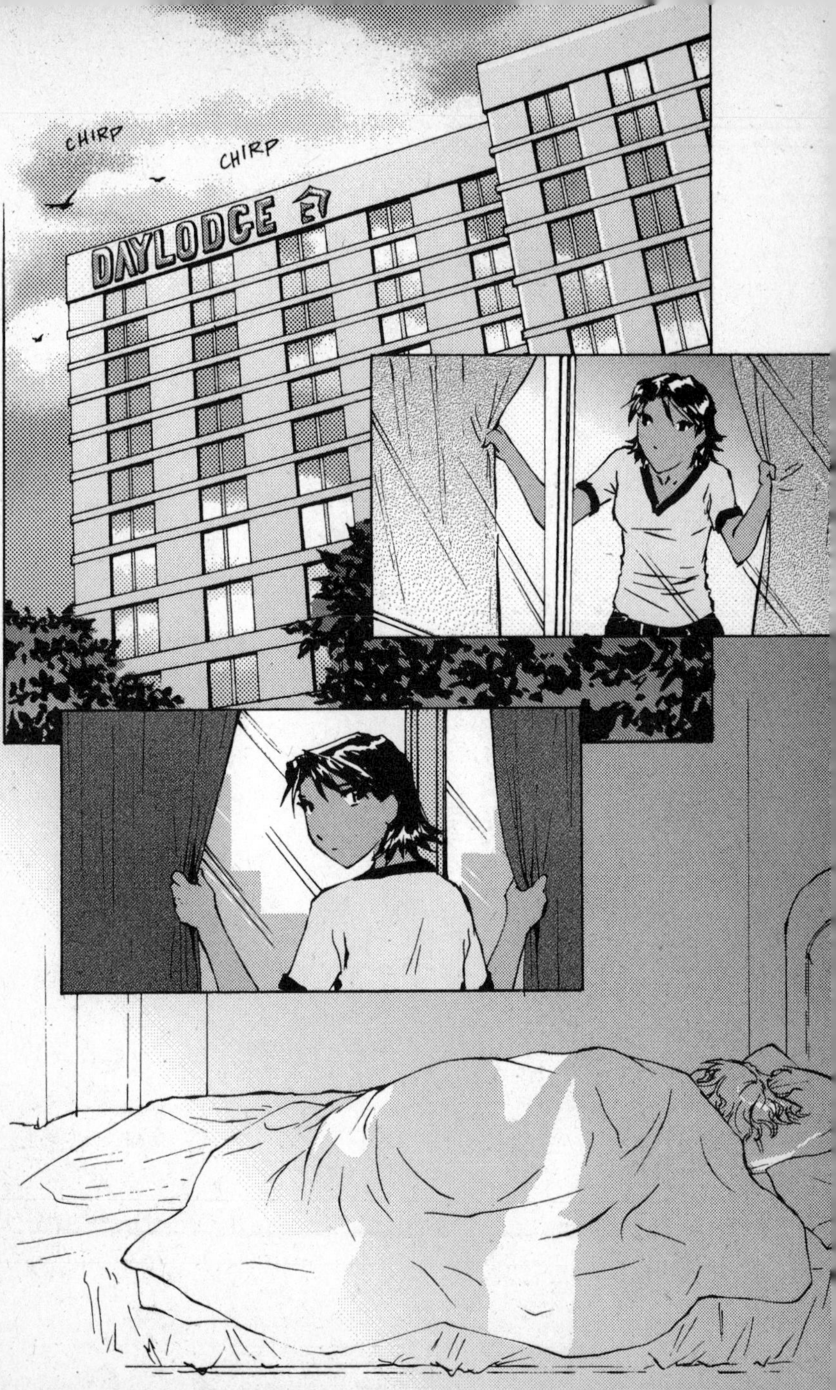
CHIRP
CHIRP
DAYLODGE

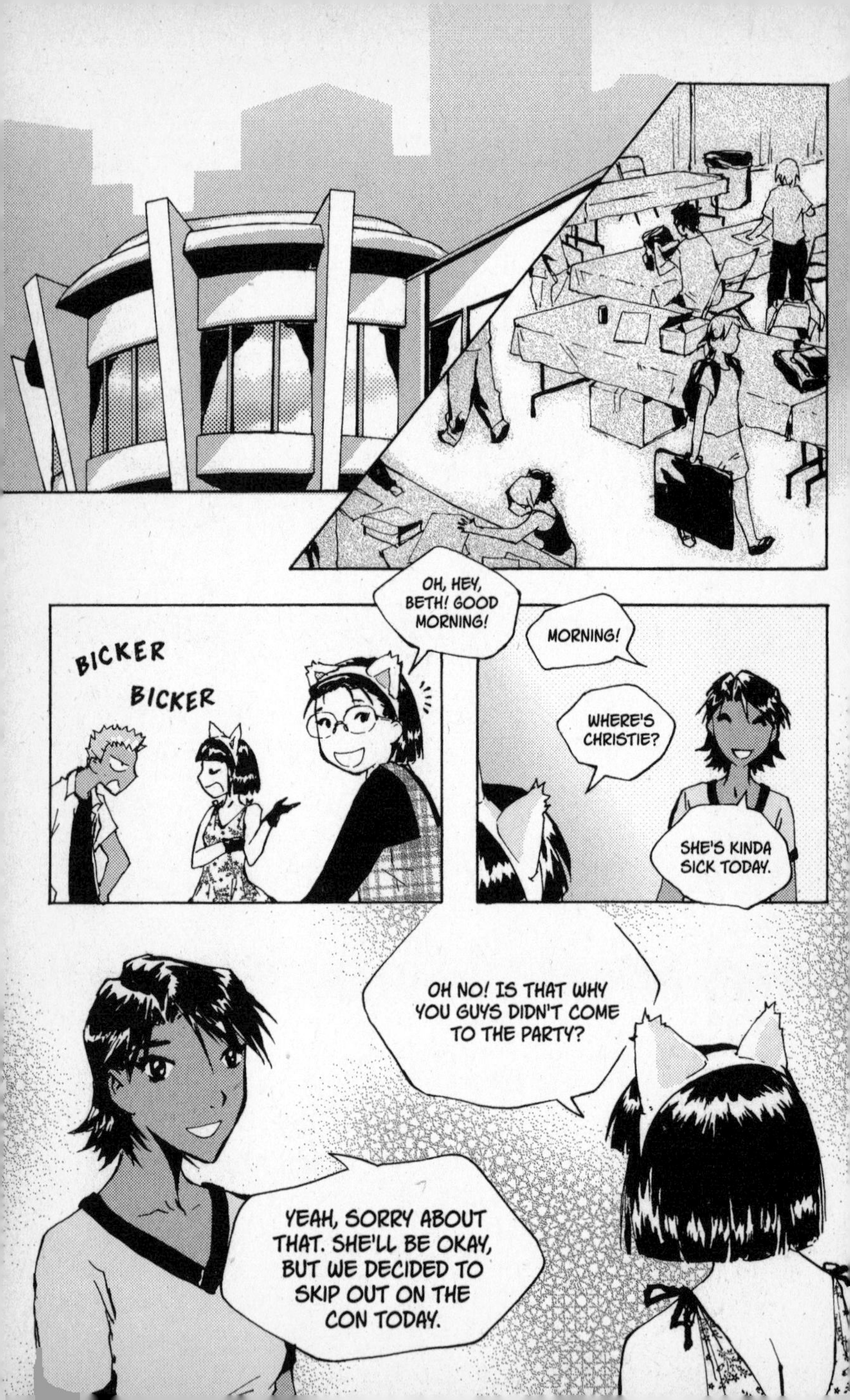
OH, HEY, BETH! GOOD MORNING!
BICKER BICKER
MORNING!
WHERE'S CHRISTIE?
SHE'S KINDA SICK TODAY.
OH NO! IS THAT WHY YOU GUYS DIDN'T COME TO THE PARTY?
YEAH, SORRY ABOUT THAT. SHE'LL BE OKAY, BUT WE DECIDED TO SKIP OUT ON THE CON TODAY.

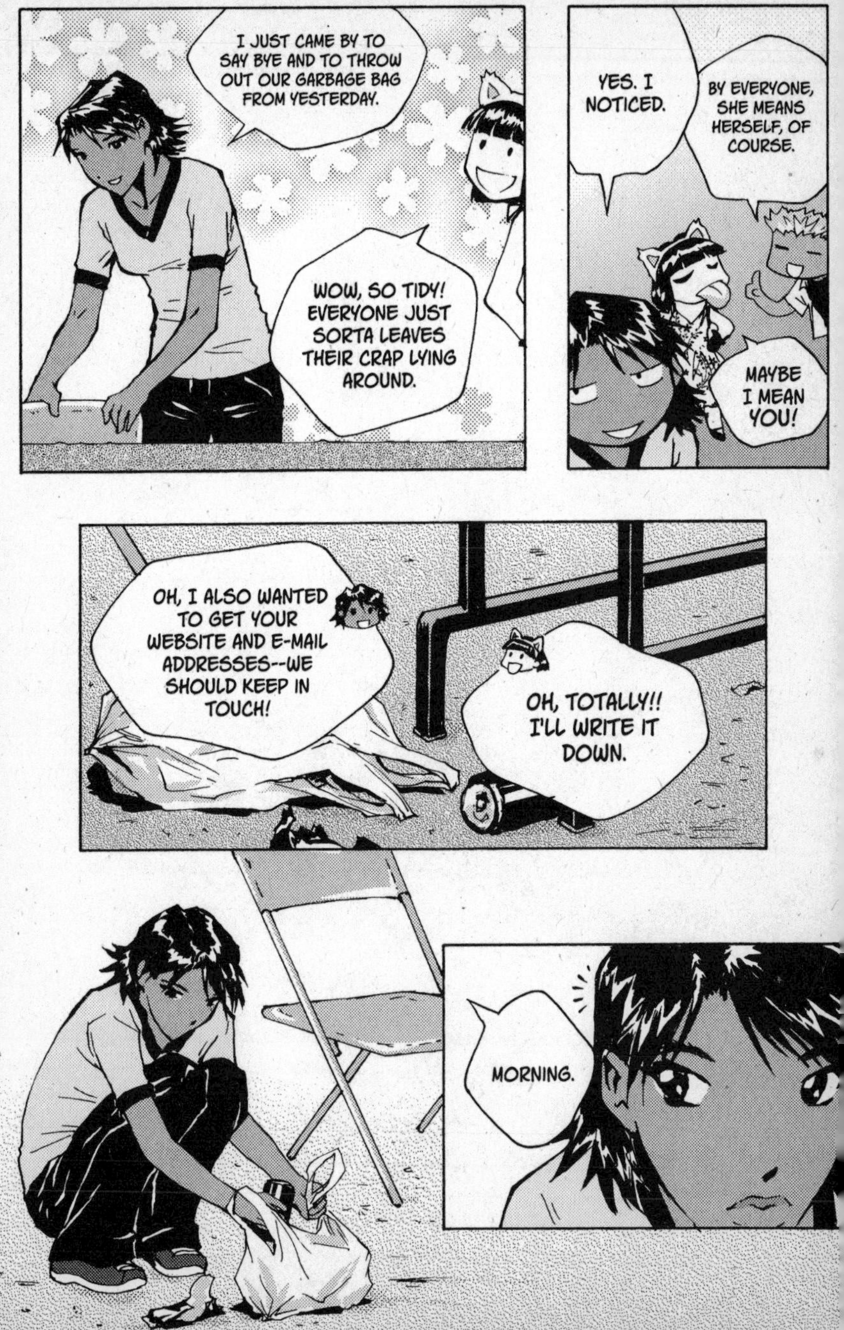
I JUST CAME BY TO SAY BYE AND TO THROW OUT OUR GARBAGE BAG FROM YESTERDAY.
WOW, SO TIDY! EVERYONE JUST SORTA LEAVES THEIR CRAP LYING AROUND.
YES. I NOTICED.
BY EVERYONE, SHE MEANS HERSELF, OF COURSE.
MAYBE I MEAN YOU!
OH, I ALSO WANTED TO GET YOUR WEBSITE AND E-MAIL ADDRESSES--WE SHOULD KEEP IN TOUCH!
OH, TOTALLY!! I'LL WRITE IT DOWN.
MORNING.

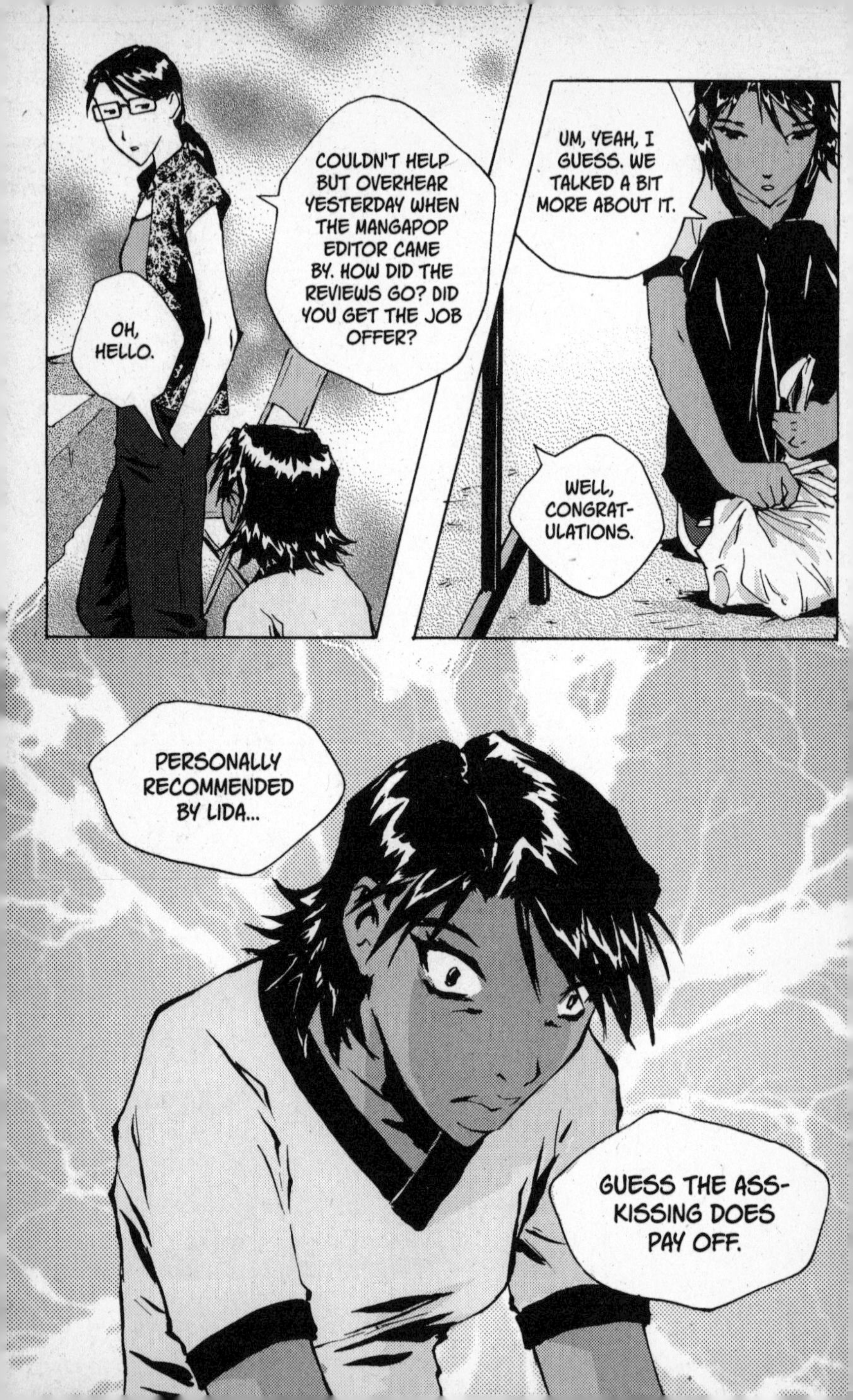
OH, HELLO.
COULDN'T HELP BUT OVERHEAR YESTERDAY WHEN THE MANGAPOP EDITOR CAME BY. HOW DID THE REVIEWS GO? DID YOU GET THE JOB OFFER?
UM, YEAH, I GUESS. WE TALKED A BIT MORE ABOUT IT.
WELL, CONGRAT-ULATIONS.
PERSONALLY RECOMMENDED BY LIDA...
GUESS THE ASS-KISSING DOES PAY OFF.

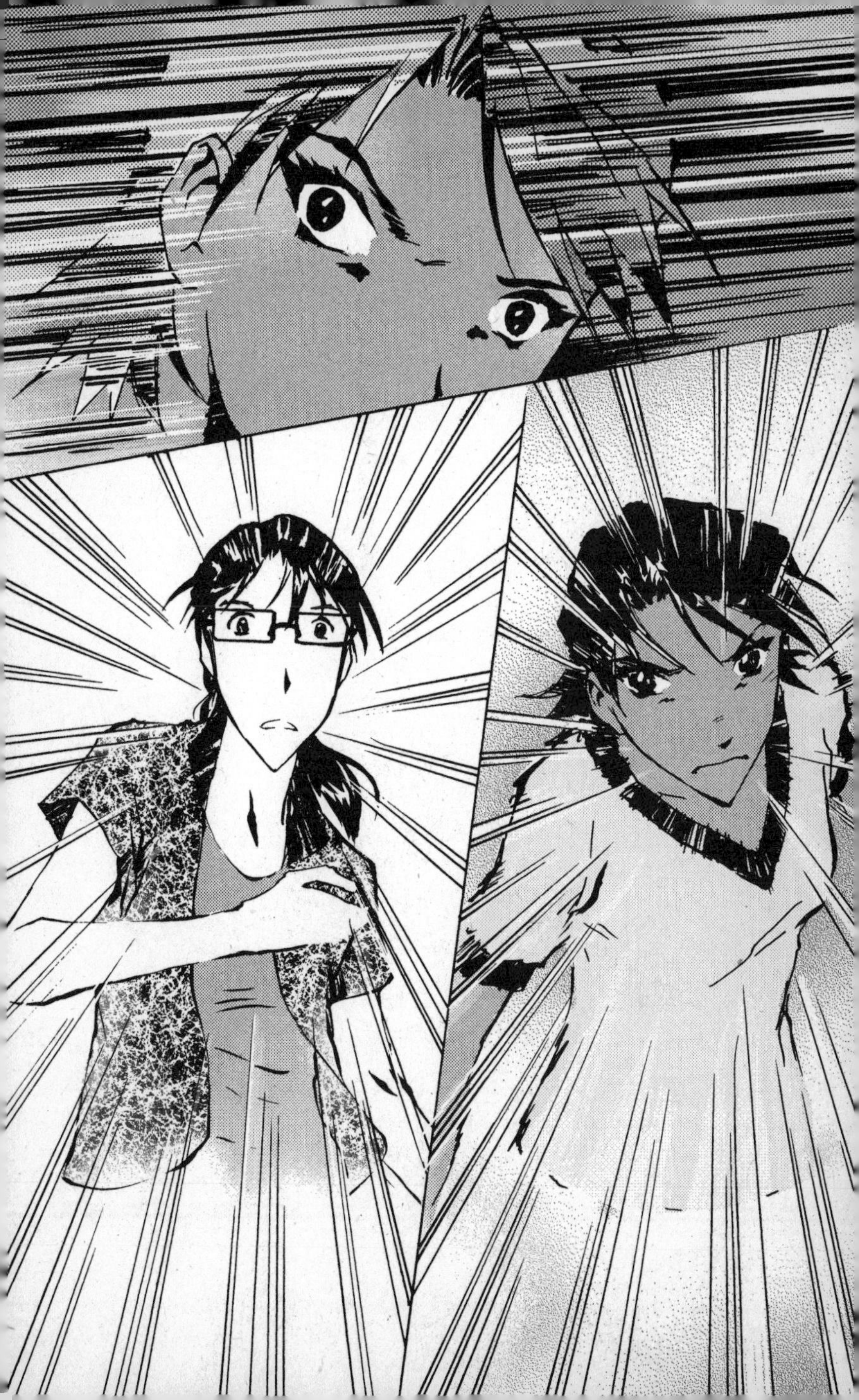

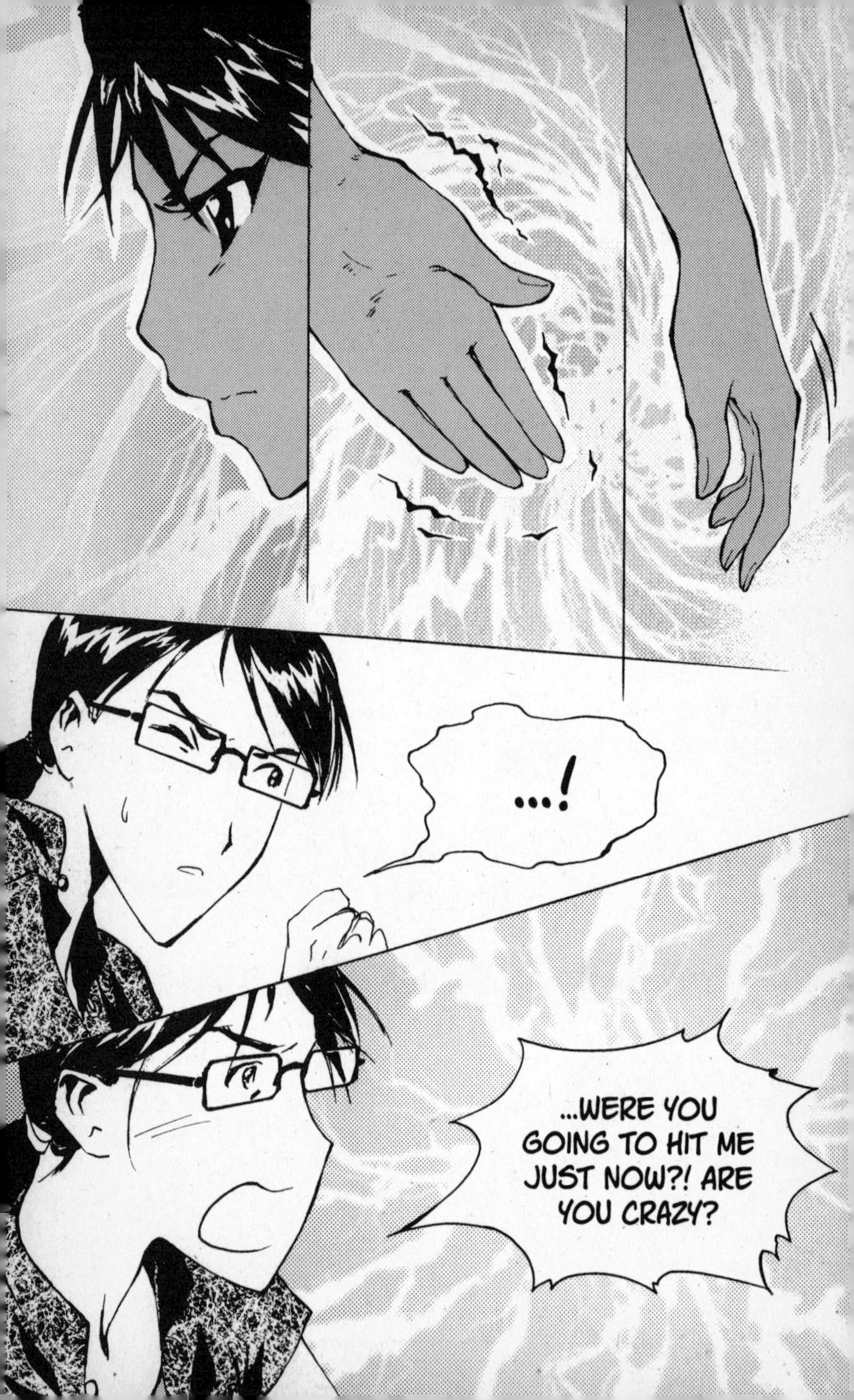
...!
...WERE YOU GOING TO HIT ME JUST NOW?! ARE YOU CRAZY?

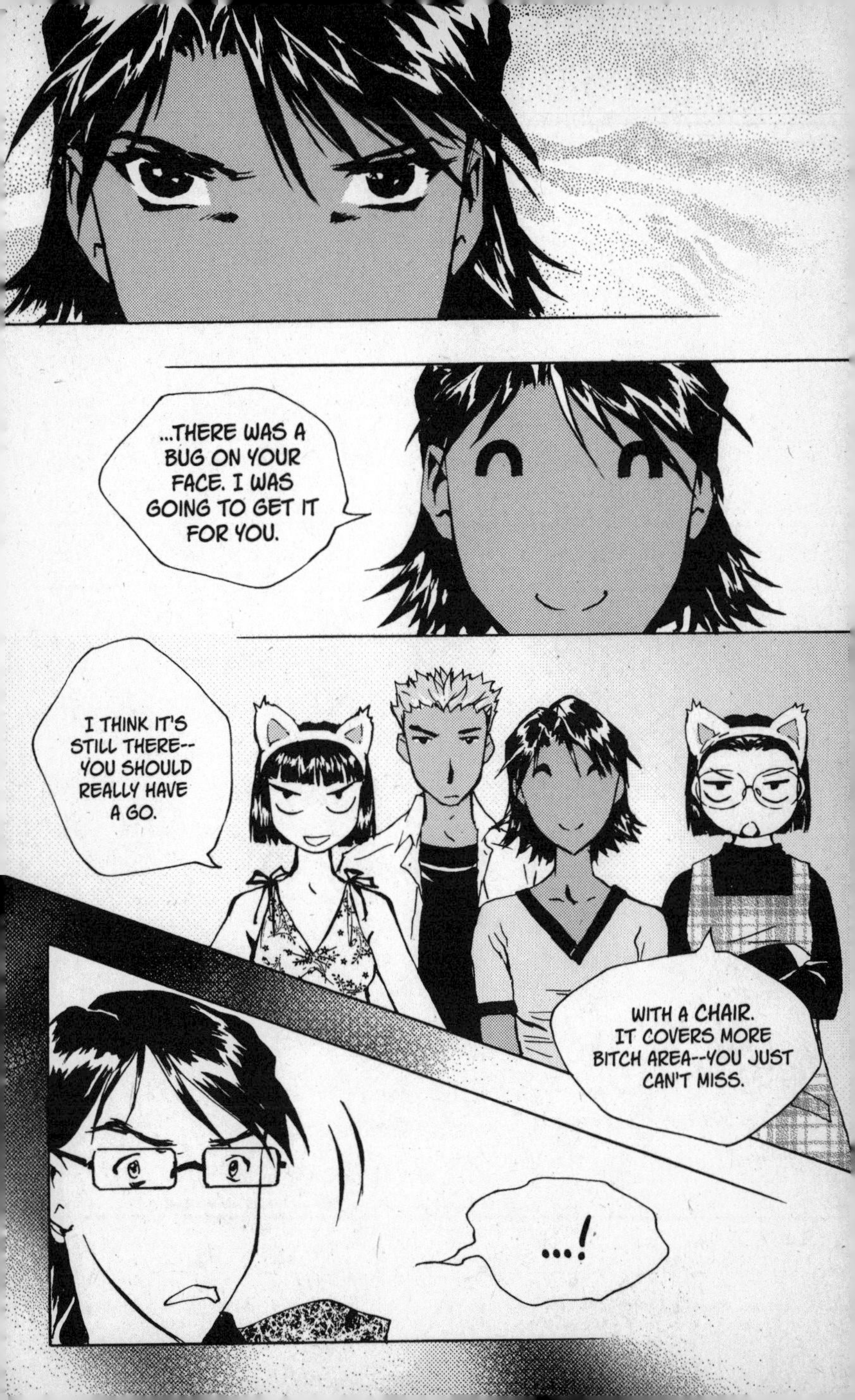
...THERE WAS A BUG ON YOUR FACE. I WAS GOING TO GET IT FOR YOU.
I THINK IT'S STILL THERE--YOU SHOULD REALLY HAVE A GO.
WITH A CHAIR. IT COVERS MORE BITCH AREA--YOU JUST CAN'T MISS.
...!

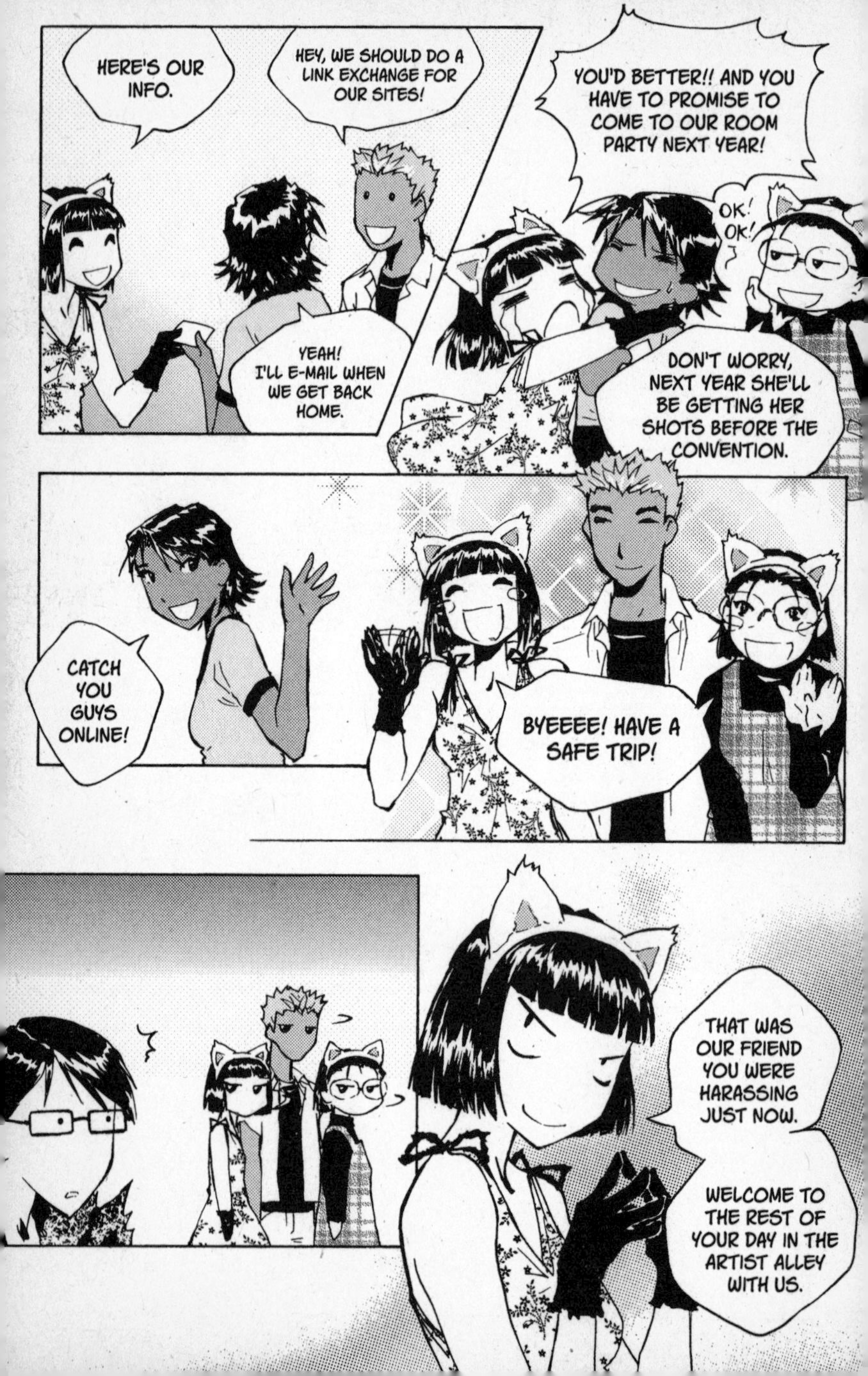
HERE'S OUR INFO.
HEY, WE SHOULD DO A LINK EXCHANGE FOR OUR SITES!
YEAH! I'LL E-MAIL WHEN WE GET BACK HOME.
YOU'D BETTER!! AND YOU HAVE TO PROMISE TO COME TO OUR ROOM PARTY NEXT YEAR!
OK! OK!
DON'T WORRY, NEXT YEAR SHE'LL BE GETTING HER SHOTS BEFORE THE CONVENTION.
CATCH YOU GUYS ONLINE!
BYEEEE! HAVE A SAFE TRIP!
THAT WAS OUR FRIEND YOU WERE HARASSING JUST NOW.
WELCOME TO THE REST OF YOUR DAY IN THE ARTIST ALLEY WITH US.

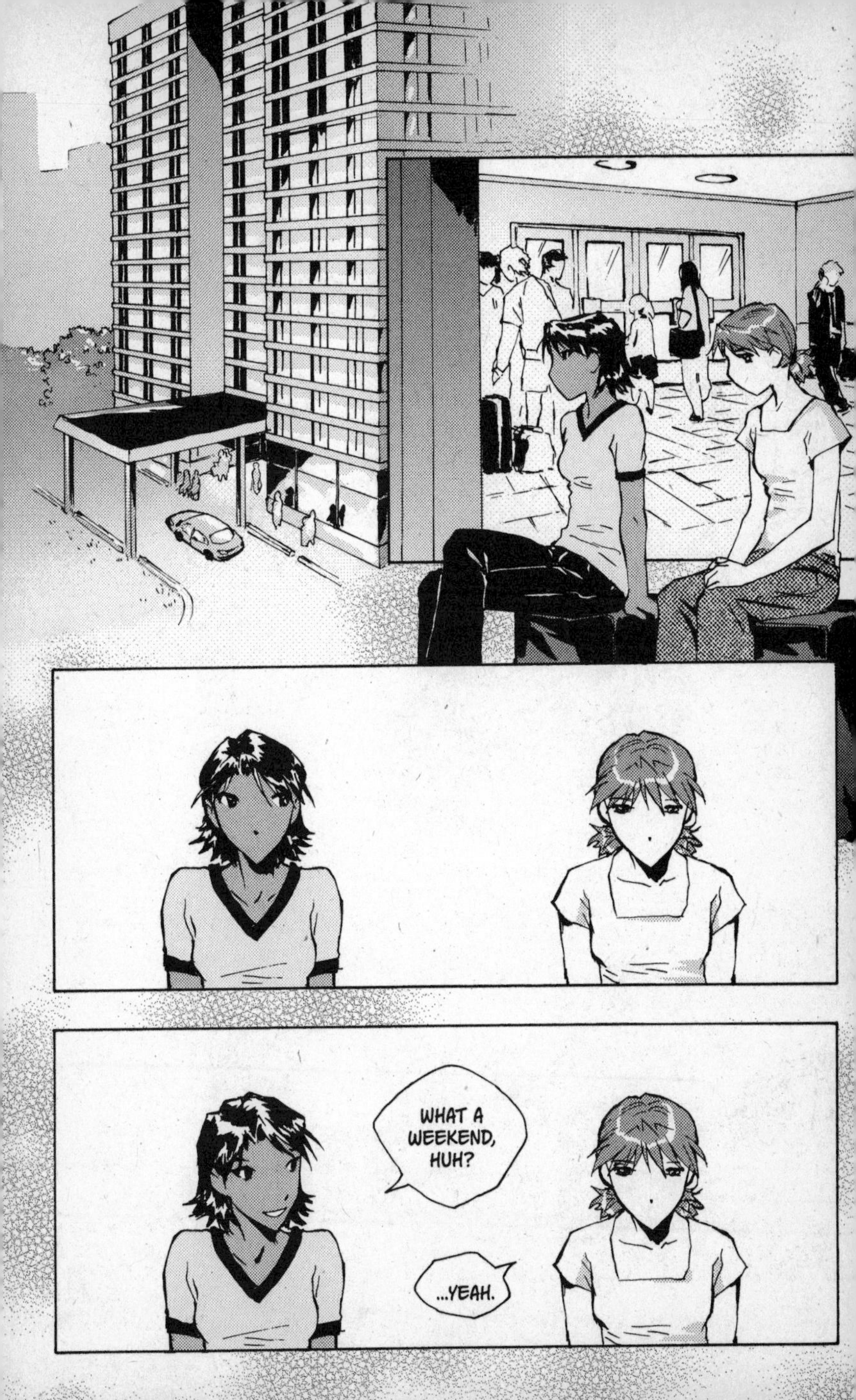
WHAT A WEEKEND, HUH?
...YEAH.

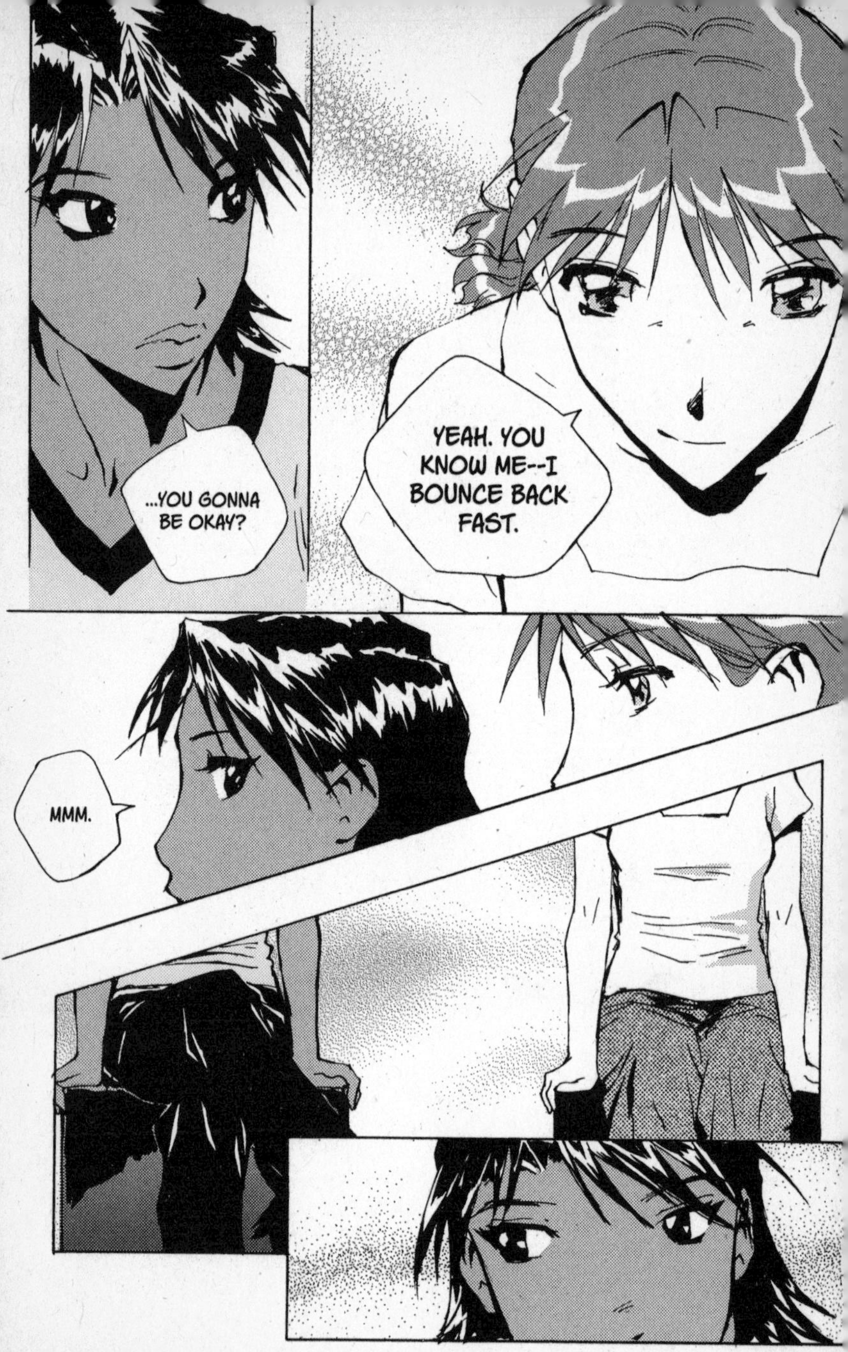
...YOU GONNA BE OKAY?
YEAH. YOU KNOW ME--I BOUNCE BACK FAST.
MMM.

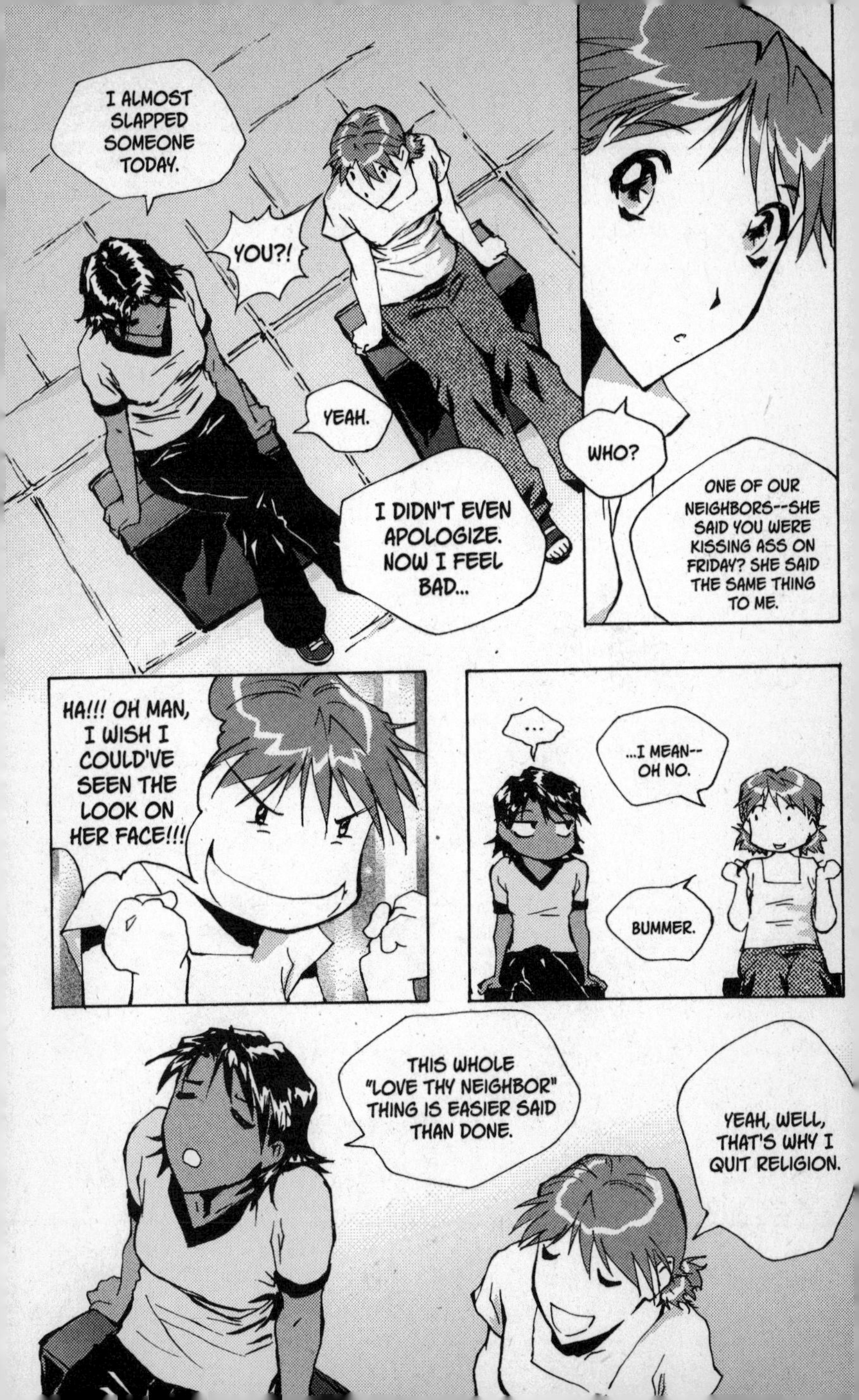
I ALMOST SLAPPED SOMEONE TODAY.
YOU?!
YEAH.
I DIDN'T EVEN APOLOGIZE. NOW I FEEL BAD...
WHO?
ONE OF OUR NEIGHBORS--SHE SAID YOU WERE KISSING ASS ON FRIDAY? SHE SAID THE SAME THING TO ME.
HA!!! OH MAN, I WISH I COULD'VE SEEN THE LOOK ON HER FACE!!!
...
...I MEAN-- OH NO.
BUMMER.
THIS WHOLE "LOVE THY NEIGHBOR" THING IS EASIER SAID THAN DONE.
YEAH, WELL, THAT'S WHY I QUIT RELIGION.

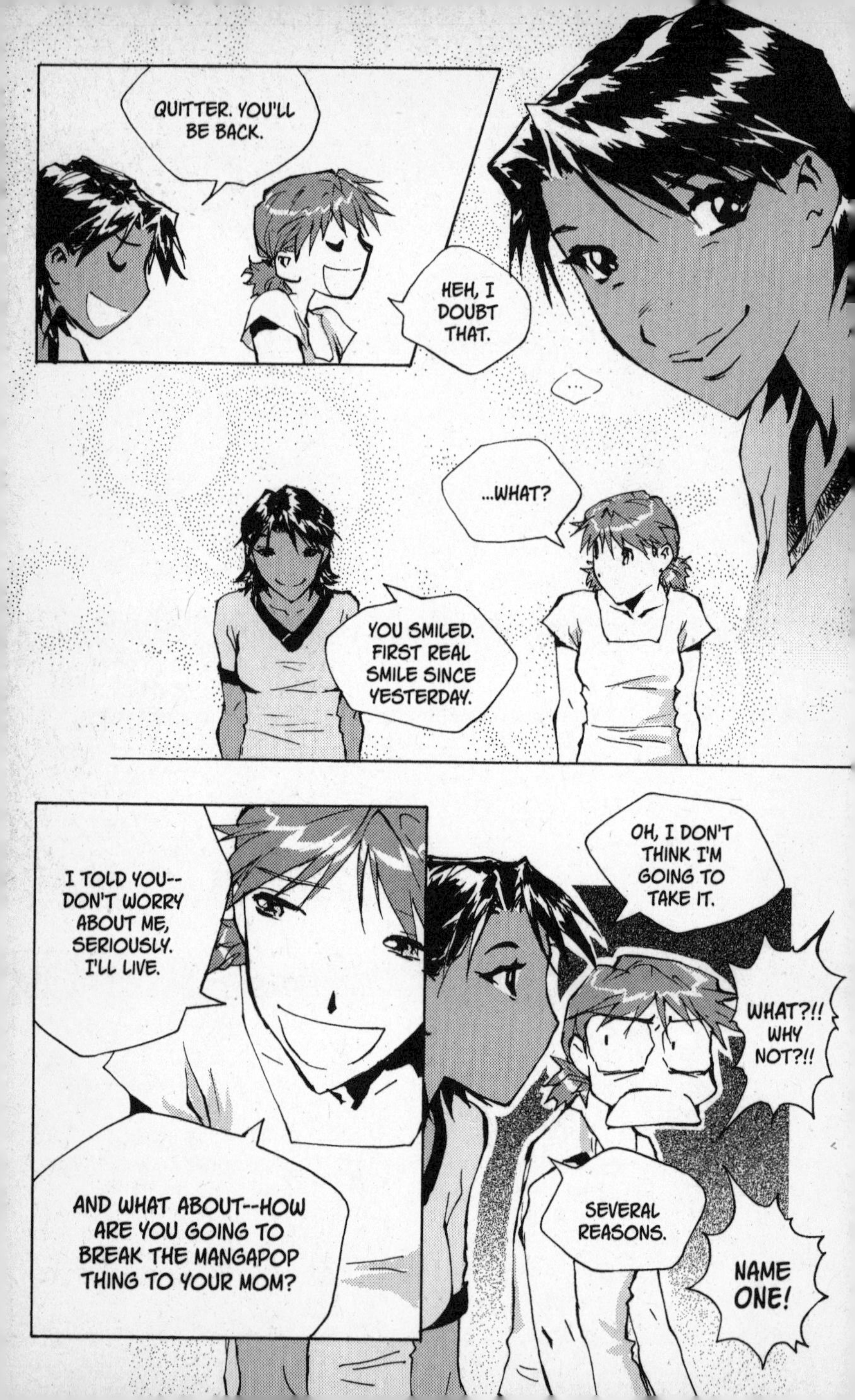
QUITTER. YOU'LL BE BACK.
HEH, I DOUBT THAT.
...
...WHAT?
YOU SMILED. FIRST REAL SMILE SINCE YESTERDAY.
I TOLD YOU-- DON'T WORRY ABOUT ME, SERIOUSLY. I'LL LIVE.
AND WHAT ABOUT--HOW ARE YOU GOING TO BREAK THE MANGAPOP THING TO YOUR MOM?
OH, I DON'T THINK I'M GOING TO TAKE IT.
WHAT?!! WHY NOT?!!
SEVERAL REASONS.
NAME ONE!

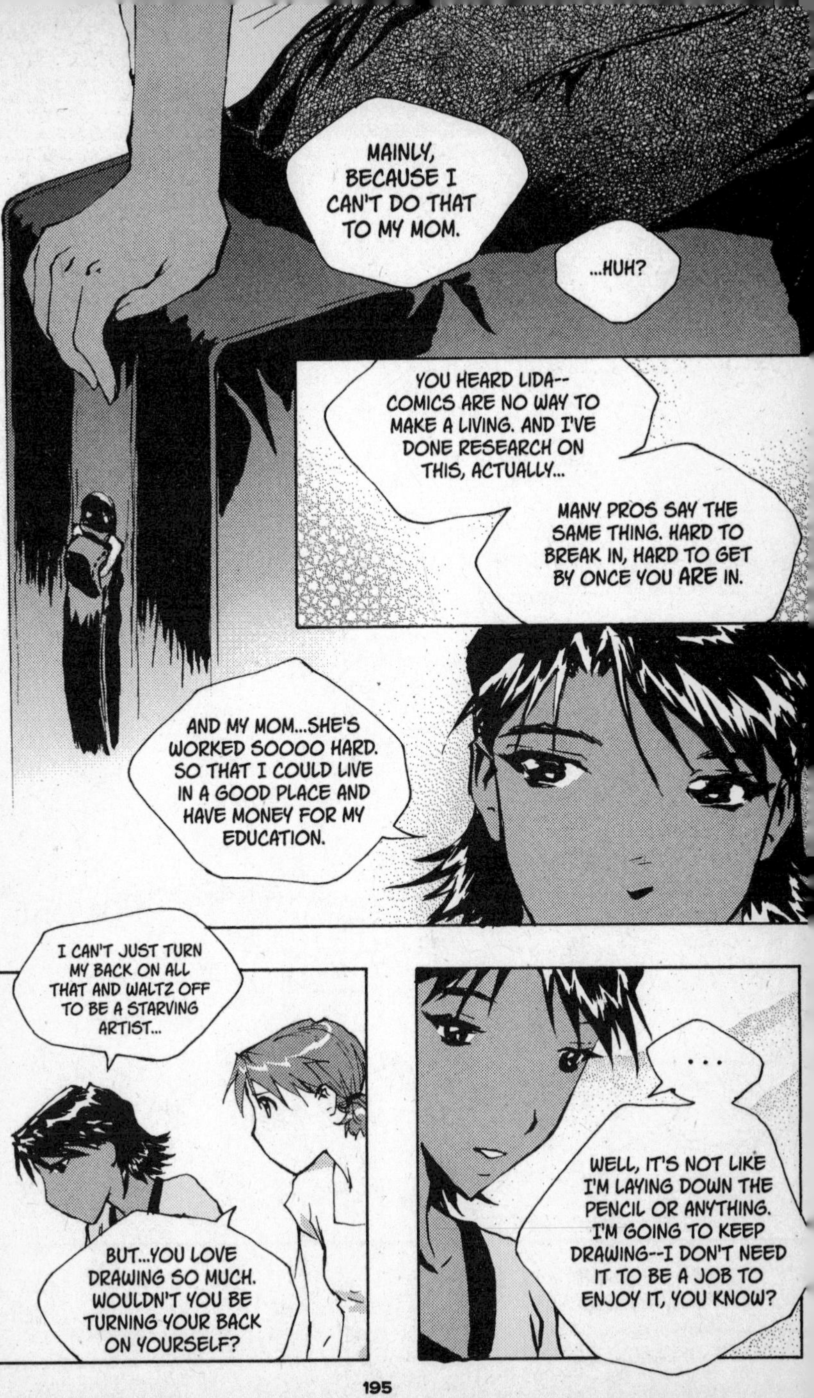
MAINLY, BECAUSE I CAN'T DO THAT TO MY MOM.
...HUH?
YOU HEARD LIDA-- COMICS ARE NO WAY TO MAKE A LIVING. AND I'VE DONE RESEARCH ON THIS, ACTUALLY...
MANY PROS SAY THE SAME THING. HARD TO BREAK IN, HARD TO GET BY ONCE YOU ARE IN.
AND MY MOM...SHE'S WORKED SOOOO HARD. SO THAT I COULD LIVE IN A GOOD PLACE AND HAVE MONEY FOR MY EDUCATION.
I CAN'T JUST TURN MY BACK ON ALL THAT AND WALTZ OFF TO BE A STARVING ARTIST...
BUT...YOU LOVE DRAWING SO MUCH. WOULDN'T YOU BE TURNING YOUR BACK ON YOURSELF?
...
WELL, IT'S NOT LIKE I'M LAYING DOWN THE PENCIL OR ANYTHING. I'M GOING TO KEEP DRAWING--I DON'T NEED IT TO BE A JOB TO ENJOY IT, YOU KNOW?

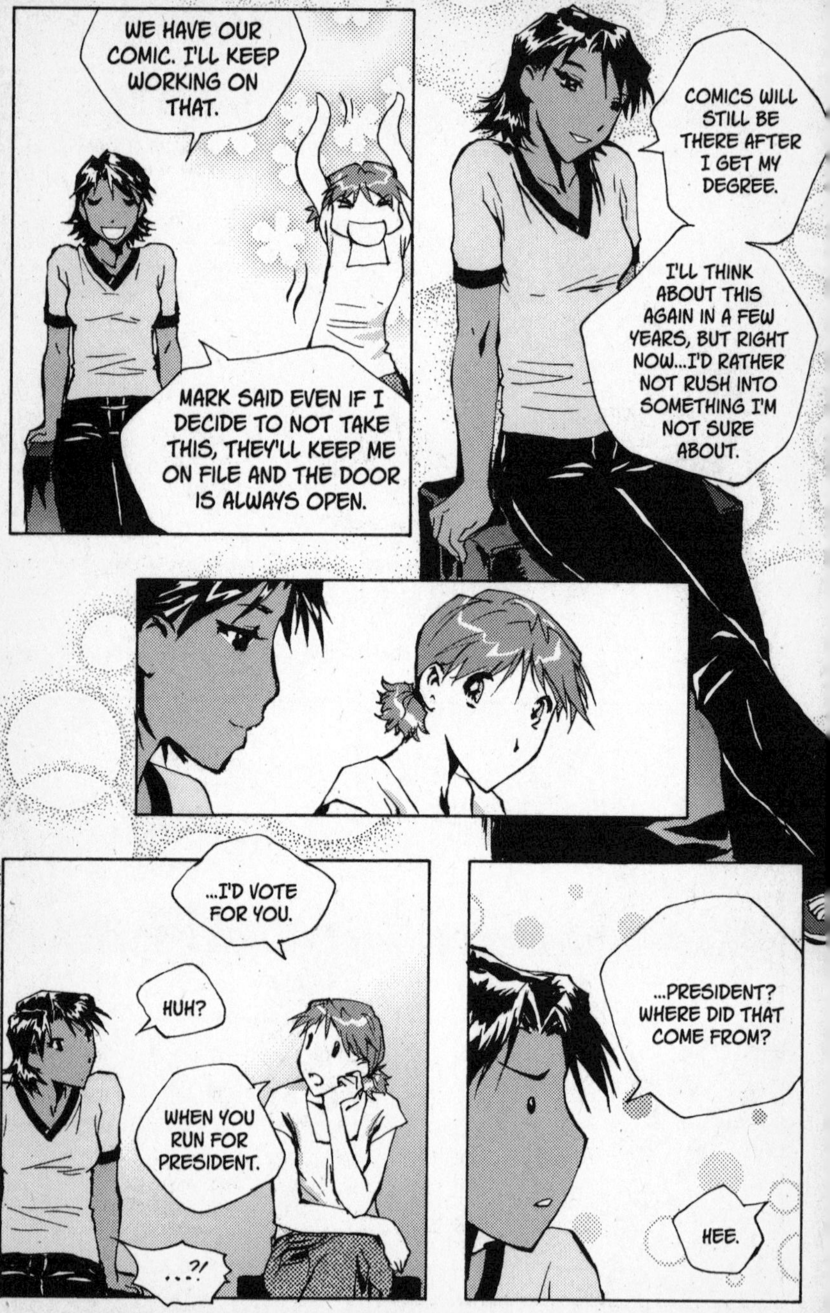
WE HAVE OUR COMIC. I'LL KEEP WORKING ON THAT.
MARK SAID EVEN IF I DECIDE TO NOT TAKE THIS, THEY'LL KEEP ME ON FILE AND THE DOOR IS ALWAYS OPEN.
COMICS WILL STILL BE THERE AFTER I GET MY DEGREE.
I'LL THINK ABOUT THIS AGAIN IN A FEW YEARS, BUT RIGHT NOW...I'D RATHER NOT RUSH INTO SOMETHING I'M NOT SURE ABOUT.
...I'D VOTE FOR YOU.
HUH?
WHEN YOU RUN FOR PRESIDENT.
...?!
...PRESIDENT? WHERE DID THAT COME FROM?
HEE.

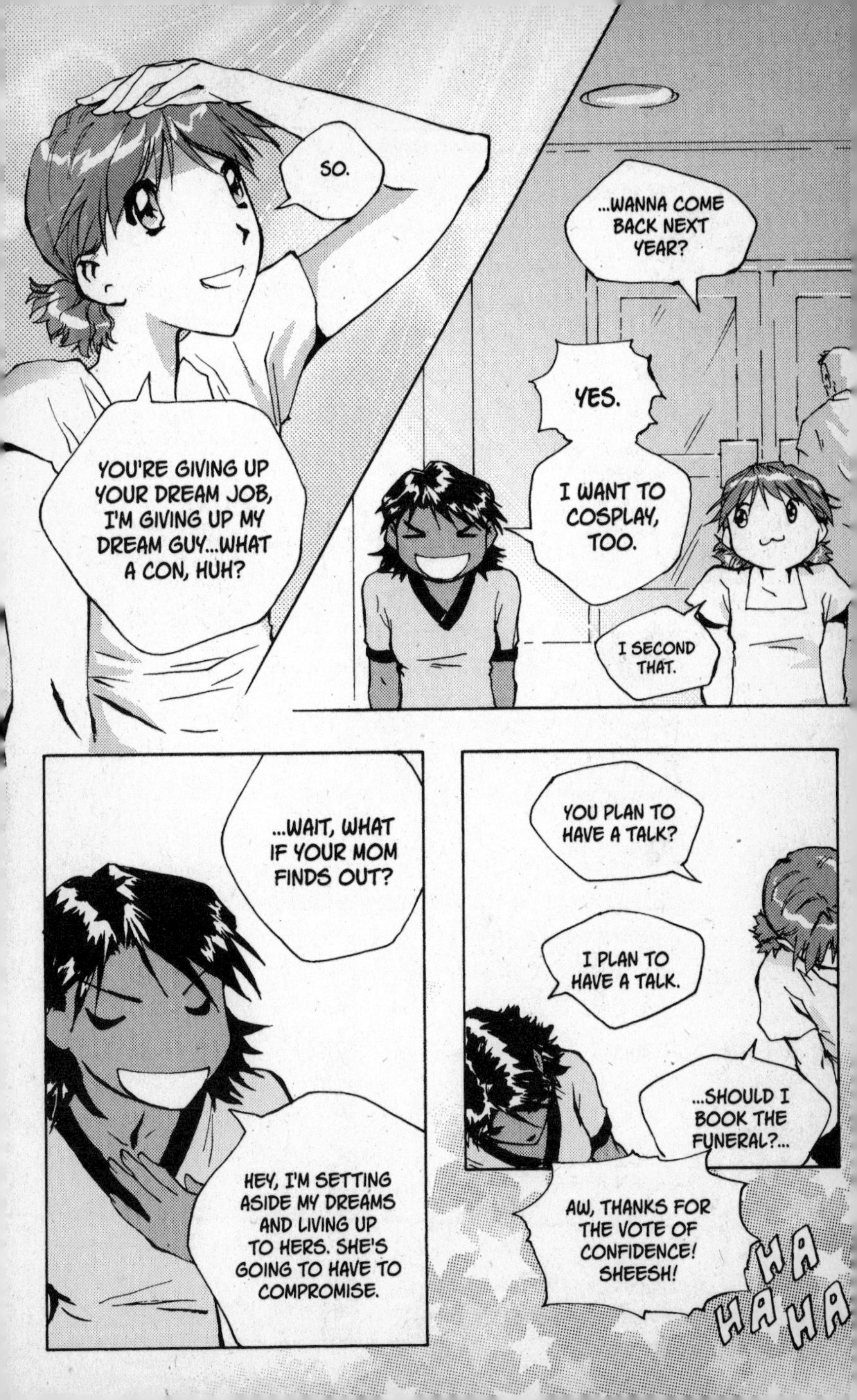
SO.
YOU'RE GIVING UP YOUR DREAM JOB, I'M GIVING UP MY DREAM GUY...WHAT A CON, HUH?
...WANNA COME BACK NEXT YEAR?
YES.
I WANT TO COSPLAY, TOO.
I SECOND THAT.
...WAIT, WHAT IF YOUR MOM FINDS OUT?
HEY, I'M SETTING ASIDE MY DREAMS AND LIVING UP TO HERS. SHE'S GOING TO HAVE TO COMPROMISE.
YOU PLAN TO HAVE A TALK?
I PLAN TO HAVE A TALK.
...SHOULD I BOOK THE FUNERAL?...
AW, THANKS FOR THE VOTE OF CONFIDENCE! SHEESH!
HA HA HAHA

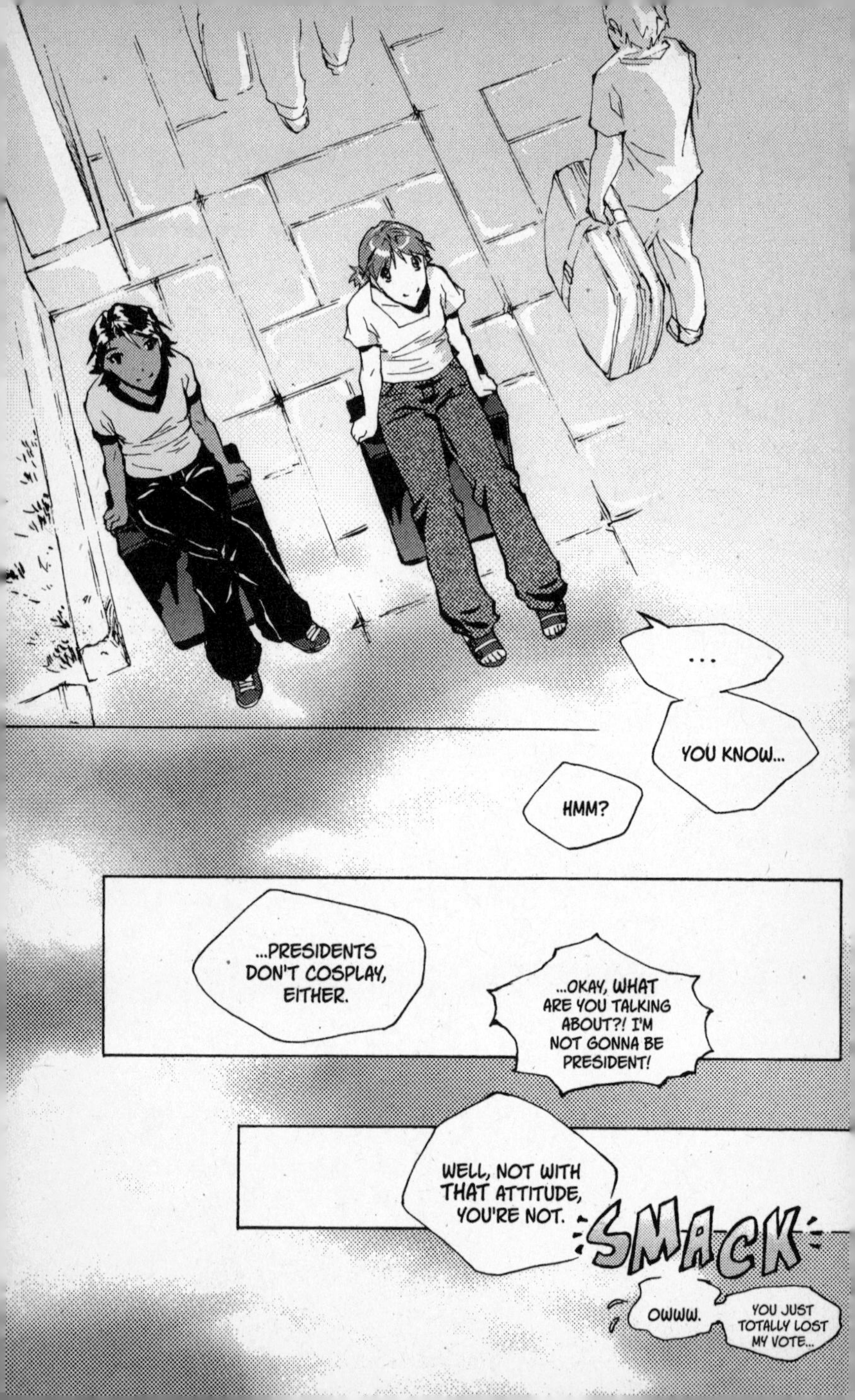
...
YOU KNOW...
HMM?
...PRESIDENTS DON'T COSPLAY, EITHER.
...OKAY, WHAT ARE YOU TALKING ABOUT?! I'M NOT GONNA BE PRESIDENT!
WELL, NOT WITH THAT ATTITUDE, YOU'RE NOT.
SMACK
OWWW.
YOU JUST TOTALLY LOST MY VOTE...

IN THE NEXT VOLUME OF...

Svetlana Chmakova's

DRAMACON

Another year, another Yatta Con, and Christie and Bethany are back for more adventure. As if sharing the hotel room with their friends from Firebird Studio wasn't adventure enough, Christie is also cosplaying for the first time ever and is up for a rollercoaster ride of a first date--with Matt. Of course, Bethany, the star of the show, with her art gracing the con t-shirts and bags, has plenty of worries of her own, with her Mom coming to see just what this festival of Japanese culture looks like. In the meantime Matt and Christie find out that the fastest way to get over a crush is to get to know them. Or, in their case, to be within earshot of each other. Will Matt and Christie's love survive the short-distance relationship?

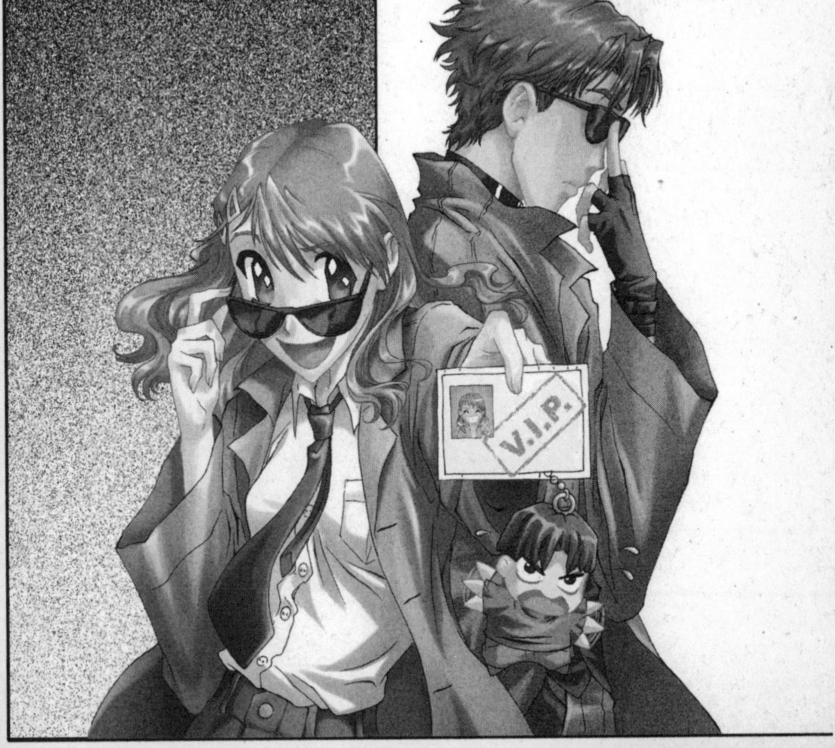
V.I.P.

DRAMACON cosplay!

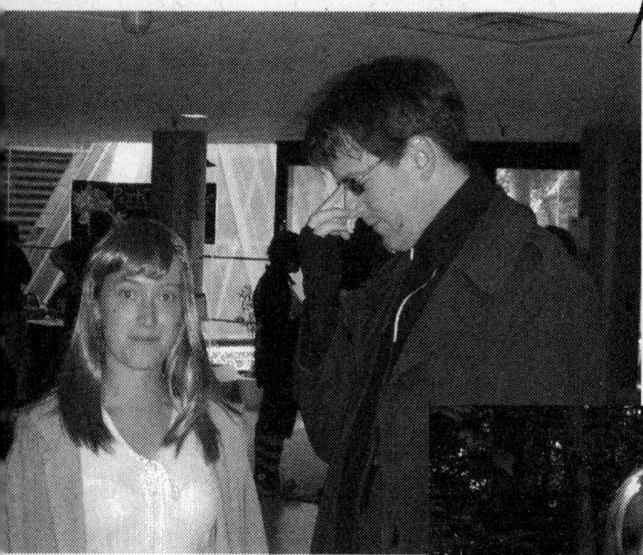

I still can't get over the fact that people are cosplaying as my characters... THANK YOU!!

Nami and PatrickD as Christie and Matt! They've got the character attitudes down pat, and the costumes, too!!

* * *

Kathy is SUCH a gorgeous Sandra, the costume was just so unbelievably good!

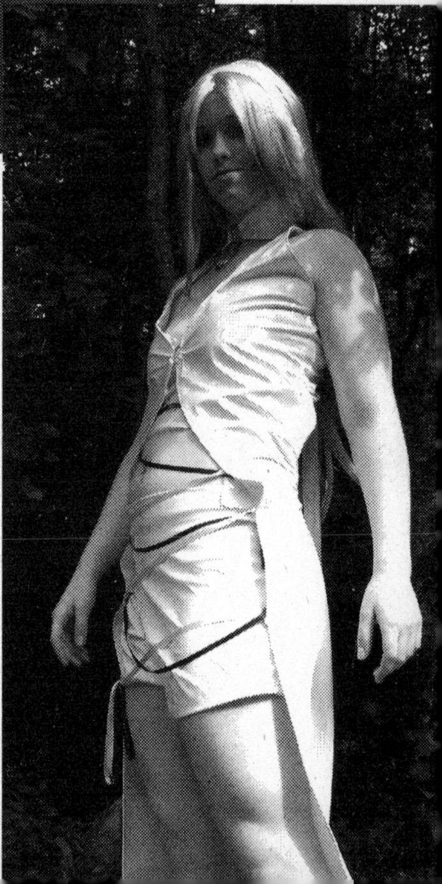

* * *

I also saw two Matt cosplayers at Anime Boston and took a picture! But I didn't have a way to contact them and ask permission to put it in the book ... Maybe next time...

See you around and thank you for reading!

THANQ's

To Dee — who deserves a shrine and then some, for staying up the long hours it took to tone this and for being amazing moral support!!

To Mom and Dad and Sasha — for too many things to count... Bestest family ever ^^

To Lillian — my poor poor editor. Thank you for the patience!!

To my friends — for always being there for me!

To my fans — WOW. So did not expect so many of you to enjoy my stuff. Thank you for all the kind words and for supporting my work!!!

~ ALSO... ~

To me. Thank you, Svet, for not running away to Alaska when the deadlines came fast and fierce... Now go and get some sleep!

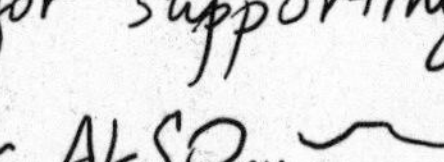

OK, YOU'RE THE BOSS!

← hasn't slept in days

(If I forgot anyone, I am sorry... See excuse ↑)

BE WELL, EVERYONE!

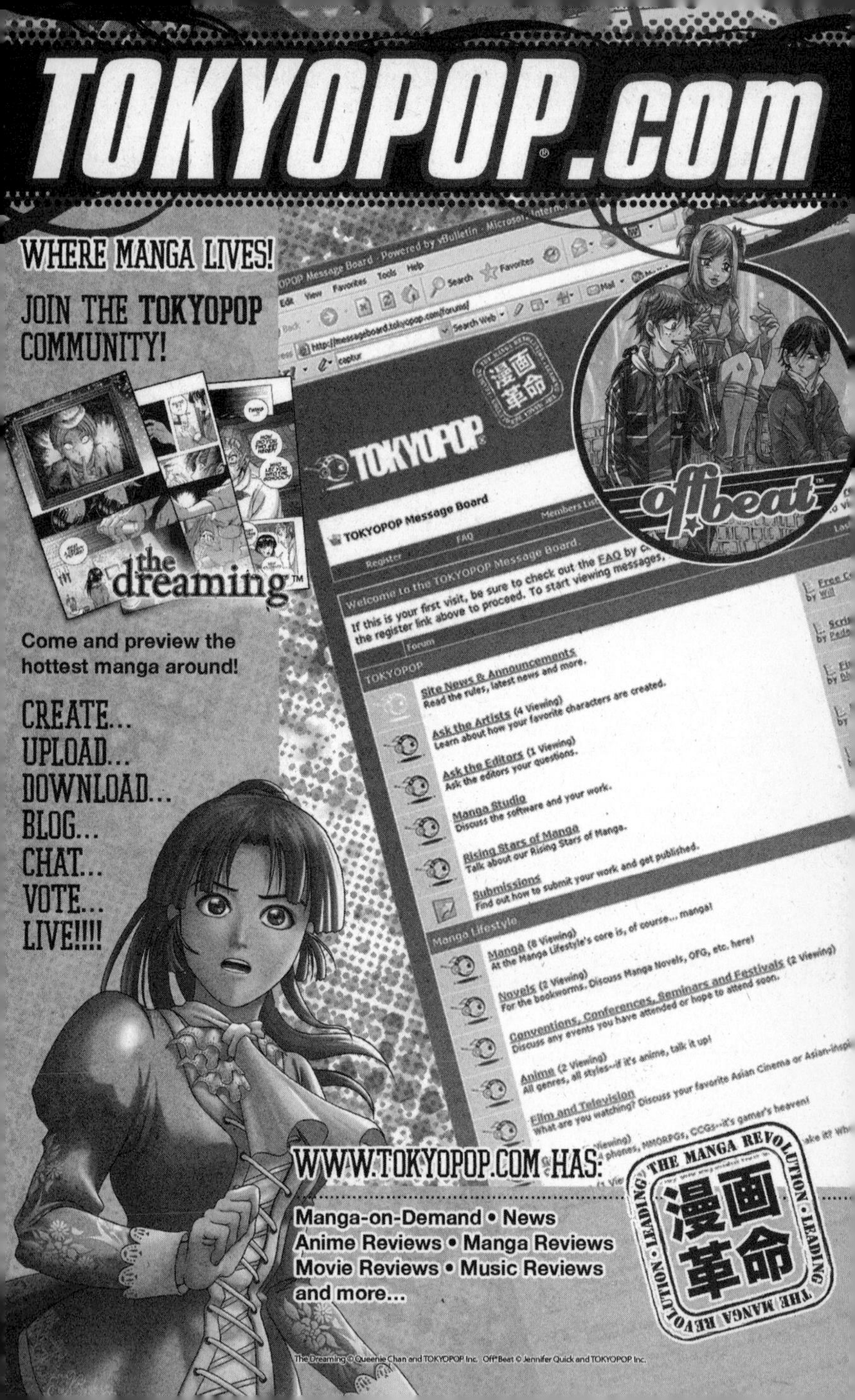
TOKYOPOP.com
WHERE MANGA LIVES!
JOIN THE TOKYOPOP COMMUNITY!
the dreaming™
Come and preview the hottest manga around!
CREATE...
UPLOAD...
DOWNLOAD...
BLOG...
CHAT...
VOTE...
LIVE!!!!
TOKYOPOP
TOKYOPOP Message Board
offbeat™
WWW.TOKYOPOP.COM HAS:
Manga-on-Demand • News
Anime Reviews • Manga Reviews
Movie Reviews • Music Reviews
and more...
THE MANGA REVOLUTION • LEADING
漫画革命
The Dreaming © Queenie Chan and TOKYOPOP Inc. Off*Beat © Jennifer Quick and TOKYOPOP Inc.

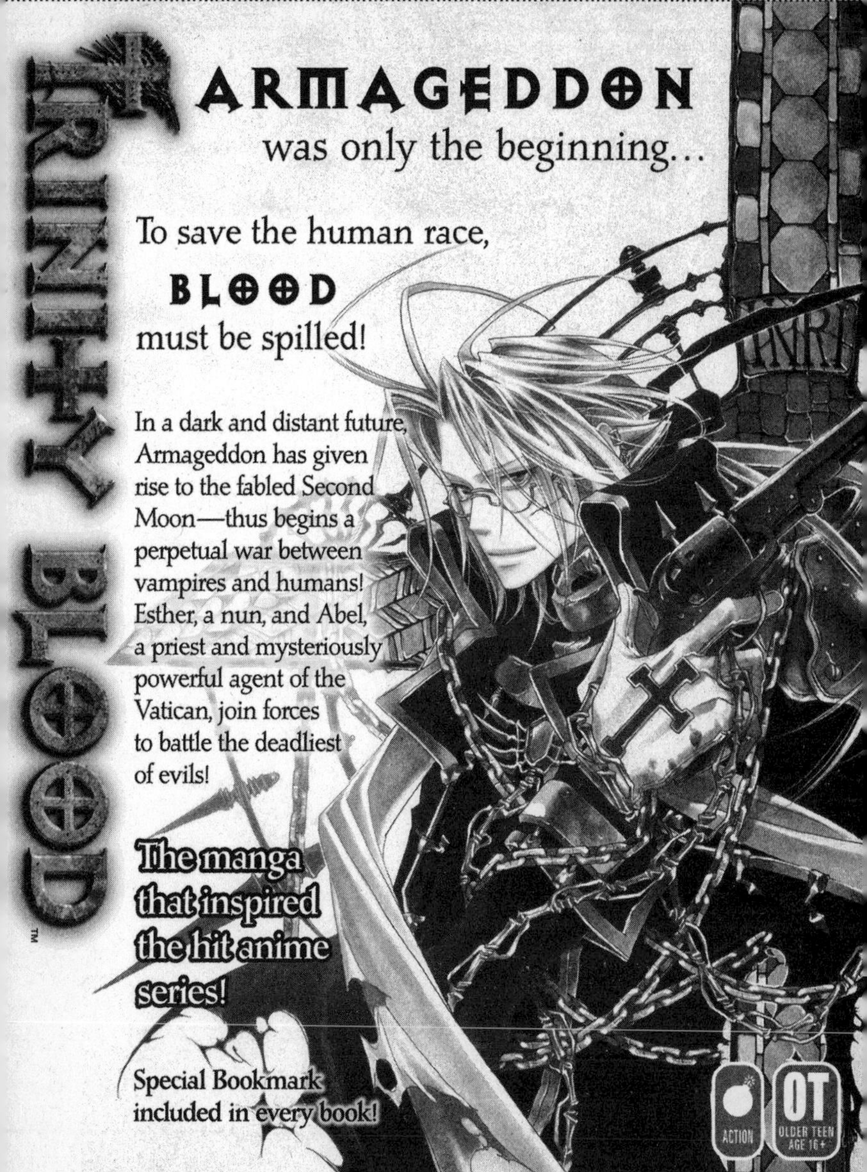
TRINITY BLOOD™
ARMAGEDDON
was only the beginning...
To save the human race,
BLOOD
must be spilled!
In a dark and distant future, Armageddon has given rise to the fabled Second Moon—thus begins a perpetual war between vampires and humans! Esther, a nun, and Abel, a priest and mysteriously powerful agent of the Vatican, join forces to battle the deadliest of evils!
The manga that inspired the hit anime series!
Special Bookmark included in every book!
INRI
ACTION
OT
OLDER TEEN AGE 16+
© Kiyo KYUJYO and Sunao YOSHIDA

How long would it take to get over...

losing the love of your life?

When Jackie's ex-lover Noah dies, she decides the quickest way to get over her is to hold a personal ritual with Noah's ashes. Jackie consumes the ashes in the form of smoothies for 12 days, hoping the pain will subside. But will that be enough?

From the internationally published illustrator June Kim.

DRAMA

OT OLDER TEEN AGE 16+

FOR MORE INFORMATION VISIT:

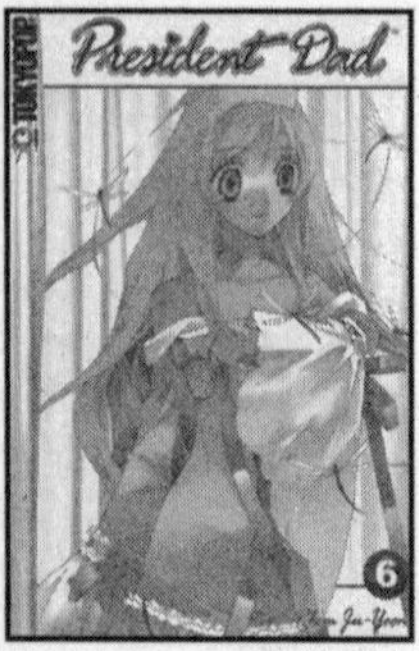
President Dad
TOKYOPOP
6

COMEDY

TEEN AGE 13+

PRESIDENT DAD

BY JU-YEON RHIM

In spite of the kind of dorky title, this book is tremendously fun and stylish. The mix of romance and truly bizarre comedy won me over in a heartbeat. When young Ami's father becomes the new president of South Korea, suddenly she is forced into a limelight that she never looked for and isn't particularly excited about. She's got your typical teenage crushes on pop idols (and a mysterious boy from her past who may be a North Korean spy! Who'd have thought there'd be global politics thrown into a shojo series?!), and more than her fair share of crazy relatives, but now she's also got a super-tough bodyguard who can disguise himself as anyone you can possibly imagine, and the eyes of the nation are upon her! This underrated manhwa totally deserves a second look!

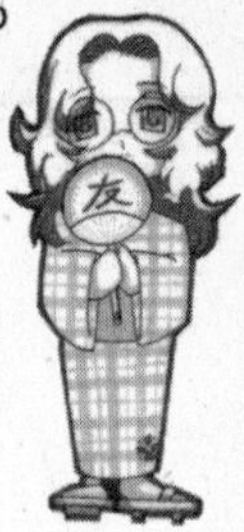

~Lillian Diaz-Pryzbyl, Editor

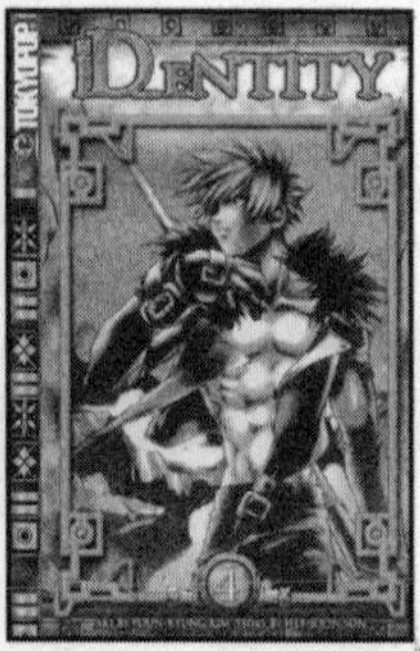
iDENTITY
TOKYOPOP

ACTION

TEEN AGE 13+

ID_ENTITY

BY HEE-JOON SON AND YOUN-KYUNG KIM

As a fan of online gaming, I've really been enjoying *iD_eNTITY.* Packed with action, intrigue and loads of laughs, *iD_eNTITY* is a raucous romp through a virtual world that's obviously written and illustrated by fellow gamers. Hee-Joon Son and Youn-Kyung Kim utilize gaming's terms and conventions while keeping the story simple and entertaining enough for noobs (a glossary of gaming terms is included in the back). Anyone else out there who has already absorbed *.hack* and is looking for a new gaming adventure to go on would do well to start here.

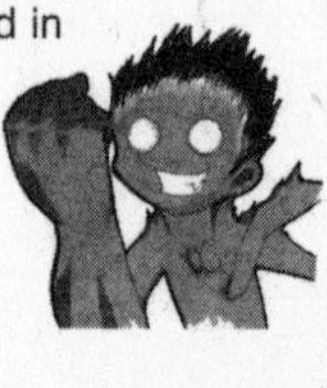

~Tim Beedle, Editor